EVER SINCE EVE

EVER SINCE EVE

*Personal Reflections
on Childbirth*

Nancy Caldwell Sorel

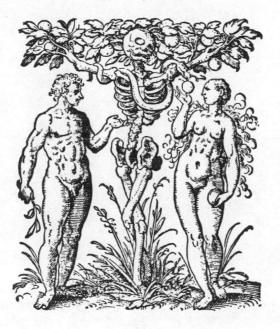

New York Oxford
OXFORD UNIVERSITY PRESS
1984

Copyright © 1984 by Oxford University Press, Inc.

Library of Congress Cataloging in Publication Data

Sorel, Nancy.
Ever since Eve.

Bibliography: p.
1. Pregnancy—Addresses, essays, lectures. 2. Childbirth—Addresses, essays, lectures. I. Title.
RG525.S645 1984   612′.63   84-916
ISBN 0-19-503460-0

Printing (last digit): 9 8 7 6 5 4 3 2 1

Printed in the United States of America

For Ed, in our lofty Eden

Acknowledgments

I gratefully acknowledge the aid and warm support of my editor, Susan Rabiner, her assistant, Naomi Schneider, and my agent, Susan Schulman; the encouragement of my father and mother; the vast facilities of that peerless institution, the New York Public Library; the regenerative benefits of a week on Martha's Vineyard à la Kathy Hourigan; the care and comfort daily extended by my husband and children; and the time, interest, and enthusiasm of all those people, named and unnamed, who freely gave a segment of their lives to make this book possible.

Introduction

Birth is that common experience we all share from a time we cannot remember; that infinitely uncommon experience many of us later repeat in fulfillment of urges and desires we only half acknowledge. The subtle workings of nine months of pregnancy, culminating in an event that never seems less than miraculous, changes us in more ways than the simple addition of a child to our lives. It puts us in touch with the past and future—a fact consoling to contemplate at those times when our present seems unbearably disrupted. Through it we become willing participants in the great cliché that life goes on.

Anyone who has been pregnant in the past ten to fifteen years is aware of the wealth of literature available on the subject of childbirth. In the course of my own first pregnancy, I read much of it, and I was enchanted because I was enchanted with myself and consumed with anticipation of the impending event. But with later repetitions of that fecund state, I found my interest waning. My gleanings from the childbirth classics were well-fixed in my mind. They were useful, valuable, wonderful books, many of them, but I didn't really need to reread them. Instead, I returned to my old standby—biography, particularly biographies and autobiographies of women who had borne children. I read about Queen Victoria and Colette, Margaret Mead and Mary Wollstonecraft, Isadora Duncan and Ingrid Bergman and Anne Boleyn. I read about fathers—Napoleon, and Picasso, and how Louis XIV was conceived because Louis XIII's bed had gone to Fountainebleau without him, and how a man could, according to Hippocrates, ensure having a son rather than a daughter by tying up the left testicle as tightly as was bearable before intercourse. I read about midwives—male and female—and couvade—ancient and modern—and how although the Egyptians from the time of the pharoahs could exactly calculate the expected date of delivery from the date of assumed conception, there were people in the world today who do not connect intercourse with pregnancy.

It began to seem to me that there was still one book on the subject of pregnancy and childbirth that had not yet been written: the book that would collect varieties of human experience throughout recorded time that were presently hidden away in scattered works—not only biographical, but anthropological, sociological, historical, and fictional— as well as some not yet written down but still very vivid in the minds of persons who had only recently taken part in the birth phenomena. The book I envisioned was not just for the presently expectant mother, but for everyone who had ever been a mother, or thought she might become one. And it would also be for fathers—those fathers who were interested in how their own experience linked with, and was foreshadowed by, the paternal past.

The subject of birth has, inevitably, its own compelling attraction. No one who has given birth or witnessed it ever quite forgets. Mothers relive it secretly, or reflect on their own experience among each other for many years afterwards. For a story that is, essentially, always the same—the long preparation of pregnancy, the varied time of labor accompanied by varying degrees of pain, the arrival of the child—the essence is always new, always dramatic. The drama stems partly, I think, from an almost inescapable wonder at life, and partly, as with death, from the sheer irreversibility of things. I remember after the birth of one of my children a moment of uncontrollable laughter at the thought of how hopelessly final it all was. This baby who had been provided for so involuntarily inside me was now outside, forcing me into responsibility. Nothing was automatic any more. Never mind, I told myself—it was the same for Cleopatra, for Marie de Medici, for Anna Magdalena Bach and Sophia Tolstoy and Sophia Loren and—Eve.

I was in good company. That is, in the end, what I would hope the reader will find in this book—good company.

January, 1984   N.S.
New York

Contents

1. One Woman's Story

My husband always said he never meant to have any children, and how he ended up with four he couldn't quite fathom. I think the instinct was there without his being willing to acknowledge it. The role of father was not one he understood automatically because his own father had not been very good at it.

When we were first married, his two children, ages four and seven, lived nearby and spent weekends and school vacations and summers with us. They were very special children, and the times we had together were wonderful times. I thought my husband was a very caring father. Of course, when I became pregnant, I was near ecstasy, but I sensed it was a little old hat for him. He was pleased, but he was more glad for *me* than for *us*.

I wanted to have natural childbirth, and he wanted to do whatever he was supposed to do so he came to one class. But I could see he was bored. He was a little older than the other fathers, and it just wasn't something he could get into. He was sure he could never bear to be present at the delivery anyway; he was convinced he would faint at the first indication of pain or blood. He had fainted when he held his son for his circumcision. When we went to get our blood tests before we were married, we both fainted. So I was sympathetic. Besides, I could see how a highly intelligent, creative man who already had two children might find breathing and counting less than thrilling. I told him I'd finish up the class and he might just as well go to a movie.

I must say that when I found myself in labor, I was unprepared for the magnitude of what everyone kept referring to as "discomfort." And, as it turned out, there were some complications in the delivery and I didn't make it through with natural childbirth anyway. I was disappointed in myself, but as for my baby, well, she was the most angelic baby in the world—just so beautiful. I nursed her for nine months, adoring every minute of it. Then when I became pregnant again, I said to myself, this time I am going to be fully prepared.

3

As the time drew near, I decided I was simply not going to allow complications. This time, I said to myself, I know what labor pains are like, and I know that I have to prepare myself better than I did last time when it was all a large unknown. I thought, this may very well be—in fact almost certainly will be—our last child, and I'm going to do it right. By "right" I didn't mean anything very unusual. I knew, for example, about a doctor in my home town in the Midwest who immersed his parturient patients in some kind of large bath until the very last stage of labor to keep them relaxed. Only sometimes the last stage came more quickly than he expected and apparently he had delivered more than one baby underwater. I wasn't after anything exotic like that. I never even seriously considered having the baby at home. I didn't feel that I would much care where I was, as long as I was totally *there*.

But I didn't talk about it much. We had moved outside the city by this time, to an old and rather isolated house in the country, but I would drive back into New York to Dr. J——, my old obstetrician—that is, my previous obstetrician, he wasn't old—because I liked him so much. He had a very relaxed, casual manner, and you always felt he was on your side. Toward the end, when I could just barely fit behind the wheel, driving seventy miles wasn't all that terrific, but, as I said, I trusted him. Along about the eighth month we had a little talk, and I explained how important it was for me to have this baby wholly and naturally, to be totally involved in its birth. He got the message. He said not to worry, that's how it would be.

I didn't even try to find natural childbirth classes in the country. Maybe I didn't want to admit that I'd already gone once and failed. I just read my Lamaze and my Guttmacher very carefully and practiced twice a day on the floor of the bedroom. Anyway, I was awfully busy— it was spring, and I had to get the whole garden planted before the baby came. Or thought I did, anyway. I remember planting the peas along the fence—peas are a particularly satisfying seed to plant, being so large—and thinking, which will happen first? Will my peas sprout or my baby arrive?

My husband was very busy too, with deadlines of one sort or another, and one Monday morning in early June, a week before the baby was due, we drove into New York, left our one-and-a-half year old with her grandmother, and I went off to the doctor. I felt enormous and uncomfortable, but peaceful somehow—that home stretch kind of feeling. I remember that as I sat in the doctor's office that morning, taking up most of a bench meant for two or three, my mind

kept going back to my grandparents' farm in Missouri where I had
spent a good portion of my childhood. As a little girl I would be sent
out by my grandmother to the chicken yard late in the afternoon to
gather the eggs, and inevitably some of the hens would still be sitting
on their nests in their little cubicles. I would have to reach my hand
very cautiously under them to try to get the eggs out of the straw
without annoying them and getting pecked. They always looked very
preoccupied and smug. Very maternal. That morning at the doctor's I
felt like one of those hens, except of course that their eggs could never
have made the commotion inside them that this baby was making
inside me. And I well knew that laying an egg not only looked, but
was, comparatively effortless.

Still, I felt very cool and unruffled when I went into the examining
room. I guess I had about another five minutes to feel that way. Then
Dr. J—— came in, took one careful look at the situation, and said
casually, "How far away did you say you live?" I said, "About seventy
miles." He said, "Well, you're six centimeters dilated. I don't think
you'll ever make it back there, much less back there and then back
here again. I certainly wouldn't want you to try." He looked again. "I
don't really think you should be walking around New York, you
know." Another look. "In fact, I think we'll just go to the hospital
right now. Together." I said, "Do you mean I'm going to have the
baby now?" He said, "I would guess in a couple of hours."

Well, how would anyone feel hearing that? Apprehensive? Excited?
Speechless? I think I felt all three. I got dressed and went back to the
waiting room where Dr. J—— was giving instructions to his nurse and
apologizing to several patients who, because of me, weren't going to
see him that morning after all. (They would see his partner instead.)
Everyone said, "How wonderful!" "How marvelous!" "Good luck!"
We walked out onto Park Avenue. I remember nothing of the conversation as we drove to the hospital, although there must have been
some. Then we were there, and my doctor was giving instructions to
nurses, and nurses were handing me gowns and things. I was in a
daze. Of course, I wasn't feeling anything yet. Just heady.

I know there are a lot of women who say you shouldn't let your
doctor induce labor, at his convenience, and basically I agree with
that, but I didn't feel that way that day. I'd had a good sleep the
night before and was feeling very rested and strong and ready. I felt
completely positive about everything that was happening. I mean, you
know, I didn't want to have the baby on Interstate 684 either. Dr.
J—— said, "Where can I reach your husband?" I said, "He's at the

Forty-second Street Library. Probably in one of the reading rooms."
He said, "Well, I don't know if I can contact him there or not, but
I'll try." He said he'd call my mother-in-law, too.

The next thing I remember I was in a bed in the labor room. The
bed was by a big window, and I had a wonderful view of the sky that
had been blue a short time before, but where big storm clouds were
now gathering. The nurse had put in the intravenous, and the contractions were beginning. I lay there and breathed and counted in
classic Lamaze style. In between I would watch the clouds building
up, and then I would wonder if my mother-in-law had told my
daughter that the baby was coming. I could picture my mother-in-law
sitting there anxiously in her West Side apartment with her mother,
my husband's grandmother, who had had five daughters in the little
town of Vatra-Dornei in Rumania before she was thirty. I thought of
my own grandmother, my mother's mother, giving birth to eight children there in the big row house in North Philadelphia. I thought of
my mother herself, transplanted to the Midwest, going to the hospital
prematurely to have a baby and it turning out to be twins. No one,
including my father, a doctor himself, had known. They had only one
name picked out, and it wasn't clear whether I would live, so they
gave it to my sister. I think almost a week passed before I was named.
And I thought of my husband, right now innocently doing whatever
it was he was doing at the library. I imagined the very efficient, very
official librarians moving among the tables, whispering, "Is there any
man here whose wife is about to have a baby?"

The contractions were picking up, and I was having to concentrate
very hard to keep on top of them. Count. Count up with it—what is
the top number you reach before you start the count back down,
gloating in the assurance of another one gone. My doctor had told the
nurses to let me strictly alone unless I asked for something, so except
for checking on my progress, they were doing just that. I know most
women want someone supportive with them, but I really didn't want
anyone. I felt absolutely complete in myself. I felt as long as no one
distracted me, I would be o.k. I had to be able to concentrate completely to handle it. The breathing, which had seemed artificial when
I practiced it on the floor of my bedroom, seemed absolutely natural
and appropriate now that I was in the situation. Several times my
doctor appeared, had a look, said a few casual words of encouragement, patted my foot, and went off again. It seemed to me he understood exactly how private the whole thing was.

By now the wind was really blowing outside—I could see the trees along upper Fifth Avenue bent against it. The clouds were the big, dark, rumbly kind. The contractions were pretty much all the time now, and I counted them up, up, up over a dark cloud and then down-n-n-n the other side. Then the time came when Dr. J—— came in and didn't go away again. He spoke to a nurse. A delivery table suddenly appeared. People were trying to move me onto it just as another contraction was beginning. "Can't you wait?" I asked, rather crossly as I remember. "I can," he said, "but the baby can't."

We were in the delivery room. My privacy was over; there seemed to be all kinds of people there, clearly intending to stay. I was concentrating on my contractions, so I hardly noticed Dr. J—— go out for a moment. When he came back in, who should be with him but my husband! All in green, head to foot! "My God," I said, "what are you doing here?" Somehow he had not only been spirited out of the New York Public Library, but here into the delivery room where he'd said he would never be. Not down where he would have to see anything, of course. Up by my head. Someone put a chair near him, just in case. He said, "Well, I called home and got the message and came right over, and then I thought, Oh, what the hell." He took my hand. I was so glad he was there—there was no time to think about it, but I was so glad.

I think I was pushing by now. Every time I had a contraction everyone said, "Push! push!" and I did. In between it was very quiet. It was as if my contractions controlled all motion and sound in the room. Between them everyone seemed to be in some kind of limbo, poised and waiting. My husband had both my hands gripped in his, but he, too, was silent. You could have heard a cotton ball drop. Then suddenly there was this great crack of thunder! Everyone jumped, and the lights flickered, and then everyone laughed. My husband said, "That must be the cue." Someone else said, "Are the candles handy?" Then I remember Dr. J—— saying, "This one should do it, make this one do it," very urgently, and I remember how hard I pushed. I was no longer aware of pain. I was aware of faces, including my husband's leaning over mine, his glasses falling off onto the pillow beside me, and voices shouting—they seemed to be shouting—"Push! push! push!" I was aware of effort. And then suddenly I was aware of something wriggling down there, and a new sort of sound, and a lot of excited voices saying, "A girl! It's a girl!"—truly excited—not, as I would have expected, just pretending for my benefit. They held her up, and my husband was saying, "You did it! You did it!" still gripping my hands, proud of me. Tears were streaming down my face—I don't know

about his. "Oh, God, look at her!" I kept saying. And then my husband—I wish I didn't remember so well what he said next, except that
it was so like him. He was sitting down on the chair, which he hadn't
needed until then, with his legs stretched out, laughing from relief
and because everyone was congratulating *him,* and he said, "Well, it
wasn't how Jimmy Stewart and Carole Lombard did it in *Made for
Each Other,* but it was a pretty good scene anyway."

It was his own kind of welcome, I guess. Typical. After all, I was
doing what was typical for me in any kind of happy situation—crying.
By now they had whisked the baby away momentarily, to aspirate
her, and weigh her—eight pounds, five ounces—and then they brought
her back to me and put her there on my stomach. And there she was.
And there I was. Lombard may have been more beautiful, but I
hardly cared at that moment. I felt absolutely, completely filled up
with it all. Exhilarated! Euphoric! I just kept looking at her, just
drinking her in, her little screwed-up face, her fingers and toes looking
disproportionately long, but the right number—I checked. I ran my
finger across the top of her head and down her little back. The kind
of thing (I thought this later) my mother missed—her tiny newborns
were hustled off to sterile incubators. But I suppose my grandmothers
had it—one in the Philadelphia town house, the other on the farm in
Missouri—and my husband's grandmother, in the house behind the
tailor shop in the little village in Rumania—now over there across
town waiting for news of this child.

2. Considering

What is this talked-of mystery of birth
But being mounted bareback on the earth?
Robert Frost, from "Riders"

Margaret Mead: "The Little Girl Has Only To Wait, To Be"

From her extensive studies of New Guinea societies Margaret Mead, in her book *Male and Female,* made the following observations of how a small girl considers the future realities of her pregnancy and motherhood.

The little girl also sees pregnancy treated with the greatest openness and simplicity. Child-birth itself may be shrouded from all but adult eyes: children may stay away from child-birth, as in Bali, because they have been frightened by tales of witches abroad to snatch the new-born; they may be firmly kept away by the adults as in Arapesh; they may be shooed away with a shower of small stones and return to peek through the cracks in the blinds, as in Samoa. But nowhere in any of these seven societies is pregnancy concealed, and indeed it requires heavy clothing and shuttered houses and an economic system that can withdraw women from almost all productive work to make it possible to conceal pregnancy from the eyes of the world as was done for certain classes in Europe in the last century. "I Wajan is pregnant, some day you will be pregnant. My! what a fat little tummy you have. Are you perhaps pregnant now?" In Bali, little girls between two and three walk much of the time with purposely thrust-out little bellies, and the older women tap them playfully as they pass. "Pregnant," they tease. So the little girl learns that although the signs of her membership in her own sex are slight, her breasts mere tiny buttons no bigger than her brothers, her genitals a simple inconspicuous fold, some day she will be pregnant, some day she will have a baby. And having a baby is, on the whole, one of the most exciting and conspicuous achievements that can be presented to the eyes of small children in these simple worlds, in some of which the largest buildings are only

fifteen feet high, the largest boat some twenty feet long. Furthermore, the little girl learns that she will have a baby not because she is
strong or energetic or initiating, not because she works and struggles
and tries, and in the end succeeds, but simply because she *is* a girl.
. . . Her sex membership may not be so conspicuous now as her
brother's, but she has only to wait, to be, and—some day—she will
have a baby.

Bacall on Bogart: "He Didn't Know What Kind of Father He'd Make"

He was twice married and more than twice her age, but when
Humphrey Bogart and Lauren Bacall played opposite each other
in *To Have and Have Not,* the romance did not end with the
filming. They were married in 1945. Bacall was determined to
have a baby, determined that Bogart be a father before he
reached fifty. Relax, said the doctor, relax. Sex is fun for its own
sake, said Bogie. In her autobiography *By Myself* Bacall describes
what happened when it happened, and how nothing can take the
tough out of a tough guy quite so cleanly as for his wife to give
birth.

We'd taken our usual trip to New York and celebrated our third anni-
versary. I remember saying we'd never had a honeymoon, to which
Bogie rightly retorted, "You've been on a three-year honeymoon—
ever since we've been married." Then I missed a period. I rushed to
the calendar, marked it, and prayed. I counted every day until I
missed the second. I'd had a false alarm once before.

I called Red Krohn and went in for my rabbit test. He called me:
"Yes, ma'am, you are pregnant." I rushed to see him, he examined me
and said absolutely—it would be around the end of December. The
joy—the joy! I'd have to set the stage for Bogie's homecoming that
evening—he'd faint when he heard. He didn't faint. I don't know
what happened, but after I told him, we had the biggest fight we'd
ever had. I was in tears—this moment I'd been hoping for, waiting for,
was a disaster. I should have learned right then never to act out a
scene before it's played. Bogie was full of sound and fury signifying
that he hadn't married me to lose me to a child—no child was going to
come between us. The next morning he wrote me a long letter apologizing for his behavior, saying he didn't know what had gotten into
him except his fear of losing me—a child was an unknown quantity to
him. He didn't know what kind of a father he'd make. He was so

afraid our closeness and incredible happiness together would be cut into by a child—but of course he wanted us to have a baby more than anything in the world, he just would have to get used to the idea. He'd spent forty-eight years childless, and had never really considered that being a father would ever become a reality at this point in his life. . . .

Harry Kurnitz gave Bogie a baby shower. If you can imagine Mike Romanoff, Paul Douglas, Dick Brooks, Jean Negulesco, Collier Young, Nunnally Johnson, Irving Lazar choosing baby presents for Bogie. It was funny—Dusty Negulesco, Ida Lupino, and I got dressed in our husbands' clothes and crashed the party late in the evening. It was a little drunk and very sentimental. My own baby shower was smaller, more sedate, more traditional. . . .

On the morning of January 6, 1949, I awakened early. I felt strange, but wasn't sure if I should start timing the pains or not. They weren't the kind of pains I expected. I casually looked at the clock and sensed a beginning regularity to them. I said nothing to Bogie, who kissed me and happily went off to work. As soon as he'd gone I sat up and started to watch the clock. When the pains seemed fairly regular I called Red Krohn, who said to wait awhile—"When they're coming every five minutes call me. I'll be here." He was the only man who mattered to me on that day. I moved to the living room with my Baby Ben clock and at last the pains started to come at five-minute intervals. . . . I called Red again, who told me to come to the office. I remember dressing and feeling very vague as I walked down the path, waving goodbye to May, saying I'd be back later. I drove to Red's office, still vague, and on examining me, the pains now coming at three-minute intervals, he said, "We'd better call Bogie—you're going into the hospital." I was still sitting on the examining table when the door opened suddenly and a panicked, green-tinged Bogart face appeared. I don't know what he expected—to find me hanging upside down by my heels? This was new territory for him. Red gave Bogie instructions, about hospital signing in, entrances, etc., and said we should get right down there, he'd meet us. Poor Bogie. He was so worried, he was afraid to touch me for fear something would go wrong. I wasn't a bit worried. . . . He was nervous enough driving—terrified something would happen in the car. He kept saying, "Are you all right, Baby? We're almost there, Baby." His face was ashen. It was much easier to be me than him that day. I was signed in, and while I was being prepared, he paced. Red brought him to the labor room to sit with me. He wore a green gown to match his face. He took my hand in his, oh, so gently—he was so helpless, so sweet, so scared. As I took my hand away to hold on to the bars of the bed above my head as instructed, he turned even greener. He didn't know what to do—after a few minutes he asked if I minded if he waited outside, he couldn't bear to see anyone he loved in pain. Things happened very quickly after that—two hours later, at 11:22 P.M., Stephen (after Steve in *To Have and Have Not*) Humphrey Bogart was born. Red showed him to me in the delivery room. He was beautiful—all six pounds, six ounces, twenty inches of him. Bogie was waiting for me when I was wheeled from the recovery room to my own room. So relieved to see me smiling at him, talking to him. I was still gaga from the anesthesia, but I knew my man when he looked at me with tears in his eyes and said, "Hello, Baby." It was the fullest, most complete moment my life has known.

Bogie had a son—after forty-nine years of living, there was another Bogart on earth. . . .

Two days before I was to bring my baby home, Los Angeles had its first snowfall in fifty years. I remember sitting in my hospital bed and looking out the window—I thought I was imagining things. What a great dividend—only right for the child of Eastern-born parents! I couldn't wait to get home. I could have a baby every nine months if it was this easy! I hoped Bogie was as happy as I was. As for me, I knew that I had it all—and Bogie had given it to me.

On January 11 the ambulance took Steve and me home. As we were carried to the front door, there on the lawn was an enormous snowman which Bogie had spent half the night building. It was odd to see snow covering camellia bushes. I was taken to our bedroom, Steve to his at the other end of the house. We had an intercom rigged so that I could hear every sound in the nursery—could talk to the nurse if I wished. It was kept on at all times. . . .

My first morning home I was having breakfast in bed when Bogie went off to work. Before he left, he stopped in to see his son—I had the intercom on and suddenly heard in a soft, new voice, "Hello, son. You're a little fella, aren't you? I'm Father. Welcome home."

A Very Caring Mother: Queen Victoria
Cautions Her Daughter Vicki

On January 25, 1858, Victoria, eldest child of Queen Victoria and Prince Albert, was married at St. James's Palace to Prince Frederick William of Prussia, soon afterwards Crown Prince and much later King of Prussia and Emperor of Germany. The bride was seventeen, the groom, twenty-six. That afternoon they left for

Windsor Castle for a week's honeymoon, and from there traveled to take up permanent residence in Berlin. The royal pair, known familiarly as Vicki and Fritz, had been gone only a few hours when Queen Victoria wrote the first in what was to become a massive correspondence. Among the thousands of admonitions to her daughter, the paramount one was to try to avoid getting pregnant; as to this, Vicki was not any more successful than her mother had been. The following epistolary excerpts (published in *Dearest Child: Letters Between Queen Victoria and the Princess Royal 1858–1861*, Roger Fulford, editor), illustrate Queen Victoria's feelings and frustrations on the subject, and reveal her as the meddling mother-in-law she frequently was.

Buckingham Palace, January 25, 1858
(the wedding day)

My own darling Child,

. . . This has been a very trying day for you, my dearest child—and you behaved excessively well. . . . It is a very solemn act, the most important and solemn in every one's life, but much more so in a woman's than in a man's. I have ever looked on the blessed day which united me to your beloved and perfect Papa . . .

Buckingham Palace, February 15, 1858

. . . there is great happiness and great blessedness in devoting oneself to another who is worthy of one's affection; still men are very selfish and the woman's devotion is always one of submission which makes our poor sex so very unenviable. . . .

March 24, 1858

. . . Now to reply to your observation that you find a married woman has much more liberty than an unmarried one; in one sense of the word she has, —but what I meant was—in a physical point of view— and if you have hereafter (as I had constantly for the first 2 years of my marriage)—aches—and sufferings and miseries and plagues—which you must struggle against—and enjoyments etc. to give up—constant precautions to take, you will feel the yoke of a married woman! . . . I had 9 times for 8 months to bear with those above-named enemies and real misery (besides many duties) and I own it tried me sorely; one feels so pinned down—one's wings clipped—in fact, at the best (and few were or are better than I was) only half oneself—particularly the first and second time. This I call the "shadow side". . . .

Windsor Castle, April 7, 1858

. . . Look what unpleasant nonsense they put into the papers about you. . . .

Buckingham Palace, April 14, 1858

. . . It is most odious but they have spread a report that you and I
are both in what I call an unhappy condition! It is odious and though
it is naturally denied by me and all who are well informed—Lady
Caroline told me—as regards me, people say they know it is so! Really
too bad. Good Sir James and all who love you—hope that you will be
spared this trial for a year yet, as you are so very young and I know
you will feel all the homesickness—and every other little trial so much
more if you were ailing and in a state of constant malaise. If I had
had a year of happy enjoyment with dear Papa, to myself—how thankful I should have been! But I was 3 years and a ½ older; and therefore I was in for it at once—and furious I was. . . .

Buckingham Palace, April 21, 1858

. . . I can not tell you how happy I am that you are not in an unenviable position. I never can rejoice by hearing that a poor young
thing is pulled down by this trial. . . .

Osborne, May 26, 1858

. . . The horrid news contained in Fritz's letter to Papa upset us
dreadfully. . . .

Osborne, May 29, 1858

. . . I am so unhappy about you! It is well Fritz is not in sight just
now or he would not be graciously received. . . . We tell everyone
your foot [Vicki had sprained her ankle] is the cause of your not going
to Coburg—and that the lying up has weakened you. I hope you do
the same—and Fritz don't allow his own people and relations to enter
into such subjects; it is so indelicate; Papa never allowed it and I
should have been frantic.

Stoneleigh Abbey, Kenilworth,
June 15, 1858

. . . What you say of the pride of giving life to an immortal soul is
very fine, dear, but I own I cannot enter into that; I think much more
of our being like a cow or a dog at such moments; when our poor
nature becomes so very animal and unecstatic—but for you, dear, if
you are sensible and reasonable not in ecstasy nor spending your day
with nurses and wet nurses, which is the ruin of many a refined and
intellectual young lady, without adding to her real maternal duties, a
child will be a great resource. . . . Think of me who at that first time,
very unreasonable, and perfectly furious as I was to be caught, having

to have drawing rooms and levees and made to sit down—and be stared at and take every sort of precaution. . . .

Buckingham Palace, June 22, 1858

You say I know you "too well" to think you would spend your day in a way unworthy of a lady and a princess—so I do, dear child, still I know your rather too great passion for very little babies, and I wish to guard you against overdoing the thing. . . .

Buckingham Palace, June 29, 1858

Promise me one thing, dear; don't stoop when you sit and write, it is very bad for you now, and later it will make you ill; remember how straight I always sit, which enables me to write without fatigue at all times. . . .

Buckingham Palace, June 30, 1858

I also send you some soothing tincture (which Mr. Saunders prescribed) which will do you great good; put a teaspoonful of it into water, and hold it in your mouth, when you have pain and it will allay it. I suffered also this way. Mr. Saunders is going to Germany and is most anxious to see you, and he is so sensible and clever and always managed your teeth so well—(and the German dentists are not famous and the German teeth are so bad) you ought to see him, for teeth suffer much from your condition, some people lose one every child they have, and you will require to have them carefully looked at. . . .

I delight in the idea of being a grandmama; to be that at 39 and to look and feel young is great fun, only I wish I could go through it for you, dear, and save you all the annoyance . . . quantities of English nurses are now in request for Germany and Russia. They are the best for babies and little children until they are five to six. . . .

Balmoral Castle, October 1, 1858

Of all the wonderful German notions that one of a lady in your condition being unable to stand godmother is the most extraordinary I ever heard! . . . I have heard of so many christenings abroad where people have been in that condition and stand as godmothers. I hope that you will break through that; but above all promise me never to do so improper and indecorous a thing as to be lying in a dressing gown on a sofa at a christening! It would shock people here very much, and as my daughter and an English Princess I expect you will not do it. . . .

Windsor Castle, November 17, 1858

I know that the little being will be a great reward for all your trouble and suffering—but I know you will not forget, dear, your promise not to indulge in "baby worship," or to neglect your other greater duties in becoming a nurse. . . . No lady, and still less a Princess, is fit for her husband or her position, if she does that. I know, dear, that you will feel and guard against this, but I only just wish to remind you and warn you, as with your great passion for little children (which are mere little plants for the first six months) it would be very natural for you to be carried away by your pleasure at having a child.

I can not bear to think Bertie [Vicki's brother, the future Edward VII] is going to you and I can't—and when I look at the baby things, and feel I shall not be where every other mother is—and I ought to be and can't—it makes me sick and almost frantic. Why in the world did you manage to choose a time when we could not be with you? . . .

Osborne, December 11, 1858

Some little further memoranda I will send you by the messenger. Mrs. Innocent has likewise copies of all the notes I put down afterwards of all I did—during my confinements—as I know you will like to know—and this will be a guide. All this I have been particularly anxious about—as my two first confinements—for want of order—and from disputes and squabbles (chiefly owing to my poor old governess who would meddle) were far from comfortable or convenient and the doctors too had not found out quite how to treat me. I am therefore particularly anxious that you should profit by my experience (which resulted in my last five confinements being as quiet and comfortable as possible) and be spared as much (as possible) all the inconveniences arising from want of experience etc. which are natural in a first confinement. So you see, dear, that though alas far away (which I shall never console myself for)—I watch over you as if I were there. . . .

Windsor Castle, January 8, 1859

By the by, let me caution you not to make too much of Mrs. Innocent or see more of her before you are confined than is necessary because these nurses are dreadfully spoilt by the ladies and full of pretensions. . . .

Windsor Castle, January 29, 1859

[The future German Kaiser was born on
January 27, a difficult birth.]

God be praised for all his mercies, and for bringing you safely through this awful time! Our joy, our gratitude knows no bounds.

My precious darling, you suffered much more than I ever did—and how I wish I could have lightened them for you! Poor dear Fritz—how he will have suffered for you! I think and feel much for him; the dear little boy if I could but see him for one minute, give you one kiss. It is hard, very hard. But we are so happy, so grateful! And people here are all in ecstasies—such pleasure, such delight—as if it was their own prince and so it is too! All the children so delighted! But don't be alarmed for the future, it never can be so bad again! Yours and baby's healths were drunk on Thursday evening. . . . Dear Papa is so happy too.

Ever your truly devoted and loving Mama.
V.R.

Barbara Berg:"I THINK WE CAN, I THINK WE CAN, I KNOW WE CAN!"

Barbara J. Berg had suffered a late miscarriage and then a still-birth when, as she relates in her very personal and moving book *Nothing to Cry About,* she started thinking about adoption. The end result was more perfect than she could have imagined—before long she, her husband Arnie, and her stepdaughter Laura had adopted a beautiful little girl, Alison, who was soon after joined by a natural son, Andrew.

When did I start thinking about adoption? I'm not really sure. Certainly right after the stillbirth, friends mentioned it. But then adoption meant admitting that I couldn't have children, that I was a failure, that I was inadequate. How could I give up, accept that I might never be pregnant again? The thought was excruciating. But it was far more painful to think that I'd never hold a sleepy baby in my arms, never feel that innocent warm flesh against mine, that I'd never be a mother. Oh, yes, that's worse—far, far worse.

I discussed it with [a friend] one evening over dinner. "Have you and Ted ever thought about adopting?"

"Sure, we've thought about it, but it's awfully hard to get a baby these days. And besides, I'd worry how intelligent it would be, what it would look like. I know it's silly, but. . . ."

Was I worried about these things? I honestly didn't think so. But maybe I was just denying. I started testing myself, by looking at children on the street. Oriental children, interracial children, blond children. Children who didn't resemble me. Children whose ancestors didn't come from Russia, whose grandma and Aunt Rose didn't study nights with damp clothes wrapped around their heads to extinguish the candle they read by in case they fell asleep.

Could I love that one? Could I love that one?

Did it really matter what your children looked like? And how important *was* my family heritage? Background? Surely I wasn't so thrilled with our medical history that I felt compelled to pass it on to our offspring.

And what did flesh of my flesh and bones of my bones mean anyway? Wasn't it really just another form of proprietorship—men of their women, women of their children?

Could I love that one? That one?

Yes, yes, *yes!*

"What do you think about adoption?" I asked Arnie casually one night.

"You mean in general, or for us?"

"Both." I was surprised at how nervous I was, waiting for his response.

"Well, I have nothing against it. I think it's terrific for some people."

"What about for us?" I held my breath.

"Maybe. But I think it's premature to give up on having our own." Arnie looked at me directly. "Besides, I thought *you* were the one who was so anxious to give birth, to have another pregnancy."

"I was—I am. But I'm trying to be realistic. It isn't happening. It may not happen." The truth may make you free, but it will also make you miserable.

Arnie thought for a few minutes, scratching his beard. "But with adoption, there's no guarantee—"

I shrugged. "There's no guarantee in anything."

Arnie nodded his head slightly. Agreeing?

So I launched my campaign. And I am nothing if not persistent. "Why don't you talk to your cousin about it? C'mon, Arnie, ask her how she feels about her kids, whether she feels any different because one is adopted." Or I'd say: "You know, Laura's not my own child and I love her." This last one was effective. I think Arnie sometimes forgot, as I did, that I hadn't given birth to Laura. "And believe me, I don't love her because half her genes are yours, and certainly not because half her genes are Charlotte's! I love her because I've helped to raise her and nurture her and because she has ripped out a piece of my heart and I a piece of hers."

It was funny how our positions were reversed in this process. Arnie, who usually embraced things immediately, hung back; and I, the cautious one, bounded on ahead. I realized there were uncertainties in adoption. But there were uncertainties in raising any children. I saw it in my friends' kids. This one had terrible temper tantrums, that one had sleep problems, this one had a stutter. And not one of them adopted.

So what did it mean? There are no guarantees, Arnie. None at all. If we're looking for guarantees, we should be thinking about buying a washing machine, not becoming parents.

What do you think, Arnie? Should we wait and try to reproduce our birthmarks and long legs, or should we *produce* life, inexorably bound to it, and sharing forever its fate?

"I can love any child," Arnie finally said as he was packing to go to California. "But I think we ought to wait a few months more."

"But we've been waiting so long already. And it could take *years* to adopt."

"I don't think it'll take years." Arnie, my perennial optimist! "And besides," he said, walking over and kissing the top of my head, "you might already be pregnant."

My period was two days late. I tried not to think about it. Okay, that was impossible. I tried not to think about it *all the time*. And I even started to do a little research on a biography I wanted to write. I'd leave the library early so I could walk for a while along Fifth Avenue enjoying the Christmas windows, the smell of hot chestnuts, and the songs of the Salvation Army volunteers before boarding the Madison Avenue bus uptown.

It was my favorite time of the year. The first week in December, the stores still not too crowded but the glow and excitement of the holidays already illuminating the streets.

Arnie would call every evening from California. "What's new?"

"Nothing."

We'd both laugh. We were bad for each other. Each saying we shouldn't get our hopes up and doing it anyway. Six days late. It had never happened before.

But on the morning of the seventh day I woke up to severe cramps and bleeding. A late period? An early miscarriage? It didn't matter. I wasn't pregnant, and the thought was too much to bear.

I wanted to phone Arnie, but it was too early. There was no one to call, no one to tell. I sat in the house and smoked.

Finally Arnie called. "You'll get pregnant," he insisted, struggling to keep the disappointment out of his voice, but we were both wondering if I ever would.

I stayed in the apartment, shielding myself from the Christmas shoppers and holiday season, once again feeling lost, desperate, and hopeless.

Motherhood is an option, not a necessity. Women can be as satisfied with their careers as with their families. Biology is not destiny.

I had written these words, argued them, and taught them. And, yes, in spite of everything, I still believed in their truth.

But I knew that for me there was another kind of reality also, a reality that had nothing to do with rhetoric or reason, one that was basic, even primitive, and haunting.

Arnie came home with a small, slim present. I ripped off the paper and into my hands fell *The Little Engine That Could.* "Let's adopt a baby," he had written on the first page. "I THINK WE CAN, I THINK WE CAN, *I KNOW WE CAN!*"

Dorothy Thompson: "I Protest!"

Dorothy Thompson was one of the most literate, and ambitiously literary, young women of her day, and it is not at all clear that she had childbearing in mind when in 1928 she married novelist Sinclair Lewis. Both were recently divorced, and it was the private opinion of not a few of their friends that neither should have married at all, much less twice, certainly not to each other. After the first year or two they spent most of their time apart. Before that, however, while they were both still in New York, Dorothy became pregnant. This somewhat alarmed her, because she considered herself, at thirty-six, too old, and felt awkward and self-conscious about her condition. In fact, nothing untoward occurred, and at the anticipated time she taxied up to Woman's Hospital at 110th Street and, on June 20, 1930, gave birth to a healthy boy.

Vincent Sheean, a close friend of the couple, later wrote a biography of their marriage, which he called *Dorothy and Red,* and in which he described his own visit to the new mother.

On the following afternoon at four thirty, according to telephoned instructions from Red, I got into a subway and went up to Woman's Hospital to see Dorothy. She was blooming—all pink and white and relieved—and she sat up in bed and harangued me.

"Here we are," said she, "in the year 1930, with every possible advancement of science already upon us in every conceivable field, and yet nothing whatsoever has been done to mitigate or diminish the boredom of childbirth. It is not difficult and it is not painful, at least it was neither difficult nor painful for me. That doctor who said that a woman of thirty-six would have trouble with a first child must have been an idiot. I had no trouble at all. I scarcely even noticed. But the length of the gestation, nine months, has not changed by so much as a moment since time began. Evolution has scarcely affected it, although it may have had a deleterious effect upon the mammary glands. A woman must be gravid, like an animal, until the unseen forces command the delivery. This is barbarous and utterly unworthy of those wise and great men who rule our universe. If they can make invisible waves bring sounds—and some say, soon, pictures—over great distances, and if they can take the heart out and put it back again, and if they can fly to the moon as they say they intend to do sometime, why in God's name can't they do something about the womb of the human woman? Why must it be subject to the same irretrievable processes as the inner organs of the horse or the cow? Ingenuity and humanitarianism and the combined resources of chemistry, medicine, psychopathology and surgery are baffled, set at naught, reduced to zero, by a mechanical automatism as familiar to prehistory as it is to you or me. What has been the practical use of all this progress through the centuries when a woman is faced with her fundamental and indeed quintessential function in the life of her species, which is to reproduce it? One might as well be a Bulgarian peasant inured to parturition in a furrow. I protest."

If these be not the precise words, they were something of the sort—very near it indeed. I can see Dorothy now in her pink silk nightie, pawing the air. I may not have every word of it but I surely have the gist of the harangue, and its general style, too.

When she ended up with "I protest" we both laughed and she rang a bell. A nurse came in. Dorothy lifted an imperious and well-arched eyebrow. She really felt well that day.

"Bring in the child," she said.

Nineteenth Century China: "A Nine Months Child Is Like a Ripe Chestnut"

In the West the cardinal rule of obstetrics has always been to observe moderation and allow nature to take its course. Apparently the same wisdom prevailed in the East, as this excerpt from an early nineteenth century Chinese work in obstetrical medicine would imply.

Birth is a consequence of the laws of heaven and earth, man is the most reasonable of all beings and his birth is the most difficult of all. Formerly an accouchement presented no difficulty, the ignorance of midwives has rendered it a very serious affair. Formerly it followed its regular course, now it is a source of great embarrassment; hence the origin of miscarriages.

General rules: To check her passions, not to sleep on one side but on both in turn, to wear a belt 12 or 14 inches wide, sufficiently tied to support the hips without injuring the child and to take it off the moment she feels the first pains of childbirth; not to pay too much attention to the advice of the midwife who is always anxious to exaggerate the gravity of the case and to display her skill: for the child grows and falls like a ripe cucumber in due season. The child turns round in the womb and we must follow his movements. To have bread, we must let the corn grow. The accouchement may be rendered complicated by the weakness of the child, in that case the mother must lie in a horizontal position as being the most conducive to repose.

There is nothing supernatural in the world and the ignorant alone see a miracle in everything.

A miscarriage may take place under the following circumstances: if the mother has been badly fed at the commencement of her pregnancy; if she has had a nervous fever, or taken too much heating substances, pepper, garlic, etc.; if she has not been moderate in the gratification of her desires; if she has lived in a damp room; if she has been often badly clothed or exposed to the cold. No accident can happen if the mother keeps herself warm, tranquil, and is not impatient. She should eat chicken, pigeon, and duck broth in preference to anything else. She should not frequent gossips who by their presence may disturb her repose.

A nine months child is like a ripe chestnut which falls of itself, a child born before its time is like bitter unripe fruits which, when plucked, carry with them a part of the tree. . . .

Do not force nature, do not insult it, for it is as if you were to open the ears of corn to make the stalks grow. If the woman feels the child moving, she must lie upon her back and if the foetus descends, if the sufferings become intense, then you must look at the radix of her middle finger, and if you feel a beating of her pulse in that part, that points out the moment of her deliverance is at hand.

Translated by Leonard Hegewald,
Chinese Medical Review, 1852

Natalia Makarova: "Most Often I Think About My Future Child"

In August 1977 prima ballerina Natalia Makarova danced her last performance of the season and settled down in her San Francisco home to await the birth of her child. There, instead of the arduous nature of her usual existence, she enjoyed "the bliss of leisure." She walked in her tiny garden, read voraciously from those books that she seldom otherwise had time for, painted, and worked on her book, *A Dance Autobiography*, from which the following excerpt is taken.

I paint and I think. And most often I think about my future child, of course. I am having it in the middle of my career, and I think: Almost none of the major ballerinas of this century had children. Pavlova, Fonteyn, Spessivtseva, Ulanova, Plisetskaya. . . . I wonder why? Was that pure egoism? Or a sacrifice they were obliged to offer to the stage, which demanded it like a pagan god? The tribute paid for total absorption in the ballet, for that unbelievable joy which it can give so generously? Or fear of losing one's form after giving birth, of losing the extension, the suppleness of the back, the shape of the feet, which could become deformed? And what if that happened to me? Could I live without the stage? I absolutely couldn't dance in bad shape, and at one stroke, wipe out everything good that I have tried to accomplish. For me, there is nothing worse than to defile the ballet by performing badly that which depends not only on a divine spark but on form as well.

The ballet . . . what essentially is this thankless art? In the dramatic theatre, the film, in the fine arts, in writing, it is possible to rest for half a year and then return and begin to create something new. But consider Marina Semyonova, who after the birth of her daughter was never able to recover her form. Tragically and slavishly we depend upon the body, upon its physical habits and caprices; we wear it out to our last ounce of strength. And our masochistic labor is wiped away like marks in the sand, and years of grinding effort—all of that single combat with the body at rehearsal and in performance—pass away into nothing, as if they had never been. Is the ballet worth such sacrifice? I don't know the answer.

I paint, bending over the easel. I paint my Madonnas, my Leda and the Swan, and think: This canvas will remain, even my amateur canvas, which is important only to me. Certainly a professional artist's canvas remains. And he imprints on it his internal experience, his relationship to life—illuminations which may be fixed or stopped in color. But what remains of our art? Of our illuminations? They are momentary, alive for only one evening; they remain only in the memory of those who were present. And even that impression is frail and changeable: the farther away it goes, the more difficult it becomes to remember *what* it really was and *how* it was. I know exactly what it is on stage to let go of my control and improvise, still supported by that control. Suddenly new details come, precisely and expressively—but I myself cannot remember them. Perhaps they remain in the memory of others.

Will the ballet take second place to my child? Will the responsibility for its life break my attachment to the stage? And how will I be able to coordinate my endless travelling from city to city and from country to country with my child's daily need of me and my need for it? Or can I possibly live completely without the ballet? . . .

I can imagine myself not being on stage—but I cannot imagine existing oustide art. Yet it is difficult to believe that there will be no more rehearsals, no more feverish agitation before performances; that there will be something else instead. I have done much, but strangely, no feeling of peace follows from that. And it seems to me at this moment that I have simply sat down for a rest, in expectation of something new.

> *Note:* On February 1, 1978, Natalia Makarova gave birth to a son whom she named André Michel after her favorite apostles, and whom she nursed herself for the first month. By the middle of May she was back at the Met, dancing Jerome Robbins' *Other Dances* with partner Mikhail Baryshnikov.

Nehru on the Confinement of His Daughter, Indira Gandhi

Jawaharlal Nehru was first imprisoned in 1921 and spent eighteen of the next twenty-five years in jail; the following letter was written from Ahmednagar Fort where he had been held since 1942. The letter is to his sister, Krishna Hutheesing—"Bets"—and concerns the confinement of his daughter, Indira Gandhi, and the birth of his first grandson, Rajiv. "Indu" had been living with her aunt in Bombay because "Bets" was the only other member of the immediate family out of prison and able to look after her.

29.8.44

Darling Bets,

Your message about the birth of the little one reached me the same afternoon as your letter giving fuller details came on the 24th. I did not write to you last week as I sent both my week's letters to Indu.

I was happy to get the news—not so excited as you must have been, for excitement is less in my line. I was particularly pleased to learn of the easy delivery Indu had. I hope that she and the baby have kept up to the mark during the days following the confinement.

In my letter to Indu I suggested to her to ask you to get a proper horoscope made by a competent person. Such permanent records of the date and time of birth are desirable. As for the time, I suppose the proper solar time should be mentioned and not the artificial time which is being used outside now. War time is at least an hour ahead of the normal time.

The birth of a new member of the family always makes one feel reminiscent and remember one's childhood days and other births. I missed your birth for I was in England then, but when Nan came and Indu, I was very much there and I have vivid recollections of the events. And then the growth of the little ones, their childhood, girlhood and womanhood. It is an unending panorama of human life with its sweet and bitterness, its ups and downs. One would think that with all this age-long experience and personal and racial memories, nothing very novel can be expected. The old cycle repeats itself again and again. And yet whenever a person arrives, it is something absolutely new, like others and still unique in its own way. Nature goes on repeating itself but there is no end to its infinite variety and every spring is a resurrection, every new birth a new beginning. Especially when that new birth is intimately connected with us, it becomes a revival of ourselves and our old hopes centre round it. . . .

Love,

Your loving brother,

JAWAHAR.

Sigmund Freud: "Birth Is the First Experience of Anxiety"

For many years Sigmund Freud was preoccupied with the importance of fantasies and unconscious thoughts about life in the womb. He came to believe that the dread of being buried alive, which some of his patients expressed, had its origin in the prebirth experience. He also theorized that the belief in survival after death had its basis in the unconscious, and was merely a projection into the future of life before birth. Most important, however, was the realization that "the act of birth is the first experience of anxiety." As he explains in his *General Introduction to Psychoanalysis,* this concept came to him through the common sense of a young student of midwifery in Vienna whose unorthodox observation sparked in him a revolutionary idea.

It may perhaps interest you to know how it was possible to arrive at such an idea as this—that birth is the source and prototype of the anxiety affect. Speculation had least of all to do with it; on the contrary, I borrowed a thought from the naive intuitive mind of the people. Many years ago a number of young house-physicians, including myself, were sitting round a dinner-table, and one of the assistants at the obstetrical clinic was telling us all the funny stories of the last midwives' examination. One of the candidates was asked what it meant when the meconium (child's excreta) was present in the waters at birth, and promptly replied: "That the child is frightened." She was ridiculed and failed. But I silently took her part and began to suspect that the poor unsophisticated woman's unerring perception had revealed a very important connection.

"Having a Baby Inside Me Is the Only Time I'm Really Alive"

A black woman who came to Boston from Georgia in the mid-1960s said:

They came telling us not to have children, and not to have children, and sweep up, and all that. There isn't anything they don't want to do to you, or tell you to do. They tell you you're bad, and worse than others, and you're lazy, and you don't know how to get along like others do. . . .

Then they say we should look different, and eat different—use more of the protein. I tell them about the prices, but they reply about "planning"—planning, planning, that's all they tell you. The worst of it is that they try to get you to plan your kids, by the year; except they mean by the ten-year plan, one every ten years. The truth is, they don't want you to have any, if they could help it.

To me, having a baby inside me is the only time I'm really alive. I know I can make something, do something, no matter what color my skin is, and what names people call me. When the baby gets born I see him, and he's full of life, or she is; and I think to myself that it doesn't make any difference what happens later, at least now we've got a chance, or the baby does. You can see the little one grow and get larger and start doing things, and you feel there must be some hope, some chance that things will get better; because there it is, right before you, a real, live, growing baby. The children and their father feel it, too, just like I do. They feel the baby is a good sign, or at least he's *some* sign. If we didn't have that, what would be the difference from death? Even without children my life would still be bad—they're not going to give us what *they* have, the birth control people. They just want us to be a poor version of them, only without our children and our faith in God and our tasty fried food, or anything.

They'll tell you we are "neglectful"; we don't take proper care of the children. But that's a lie, because we do, until we can't any longer, because the time has come for the street to claim them. . . . So I turn my eyes on the little children, and keep on praying that one of them will grow up at the right second, when the school teachers have time to say hello and give him the lessons he needs, and when they get rid of the building here and let us have a place you can breathe in and not get bitten all the time, and when the men can find work—because *they* can't have children, and so they have to drink or get on drugs to find some happy moments, and some hope about things.

From Robert Coles, *Children of Crisis*

Pablo Picasso: "What You Need Is a Child"

Picasso already had two children—a son by his wife Olga and a daughter by his mistress Marie-Thérèse—when Françoise Gilot came into his life. It was May, 1943, during the German occupation of Paris; she was twenty-one, he nearly three times that. After the war she went to live with him, but she soon found that coping with the artist on a daily basis was not easy. As she put it later: "Life for Pablo was always a game one played with no holds barred." On a summer afternoon at Ménerbes her frustration reached the breaking point and she started hitchhiking to Marseilles, final destination North Africa. The first car to come along, however, was Picasso himself. Furious, he pushed her into the car and, while the chauffeur drove, railed at her for even considering leaving. Then as she later described in her book *Life with Picasso:*

. . . he drew me close to him. After a moment he turned toward me, relaxed his grip, and kissed me. He didn't speak right away, but when he began he spoke more softly.

"You mustn't listen to your head for things like that," he said. "You'll talk yourself out of the deepest things in life. What you need is a child. That will bring you back to nature and put you in tune with the rest of the world."

I told him nothing was more simple than to have a child at my age; it was only a matter of choice. But I didn't feel that having one would add anything that was especially relevant to the experience I was right now coming to grips with. Children were useful in a negative rather than a positive sense, I said, in that when one becomes mature and there are none, the lack makes itself felt, because by that time one must get out of oneself, and being occupied with the problems of others helps to ease one's own anguish. But children, I told him, were only one solution among several. After all, there were other forms of creation. The fact that I had undertaken to become a painter and, on top of that, to live with him and help bear the burden of his solitude showed that I was trying to make something creative out of my life, and to get out of myself. Each one of those steps had forced itself on me, and I felt I had no choice; but the idea of having a child was something that up to now had never crossed my mind, and it seemed to me entirely irrelevant. It was just as though he had told me that I ought to learn how to sole shoes. I would have said yes, I was sure it was a very practical thing to know but not at all urgent just at the moment. And that was the way I felt about having a child, I tried to explain.

Pablo sighed. "Words, words, words," he said. "You are developed only on the intellectual level. Everywhere else you're retarded. You won't know what it means to be a woman until you have a child."

I didn't feel altogether sanguine about that, considering the effects to date of my radical attempts to stand on my own feet like a grown woman, and I told him so. He brushed me aside. "I've seen it work before and I assure you that you'll be completely transformed. Please don't deny it until you've at least tried."

I couldn't feel, all at once, the same kind of buoyant enthusiasm that Pablo was displaying but before he dropped the subject, I had decided to take his advice, and to stop listening to my head. Since Pablo, I was convinced, had been talking with his heart, I could at least listen with mine. I put Marie-Thérèse and all the other negative elements out of my mind and I took the rest of Pablo's advice: I tried. . . . In a few weeks I knew I was pregnant.

> Once the transformation was accomplished, however, Picasso believed in letting well enough alone. He shared the primitive belief that to exhibit too much concern about a pregnancy is to invite disaster. The baby, they figured, was due in May, and in March Francoise had not yet seen a doctor.

Pablo was against the idea because he felt that if one looked after such things too carefully, it might bring bad luck. The only medical person I had seen during that winter was the psychoanalyst Doctor Lacan. Pablo always felt you should use people for things that lay outside their area of specialization. Since Lacan was a psychoanalyst, Pablo had adopted him as his general medical practitioner. He took his troubles to him and Lacan prescribed very little, saying, as a rule, that everything was fine. One time, a little earlier, I had had what seemed to be a bad grippe and was coughing a great deal. Doctor Lacan said it was a combination of fatigue and nervousness and simply gave me some pills to make me sleep and I did, in fact, sleep for most of two days and two nights as a result. When I got up, the grippe was gone and the cough with it.

About a week before the baby was to be born I was beginning to be quite excited and I decided it was time to do something. I kept talking about it until Pablo finally agreed we should think about an obstetrician and a clinic. He called Doctor Lacan, who was astounded to learn that I hadn't been seeing an obstetrician. He got Doctor Lamaze for me and he, even more flabbergasted, arranged for a bed in a clinic in Boulogne called *Le Belvedere*.

A year or two before I met Pablo I had begun to note down the details of any dreams I had that seemed out of the ordinary. Just before we met I dreamed one night that I was taking a bus trip, the sort of thing organized to show tourists famous monuments. In my dream we stopped at a museum. When we got out they herded us into a goatshed. It was very dark inside but I could see there were no goats. I was beginning to wonder why they had brought us there when I saw, right in the middle of the shed, a baby carriage. In it and hanging from it were two paintings: the portrait of Mademoiselle Rivière by Ingres, and a small painting by the Douanier Rousseau called *Les Representants des puissances étrangères venant saluer la République en signe de paix*. Both of them were smaller than their actual size; the Ingres was dangling from the handle of the baby carriage and the Douanier Rousseau was nestling inside it.

A few months after I met Pablo I had shown him the notebook in which I wrote about my dreams. He had thought that one particularly interesting; all the more so since the Douanier Rousseau painting I had dreamed about belonged to him, although I hadn't known it at the time. The day I went to the clinic for the delivery, Doctor Lamaze was delayed in arriving and when I got there, instead of finding him, I had a nurse and a midwife waiting for me. One of them was named Mademoiselle Ingres and the other, Madame Rousseau. Mademoiselle Ingres had black hair parted in the middle and pulled down severely on each side, like so many of Monsieur Ingres's female sitters. Pablo remembered reading what I had written about the dream and when Lacan arrived he asked him the meaning, in analysis, of a goatshed. Lacan told him it was a symbol for the birth of a child.

The baby—a boy—was born without difficulty on May 15, 1947.

Pablo wanted him to be named Pablo but since his first son had been named Paul—the French equivalent—I thought we should try something different. I remembered that Watteau's teacher had been called Claude Gillot, and that he had done many paintings of harlequins, just as Pablo himself had, even before the Blue Period and long after, so we named the baby Claude.

3. Conceiving

Go, and catch a falling star,
  Get with child a mandrake root,
Tell me, where all past years are,
  Or who cleft the Devil's foot.

John Donne

It is hitherto inexplicable, the manner in which the animalculum gains admission into the ovum, and the method by
which the vessels of the navel-string are inosculated with those
of the animalculum. Indeed, these points are so intricate that
every different theorist has started different opinions concerning them, some of which are rather jocular than instructive.

William Smellie, c. 1750

The Dionne Quintuplets: Five Tiny Baby Girls in a Butcher Basket

On May 28, 1934, the Associated Press in New York received the following dispatch from the Canadian Press:

> North Bay, Ontario, May 28—Mrs. Oliva Dionne, residing within a few miles of Callander, nine miles south of here, gave birth to five girls today. All were healthy, said Dr. A. R. Dafoe, Callander, attending physician. Mrs. Dionne is 26 years of age and previously had given birth to six children.

In light of what happened later that early communication becomes a rare instance of media understatement. But then in spite of the doctor's avowal of health, no one knew if any, much less all, of the babies would live till the news hit the papers. No one really thought it possible. Before the advent of fertility drugs fraternal quintuplets were extremely infrequent, 54 million to one, and the statistical probability of identical quintuplets was incalculable. There were only two cases in recorded history, and they had not survived. There have been none since.

But if the birth of the Dionne quintuplets was the miracle it was soon to be called, the fact that they survived was even more so. They were born in the depths of the Depression to a French Canadian farm couple in a remote part of northern Ontario, halfway between the old lumber mill town of Callander, where seventy percent of the population was on relief, and the farming community of Corbeil, where the inhabitants ate better but had no electric power, telephone service, running water, post office, or medical services. Oliva Dionne, the papa, was sophisticated compared with most of his neighbors; he had had nine years of schooling, could speak English, and owned a car. Elzire Dionne, his wife, understood English but did not speak it. It was not germane to her life. She was sixteen when she married, seventeen when her first child was born, twenty-six when in May of 1934 she entered the seventh month of her seventh pregnancy and wondered why she was experiencing so many problems with what had become for her such a normal state of affairs.

Another example of Oliva Dionne's relative sophistication was the fact that he had called in a doctor for four of his wife's six previous deliveries instead of relying exclusively (as did most of his neighbors) on the local midwife, Mme Benoit Labelle. Mme Labelle was quite competent and certainly experienced—ten children for the farming families of the area was average; she herself had had eighteen, thirteen of them without help. But Oliva Dionne, or perhaps it was Elzire, had felt more secure with the doctor present. So when in that spring of 1934 his wife's pregnancy developed disturbing complications—when her weight (she had never been slim) reached 200 pounds, her legs swelled to double their normal size, and the pain was almost constant—Oliva Dionne dropped by the doctor's office in Callander to see what he thought.

Allan Roy Dafoe, M.D., was the archetypal country doctor, minus the twinkle in the eye. He was brusque, direct, intent on his calling, unheeding of distances, weather, times of day or night, or ability to pay a fee. He had little sense of humor, even less of the subtleties of human psychology. He was basically compassionate, but an autocrat, a man with a mission. After his wife's death eight years before, he had withdrawn behind the sheltering confines of his profession, losing himself in the daily crises of a rural practitioner.

He could not know as he listened to Oliva Dionne that morning that he, Dafoe, was about to become (with the possible exception of Albert Schweitzer) the most famous doctor in the world. From Dionne's description of his wife's complaints, Dafoe suspected dropsy. He had no doubt that her case was serious, and he did his best to impress that on Dionne. His wife must—*must*—get off her feet. No more farm chores, cooking, housework. A hired girl should be brought in to take care of the children. Dionne nodded, but Dafoe knew what these farm families were like, knew where their priorities lay and that in hard times a hired girl would be considered an unaffordable luxury no matter what the alternative. So he himself drove out to the Dionne farmhouse the next day. He found, as he knew he would, that no one was paying him any mind. He shouted, he scolded. He deplored what he considered a fatalistic Catholic obstinancy opposing his scientific wisdom and authority. He insisted that if his directives were not carried out, Elzire Dionne would surely die.

A hired girl was engaged, and Elzire did, to some extent at least, retire to her bed. Her length of stay there was not long. At one A.M. on the morning of May 28, some eight weeks ahead of schedule, she went into labor. Her husband lit the coal oil lamp in the little room off the kitchen where she lay, and ran across the field for the nearest help—Mme Legros, Elzire's uncle's wife, who helped with births but did not charge a fee. Having secured that assistance, he hustled the children off to sympathetic neighbors, all except for eleven-month-old Pauline who was bedded down in a corner of the kitchen. But he continued to be alarmed by his wife's physical aspect and her mental state—she was convinced that this time she would not survive and murmured Hail Marys between contractions—so he set off after Mme Labelle. That good midwife was experienced enough to recognize clear and present danger when she saw it, and she in turn sent Dionne off to Callander after Dr. Dafoe. The doctor, of course, had a telephone, but the farmhouse did not.

In the interim before Dafoe's arrival (he had already delivered one baby that night), the first two of the quintuplets were born. Later Mme Labelle would describe how just before dawn the first baby arrived, grotesquely proportioned, with spider-like legs and a large head, bright blue in color, not breathing. The women might have been excused assuming the baby still born, but it was not their habit to give up so easily. Mme Labelle opened the oven door in the kitchen and holding the baby in front of the heat, massaged its little wrinkled back and blew air into its tiny mouth. She was rewarded with a cry more like the mew of a kitten than human. Assured that for the moment, anyway, it was alive, she wrapped the baby quickly in whatever she could find because it was apparent that another was about to emerge. This one, too, was blue. Mme Labelle repeated her ministrations and Mme Legros hurriedly baptized both. Dafoe arrived to find two miniscule beings wrapped in tattered bits of blanket at the foot of the bed and the night's activities clearly not yet finished.

The combined amazement of those present at what happened during the next half hour is surely beyond imagining. Outside in the May dawn the birds were singing and the farmyard noises were just beginning. Inside little Pauline slept in her corner, Oliva Dionne paced about, Mme Labelle heated more water, Mme Legros hunted out more scraps of blanket, and Dr. Dafoe barked orders at everyone.

A third baby emerged; then in quick succession, a fourth and fifth. The last two were still encased in their amniotic sacs like tiny water sprites. The doctor ruptured the sacs and turned the babies over to the midwives. He doubted any of them would live, but he would try to save the mother if he could.

Elzire Dionne lay seemingly close to death. The tips of her fingers were black, as if the blood had already ceased circulating in her limbs. Dafoe injected a dose of pituitary to try to raise her blood pressure, and followed it with one of ergot to guard against post-natal hemorrhage. When she had somewhat revived, they gently informed her that she had given birth to five tiny baby girls. She could barely take it in. "Holy Mary!" she whispered.

Oliva Dionne went into similar shock, but whereas Elzire was awed, Oliva was from the first overwhelmed by practical considerations. He seemed less concerned that the babies should die than they might live. It would be unfair to condemn him for that—the Depression had already swallowed up the meager savings he had once had, and now in a few short hours the number of his dependents had almost doubled. He was heard appealing to the Almighty: "What am I going to do with five babies? It was bad enough to look after one; but how are we going to manage to look after five?" Bordering on nervous prostration, he was in no condition to go for the priest, which the good Catholic midwives wanted in case Elzire Dionne grew worse. So the weary doctor, the only other person who could drive, went off to perform that function. He may have welcomed the opportunity to see firsthand the reaction of a man of God to the miracle just wrought.

By eight o'clock things were in some kind of order. Elzire had sipped a cup of tea and Mme Labelle had gruel and chicken broth simmering on the stove. Little Pauline was awake. Mme Legros had gone back across the field and returned with a blanket, flatirons, a bottle of olive oil, and a butcher's basket. One by one each baby had been patted with the warm oil, wrapped up again, and laid crosswise next to her sisters in the basket, which was placed between two chairs in front of the warm oven. Another blanket was heated and hung over the backs of the chairs. Before he left to go back to Callander to get some breakfast and, who can doubt it, spread the word, Dr. Dafoe left exact instructions as to the care—or non-care—of the babies. They were, if they lived, to be kept warm and given a couple of drops of warm water every two hours. Other than that, they were to be left absolutely alone.

Afterward it was agreed that it was this very lack of attention that

allowed the babies to survive. They were so fragile—ranging in weight
between one and a half and two and a half pounds—that any extra
handling would itself have been fatal. The other children drifted
home, the neighbors dropped by, but the basket with its five mummy-
like occupants was so awe-inspiring that people tended to look from
some distance. A nurse was summoned; when the babies continued to
live, more were called in. The nurses faced a gargantuan task—not
only were there five "patients" in the most delicate condition imaginable, but there was no electricity, no running water, no screens, and a
plethora of farm-bred flies and mosquitos circulating between house
and barn. After the first twenty-four hour period, Dafoe devised a
formula of seven parts cow's milk to twenty parts sterilized water and
two parts corn syrup, which was fed the babies from an eyedropper a
few drops at a time every two hours. It was imperative that the temperature be kept constant—the slightest increase caused them to gasp
for breath; a decrease, and the rate of their breathing accelerated
alarmingly. They could not be touched, but they had to be watched
unceasingly.

In the first few days the babies were named—Yvonne, Cécile, Annette, Emilie, and Marie—and after that they acquired personalities
related to their individual needs. Emilie and Marie, the smallest, were
the quickest to react to any change in their environment. If he saw
them begin to turn blue around the sides of their mouth or nose,
Dafoe would doctor them with a solution of two parts rum to ten
parts warm water. Later he was questioned why he used rum rather
than the traditional brandy; it was, he replied, all a matter of economics. In northern Ontario in 1934 rum was all anyone could afford.
There wasn't any brandy to be had.

By the third night Dafoe, peering at his tiny charges, concluded that
Emilie and Marie were barely hanging on to life and would not make
it until morning unless something drastic were done. To the horror of
the nurse then in attendance, he took a two-inch hypodermic syringe
out of his bag, fit a small section of rubber tubing over it, and prepared to give them an enema. The nurse was convinced it would kill
them; Dafoe countered that without it, they would die. He completed
the operation and then fed ten drops of rum into each little mouth.
They lived.

Gradually it began to dawn on the world that something quite out
of the ordinary had happened up there in the Canadian backwoods.
Dr. Dafoe's phone began to ring; he was seldom at home, but when
he was, he spent all his time answering calls. One of the first was from

a Dr. Bundeson, a Chicago expert on premature babies. At first he
refused to believe the babies were still living, but when Dafoe told
him to go to hell and hung up, Bundeson revised his approach and
called back. He immediately started dispensing advice. The babies
would, of course, need incubators. Impossible, said Dafoe, there was
no electricity in the farmhouse. Then he, Bundeson, would hunt out
an old-style, gas-operated one. Now, what about breast milk? The
babies would not be able to tolerate anything else, but a bevy of wet
nurses, even should they be rounded up, was out of the question. He
would take it upon himself to find donors there in Chicago, pack
the milk in dry ice, and send it regularly via plane and train to
Callander.

In the meantime an enterprising Hearst reporter had located a
nineteenth century kerosene-burning incubator, which he personally
conducted up to the farmhouse. Made for one baby, it could accommodate the three smallest quints. The *Toronto Star* sent an entire
news team bearing gifts—hot water bottles, sheets, blankets and coverlets, soap, absorbent cotton, vaseline, a large tin of olive oil and another of talcum powder, dozens of diapers, and a complete wardrobe
of the smallest size baby clothes which were still, of course, much too
large. For the "proud parents" there was a great basket of goodies
ranging from jellies, biscuits, and cream cheese to fresh strawberries,
cantalope, tomatoes, celery, and sponge cake.

At this stage, however, the "proud parents" were not all that proud.
Although Oliva Dionne had begun to be aware that supporting his
new daughters might pose less of a problem than he had first supposed, this did not reconcile him to their birth. He hated the reporters
rushing about asking questions, the photographers flashing magnesium
powder in everyone's face. He felt more humiliated than proud. He
and Elzire were simple people, farm people, and giving birth to five
babies was much too close to an animal producing a litter. Oliva felt
that the fault was his. The act of impregnation had been his act; it
was he who had done this thing to his wife—indeed, to his whole
family. "What will the neighbors say?" Elzire had asked him when he
gathered enough courage to come to her bedside that first morning.
"They will think we are pigs." It was bewildering enough that it
should have happened, and now here were all these reporters, more
every day, recording and publicizing his disgrace.

The rest of the story—everything that happened after those first few
days of tenuous life—is not relevant here. The quints did survive, and

then thrive. For various reasons—some real, some concocted—they were taken away from their parents and made wards of the state. Their goldfish-bowl childhood is well known. Times were hard, and their very existence—five adorable little girls with enormous black eyes—brought millions of tourist dollars into Depression-torn Ontario.

The quintuplets grew up estranged from their parents and older brothers and sisters in the old farmhouse across the road from their own custom-built habitation. Eventually a large new family home was constructed, and for a while the family was united, but only physically. Early habits are strong, and emotionally the quints always lived apart. They were complete within themselves, and famous beyond exaggeration: there were people all over the world who knew absolutely nothing else about Canada except that the quintuplets lived there. Their wide visibility held unexpected benefits—in Nigeria missionaries pasted their pictures on the church walls to try to halt the native practice of killing one or both of a pair of twins—and were at least partially successful. As the miracle doctor who had kept them alive, Dr. Dafoe acquired his own, independent celebrity, and others who had by chance been part of that extraordinary birth found they could capitalize on it almost endlessly. The quints possessed the infinite fascination of royal children, but they were less protected from the obvious drawbacks, and probably suffered more. And their parents—poor God-fearing Elzire who had almost given her life for theirs, and Oliva, an ordinary French-Canadian farmer, a family man who lost half his family and all his self-respect—for them the miracle had been something less than blessed.

Postscript: Only three of the Dionne quintuplets are still alive to celebrate the half-century of their birth on May 28, 1984. The last two born, Emilie and Marie, neither of whom were ever strong, died at the ages of twenty and thirty-five, respectively. Yvonne, the eldest, studied nursing for a while and made several unsuccessful attempts to become a nun. Annette, Cécile, and Marie (before her death) all married and had children of their own. Today the three surviving quints live not far from each other in the Montreal suburb of St Bruno, existing mostly on the somewhat meager interest from their trust fund. Considering the enormous sums they brought into the province of Ontario during their childhood, they are barely comfortable by current standards. They live quiet lives, go about largely unrecognized, as they prefer, and are still closely bound to each other, as they also prefer.

Louis XIII Loses a Bed and Gains a Son

Marriages of princes take place not, Charles Perrault to the contrary, in order to live happily ever after, but rather in order to beget sons, legitimate heirs to continue the monarchial line. Seventeenth century French sovereigns were a case in point. Louis XIII inherited the throne at the age of nine, was crowned on his thirteenth birthday, and almost at once had to confront the question of the succession. Thirteen is young for marriage, and this was especially true of Louis whose development was a little more delayed than average. Temperamentally, he was brooding, secretive. And his mother, the ogress Marie de Medici, had soured him on women.

But a king must marry, even an immature one. Louis was contracted the following year to Philip III of Spain's daughter known (somewhat inexplicably) as Anne of Austria. Anne, also fourteen, romped out of the court of Madrid and into that of Paris accompanied by her little maids-of-honor, all hardly more than children. Her French was terrible and she had a decided underbite, but Louis probably would not have liked her in any case. He clearly preferred hunting to husbandry. Even after she was at last pregnant (the marriage was not consummated until they were eighteen), he continued to hunt and she to romp, and so it came as no surprise when one day while sliding with a companion down the long shiny halls of the Louvre, Anne fell and suffered a miscarriage.

A *contretemps*, to be sure, but *c'est la vie*. The little queen was young, and there seemed no undue cause for alarm. She would have a child next year, the court reasoned, but they reasoned without Louis. The young king chose to take the accident as a personal affront. Lose his child, would she?! Waste his seed? He would show her! And for the next eighteen years, Bourbon line be damned, the king slept apart from the queen.

The matter should not be misconstrued. No progression of mistresses filed through the king's apartments, nor did a great romantic passion absorb his attention. Son of one licentious king, eventual father to another, Louis avoided women. He preferred male companionship, or often none at all; he liked to ride and hunt, to putter around with his guns and clocks, to whip up the odd omelet in the palace kitchen. Not exactly a misogynist, but a misfit at the very least.

Then one December day in 1637 Louis prepared to set off with his retinue for Fountainebleau and a week or two of hunting. In that age when a king traveled from one residence to another, his furniture went with him. On this particular day (his bed, etc., having gone off that morning), the king was detained, and before he could leave a violent storm came up and forced him to postpone his departure.

But the delay created its own difficulties. A king is a king; he cannot, after all, sleep in just any bed. He cannot simply stretch out on a couch somewhere. There are only two royal possibilities open to a king in regard to beds—his own, or the queen's.

Thus it was that on that stormy December night nearly 350 years ago the king once again slept with the queen. The next day, as far as is known, he set off for Fountainebleau. And the next September was born Louis XIV.

The story might well end there with its happily ever after, but there is a postscript. The king was not at all displeased with the whole affair. He repeated the experiment a year or so later, and in due course the young prince had a brother. Who knows where it all might not have led, had the king not died soon thereafter, leaving Louis XIV, aged five, to begin his own long and stormy reign.

The Centuries-old Riddle of Conception

Perhaps none of life's mysteries has ever so engrossed the human mind as the mystery of conception. The true facts have only been known for about a hundred years; before that there were centuries and millennium in which various theories were put forward within the civilized world, not to mention the numerous and often poetic explanations of the primitive.

The earliest Hebrews, Egyptians, and Greeks of whom we have records believed that the embryo was formed from the semen of the father housed in the receptacle of the mother. The Greek philosopher Anaxagorus (c. 475 B.C.) translated it into terms his fellow Greeks would understand: the embryo "grew" when the "seed" of the father was "planted" in the "soil" of the mother. He was immediately followed by the physician Hippocrates who refined the theory according to his observations. Hippocrates said that both men and women produced seed, and that both produced both male and female seed. Fertilization came about when the two were combined. Male seed was stronger than female seed; if there was more of the stronger seed in the mixture, the child would be a boy; if more of the weaker, a girl. Whichever seed was most abundant would affect and transform the other. Hippocrates was unique in this explanation—it would be centuries before anyone else would suggest that the female actually contributed on a par with the male.

Aristotle lost no time in returning woman to her place. The female contribution, he said, was mere "matter," a substance constituted of menstrual fluid, to which the man gave form and life and energy. Much in the way, he said, that a bedstead is carved from wood by the carpenter. This theory held for generations. The early Christians liked it because of the analogy to God generating life in the Virgin Mary. Thomas Aquinas gave it his stamp of approval—"the power of the female generative virtue provides the substance but the active male virtue makes it into the finished product"—indicating that science, under the influence of the Church, had made no advancement at all in fifteen centuries. In the years following, several men less known for their religious bias, including Leonardo, did suggest that men and women appeared to contribute equally to the heredity of a child, but they did not know how it was done. The breakthrough did not come until 1677 when the Dutch scientist Leeuwenhoek developed a new and powerful microscope and put a specimen of semen under it. The spermatozoa that Leeuwenhoek observed, he called "animalcules," misinterpreting them as actual human babies in minuscule form, which he thought were transported through the semen into the mother for nurturing.

Even after the ovum was discovered 150 years later, the Aristotelian theory of man's dominance prevailed. The ovum was believed inert until activated by the man's semen. Only in the last century has it been irrefutably demonstrated that the egg—ovum—is an equal partner with the sperm in the fertilization of the embryo.

Alice Roosevelt Longworth Explains the Facts of Life to her Cousin Eleanor

As a young woman Alice Roosevelt Longworth seemed to have everything—beauty, brains, aristocratic family connections, and enough money not to have to think about it. She lived most of her long life in Washington, and saw eighteen different presidents occupy the White House, including her father, Theodore, and her cousin, Franklin. In the following brief excerpt from Michael Teague's *Mrs. L: Conversations with Alice Roosevelt Longworth,* she looks back to her childhood with its carefully nurtured innocence, and recalls how differently she and her cousin, Eleanor Roosevelt, reacted to the adolescent nescience that convention insisted upon.

My father's library was enchanting. He had an enormous variety of books, including many we were told not to read, such as *The Heart of Midlothian* (because it had an illegitimate child in it). Even some of Kipling's works were doctored for us for reasons I could never discover. To give my father credit, he detested sham, especially euphemisms like "enceinte" for pregnant and things like that. But he did have Principles.

Anything to do with sex or childbirth was just not discussed. Yet it was curious how much surreptitious attention was paid to the consequences of sex in those days. For instance, I never discussed such matters with my stepmother when I was a teenager, although she did come to me before I was married and said, "You know, before you were born, your mother had to have a little something done in order to have you, so if you need anything let me know." It was couched in just those words. And I said, "Thank you very much." And that was that.

By the age of fifteen I knew quite a bit from the Bible and from my rabbits and guinea pigs. Living in the country as I did, you take these things for granted. They wouldn't admit that the Bible was a good place to learn the facts of life but I did just that.

However, when I tried to pass some of the information on to my cousin Eleanor, I almost came to grief. We were in the back bedroom at Auntie Bye's just after I had been "expelled" from Washington and I started imparting some of my newly found biblical knowledge . . . probably nothing more explosive than the "begat" series . . . when she suddenly leapt on me and tried to sit on my head and smother me with a pillow, saying I was being blasphemous. So I shut up and I think she probably went to her wedding not knowing anything about the subject at all. It was that kind of difference between us from the start.

Moon-Struck and Moon-Begotten

The moon, it was believed, controls more than the tides; it also controls the fertility of women. In his voluminous and extraordinary work *The Mothers*, Robert Briffault collected a great mass of lunar lore, from which the following observations on conceiving may be drawn.

Many primitive tribes attribute the onset of menstruation to the moon which, they say, defiles young girls. But the moon does not stop there. As the girl becomes a woman and marries, the moon controls whether or not she will conceive, and sometimes is counted responsible for the pregnancy itself. The Papuan natives of New Guinea believe that; the Maori go on to argue that the moon is every woman's real husband, the man living with her being only a (generally poor) substitute. The aborigines of Australia maintain that women belong to the moon by right. At the diametrically opposite point of the globe, the Eskimos of Greenland also claim that the moon makes love to their women; they warn young girls not to stare at it for fear of leading it on and getting a child in the bargain.

In other parts of the globe moon-rape appears less of a problem, but its influence is still considerable. The Saorias of the Rajmaha Hills are convinced that intercourse at the dark of the moon will never lead to pregnancy. An Indian woman of the American Southwest who wants to become pregnant will stand naked straddling a bucket of water in which the rays of the moon are reflected. In Central Europe she might drink water from such a container, thus "swallowing the moon," or if she is more daring, or more desperate, she will expose the lower part of her body to the moon's rays when it is in its first and last quarters—when it is "horned."

Many mothers in primitive cultures hold their newborn babies up to the sun or moon—the "father" from whom they will receive health and strength. The Isubu mother of the Cameroon is less ready to write off her husband; she compromises and introduces the moon to her newborn child as its "grandfather."

All such practices extend back to Egyptian and Babylonian times. Ancient peoples also believed that the moon governed a woman's fertility; the Babylonians even said that the sex of the child depended on whether or not the moon had a halo at the time of conception. The Vedic believed that the moon was the real husband of women, a concept that passed over into Buddhism where, in one legend, Buddha is himself moon-begotten.

A Ceremony of Hope in India

The woman who does not conceive a child has always been at a special disadvantage in India. Not only is she denied personal fulfillment, but her position in society as a whole is nebulous, undefined. She has no status. Although the educated urban woman will feel this less, it is doubtful that even she can escape it entirely. In her book *The Hindu Woman* Margaret Cormack, who was born and grew up in India, recalls how along the roadsides

the trees are festooned with fertility offerings, and describes the
annual "ceremony for barren women" in a South Indian village.

The barren women, most of them young, were first bathed by their
families in the village tank—many of them stood in the water for several hours, as the proceedings in the temple took a long time. They
were then placed prone, face down, on the main village road, their
arms extended above their heads, their hands together and holding
plantains, coconut, and betel leaves. For a long time there had been
drumming and music at the temple, where the Priest was "getting
ready," and the bulk of the swarming crowd was concentrated at the
temple. Finally, accompanied by shouting and frenzied tom-tomming,
the priest came out, holding on his head a tall phallic symbol covered
with marigolds. Supported by two men, the priest, seemingly in semi-
trance, walked along the road, stepping on the backs of the prone
women. Many of the women were limp, some were rigid and foaming
at the mouth. Their husbands picked them up, sometimes carrying
them down the road for a second "step." This ceremony took many
hours altogether, and the women involved were in a state of cataleptic
exhaustion at the end.

Sylvia Plath: "I Want a House of Our Children"

Sylvia Plath kept a journal from the time she was a young child.
She wrote in it steadily through her years at Smith, during her
term as a Fulbright scholar at Cambridge when she married poet
Ted Hughes, right up until the time she and Hughes returned to
England to await the birth of their first child. That baby was followed by a second, not long after which, as the world knows, her
warring selves became too much for her and she committed sui-
cide. The following excerpt from *The Journals of Sylvia Plath*
dates from the period when she was trying—as yet unsuccessfully—
to become pregnant.

Saturday, June 20 1959. Everything has gone barren. I am part of
the world's ash, something from which nothing can grow, nothing can
flower or come to fruit. In the lovely words of 20th century medicine,
I can't ovulate. Or don't. Didn't this month, didn't last month. For
ten years I may have been having cramps and for nothing. I have
worked, bled, knocked my head on walls to break through to where I
am now. With the one man in the world right for me, the one man I
could love. I would bear children until my change of life if that were
possible. I want a house of our children, little animals, flowers, vege-

tables, fruits. I want to be an Earth Mother in the deepest richest sense.
I have turned from being an intellectual, a career woman: all that is
ash to me. And what do I meet in myself? Ash. Ash and more ash.

I will enter in to the horrible clinical cycle of diagramming intercourse, rushing to be analyzed when I've had a period, when I've had
intercourse. Getting injections of this and that, hormones, thyroid,
becoming something other than myself, becoming synthetic. My body
a test tube. "People who haven't conceived in six months have a problem, dearie," the doctor said. And, taking out the little stick with
cotton on the end from my cervix, held it up to his assistant nurse:
"Black as black." If I had ovulated it would be green. Same test, iron-
ically, used to diagnose diabetes. Green, the color of life and eggs and
sugar fluid. "He found the exact day I ovulated," the nurse told me.
"It's a wonderful test, less expensive, easier." Ha. Suddenly the deep
foundations of my being are gnawn. I have come, with great pain and
effort, to the point where my desires and emotions and thoughts center
around what the normal woman's center around, and what do I find?
Barrenness.

Suddenly everything is ominous, ironic, deadly. If I could not have
children—and if I do not ovulate how can I?—how can they make
me?— I would be dead. Dead to my woman's body. Intercourse would
be dead, a dead end. My pleasure no pleasure, a mockery. My writing
a hollow and failing substitute for real life, real feeling, instead of a
pleasant extra, a bonus flowering and fruiting. Ted should be a pa-
triarch. I a mother. My love for him, to express our love, us, through
my body, the doors of my body, utterly thwarted. To say I am abnor-
mally pessimistic about this is to say that any woman should face not
ovulating with a cavalier grin. Or "a sense of humor." Ha again.

I see no mailman. A lovely clear morning. I cried and cried. Last
night, today. How can I keep Ted wedded to a barren woman? Barren
barren. His last poem, the title poem of his book, being a ceremony to
make a barren woman fertile: "Flung from the chain of the living, the
Past killed in her, the Future plucked out." "Touch this frozen
one." . . . My god. This is the one thing in the world I can't face.

Inside Every Woman Is the "Baby Putting Place"

In Nepal they say that inside the stomach of every woman is a folded
area known as the "baby putting place." Secreted there is a piece of
"flesh," which, when joined by the "pus" of the man, may unite and
form a baby. As the baby grows, the "baby putting place" grows with

it. A man and woman may continue to have intercourse right up until the time of the birth, but afterwards they should abstain for a week or two so that the "baby putting place," which has been loosened by the birth, will not fall out. Eventually it will shrink back to its former size and re-attach itself firmly to the stomach.

Since it took several thousand years for the civilized world to arrive at a sound theory of procreation, it is hardly to be wondered that primitive societies still cling at least in part to the old beliefs. The Balinese, for example, say that not only the man, but the woman, too, produces semen, which after intercourse may join with the man's to form a ball. When fed by the woman's blood, it will gradually take on human characteristics and develop into a child. At the same time the child is a reincarnation of an ancestor whose spirit has returned to earth in the form of dew that has been inadvertently consumed by the parents.

The Mundurucu tribe of Amazonian Brazil, on the other hand, believe that only the father produces semen, but that it takes a lot of it to make a child. The accumulation of just one or two passionate episodes will never yield enough; there is, therefore, little danger involved in the occasional extramarital fling. Continuous and persistent love-making is the only way to ensure an adequate supply. When accomplished, the hero-god Karusakaibo will enter the womb and form the accumulated semen into a tiny likeness of the child.

But by far the most extraordinary beliefs are those that prevailed in the Australian bush until very recent times, and which perhaps in the most remote areas continue still.

For centuries the Australian aborigines avoided making the obvious connection between fornication and procreation. This fact was validated by a number of different research teams that went into the bush in the 1920s and 1930s, seeking out the aborigines as almost the only truly primitive peoples left. These scientists all returned with the same data—that the bushmen believe that conception occurs when a spirit enters the woman, and that spirit might be the moon or stars, wind or water or tree, lizard or bird, but assuredly is not something contained in the semen of a man.

Even now, when most aborigines will admit to the view that the conception of a child may be distantly related to biology, they still connect it with the totem—or, more accurately, with the father's totem. This totem—animal, bird, plant, or other natural object—binds the family or clan together in blood relationship and ensures a vaguely mystical connection to a particular land area where the totem resides.

All the approximately five hundred tribes still inhabiting the Australian outback are patrilineal in structure. The child always descends from the father. The mother, far from being a star in the drama of childbirth, barely holds a supporting role.

Australian aborigines do not so much deny a blood link between parent and child as simply ignore it. It becomes of little consequence; it is the spiritual relationship that is significant. Ritual defloration, which initiates the young girl into womanhood and readies her spiritually to conceive, and which is followed by marriage to a man usually twice her age, is designed to prepare her to carry the already formed "spirit child" who is waiting in one of the totem centers. The young wife will be followed by the "spirit children" of her husband's totem, one of which will enter her body and lodge in her womb. Just as with the Mundurucu who believe that the lover will not have adequate opportunity to leave enough semen with a woman to make a child, so the Australian aborigines hold that the woman's body is the exclusive property of her husband and will not, as a result, accept the spirit child of anyone else's totem. This philosophy allows for considerable promiscuity without paternity becoming an issue.

It also makes for an unusually strong bond between the father and his children, since they are of his totem rather than their mother's. The souls of his children are part of his soul—not part of hers, and assuredly not part of the soul of some other man that she may, through his generosity in lending her out, have slept with recently. The same conviction has the added advantage of eliminating the social problem of illegitimate children. They do not exist. All women are married; if a woman's husband dies, she is acquired as an extra wife by his brother, and any child she bears is automatically the child of her current mate.

Christian missionaries generally failed in their attempts to upgrade sexual morals by imparting the biological truths of pregnancy. But although recent incursions of civilization may have erased that innocence in the contemporary aborigine, most clearly prefer their traditional explanations of conception that allow them to continue the kind of gentle philandering they also prefer. We might therefore assume that the old theories have not been laid to rest, but exist side by side with the new. In North Queensland a man who wants his wife to conceive will formally present her with food he has prepared and stand over her while she eats it. The old men of Port Darwin tell of evil spirits that reach into the fire for babies that they install in the wombs of women who then have no choice but to give birth to them.

The natives of the Pennefather River area believe that babies are molded from swamp mud and then implanted in women by a being called "Anjea" who provides the spirit for the child. A boy will be animated with a piece of his father's spirit; a girl, with a piece from her father's sister. These spirit-pieces are retrieved by Anjea from the afterbirth of the father or his sister which long ago, at the time of their own birth, was buried in the sand by their grandmother and marked with sticks for this eventual purpose. The father or his sister may have wandered extensively in the interval, but Anjea will always know where to find the appropriate afterbirth.

Admittedly, that is strong competition for the bare facts of biology.

Brendan Gill: Unexpected Fruits
of the Labor of Youth

In his autobiographical *Here at The New Yorker* Brendan Gill describes how the academic fruits of his senior year at Yale affected the lives of some English houseguests thirty years later.

At Yale . . . by judicious planning in earlier years I had reduced the number of classes I was obliged to attend in senior year to one: a survey of English lyric poetry. And this class met but once a week, and I was the only student in the class. My professor, F. E. Pierce, had suffered a stroke and was confined to his house. . . . One day he managed to get out of the house, shuffle his way to a gunsmith's shop, purchase a revolver, shuffle home, put the revolver against the roof of his mouth, and blow his brains out. Shocked as I was by the violence of his death—a violence all the more unexpected in so gentle and smiling a man—I thought it admirable. . . .

In the months following Pierce's death, I wrote a long sonnet-sequence, based on what I imagined to be Pierce's feelings in respect to his late wife. The sequence won a prize, which consisted of a comparatively large sum of money. One of the stipulations of the prize was that the poem that won it must be published, so I decided to spend all the money on the printing of a distinguished-looking little book—my first—called *Death in April*. It contained, in handset type upon hand-made paper, the sonnet-sequence, a dozen or so love poems, and other tender scraps. I have taken pains not to look at it since, but all books have lives of their own and their own consequences, and that book helped teach me a lesson: never accept a compliment until it has been completed.

A few years ago, an English friend of mine saw me among a group of people in Washington. He came up and began telling the group how the Gills, meeting him and his wife on their first visit to America, had kindly offered them the use of the Gills' country house for an autumn holiday. Late one night during the holiday, he was glancing over our shelves in search of something to read and stumbled on my little book. He read some of the love poems aloud to his wife; they were so moved by them that they immediately made love and she conceived a child. I broke in at that point to say how delighted I was to think that any word of mine could have led not only to love-making but to a birth as well. "And furthermore," my friend went on, interrupting my interruption, "I think those poems of yours are the very best work you've ever done." So from the heights, the depths: his compliment had dismissed thirty years of my life's work in a single breath.

4. Expecting

Send us, bright one, light one, Horhorn, quickening and wombfruit. Send us, bright one, light one, Horhorn, quickening and wombfruit. Send us bright one, light one, Horhorn, quickening and wombfruit.

James Joyce, *Ulysses*

Pregnancy permits woman to rationalize performances which otherwise would appear absurd.

Helene Deutsch

Mary Wollstonecraft: "I Have Felt Some Gentle Twitches"

Mary Wollstonecraft was a true daughter of the eighteenth century as her well-reasoned appeal for the independence of her sex, *A Vindication of the Rights of Woman,* demonstrates. She was also, however, a woman of passionate emotion. Soon after the publication of her *Vindication* she fell in love with an American, Gilbert Imlay, and the realization that she was carrying his child, plus her uncertainty as to what his reaction to that news would be, prompted the following letter:

Paris, November, 1793
Sunday Night

I have just received your letter, and feel as if I could not go to bed tranquilly without saying a few words in reply, merely to tell you that my mind is serene, and my heart affectionate.

Ever since you last saw me inclined to faint, I have felt some gentle twitches, which make me begin to think that I am nourishing a creature who will soon be sensible of my care. This thought has not only produced an overflowing of tenderness to you, but made me very attentive to calm my mind and take exercise, lest I should destroy an object, in whom we are to have a mutual interest, you know. Yesterday—do not smile!—finding that I had hurt myself by lifting precipitately a large log of wood, I sat down in an agony, till I felt those said twitches again. . . .

Write to me, my best love, and bid me be patient—kindly—and the expressions of kindness will again beguile the time, as sweetly as they have done tonight. Tell me also over and over again, that your happiness (and you deserve to be happy!) is closely connected with mine. . . . Take care of yourself, and remember with tenderness your affectionate

Mary

Colette: Having a Masculine Pregnancy

Colette is best known as a French novelist, creator of such memo-
rable fictional heroines as Claudine, Cherí, and Gigi, but she published a large body of autobiographical writings as well. After her
death these were collected, translated, and published in English
under the title *Earthly Paradise*. The following selection from
that work concerns her pregnancy—at forty—and the birth of her
only child. It is interesting, and not unexpected, that the baby's
father—Henri de Jouvenel, editor of the leading Paris newspaper
Le Matin and Colette's second husband—is never mentioned.

I was forty, and I remember greeting the certitude of the belated
child's presence with serious mistrust, while saying nothing about it.
Physical apprehension had nothing to do with my behavior; I was
simply afraid that at my age I would not know how to give a child
the proper love and care, devotion and understanding. Love—so I believed—had already hurt me a great deal by monopolizing me for the
past twenty years.

It is neither wise nor good to start a child with too much thought.
Little used to worrying about the future, I found myself for the first
time preparing for an exact date that it would have been quite
enough to think about only four weeks beforehand. I meditated, I
tried to think clearly and reasonably, but I was struck by the recollec-
tion that intelligent cats are usually bad mothers, sinning by inad-
vertence or by excess of zeal, constantly moving their kittens from
place to place, holding them by the nape of the neck, pinched between their teeth, hesitating where to deposit them. What a comfortable nest that sagging seat of an armchair! However, less so than
under the down quilt, perhaps? But surely the acme of comfort would
be the second drawer of the commode?

During the first three months I told almost no one of my condition
or my worries. I did tell Charles Sauerwein and was struck by his comment. "Do you know what you're doing?" he exclaimed. "You're behaving as a man would, you're having a masculine pregnancy! You
must take it more lightheartedly than this. Come, put on your hat,
we'll go to the Poirée-Blanche and have some strawberry ice
cream."

Fortunately I changed, without realizing it at first. Soon everyone
around me began to exclaim how well I looked and how cheerful I
was. The half-hidden and involuntary smile of pregnant women

showed even through my makeup as the Optimistic Owl—for I was serenely continuing to play my part in *L'Oiseau de Nuit*. . . .

Insidiously, unhurriedly, the beatitude of pregnant females spread through me. I was no longer subjected to any discomfort, any unease. This purring contentment, this euphoria—how give a name either scientific or familiar to this state of preservation?—must certainly have penetrated me, since I have not forgotten it and am recalling it now, when life can never again bring me plenitude. . . .

Every night I bade farewell, more or less, to one of the happiest periods of my life, knowing well how I was going to regret it. But the cheerfulness, the purring contentment, the euphoria submerged everything and over me reigned the sweet animal innocence and unconcern arising from my added weight and the muffled appeals of the new life being formed within me.

The sixth month, the seventh month. . . . Suitcases to pack, the departure for Limoges, a lightheartedness that disdained rest. . . . But how heavy I became, especially at night! When climbing back up the road winding around the hill toward my lodgings, I let my two shepherd dogs, Bagheera and Son, haul me, by pulling on their two leashes. The first strawberries, the first roses. . . . Can I regard my pregnancy as anything but one long festival? We forget the anguish of the labor pains but do not forget the long and singular festival; I have certainly not forgotten any detail. I especially remember how at odd hours sleep overwhelmed me and how I was seized again, as in my infancy, by the need to sleep on the ground, on the grass, on the sun-warmed hay. A unique and healthy craving.

When I had almost reached my term, I looked like a rat dragging a stolen egg. Feeling unwieldy, I sometimes was too tired out to lie down, and would sit in a comfortable armchair to exhaust the resources of a book or newspaper before going to bed. . . .

Beneath the weight and beneath the fatigue, my long festival was not yet interrupted. I was borne on a shield of privileges and attentions. "Take this armchair! No, it's too low, take this other one instead." "I've made a strawberry tart for you." "Here is the pattern for the booties, you begin by casting on fifteen stitches. . . ."

Neither fifteen nor ten. I would neither embroider a bib nor cut out a vest, nor gloat over white woolies. When I tried to visualize my little babe, I saw it naked, not all dressed up. It had to be content with a plain and practical English layette, without any frills or lace or smocking, and even that was bought—out of superstition—at the very last minute.

The "masculine pregnancy" did not lose all its rights; I was working on the last part of *L'Entrave*. The child and the novel were both rushing me, and the *Vie Parisienne*, which was serializing my unfinished novel, was catching up with me. The baby showed signs that it would win the race, and I screwed on the cap of my fountain pen.

My long festival came to an end on a cloudless day in July. The imperious child, on its way to its second life, maltreated a body no less eager than itself. In my little garden surrounded by other gardens, sheltered from the sun, provided with books and newspapers, I waited. I listened to the neighbors' cocks crowing and to the accelerated beating of my heart. When no one was looking, I took down the garden hose and gave the thirsty garden—which I would not be able to succor the next day or the following days—a token watering.

What followed. . . . What followed doesn't matter, and I will give it no place here. What followed was the prolonged scream that issues from all women in childbed. If I like, this very day, to hear its echo, I need only open the window overlooking the Palais-Royal: from beneath the arcade rises the humble clamor of a neighbor woman who is pushing out into the world her sixth child. What followed was a restorative sleep and selfish appetite. But what followed was also, once, an effort to crawl toward me made by my bundled-up little larva that had been laid down for a moment on my bed. . . . What followed was the contemplation of a new person who had appeared in the house without coming from the outside. . . .

In the competition between the book and the birth, it was the novel, thank God, which got the worst of it. Conscientiously I went back to work on the unfinished *L'Entrave*, but it could not recover from the blows dealt by the weak and triumphant infant. Please note, O my hypothetical readers, how skimped is that ending, how insufficient the corridor through which I wanted my pared-down heroes to pass. Observe, too, the empty tone of a conclusion in which those heroes do not believe, an ending like a subdominant chord—the cadence a musician would call plagal—too hurriedly struck.

Since then, I have tried to rewrite the ending of *L'Entrave*, but have never succeeded. Between the interruption of the work and its resumption, I had performed the laborious delectation of procreating. My jot of virility saved me from the danger to which the writer promoted to the status of happy and loving parent is exposed, a danger that can turn him into a mediocre author, thenceforth preferring the rewards of a visible and material growth: the cult of children, of plants, of breeding life in some form or other. An old boy of forty under the surface of the still young woman that I was, kept a sharp watch on the safety of a perhaps precious part of me.

When I was a young girl, if I ever happened to occupy myself with some needlework, Sido [Colette's mother] always shook her sooth-sayer's head and commented, "You will never look like anything but a boy who is sewing." She would now have said, "You will never be any-thing but a writer who gave birth to a child," for she would not have failed to see the accidental character of my maternity.

Irrational Whims and Uncontrollable Appetites

From the time of the ancient Greeks pregnant women were held to be largely governed by irrational whims and uncontrollable appetites. Jacques Guillemeau in his *Child-birth, or the Happie Deliverie of Women* combined the obstetrical theories of his great teacher Ambroise Paré with the assorted teachings of the ancients in one of the earliest birth manuals (translated and published in English in 1612). He ad-vises the pregnant woman neither to eat so much that the child will grow too big to "keepe himselfe in his place" nor so little that he will "be borne before his time, seeking after nourishment" (everyone at that time believed it was the fetus that initiated labor, usually from hunger).

Guillemeau laments the "disordinate appetite" that makes her "de-sire to eate Coles, Chalke, Ashes, Waxe, Salt-fish raw, yea and un-watred, and to drinke Verjuice, and Vinegar, yea very dregs." She is, he says, to avoid violent exercise, also fretting, scolding, and immod-erate laughing. She may sleep in the morning but not after dinner. She is to abstain from all sexual relations in the first through the fourth month and in the sixth and eighth months; she may, however, indulge in the fifth, seventh, and ninth months, particularly the last, "thereby to shake the child, and make him come the more readily forth; for comming into the world after this acte, he is commonly en-wrapped and compassed with slime, which helpeth his comming forth."

It is interesting that Guillemeau has nothing to say to the husband in the matter of sexual denial. He does take note of the fact that "some women when they be with child hate the companie of their husbands: which quality is said also to be in brute beasts when they be great with yong, who commonly shun the companie of the Male." But, he concludes, "I know well the answere that those two noble Ladies, Poppea the daughter of Agrippina, and Julia the daughter of Augustus made concerning this matter. The one sayd, that brute beasts

cannot taste the delight which women receive that are with child, because they are without reason: and the other sayd, that when her ship
was laden with wares, then she could take in passengers."

Malcolm X: His Pregnant Mother
Confronts the Klan

When my mother was pregnant with me, she told me later, a party of
hooded Ku Klux Klan riders galloped up to our home in Omaha,
Nebraska, one night. Surrounding the house, brandishing their shot-
guns and rifles, they shouted for my father to come out. My mother
went to the front door and opened it. Standing where they could see
her pregnant condition, she told them that she was alone with her
three small children, and that my father was away, preaching, in Mil-
waukee. The Klansmen shouted threats and warnings at her that we
had better get out of town because "the good Christian white people"
were not going to stand for my father's "spreading trouble" among
the "good" Negroes of Omaha with the "back to Africa" preachings
. . . exhorting the Negro masses to return to their ancestral African
homeland. . . .

Still shouting threats, the Klansmen finally spurred their horses and
galloped around the house, shattering every window pane with their
gun butts. Then they rode off into the night, their torches flaring, as
suddenly as they had come.

From *The Autobiography of Malcom X*

A Vice President in Investment Banking
Conducts Business from the Bedside

When Jane Metzroth, a tall and charming vice president of the
international investment banking firm of Salomon Brothers, in
New York City, decided to have a second child, she carefully
weighed the impact of a new baby on her life. What she did not
consider was all that could happen before the baby was even born.

There were a couple of years worth of thinking that went into the
decision to have another child. We already had a school-age son, and
for a long time I thought we'd just have one child, because working
and raising a family and trying to have a normal kind of life, too, was
kind of hard work. But after Erik was in school, and I saw him de-
veloping into a really neat little person, I kept trying to decide in my
own mind whether to do it again. He would come home and say,

"How come I don't have brothers or sisters?" I saw that he was looking, really striving to add to the family, and my husband and I, after being married twelve years, really wrestled with the idea. The point at which we said, "We really think it's time to do this again," was when I felt comfortable that my career was going the way I wanted it to be going, when I was happy with what I was doing, and am doing, as is the case now. I felt if we were going to add to the family, this would be the time. There were also financial considerations, and child care arrangements; we've had the same lady for almost four years now, and she's really terrific. And that helped me make the decision. She loves Erik, and she said it would be so nice if there were another one, a baby. "I love babies," she'd say. So with all those things combined, we said, "Now's the time." Plus, I'm in my thirties now, so I didn't want to put it off and then find out it wouldn't be possible.

I became pregnant shortly thereafter, but I had a miscarriage. That was a real surprise; I don't know why I thought that it could never happen to me. I had gone out to California on a business trip, and I got on a plane to come home and had the miscarriage on the plane. The plane stopped in Denver and I got off and went to some hospital where I didn't know anybody—I was miserable. It was early on, between the second and third month, but after that I started getting a little gun-shy, thought maybe I had waited too long; maybe I couldn't have any more children. I went through the usual precautions—wait a few months and try again, make sure I'm healthy before I start. So in August we thought o.k., we'd try again, and in September I was pregnant.

Then I was kind of nervous about the whole thing, afraid that maybe I would miscarry again. We were scheduled to go to Florida over Thanksgiving, and I was afraid to get on an airplane. I sent the family on the plane, and I got on Amtrak, which was horrendous. I took the train back, too, and that was even worse because I knew then what it was like. I really took care of myself during the first three months, because from everything I'd read, I figured if you get past that point, you're home free. So I got past the first three months, and then the next three months, and then suddenly I was faced with a new problem.

Again, I had no idea that I had a problem. I was leaving on another business trip, and I figured I could fly now. I went to the obstetrician and asked him to check me out thoroughly before I got on the plane. I just wanted to know everything was o.k. So he examined me, and—I think he was as shocked as I was—all he said was, "Look, you've got to go to the hospital. I'm going to send my nurse with you." One of the other doctors (of the four who work together) was already there, on duty that night. My doctor said, "You need to have a stitch put in, because you're already starting to dilate. Otherwise, you'll lose the baby."

My first reaction was that I was scared. I just followed the nurse into the cab; I didn't even call my husband. I just *went*. I ended up on the labor floor at Mt. Sinai. The doctor came in and explained that he was going to put this stitch in and give me a drug that would stop any contractions, although I didn't feel any. He said I had a condition called "incompetent os"—a weakening of the cervix area—but that if I stayed off my feet and followed all their instructions, they would try to hold everything together for as long as they possibly could. That was the end of the business trip—the end of everything for a while.

It was the twenty-sixth week when this happened. That night my husband came to the hospital, and I was very, very upset. The part about remaining flat on my back didn't sink in for about a day. Then suddenly I said, "Flat on my back! I can't even go to the office?" Then I said, "How about if I go to the office and keep my feet up?" They said, "No, you don't understand. You don't go anywhere!"

During that first week in the hopsital, people came, and all these flowers kept arriving, and everybody tried to keep my mind off my situation. The doctors said it looked as if the surgery was successful. They did a sonogram, and the baby looked fine. So I was happy that that was o.k. But the day I got home and looked around and started thinking about not being able to get up—I spent the first day in tears. I thought I was never going to be able to do this. This was the worst thing in the whole world. That's when I decided I had to think of a way to get around the fact that I wasn't moving around. I decided to run the office from home.

Doing that really carried me through. It kept my mind off thinking about the situation. I rented a hospital bed, because the bed in my bedroom is a platform bed and difficult to get in and out of, and I needed something with a back that could be raised and lowered. So I rented this thing, but there was no room in the bedroom for it, so I put it in the living room. Then I got the phone set up. The company was very, very kind to me during this whole period of time and helped me out every way they could, and they ran a phone line from this office to my apartment so that I could have direct access to the people there, and they to me. I had that next to the bed, and I set up a working area that I could reach without moving. Twice a day, or sometimes three times, there was courier service that would go between my apartment on Eighty-seventh Street and the office down at the tip of Manhattan. They'd bring me work; they'd take back work that was completed; they'd bring me more work. Every day at lunchtime one of my managers would come up and tell me in person what was going on, and then he or she would go back downtown and fill everyone in on the visit and what messages I had. Two or three times a week my administrative assistant would come up and take letters and bring me things to sign. And my boss would come periodically and really kind of reassure me that things were going o.k., that the place was functioning and the work getting out. The staff of people who work with me carried it off beautifully.

Otherwise, life was, well—different. My son was never used to having his mother at home, because I had gone back to work right after he was born. He would bring his friends home after school, and I was part of the tour of the apartment. "Here's my mother, working," he'd say. The kids could never figure out why his working mother was always in bed.

The first week he thought it was fun that I was there, and he would come in and want to sit, and I would have to say, "This is my office; you have to understand that between this hour and this hour I have to work in here, and you can come in at the time I would be coming home from work to visit." Sometimes, like on Fridays when he gets off at twelve o'clock, he'd have lunch with me. The housekeeper took care of my son and of me. She had two kids at that point.

I was allowed up thirty minutes a day in total. What I would do was get up in the morning when my husband got up, which was my old getting-up-for-work time, get in the shower while he was there to make sure I got back out again, and spend about ten or fifteen minutes getting cleaned up. Then I'd drag all my make-up and my rollers and such back to bed. I would get dressed in my office clothes every day, because I knew people would be coming, and I had interviews to do and consultants to see. It was better psychologically, too, that I was dressed and felt like a human being. My meals were brought to me, and taken away, and on weekends my husband was responsible for feeding. So we ate a lot of take-outs.

My husband did real well. He did a lot better than I had expected. He has always been used to chipping in around the house. I've always worked, and ever since Erik was born, he's done fifty percent of what has to be done around there. So now he had to do one hundred percent. But he held up real well. He would take Erik out on the week-

ends; they'd go to the movies and other places together. So home life
was different, but we coped. We managed. I think my son kind of
liked it—the fact that I was around. A few times he said he wished I'd
go back to work—when he'd have a friend over and they'd be hollering
and I couldn't hear on the phone, and I'd be saying, "Keep it down!
Keep it quiet!" Then he'd make a comment like, "When are you going back to work?"

But the whole group of them adjusted real well. My cats loved it;
they were in bed with me all the time. Ordinarily they wouldn't be
allowed on the beds, but they'd be in bed with me, under the covers—
in seventh heaven!

I had a couple of flare-ups during those ten weeks when I'd be back
in the hospital again. I think I had a total of five weeks in the hospital
out of the ten. The hospital was the worst part, because then I was
subject to the hours that the hospital imposed. I was on the maternity
floor, and on that floor, as opposed to the other floors of the hospital
where you can visit from ten in the morning to ten at night, you could
only come in when the babies weren't out. That was kind of hard, too,
because I was the outcast. I was the only one on the floor who hadn't
had a baby. I had a private room in a corner—the same room every
time I went back. But no one from the floor ever came in to see me.
All the other new mothers were always bustling around, and they'd
meet at the baby window, but they didn't really know what was wrong
with me, and they didn't come find out. Towards the end the nurses
would wheel me in the wheelchair down to the shower, and I'd get to
pass by the baby window and see them, and then it started to seem
like it was almost really going to happen. Every day that ticked away,
I'd think, well, I've made it through another one. Then I would look
more and more at the babies. In the beginning I was afraid even to
look. I didn't want to see them all there, in case something went
wrong, and I didn't get to have what everybody else got to have.

One of the characteristics of my condition is that you don't feel any
of the things that are happening to you. You have to look for other
kinds of signs. During the second hospitalization, they put me on a
drug called Ritodrene to control the contractions. I would take it
every two hours, which meant setting the alarm and getting up in the
night. But I got to be pretty smart at figuring out when it wasn't
working any more. I wouldn't feel anything, but I wouldn't feel right
either. I would always know when the contractions had started again.
They had said all along, "One day this drug won't work."

The day the baby was born—I was home, and I took my one A.M.

drug, and when I woke up at three, I said, "Jeez, I don't feel right. I wonder if the one o'clock one worked." So I took the three o'clock one, and then stayed awake. It didn't seem like it was working. I woke my husband up about four and said, "I think we have to go back to the hospital again." I thought what I'd like to do was to get up, take a shower, get all cleaned up, set my hair—somewhere subconsciously I must have known. I said, "I want to get right before we go up there instead of just dashing up." I knew an hour wasn't going to make any difference. About five o'clock I called my housekeeper and said I thought this might be it. And I called my family. All those other times I never did that, but this time I did. I still couldn't really feel any contractions, but I just knew something wasn't right again. I called the doctor and told him I was going. I even took a suitcase this time, which I had never done before. Always before I had been convinced I was coming home again.

When I got there they put the fetal monitor on to see if there were contractions, and there were. They were coming every two minutes, although, of course, I couldn't feel them. When Erik was born, I thought I had this wonderfully easy delivery, that I was one of those fortunate people, but really what it was was the beginning of this condition. I had gone to the doctor on a regular visit that day, too, and he said, "You know, you're halfway through labor. Do you feel anything?" I said, "No." He said, "Well, you'd better go to the hospital." I did, and two hours later he was born.

Since it was now the thirty-sixth week, and the contractions were two minutes apart when we got there, I thought they would just leave me be and let me have the baby. But the doctor said, "Let me try to stop this one more time." I was real upset. That's the only time I think I cried, after the initial time of finding out about it all. I'd had enough of all the poking and the prodding. It was just awful. It hurt when they'd stick all the intravenous things into me, because they could never seem to get it on the first try, so I was covered with bruises. I said, "Why won't you just let me have the baby?" But they thought it would be better if I could get two more weeks. So they hooked me all up and left the monitor on to see how the drug was working. But it didn't work at all. It was just as if it wasn't there, so they increased the dosage. The problem is that the drug has other kinds of side effects— heart palpitations, for openers. And the stronger the dosage, the worse that gets. You can hear it in your ears after a while. So they finally said, "O.K., you win."

They disconnected everything. I was thrilled. I didn't know how

long the labor was going to last—it was about one o'clock in the afternoon by then. He was born at 5:39. With all the problems of the pregnancy, they didn't want to stress me, or strain me, any more than had
already happened, so they gave me an epidural. I was numb from the
waist down. I took a nap, and when I woke up—the doctor had come
by to check on things—the head was already out. We zipped off to the
delivery room, and he was born about thirty seconds after we got
there. You can't imagine how wonderful it felt to have him there! He
weighed six pounds—a nice size, and he looked good. But it turned
out he wasn't so good. He had the problem a lot of premature babies
have with their lungs, where he was not breathing properly. He was
fine when he was first born, but then a couple of hours later he wasn't
so fine. They have a terrific neo-natal nursery at Sinai, and they put
him there and told me I could visit him. And there I was back on the
maternity floor again with no baby.

That might have been the worst part of the whole ordeal. For me it
was the worst part. That neo-natal nursery, although it's a marvelous
place, and they save lots and lots of little babies' lives, is a scary place
to sit in. Alexander was the biggest baby there. He looked like the
grandfather of all the other babies—there were a lot of two-pound babies. But he was in an incubator with all this equipment—tubes and
needles—and I just went to pieces. They have those monitors there for
breathing, and when they stop breathing, it makes a beeping sound.
Sounds are going off all over the room, and I'd sit there and the thing
would go off on Alexander. Sometimes if he would move around in a
certain way, he would lie on the wires, which would set off the beep.
And I never knew if he wasn't breathing or if it was just the ma-
chinery. And then he got jaundice, so something that probably should
have taken two days dragged itself out to ten days. Of course, I'm
thankful that he was as healthy as he really was, and that it was over
in ten days, because there were other parents who had been there for
a long, long time.

But Alexander came home, and lived happily ever after. Now he's
six months old, and more than robust. It was the best decision, even
with everything that happened, we've made in a long time. Erik
adores him, and the baby looks for Erik in the room; he recognizes
that Erik is a child. They have an understanding on some level there.
Makes me think about having a third—but not for a while.

But when I think about how supportive everybody was—my family,
and the friends we have, and the people I work with. They made it
tolerable, and sometimes even fun. They kept my mind off how scared

I was for the baby, and for us as a family. They really carried me through.

Pregnancy Is a Precarious Business

Pregnancy in primitive societies is often a precarious business. Dangers lurk everywhere, and nine months is a long time to be on guard. If the woman is young and this is her first—or even her second or third—child, she may be pleased, delighted at her condition, but she will do well not to dwell on it. Among many peoples—the Wolof of Dakar (Senegal) are an example—she will make no preparations at all for the child's arrival. To do so would be equivalent to wishing it not to be born. In colder climates women are less apt to delay to that extent, but an expectant Chukchee woman of northeast Siberia will sew her little furry garments in secret and refer to them by a special name.

Taboos abound. In Bali a pregnant woman may not approach too closely to a priest, or go into houses where certain gods are kept. An expectant mother of the Munduruçu tribe in Brazil must avoid the sight of a jaguar, a fresh-water porpoise, or a snake, any one of which might cause her or her child's death. Turtles and alligators are less malignant, but might prevent the child's learning to walk properly. The pregnant Tiwi woman of North Australia will forego bathing in the sea for fear of offending the *Maritji* (rainbow spirits), and the Chukchee woman will, with her husband, get up before dawn, dress, go out to look at the rising sun, and then walk around the tent in the direction of the sun's path.

Many foods are forbidden during pregnancy, most for reasons now long forgotten. A Tiwi woman may not eat carpet snakes, hawksbill turtle, or crocodile eggs. In New Guinea the Arapesh women are not permitted eel, frog, or bandicoot, and the Azande must avoid red pig, waterbuck, and eggs. In Bali eggplant and octopus are forbidden.

Certain precautions are taken with an eye to the ordeal ahead. The Japanese have a superstition by which two pregnant women should not occupy the same house for fear that one or the other will die in childbirth; this admonishment is also found among the Yukaghir, a Turkic-speaking people of East Siberia, who reason that the unborn children, apparently of a diabolic nature, will communicate with each other and conspire between them which mother is to die. The Yukaghir have, in fact, an extensive accumulation of do's and don'ts. The expectant mother is not to eat larch-gum, or the fat of the cow or reindeer, as any of these will thicken in the stomach like glue, and "fasten" the child to the inside of the womb. She is instead to choose butter or horse fat, both of which will melt and facilitate the baby's emergence. She must be active and energetic so as to pass on these attributes to the child who will then make an energetic exit from the womb. But when she goes out for a walk—part of keeping active—she must be sure to kick away any stones or lumps of earth that lie in her path, in order that there will be no obstructions during her delivery, and once she has set out, she must on no account turn back, as this might cause the labor to begin and then stop before completion.

Knots are not usually considered a problem until the onset of labor, but in some cultures they are to be avoided throughout pregnancy as well. To braid one's hair, to tie a knot, or even to cross one's legs while sitting, may affect the impending birth. The father, too, must be careful. In the Toumbuluh tribe of North Celebes, Indonesia, after the fourth or fifth month, both prospective parents are forbidden to tie knots or sit with their legs crossed. The proscription is actually an ancient one. Pliny sternly admonishes us that to sit beside a pregnant woman with clasped hands or crossed legs, or, even worse, to cross one leg over the other and then nurse the upper knee with clasped hands, is to cast a malignant spell over the poor woman. Nor should we forget Alcmena, Hercules' unfortunate mother. She was in labor for seven days and seven nights, all because the hardhearted goddess Lucina sat there in front of the house with crossed legs and clasped hands, refusing to move, and the baby Hercules could not be born until she had been persuaded to change her attitude.

The *leyaks* (witches) of Bali are equally vicious; their preferred diet is the blood of pregnant women and the entrails of unborn children. Fortunately, there are amulets, purchasable from the local priest or witch doctor, to protect the prospective mother.

It is hard to find a primitive society where pregnancy is not beset with anxiety. The Mbuti of Zaire might be that rare exception, or so Colin Turnbull tells us in *The Human Cycle*. Indeed, his observations of the nine months of gestation in a Mbuti woman's life sound like pure bliss. Pregnancy there has the dreamy, unreal quality of the great protective forests and slow-moving rivers of the surroundings. There seem to be no taboos; the pregnant woman follows her own intuitions, does whatever makes her and her baby "feel good." She relaxes, avoids strenuous activity and emotional scenes. And she takes to singing:

The lullaby that she sings is special in several ways. It is the only form of song that can be sung as a solo and is composed by the mother for that particular child within her womb. It is sung for no other, it is sung by no other. The young mother sings it quietly, reassuringly, rocking herself, sometimes with her hands on her belly, or gently splashing her hands or feet in the water of her favorite stream or river, or rustling them through leaves, or warming herself at a fire. In a similar way she talks to the child, according it the intelligence, though not the knowledge, of an adult. There is no baby talk. What she says to the child is clear, informative, reassuring, and comforting. She tells it of the forest world into which it will soon emerge, repeating simple phrases such as those perhaps already "heard" by the unborn baby while its mother was off on the hunt: "the forest is good, the forest is kind; mother forest, father forest."

Some mothers describe the place where the child will be born, the other children it will meet and play with, grow up with; and tell the womb-child that if he is a boy, somewhere there is an unborn girl baby that one day he will marry. Both the physical and the social world may be described to children in this way. And once the children are born and begin to learn to speak they hear these stories over and over again and it all becomes so familiar that it is as if they were conscious of being conceived at that place and at that time of day, and of all that went on around them as they were being carried through the forest in their mothers' wombs. Mbuti see their life as beginning the moment they were wanted, for that is when they were conceived, and from these stories told them throughout childhood all Mbuti have a detailed, though not necessarily exact or verifiable, knowledge of their earliest beginnings.

In one sense it is not of the slightest importance that the unborn child can hardly be expected to understand what is being said to it. Nor does it matter whether or not the emotional content of what the mother is thinking and doing and saying and singing is in any way transferred to the unborn baby's consciousness. It is enough that the mother, at least, is reinforcing *her* own concept of the world and is readying *her*self for the creative act about to unfold, giving *her*self confidence that the forest will be as good and as kind to her child as it has been to her; providing food, shelter, clothing, warmth, and affection. That confidence alone would be an auspicious beginning to any life.

Beverly Sills: "Why Me? Why Them?"

Beverly Sills and her husband Peter Greenough have two children: their daughter Muffy, who was born deaf, and their son

Bucky, who is mentally retarded. That the children live as normal and constructive lives as they do can be attributed to the enormous courage and concern and love of their parents. *And* to their mother's sense of humor—which apparently never leaves her, as the following selection taken from her autobiography *Bubbles* would indicate.

Peter and I decided that it was time to have a baby. I was six months pregnant when I appeared at the New York City Opera in April 1959 to play the character of The Prima Donna in the world premiere of Hugo Weisgall's *Six Characters in Search of an Author,* based on the Pirandello play. The opera was rather interesting and a personal success for me but it was not very well received.

The real hero of the production may have been Edgar Joseph, head of the City Opera's costume department, for the imaginative lengths he went to conceal my pregnancy. He redesigned a copy of a Dior dress I owned, gathered it high in front, and draped me in an enormous mink cape that Peter had bought me or in large stoles or shawls. I was never allowed on stage without a prop—usually a hatbox or an umbrella. One night the stage director, William Ball, had the brilliant idea of my entering carrying a tiny French poodle; it would not only effectively cover my tummy but would also be the kind of item my character would normally own. On opening night, the lady who lent us the poodle was very nervous that the poodle would be nervous, so she gave it a tranquilizer. As a result the dog looked dead, but at least, I thought, he'll be quiet. Suddenly, during one of my arias, I felt a warm trickle down the front of my dress; the dog, naturally, was peeing all over me. When I pulled him away from the dress, he woke up, startled, and howled at the top of his lungs throughout the whole aria, off-key. The audience was hysterical, and as far as I was concerned, *that* poodle's operatic career was finished. I never sang with a dog again.

Back home in Cleveland that summer, awaiting the birth of my baby, I got a call from Julius Rudel: Leopold Stokowski is opening our fall season with *Carmina Burana* and it would be nice if you could be in it. I went to New York to audition for Mr. Stokowski. I was very pregnant and he asked me if I were practicing breathing exercises. With his accent, it sounded like "breeding" exercises, so I replied, Obviously I practice breeding exercises. It was an Abbott and Costello routine—he said "breathing" and I thought "breeding." He offered me a role in *Carmina Burana* provided my baby was born on schedule, by July 25. She was not and I was never able to take that job with Stokowski.

Meredith "Muffy" Greenough was born August 4, 1959, and I became an asterisk on the City Opera roster—"On leave of absence." . . .
That [next] fall my husband announced that we were moving to Boston: he was leaving the Cleveland Plain Dealer to write a financial
column for a Boston newspaper. We settled in a nineteen-room house
in Milton, Massachusetts, about ten miles south of Boston, and decided to have a second child. In April of 1961, when I was seven
months pregnant, the phone rang and a deep voice said: "This is Sarah Caldwell." I had never met Sarah but I knew, of course, who she
was. . . . Sarah was planning a production of *Die Fledermaus* with
Arthur Fiedler conducting. Would I play Rosalinda? "I'd be delighted," I said. "When?" In a few weeks, with rehearsals beginning
in a few days. Wonderful, I said, and we hung up. My husband, who
had been listening to this, asked dryly: "What are you planning to
wear?" "Oh, costumes," I said airily. Then I looked down and realized
what a shape I was in. I called Sarah back and said, "Miss Caldwell,
I'm terribly sorry but I can't do your *Fledermaus* because I'm pregnant." There was a pause and then: "Weren't you pregnant five minutes ago?"

Our son, Peter Jr. (Bucky), was born June 29, 1961, weighing nearly
ten pounds. We were on Cloud Nine: he was the first boy to be born
into the Greenough family in forty-seven years and we at last had
someone to carry on the name. A month later we suffered a tremendous shock: we learned that our daughter Muffy, who was then
twenty-three months old, was deaf. . . . "This is the worst day of my
life," I said to Peter. "At least," he said, "it's over."

But it was not: shortly after the discovery of Muffy's loss of hearing,
we learned that Bucky was mentally retarded. . . .

I was now only thirty-four, but a very mature thirty-four. In a
strange way, my children had brought me an inner peace. The first
question I had asked when I learned of their tragedies was a self-
pitying "Why *me?*" Then gradually it changed to a much more important "Why *them?*"

Margaret Cavendish: "They Take More Pride in Being with Child Than in Having a Child"

Margaret Cavendish, Duchess of Newcastle, was a brilliant and
talented seventeenth century Englishwoman who, because no
other women of her acquaintance could begin to match her in
wit or learning, accepted the generally held belief that woman

was man's inferior and she herself but an oddball exception. She dressed outlandishly, composed poetry and plays, wrote scientific treatises and philosophical works, compiled a biography of her husband William and an autobiography of herself, and saw to it that they were published. She also composed letters to an unidentified *Madam* in which she explored her thinking on a variety of subjects, of which the following is an example:

Madam,

The other day the Lady S.M. was to visit me, and I gave her joy. She said she should have joy indeed if it were a son. I said I bid her joy of her marriage, for I had not seen her since she was a wife and had been married, which was some four weeks ago, wherefore I did not know she was with child. But she, rasping wind out of her stomach, as childing women usually do, making sickly faces to express a sickly stomach, and fetching her breath short, and bearing out her body, drawing her neck downward, and standing in a weak and faint posture, as great-bellied wives do bearing a heavy burden in them, told me she had been with child a fortnight, though by her behavior one would not have thought she had above a week to go, or to reckon. But she is so pleased with the belief she is with child (for I think she cannot perfectly know herself; at most it is but breeding child), as she makes or believes herself bigger than she appears, and says she longs for every meat that is difficult to be gotten, and eats and drinks from morning till night, with very little intermission, and sometimes in the night. Whereupon I told her if she did so, I believed she would be bigger bellied and greater bodied whether she were with child or not. Besides, eating so much would make her sick if she were not with child. She answered that women with child might eat anything and as much as they would or could, and it would do them no harm.

But I have observed that generally women take more pleasure when they are with child than when they are not with child, not only in eating more and feeding more luxuriously, but taking a pride in their great bellies, although it be a natural effect of a natural cause. For like as women take a greater pride in their beauty than pleasure or content in their virtue, so they take more pride in being with child than in having a child. For when they are brought to bed and up from their lying-in, they seem nothing so well pleased, nor so proud as when they were great with child. And to prove they are prouder and take more pleasure in being with child and in lying in than in having a child is their care, pains, and cost in getting, making and buying fine and costly childbed linen, swaddling clothes, mantles, and the like, as also fine beds, cradles, baskets, and other furniture for their chambers, as hangings, cabinets, plates, artificial flowers, looking glasses, screens, and many such like things of great cost and charge. . . . And their children being christened are like some brides and bridegrooms that are so fine on their wedding day, as they are forced to go in rags all their lives after, which methinks is very strange, that for the vanity and show of one day they will spend so much as to be beggars all their lives after.

But as I said, this proves that women take a greater pride and pleasure in being with child than in having children well-bred and well-bestowed or maintained when grown to years. And that which makes me wonder more is that wise men will suffer their foolish wives to be so foolishly and imprudently expensive. . . . But leaving the Lady S.M. to her breeding pride or pride of breeding, to her sick pleasure of pleasurable sickness, to her luxurious feeding and vain providing, and wishing her a good gossiping, I rest,

Madam,

Your faithful friend and servant

Colonial Dames: Their Trousseaus Included Childbed Linen

Brides of "better families" in the American colonies brought to the marriage not only a trousseau of their own clothes and an assortment of pots and kettles, but a set of "childbed linen" as well, carefully set aside for them by their own mothers. This mysterious collection of items might range from embroidered maternity petticoats and chemises (clearly not meant for everyday use) to damask pillowcases for the "lying-in" and an assortment of lace-edged baby garments and knitted coverlets. Not infrequently, however—colonial fertility being exceptionally high—a mother would have to request, with some embarrassment, the return of same, having unexpectedly found herself once again "in that way." Nelly Custis Lewis already had several children of her own when she wrote a friend: "My Dear Mother has just recovered from her confinement with her twentieth Child, it is a very fine Girl, large and healthy. Mamma has suffered extremely, and is still weak."

Maya Angelou: I Had Had an Immaculate Pregnancy

Marguerite "Maya" Angelou—dancer, actress, director, political activist, writer—was only sixteen when she became pregnant after a casual encounter she herself had instigated. How she incorporated her pregnancy into a scramble for independence is described with much love and no little anguish in her autobiographical *I Know Why the Caged Bird Sings*.

The world had ended, and I was the only person who knew it. People walked along the streets as if the pavements hadn't crumbled beneath their feet. They pretended to breathe in and out while all the time I knew the air had been sucked away in a monstrous inhalation from God Himself. I alone was suffocating in the nightmare. . . .

For eons, it seemed, I had accepted my plight as the hapless, put-upon victim of fate and the Furies, but this time I had to face the fact that I had brought my new catastrophe upon myself. How was I to blame the innocent man whom I had lured into making love to me? In order to be profoundly dishonest, a person must have one of two qualities: either he is unscrupulously ambitious, or he is unswervingly egocentric. He must believe that for his ends to be served all things and people can justifiably be shifted about, or that he is the center not only of his own world but of the worlds which others inhabit. I had neither element in my personality, so I hefted the burden of pregnancy at sixteen onto my own shoulders where it belonged. Admittedly, I staggered under the weight. . . .

The first three months, while I was adapting myself to the fact of pregnancy (I didn't really link pregnancy to the possibility of my having a baby until weeks before my confinement), were a hazy period in which days seemed to lie just below the water level, never emerging fully.

Fortunately, Mother was tied up . . . in the weave of her own life. She noticed me, as usual, out of the corner of her existence. As long as I was healthy, clothed and smiling she felt no need to focus her attention on me. As always, her major concern was to live the life given to her, and her children were expected to do the same. And to do it without too much brouhaha.

Under her loose scrutiny I grew more buxom, and my brown skin smoothed and tightpore, like pancakes fried on an unoiled skillet. And still she didn't suspect. Some years before, I had established a code which never varied. I didn't lie. It was understood that I didn't lie because I was too proud to be caught and forced to admit that I was capable of a less than Olympian action. Mother must have concluded that since I was above out-and-out lying I was also beyond deceit. She was deceived.

All my motions focalized on pretending to be that guileless school girl who had nothing more wearying to think about than mid-term exams. Strangely enough, I very nearly caught the essence of teenage capriciousness as I played the role. Except that there were times when physically I couldn't deny to myself that something very important was taking place in my body.

Mornings, I never knew if I would have to jump off the streetcar one step ahead of the warm sea of nausea that threatened to sweep me away. On solid ground, away from the ship-motioned vehicle and the smell of hands coated with recent breakfasts, I regained my balance and waited for the next trolley.

School recovered its lost magic. . . . I burrowed myself into caves of facts, and found delight in the logical resolutions of mathematics.

I credit my new reactions (although I didn't know at the time that I had learned anything from them) to the fact that during what surely must have been a critical period I was not dragged down by hopelessness. Life had a conveyor-belt quality. It went on unpursued and unpursuing, and my only thought was to remain erect, and keep my secret along with my balance. . . .

Two days after V-Day, I stood with the San Francisco Summer School class at Mission High School and received my diploma. That evening, in the bosom of the now-dear family home I uncoiled my fearful secret and in a brave gesture left a note on Daddy Clidell's bed. It read: *Dear Parents, I am sorry to bring this disgrace on the family, but I am pregnant. Marguerite.*

The confusion that ensued when I explained to my stepfather that I expected to deliver the baby in three weeks, more or less, was reminiscent of a Molière comedy. Except that it was funny only years later. Daddy Clidell told Mother that I was "three weeks gone." Mother, regarding me as a woman for the first time, said indignantly, "She's more than any three weeks." They both accepted the fact that I was further along than they had first been told but found it nearly impossible to believe that I had carried a baby, eight months and one week, without their being any the wiser.

Mother asked, "Who is the boy?" I told her. She recalled him, faintly.

"Do you want to marry him?"

"No."

"Does he want to marry you?" The father had stopped speaking to me during my fourth month.

"No."

"Well, that's that. No use ruining three lives." There was no overt or subtle condemnation. She was Vivian Baxter Jackson. Hoping for the best, prepared for the worst, and unsurprised by anything in between.

Daddy Clidell assured me that I had nothing to worry about. That "women been gittin' pregnant ever since Eve ate that apple." He sent one of his waitresses to I. Magnin's to buy maternity dresses for me. For the next two weeks I whirled around the city going to doctors, taking vitamin shots and pills, buying clothes for the baby, and except for the rare moments alone, enjoying the imminent blessed event.

After a short labor, and without too much pain (I decided that the pain of delivery was overrated), my son was born. Just as gratefulness was confused in my mind with love, so possession became mixed up with motherhood. I had a baby. He was beautiful and mine. Totally mine. No one had bought him for me. No one had helped me endure the sickly gray months. I had had help in the child's conception, but no one could deny that I had had an immaculate pregnancy.

Anne Boleyn: "I Had a Wild Desire To Eat Apples"

For six years Anne Boleyn had resisted King Henry VIII, but during the Christmas court of 1532, believing her hold on him to be slackening, she gave in to his entreaties. In January she jubilantly informed him that she was with child. The immediate assumption on both their parts was that the child would be, must be, the hoped for, long-awaited son.

In February, her second month, basking in her private glory (Henry had married her secretly), she could not restrain herself from dropping hints as to her condition. "If I find I am not with child, I shall go on a pilgrimage immediately after Easter," she told her astounded uncle, the Duke of Norfolk, in a room crowded with people. And when Sir Thomas Wyatt, rumored once to have been her lover, came upon her in the castle hall one day, she did not even bother to lower her voice. "Three days ago," she told him, "I had an inestimable wild desire to eat apples. I have never liked them before. The King says it is a sign that I must be with child. I tell him no. I cannot be!"

By March, the third month, gossip was rife and Anne's craving for apples had given way to less pleasant symptoms. Bouts of nausea were difficult to hide. That month a bill was passed in Parliament enabling the new Archbishop of Canterbury to pronounce sentence for Henry's divorce from Catherine of Aragon and provide for his marriage to Anne without papal consent. That eliminated the necessity for keeping the marriage secret, which was fortunate since one aspect of it could not have been kept secret much longer anyway.

On the fourteenth of April Anne, now in her fourth month, attended mass dressed in cloth of gold and accompanied by no less than sixty ladies. After the service, just in case there should be anyone who still missed the point, she held court, while Henry stood by glowering at any noble who so much as hesitated before kneeling and kissing her hand. Later that month he sent out instructions that prayers be offered in all churches throughout the realm for Anne's well-being. This was not received with enthusiasm by the populace at large, and in London at least one congregation—with, it was reported, "great murmuring and ill looks"—marched out in a body.

In May, now five months pregnant, Anne took part in the elaborate water pageant by which the King was attempting to beguile Londoners into acceptance of his new wife. She and her ladies floated down the Thames to the Tower where Henry waited. Cannon boomed. While the assembled populace watched without noticeable enthusiasm, Anne disembarked, ascended the main stairway, and knelt before the King. Raising her gently, Henry kissed her and placed his hands on either side of her rounding tummy to indicate approval of her condition. Then they turned and with their entourage disappeared into the royal apartments. That evening there were fireworks on the river, and music played from the barges through half the night.

Anne's coronation was set for Whitsunday, which fell that year on the first of June. The procession from the Tower to Westminster would take place the day before. Well into her sixth month, Anne was plagued by continued nausea, by salivation—she constantly needed to spit—and by pressure on her bladder. In the six years she had dreamed of being crowned Queen of England, she had never thought of it accompanied by problems such as these. In an open litter draped with cloth of gold, cloaked in ermine and bejeweled with diamonds, Anne sat very straight throughout the long procession, turning from side to side, smiling as if she were being met by cheers instead of by hostile silence from men who kept their caps on their heads and women who stared grimly. At various points along the way statues of St. Anne, mother of the Virgin, were on display, which ought to have encouraged her, except that she could not help but recall that St. Anne had borne only one child, and that a girl.

The coronation ceremony lasted some eight hours, and was followed by a banquet during which the newly crowned queen sat on a dais at one end of the hall and could not leave her place until the entire affair was over. The Countesses of Oxford and Worcester stood on either side of her throughout the meal; it was their job to "hold a fine cloth" before her face should she need to spit or vomit, just as it was the job of the two lesser ladies-in-waiting at her feet to provide for her as unobtrusively as possible should she have to pee. Through it all trumpets sounded and fountains flowed with wine.

It must have seemed to Anne, as she entered the last trimester of her pregnancy, that at last her star had risen to its proper place in the firmament. She saw no reason why it should not remain there. If in the recesses of her mind there was any nagging reminder that the perpetuation of all this was perhaps contingent on something else that had not yet occurred—something that was, in fact, only a summer's breath away—she pushed the thought away. She could, she was sure, turn whatever outcome to her advantage.

In truth, her star was already starting its downward course. Much of the seventh month Anne spent with Henry at Windsor, a great drafty castle seldom used except in summer. An unsettling event occurred. Ex-Queen Catherine, having been ordered to move to a remote dwelling in Huntingdonshire, found her way thronged with villagers weeping and crying, "God save the Queen! God save Queen Catherine!" Anne complained, then nagged at Henry to do something. Henry did not like to be nagged at. Still, he was anxious to pacify her—she was, he reminded himself, carrying his son—so he had an edict drawn up and proclaimed by trumpet call. Hear ye, hear ye, hear ye. Only Anne was to be called "queen"; to use the term with "the Lady Catherine" was punishable by death. But the edict had little effect since Henry did nothing to enforce it.

In August, Anne's eighth month, came the news from Rome. Pope Clement had at last acted: King Henry's marriage to the so-called Queen Anne was declared null and void, any issue from that marriage illegitimate, and Henry himself excommunicated. About the same time Anne discovered that Henry was having an affair. History does not record who the lady was—just that she was at court and was "very beautiful," something that at this stage of the game Anne knew she was not. Her pride was badly bruised. She flew at Henry, used—it was said—"certain words which he very much disliked," and was commanded in return to "shut her eyes and endure, as those who were better than herself had done." For several days they did not speak.

Near the beginning of the ninth month came word that, although all the soothsayers, doctors, and astrologers were in agreement that Anne would give birth to a boy, one man, a servant to Thomas Wyatt's father, had had a vision that the child would be a girl. Its effect on him was apparently so strong that he risked reporting it, which was why it was disturbing. Only if the child were a boy could Parliament be persuaded to honor it over the Princess Mary, Catherine's daughter, and would the people of England accept the new marriage.

Meanwhile, the traditional preparations had been going on at Greenwich where, it had been decided, the confinement would take place. Henry VII, the King's father, had laid down exact stipulations for the lying-in of a queen, and these were being meticulously observed. There were, for example, three beds—a great bed of state in the Chamber of Presence, an ornate French bed, the ransom of a Duke d'Alençon, in the Bed Chamber, and a third bed with embroidered crimson satin canopy where Anne would hold court and receive congratulations after the event. The sheets were of fine lawn, the spreads of scarlet bordered with ermine and blue velvet, or of ermine embroidered with cloth of gold.

For the new heir to the throne there were two cradles: a magnificently carved and gilded one as large as a bed, and another less lavish and more appropriately sized for a newborn. The notices of the birth were written out, all ready to send off to the nobility, informing them of the "deliverance and bringing forth of a prince," and with space left to make it "princess" should fate so dictate. But fate could not be so perverse. The prince would be named either "Henry" or "Edward," the King had not yet decided which, and a tournament would be held almost immediately in his honor.

Anne arrived at Greenwich in early September. She was conducted to her chapel for communion, and then, accompanied by various noblemen and ladies, to the Chamber of Presence where her Chamberlain offered prayers that God would send her a good hour. After that she was formally led by two noblemen to her chamber door. Her ladies could come and go, but no man could enter there, and Anne, once she had entered, could not leave until after the child was born. The room was magnificently decorated but dark and airless, an uncomfortable place to spend the tedious last days waiting for her "good hour."

The first pains came early in the morning on Sunday, September 7. Between three and four in the afternoon the baby was born and the King informed. The child, of course, was a girl.

A Proposal for Mothergartens

The nineteenth century American wife was expected to exist free of carnal thoughts while submitting to her husband's every whim, but when she was pregnant, restraint was required of him as well. What had been natural appetite in him before was suddenly unnatural lust. Ladies of the temperance movement took the position that alcohol led otherwise good husbands to rape their wives, and one reformer wrote in despair of "the millions of pregnant women in the world, bowed down under the burdens of manual toil, and yet compelled to satisfy the demands of lust, intensified by drink and by tobacco." In an attempt to provide sanctuary to the thus-oppressed, Catharine Beecher, sister of Harriet Beecher Stowe, submitted to the International Council of Women in 1888 a proposal for "mothergartens"—havens where pregnant wives could take refuge from the "lustful selfish propensities" of their husbands.

Isadora Duncan: "My Beautiful Marble Body Softened and Broken and Stretched and Deformed"

Early in 1906 Isadora Duncan found she was pregnant from her liaison with stage designer and director, Gordon Craig. Although she frequently denounced marriage, especially for artists, and advocated that women choose at will the fathers of their children, she had her own inner fears about bearing an illegitimate child. She valued her mother's good opinion, and her mother strongly disapproved. Craig, she knew, had no intention of marrying her. Always low on funds, Isadora continued touring, dancing as long as her loosely draped costumes and filmy scarves would hide her figure. Then she retired to a tiny Dutch village where she hid herself away in a house that could be reached only by climbing a flight of nearly a hundred steps. She was not as secure in her impending motherhood as she pretended.

In her autobiography *My Life* Isadora describes the months of alternating loneliness, elation, and despair that preceded the birth of her baby in September.

I had an intense desire to be near the sea. I went first to The Hague, and from there to a little village called Nordwyck, on the shores of the North Sea. Here I rented a little white villa in the dunes, called Villa Maria.

I was so inexperienced as to think that having a baby was a perfectly natural process. I went to live in this villa, which was a hundred miles from any town, and I engaged a village doctor. In my ignorance I was quite content to have this village doctor who, I think, was only used to peasant women.

From Nordwyck to the nearest village, Kadwyck, was about three kilometres. Here I lived, all by myself. Each day I walked from Nordwyck to Kadwyck and back. Always I had this longing for the sea; to be alone in Nordwyck, in the little white villa, quite isolated among the sand dunes which stretched for miles on either side of the lovely country. I lived in the Villa Maria for June, July and August. . . .

Craig was restless. He came and went. But I was no longer alone. The child asserted itself now, more and more. It was strange to see my beautiful marble body softened and broken and stretched and deformed. It is an uncanny revenge of Nature, that the more refined the nerves, the more sensitive the brain, the more all this tends to suffering. Sleepless nights, painful hours. But joy too. Boundless, unlimited joy, when I strode every day over the sands between Nordwyck and Kadwyck, with the sea, the great waves, looming on one side, and the swelling dunes on the other, along the deserted beach. Almost always, on that coast, the wind blows, sometimes a gentle, billowing zephyr, sometimes a breeze so strong that I had to struggle against it. Occasionally the storms grew terrific, and the Villa Maria was rocked and buffeted all night like a ship at sea.

I grew to dread any society. People said such banalities. How little is appreciated the sanctity of the pregnant mother. I once saw a woman walking alone along the street, carrying a child within her. The passers-by did not regard her with reverence, but smiled at one another derisively, as though this woman, carrying the burden of coming life, was an excellent joke. . . .

As I walked beside the sea, I sometimes felt an excess of strength and prowess, and I thought this creature would be mine, mine alone, but on other days, when the sky was grey and the cold North Sea waves were angry, I had sudden, sinking moods when I felt myself some poor animal in a mighty trap, and I struggled with an overwhelming desire to escape, escape. Where? Perhaps even into the midst of the sullen waves. I struggled against such moods and bravely overcame them, nor did I ever let any one suspect what I felt, but nevertheless, such moods were waiting for me at odd hours, and were difficult to avoid. Also I thought that most people were receding from me. My mother seemed thousands of miles away. Craig was also strangely remote, and always immersed in his art, whereas I could think less and less of my art, and was only absorbed in this fearful, monstrous task which had fallen to me; this maddening, joy-giving, pain-giving mystery. . . .

In August there came to stay with me, as a nurse, a woman who afterwards became my very dear friend, Marie Kist. I have never met a more patient, sweeter or kinder one. She was a great comfort. From

now on, I confess, I began to be assailed with all sorts of fears. In vain
I told myself that every woman had children. My grandmother had
eight. My mother had four. It was all in the course of life, etc. I was,
nevertheless, conscious of fear. Of what? Certainly not of death, nor
even of pain—some unknown fear, of what I did not know.

August waned. September came. My burden had become very
heavy. . . . More and more my lovely body bulged under my astonished gaze. My hard little breasts grew large and soft and fell. My
nimble feet grew slower, my ankles swelled, my hips were painful.
Where was my lovely, youthful Naiad form? Where my ambition? . . .

One day . . . a sweet friend I had known in Paris—her name was
Kathleen—came from Paris and said she had the intention of staying
with me. . . . We were all sitting at tea one afternoon, when I felt a
thud as if some one had pounded me in the middle of the back, and
then a fearful pain, as if some one had put a gimlet into my spine and
was trying to break it open. From that moment the torture began, as
if I, poor victim, were in the hands of some mighty and pitiless execu-
tioner. No sooner had I recovered from one assault than another began. Talk about the Spanish Inquisition! . . .

For two days and two nights this unspeakable horror continued.
And, on the third morning, this absurd doctor brought out an immense pair of forceps and without an anaesthetic of any sort, achieved
the butchery. . . .

Well, I did not die because of it. No, I didn't die—nor does the poor
victim taken timely from the rack. And then, you may say, when I saw
the baby I was repaid. . . .

During the first weeks, I used to lie long hours with the baby in my
arms, watching her asleep; sometimes catching a gaze from her eyes;
feeling very near the edge, the mystery, perhaps the knowledge of
Life. . . .

Little by little my strength came back. Often I stood before the wonderful Amazon, our votive statue, with sympathetic understanding, for
she, too, was never to be so gloriously fit for the battle again.

"I Love Lucy": TV's First Prime Time Pregnancy

In the course of a single recent month I (who only watch television occasionally) have viewed three actual deliveries, including
one of twins and one Caesarean, all with father present; two
pseudo-deliveries on reruns of "M*A*S*H" and another on Mas-
terpiece Theater; various women in varying states of pregnancy

in dramas and sit-coms including one teenager on an afternoon special; and discussions of the ultra-sound scanner, amniocentesis, prenatal diagnoses of problems, operations on the fetus in the womb including brain surgery, treatment of hydrocephalus and congestive heart failure in utero, and "prenatal adoption" by which, when a woman does not conceive, her husband may inseminate the egg of another woman that, when grown to about one hundred cells, will be transferred into his wife's uterus.

All this via a medium that thirty years ago did not permit the use of the word "pregnant" over the air.

The case that broke the media barrier was, as everyone old enough will readily remember, that of Lucille Ball and Desi Arnaz who in 1952, just as they were about to start filming their second season of "I Love Lucy" shows, discovered that the heroine was pregnant. They had been married for ten years when their first child, a girl, was born, and now only nine months later Lucy was pregnant again. In that interim the first season had been shot and had appeared to top ratings, and expectations of course were that the second season would match the first. But this new turn of events altered everything.

From the Ball–Arnaz point of view there could be nothing more natural than for the ordinary American couple that they depicted on their show to have a baby. They proposed to lead up to the event with eight or ten shows in which Lucy was obviously pregnant and preparations were made for the baby's arrival, followed by a show on which the baby was born (off screen), scheduled as closely as possible to the time of the actual birth.

The advertising agency, however, was strongly opposed. The client, Philip Morris cigarettes, was opposed. The network, CBS, was opposed. No pregnant woman had ever been featured on TV before. The words "pregnant" and "pregnancy" had never been spoken on the air. It could not be done.

Confronted by such solid opposition, Arnaz decided that the time had come to go to the top. He wrote a letter to the chairman of the board of Philip Morris in England, explaining the situation of Lucy's pregnancy, reminding him of the show's top rating, and withdrawing all responsibility for future ratings if the show were not allowed to go on as they, its stars, proposed. Arnaz received no direct answer, but opposition to their plans abruptly ceased. Episodes were written in which Lucy informed a jubilant Ricky that he was going to become a father, Lucy craved this or that exotic food combination, Lucy could not tie her shoes, Ricky developed labor pains.

The real baby's birth was anticipated for mid-January. The delivery, like Lucy's previous one, would be a Caesarean, and as the doctor generally performed Caesareans on Mondays, and the show ran on Monday nights, the timing was perfect. The only thing that could not be predicted in 1952, before the development of amniocentesis, was the sex of the child.

The show in which the Ricardo baby was born was shot in October. The Arnazes had decided that the TV baby would be a boy, no matter what the real baby turned out to be. So a typical comedy routine of trip to the hospital, waiting room anxiety, etc., was filmed in which Ricky, when informed that the baby was a boy, fainted from joy. In fact, Arnaz very much wanted a son in real life, too. Not only did they already have a daughter, but there were no sons in his generation of the Arnaz family, and, since Lucy should not, said the doctor, have another child, this was their last chance.

On Monday evening, January 19, 1953, Lucy Ricardo gave birth (off screen) while a record-breaking television audience celebrated with Ricky. Only twelve hours earlier Lucille Ball Arnaz had also given birth to a son.

Ernest Hemingway: "I'm Not Going To Be Married in This Splendid Matronly State"

Catherine Barkley's pregnancy in Ernest Hemingway's *A Farewell to Arms* was a time of physical and emotional regeneration for both her and Frederick Henry. Catherine is in her sixth month in the following scene which takes place shortly after their escape to Switzerland. There is no hint here of the tragedy to come—the death of both mother and child.

We did not know any one in Montreux. . . . We walked along the main street and looked in the windows of the shops. There were many big hotels that were closed but most of the shops were open and the people were very glad to see us. There was a fine coiffeur's place where Catherine went to have her hair done. The woman who ran it was very cheerful and the only person we knew in Montreux. While Catherine was there I went up to a beer place and drank dark Munich beer and read the papers. . . .

We went out and up the street. It was cold and wintry and the wind was blowing. "Oh, darling, I love you so," I said.

"Don't we have a fine time?" Catherine said. "Look. Let's go some place and have beer instead of tea. It's very good for young Catherine. It keeps her small."

"Young Catherine," I said. "That loafer."

"She's been very good," Catherine said. "She makes very little trouble. The doctor says beer will be good for me and keep her small."

"If you keep her small enough and she's a boy, maybe he will be a jockey."

"I suppose if we really have this child we ought to get married," Catherine said. We were in the beer place at the corner table. It was getting dark outside. It was still early but the day was dark and the dusk was coming early.

"Let's get married now," I said.

"No," Catherine said. "It's too embarrassing now. I show too plainly. I won't go before any one and be married in this state."

"I wish we'd gotten married."

"I suppose it would have been better. But when could we, darling?"

"I don't know."

"I know one thing. I'm not going to be married in this splendid matronly state."

"You're not matronly."

"Oh yes, I am, darling. The hairdresser asked me if this was our first. I lied and said no, we had two boys and two girls."

"When will we be married?"

"Any time after I'm thin again. We want to have a splendid wedding with every one thinking what a handsome young couple."

"And you're not worried?"

"Darling, why should I be worried? The only time I ever felt badly was when I felt like a whore in Milan and that only lasted seven minutes and besides it was the room furnishings. Don't I make you a good wife?"

"You're a lovely wife."

"Then don't be too technical, darling. I'll marry you as soon as I'm thin again."

"All right."

"Do you think I ought to drink another beer? The doctor said I was rather narrow in the hips and it's all for the best if we keep young Catherine small."

"What else did he say?" I was worried.

"Nothing. I have a wonderful blood-pressure, darling. He admired my blood-pressure greatly."

"What did he say about you being too narrow in the hips?"

"Nothing. Nothing at all. He said I shouldn't ski."

"Quite right."

"He said it was too late to start if I'd never done it before. He said I could ski if I wouldn't fall down."

"He's just a big-hearted joker."

"Really he was very nice. We'll have him when the baby comes."

"Did you ask him if you ought to get married?"

"No. I told him we'd been married four years. You see, darling, if I marry you I'll be an American and any time we're married under American law the child is legitimate."

"Where did you find that out?"

"In the New York World Almanac in the library."

"You're a grand girl." . . .

"Now let's go up the mountain. Should we? Can we get the M.O.B.?"

"There's a train a little after five."

"Let's get that."

"All right. I'll drink one more beer first."

When we went out to go up the street and climb the stairs to the station it was very cold. A cold wind was coming down the Rhone Valley. There were lights in the shop windows and we climbed the steep stone stairway to the upper street, then up another stairs to the station. The electric train was there waiting, all the lights on. There was a dial that showed when it left. The clock hands pointed to ten minutes after five. I looked at the station clock. It was five minutes after. As we got on board I saw the motorman and conductor coming out of the station wine-shop. We sat down and opened the window. The train was electrically heated and stuffy but fresh cold air came in through the window.

"Are you tired, Cat?" I asked.

"No. I feel splendid."

"It isn't a long ride."

"I like the ride," she said. "Don't worry about me, darling."

5. Laboring / Delivering

Being pregnant was horrible. I worried myself ill about eating and drinking the wrong things, and fainted in telephone kiosks. I didn't feel much sense of communion with the unborn, though I know others do. Labor wasn't much fun either, until the last stages. But the last stages were spectacular. Ah, what an incomparable thrill. All that heaving, the amazing damp slippery wetness and hotness, the confused sight of dark gray ropes of cord, the blood, the baby's cry. The sheer pleasure of the feeling of a born baby on one's thighs is like nothing on earth.

Margaret Drabble,
"With All My Love, (Signed) Mama"

Among the Hudson Bay Eskimos, Birth
Is at Most "Inconvenient"

Peter Freuchen's fifty-year love affair with the Eskimos began
when he went as a member of the Danish Expedition to Greenland in 1906. Later he was founder and administrator of the trading station of Thule; it was during this period that he married
the beautiful Navarana, by whom he had two children. (She died
of Spanish flu in 1921.) In the following excerpt from his autobiographical *Book of the Eskimos* he describes the birth of
Mequsaq, his son.

Eskimo women used to talk about giving birth as being "inconvenient." This is not to say that it was any fun, but they had a remarkably short period of confinement. The women used to sit on their
knees while giving birth. If the woman was in a tent or a house when
her time came, she would most often dig a hole in the ground and
place a box on either side of it to support her arms, and then let the
baby drop down into the hole. If she was in an igloo, the baby had to
be content with the cold snow for its first resting place. If the birth
seemed to take long, the husband would very often place himself
behind his wife, thrust his arms around her, and help press the baby
out.

Among the Hudson Bay Eskimos, things were a little more difficult.
In that community, childbirth was surrounded by a number of taboos
that virtually isolated the poor woman. Nobody, for instance, was
allowed to touch her. So if the husband had to help her, he would
place a strip of skins around her just above the fetus, tie it with a loop
at her back, and pull it tight. The baby was immediately wiped clean
with a piece of skin and placed in the *amaut* where it would spend its
first year. The skin piece was guarded as a precious amulet to ward
off evil.

At Thule, in one case, I gave some skins to a woman to prepare in the morning. She brought them back in the afternoon deploring that it had taken so long, but she had had a baby in the meantime!

Another time we were traversing a glacier while traveling in the company of an Eskimo couple. While up there, the husband came and told us that his wife was going to give birth. I told her that this was very inconvenient, since there was no snow from which to build an igloo. Couldn't she wait? She said she might, and in two hours we managed to get down from the glacier, and we all helped build the igloo while everybody joked about the event.

As soon as the igloo was finished she went inside with her husband, and we waited about an hour. Then the man came out and told us that he had a son. But the mother was a bit tired, and they had decided not to go any farther that day. We went across the bay, and the next morning, when we woke up, there were the happy parents with their newborn child waiting for us.

Navarana was true to form regarding these things. One day, while I was sleeping she came to tell me that Itukusuk had caught a narwhale. Did I want to go down there and eat *mattak*? I said that I was sleepy, I had just returned from the hunt, but I would come later. It was during the summer, daylight lasted through twenty-four hours, and every man had his own sleeping period in that part of the world. Later I woke up again when she came back home. I asked if the mattak feast was over already, but she said that she had an upset stomach, and so she had come home to sleep. After a while, Arnan-guaq [the servant woman] came to report that Navarana was in labor.

I became very excited and called Knud [Knud Rasmussen, a fellow Dane and partner in the Thule enterprise], who was sleeping in the loft. He had himself taken an Eskimo wife. His wife had borne him two girls; he had experience in those matters, and I wanted to ask him what to do.

He said that, as far as he knew, coffee had always played a role in the proceedings. It was during the first world war, we had not received supplies (especially coffee) for a long time, so I said that this was quite impossible. Knud then revealed that he had preserved some coffee beans tied up in a piece of cloth for the occasion. Consequently, we resolved to go to the brook for water.

Before we could leave the house, though, we heard a loud yell: "Anguterssuaq! A big boy!" It was Arnanguaq acting as midwife. Somewhat dazed, I went with Knud for the water, and when we returned, we went inside to see Navarana. She said that it was more tiresome than she had imagined to bear boys and so she wanted to be left alone. It was only three in the morning, she still had time to get a nice sleep.

Knud was sleepy too, and the coffee was forgotten. I was too happy to sleep. I went outside and sat down on a rock and started laying all kinds of plans for my boy. I resolved to stay in Thule the rest of my days, to teach him hunting, economy, and industry, and to be to him everything that a father could be. He was to avoid all the stumbling blocks I had run into myself. In short, I sat there daydreaming about my newborn boy that I hadn't even seen. And I stayed there until Navarana came out herself and told me to come in and see him. She got out of bed at the usual hour and tidied up the house.

In the evening, Knud threw his coffee party. The entire Thule population was there, of course, and he opened the dance with Navarana. She didn't stop dancing till very late. Our firstborn had arrived in style.

Remedy To Cause a Woman To Be Delivered: Peppermint

Georg Ebers was a well-known German archeologist and Egyptologist who was on a dig in Thebes one winter day in 1872 when he was approached by an anonymous but clearly wealthy Egyptian. The Egyptian had, he said, something that he thought might interest Ebers—for a price. That "something" turned out to be a huge papyrus wrapped in mummy cloth and in a nearly perfect state of preservation. Ebers raised the money, paid the price, and thus acquired the oldest medical work in existence, dating from the reign of Amenhotep I, c. 1550 B.C. Moses himself might have studied it. It achieved celebrity as the "Papyrus Ebers" and was translated in 1890. Among its many and varied prescriptions were the following for expediting a speedy delivery in childbirth.

> Remedy to cause a woman to be delivered:
>   Peppermint
>   Let the woman apply it to her bare posterior.
>
> Remedy to loosen a child in the body of a woman:
>   Sea-salt, Clean Grain-of-Wheat, Female Reed
>   Plaster the abdomen therewith.
>
> Another:
>   Fennel, Incense, Garlic, sert-juice, Fresh Salt,
>   Wasp's dung
>   Make into a ball and put in the Vagina.

Another:
> Tail-of-a-Tortoise, Shell-of-a-Beetle, sefet-oil,
>   sert-juice, Oil
> Crush into one and poultice therewith.

Childbearing on the Mayflower

Childbirth in America (Indians excepted) begins with the obvious.
When after many delays the *Mayflower* finally sailed on September
16, 1620, there were three pregnant women on board: Elizabeth Hopkins and Susanna White, both probably in their seventh month, and
Mary Norris Allerton in her second or third.

Whatever the feelings of these three women when they embarked,
they are easy to imagine by mid-voyage. The *Mayflower* was tiny by
any standards. Of the nine-and-half weeks on the gray Atlantic, six
weeks were in storm or squall. For the passengers that meant six weeks
unrelievedly below deck, everybody wet and cold and huddled together in the unlit, poorly ventilated interior that could not help but
have reeked with sweat, vomit, and bilge, while the little ship pitched
and wallowed in a malignant sea. Not to mention the constant noise—
sails slamming, wind howling in the rigging, timbers creaking, and an
unrelenting thud, thud, thud of the waves against the side. It was
awful for everyone; how then must it have been for Mary, no doubt
combining seasickness with morning sickness, and for Elizabeth and
Susanna, additionally plagued by the discomforts of advanced pregnancy and fears for what was to come.

Day after gray day the little ship moved steadily, or unsteadily, westward. Sometime in what was probably the seventh or eighth week,
Elizabeth Hopkins gave birth. William Bradford recorded no more of
the event than that; journal keeping on a rough sea is not easy. It may
have been a first baby for Elizabeth; there were older Hopkins children, but there were also suggestions that Elizabeth was a second wife.
There is no mention of the state of the weather that day—if during a
storm privacy would have been virtually nonexistent, while should
there have been a lull, men and children might presumably have been
on deck. Nor do we know whether it happened during the black—
really black—of night, or by the dim light that below deck served for
day. How long was her labor—three hours? Three days? Did the baby
lurch into life, or did God grant her a rare hour of calm? Had she
managed to keep the baby's little clothes, which she would have
brought with her, in some spot where they might have stayed dry, as
opposed to the state of almost everything else? The only thing Eliza-

beth would assuredly not have lacked was feminine aid and comfort: there would have been plenty of that, including a young midwife, Bridget Lee Fuller, known to have been on board and to have continued her practice in Plymouth until her death forty-five years later. And she would not have lacked for prayers. William Bradford would unquestionably have led her fellow Pilgrims in heartfelt entreaties for her safe deliverance.

The baby was a boy, appropriately christened Oceanus. Susanna White had a boy, too, born in the relative calm of Cape Cod bay some two weeks later. He was named Peregrine, meaning pilgrim. Oceanus Hopkins was one of the casualties of that first devastating winter, but Peregrine White was still alive in 1700—he would have been eighty that year. Poor Mary Allerton—she died the following spring giving birth to her baby, which was itself stillborn.

Ingrid Bergman, in Advanced Labor, Writes to Her Daughter Pia

In 1949 Ingrid Bergman left her husband of twelve years, Petter Lindstrom, and her ten-year-old daughter Pia, and flew to Rome to make a movie with Italian film director Roberto Rossellini. The movie was filmed on the remote volcanic island of Stromboli. It took more than twice the scheduled time to make, and before it was finished Ingrid wrote to Lindstrom that she would not be returning. She made a great and largely futile effort to maintain her relationship with Pia, but she did not write that she was pregnant. Her husband and daughter would learn that in good time from the press.

The American press had, in fact, been having a heyday over the affair of Bergman and Rossellini, both of whom were still married. When the pregnancy story broke, all other news, including President Truman's announcement of the invention of the hydrogen bomb, was pushed to the bottom of the page. Their friend Ernest Hemingway tried to put the matter in perspective. "What is all this nonsense?" he was reported saying. "She's going to have a child. So what? Women are always having children. I'm proud of her and happy for her. She loves Roberto and he loves her, and they want the child. We should celebrate with her not condemn her." But the hounding of reporters and photographers still necessitated her living behind locked doors and shuttered windows until the day finally came. It happened, as she describes in *Ingrid Bergman: My Story* (by Ingrid Bergman and Alan Burgess) in this way:

The phone rang in our apartment. It was getting on toward noon and the date was February 2, 1950. I remember that date very well. It was Mrs. Lydia Vernon, the wife of our business manager, and she was ringing from Beverly Hills. She started right in: "What's the matter with you? You really must pull yourself together and come back and see Pia. Do you understand that? You have to come back to America to see Pia. She is crying for you all the time. She's dreadfully unhappy. Get on a plane and come back at once."

I was so upset I was crying, and kept trying to interrupt, "But I can't come now. Don't you understand? As soon as I can, I'll arrange something."

But she went on and on just raving at me, and when I finally managed to put the phone down, I felt the first contractional pain of the birth starting. And I had this terrible presentiment. I was going into the hospital to have this baby and perhaps I wouldn't come out of it alive. It had something to do with being brought up on movies, I think. I had to pay for my sins: you either died or went to prison if you sinned.

I had to write, I just had to write to Pia to tell her I loved her, that even at this moment, if it should be my last, she would know I had been thinking about her. I had to have some document to prove that. So I got to my typewriter and put in carbon and paper: if the letter got lost at least the carbon copy would get to her somehow. And now what did I say? How to tell a ten-year-old child that I was expecting another baby, why I couldn't come home and have the baby with her and Papa. How to tell her I'd fallen in love with another man; he was the father of the child, and I would stay in Italy, and she would come and visit me and I would visit her. . . .

Then Elena Di Montis, the maid who'd been with me ever since I first arrived in Italy, rushed in and took one look at me, all curled up and typing away, and cried, "For pity's sake, we can't have the baby *here!* I can't handle such things. We must call the doctor. Please call the doctor." And I was saying, "No, No, I must write this letter first."

I looked at the clock on the wall. I knew from Pia's birth that these contracting pains come regularly, every four minutes for the first period, then three minutes, and so on, and between them peace and you feel absolutely fine. So I plugged away at the letter and then I glanced up at the clock and oh . . . oh . . . oohhhh, here we go again. Every four minutes I was literally hanging on to the chair, and then back to the typing. Now the spasms were coming every three minutes and Elena was hopping round going mad, moaning "Signora, the doctor, the doctor! Please call the doctor! I can't help you . . . I have no experience."

"I haven't finished the letter yet, I haven't finished the letter. I must finish the letter."

"But you'll have the baby here, and I don't know what to do. Let me call the doctor. I'll call the doctor? . . ."

I finally finished it, literally hanging over the chair. I wiped the sweat away and said, "All right, call the doctor now."

Roberto was away in the mountains outside Rome shooting *Flowers of St. Francis,* so he was also telephoned. I expect he jumped into his Ferrari and might even have got to the clinic before I did.

The car arrived. I sneaked into it and off we went. Then when we were halfway there, I suddenly realized I wasn't wearing my green emerald ring which Roberto had given me, and which I never took off. I had washed my hands and left it in the bathroom. That really threw me. In the hospital I rushed for the phone. Poor Elena; there I was raving at her again: "I can't have this baby without that green ring on my finger! It is in the bathroom! Throw yourself in a taxi and rush it to the hospital. I shall not have the baby without it. Hurry! Hurry!"

The pains were now arriving so regularly that all my time schedules had gone astray. And I had gone astray too because the last thing I remembered was dear Elena slipping the ring on my finger and smiling at me. Then I was in the delivery room and Robertino was born at seven o'clock in the evening.

"I Granny for All the Women Around Here"

Today there are hardly any white tenant farmers in the American South, but in 1935, in the middle of the Depression decade, there were three-quarters of a million in North Carolina alone. The most obvious harvest was children, a fact amply evident to anyone traveling the rural by-roads of the region.

One such person was Georgia-born Margaret Jarman Hagood, who over a sixteen month period conducted an extensive survey of white tenant farm mothers in the Carolina piedmont, Georgia, and Alabama. She encouraged these normally reticent women to talk of their lives, especially their experiences with childbirth.

During her visits children wandered in and out, babies were nursed, neighbors dropped by, the husband returned for supper. Only three of the 129 mothers had completed high school. Semantics were sometimes problematical and always colorful: midwives were "grannies," menopause was "when nature leaves you," a "knee baby" was the next-to-youngest child, no matter what its age. The past tense of "help" took its Old English form "holp." The baby that didn't cry was "smart"; the child that did well in school was "shrewd." An opinion was usually expressed with the opener "I tells 'em" or "I allus say." Few mothers did more reading than an occasional dip into the Bible or their children's schoolbooks. Knowledge of international affairs was vague at best; although most women were aware that something was brewing in Germany, they had little understanding of what it was, and one couple argued heatedly over whether the Kaiser and Hitler were the same person.

For these women, like the poor in many parts of the world, their wealth was their children. Only the youngest women wanted more children than they already had; still, whatever number that was was a source of great pride, as is clear from the following selection from Hagood's book, *Mothers of the South.*

Almost every mother described the birth of a child, varying in fullness of detail according to the presence or absence of children and their age and sex. It was often interesting to notice the immediate shifting to the biological and especially to the obstetrical features the moment a husband or child left the room and there was privacy. Older women took the precaution of inquiring about marital status. An affirmative reply to "Air you a married woman?" assured them on this point and the relationship became more nearly one of equals in the discussion of this subject. Childbirth is regarded as an achievement for which the tenant mother need make no apologies as she might for housekeeping or her children's clothes. There is more often than not a touch of pride in her voice as she relates her experiences in "having a baby." Lines of class distinction vanish in sharing reminiscences about this most fundamental of realities. Upon hearing that the visitor had only one child and that with little difficulty, one woman could not restrain herself: "Then you don't know *nothing* about having babies—you just listen to *me*. I 'granny' for all the women around here. . . ." With gusto she continued accounts of general practices interspersed with vivid illustrations from her own experience and that of other women she had "grannied" for.

The place of childbirth is the home, occasionally that of the mother's or father's parents for the first child, or rarely the hospital. This means interrupting the household routine in several ways. First, the other children must be disposed of for the actual duration of labor.

The most common practice is sending them off to their grandmother's or their aunt's or a neighbor's. As soon as one mother felt the first pain, she would rush with the children down the road about a quarter of a mile to her mother-in-law's, leave them there, and hurry back with the mother-in-law, who was a "granny." Speed was necessary because she was never in labor more than an hour except once. Another who took much longer could pack up her children's things more leisurely and have her husband take them off to a relative's for a few days' visit when she decided it was time for him to go for the doctor. Seven of another's eight children were born at night and so all she had to do was to move the children back into the kitchen and let them go on sleeping. Another can't bear to have her children sleep away from her and has never sent them off. When she had to be taken to the hospital for an instrumental delivery of her baby, now two months old, she insisted on coming home the next day to be with her children, even though it meant having an ambulance. . . .

Eighty-five percent of the children of these mothers were delivered by doctors, but several mothers had never had doctors and several others had had them only for the first child. When a midwife is employed she is paid $5 to $10 for her services during labor, birth, and for a few hours afterwards. There her duties end unless there is an overlapping of the "grannying" and the "staying with" functions. Midwives are usually Negroes now, although one woman's mother and mother-in-law were both "regular grannies." The qualifying adjective, "regular," may technically connote "licensed," but in ordinary usage it distinguishes midwives, who deliver babies alone, from nonprofessional women, as often white as Negro, who are not licensed and who do not actually deliver except in an emergency, but who go to assist the doctor and to perform the duties of a nurse under his supervision. Such women "granny" but are not "regular grannies" and usually receive no pay, although sometimes they get presents. . . .

Several mothers had borne children with no help because the doctor or midwife did not get there in time. A woman's sixth baby was born one night after the worst snow storm in years. She had always used midwives, but there was none around in that community—it was just four miles from town. Her husband walked to town to get the doctor after they put the children back in the kitchen. Because of the snow and a crust on it which broke through, the doctor could not get any nearer than the highway in his car and had to find a mule to ride on for the last mile and a half. The baby had been born a half hour when he and the husband finally arrived. The mother had been all alone so she just covered the newborn baby with a quilt and without cutting the cord let it lie there until the doctor came. Having babies alone is a fast fading practice, but, if we go back a generation, many can tell of their mothers' experiences—several of whom preferred having them while sitting on slop jars instead of lying in bed. One woman's mother had a doctor with her first and watched everything he did very carefully. After that she always had her own alone. She wouldn't even let a neighbor woman come in to "granny" because she didn't like having anybody around. She would call her husband in when she wanted him to hand her things. She had ten children and learned the art of delivery so well on herself that "after nature left her," she started "regular grannying." Although she is nearly eighty now, she helped one young girl this fall.

In describing labor and the actual process of giving birth, the points featured are those to which some pride in achievement can be attached. The duration of labor is a matter where either extreme seems to be a basis for prestige. One mother with an air of condescension and pity for her weaker sisters claimed, "I *never* took over a few hours except with my first, and this knee-baby, here, was born in less than a half hour." Another described almost hour by hour nearly a week of labor with the implication that only a courageous person could have lived through it. The one who "grannies" said anyone can stand a day of being in labor; it's on the second and third and fourth days when you're "plum wore out" and "feel like you can't do nothing else" that you wish you could die. . . .

The other bragging point is not yelling. One explained that she could keep her children right in the house because she never "carried on." Another says she always "grunted it out" with no other noise. One shamefacedly confessed to weakness in this respect although she justified herself by claiming that anyone would have to holler that went through what she did. One woman telling of a spoiled sister with implied condemnation said she screamed so loud that her children, who were nearly a mile away, heard her. . . .

The sanitary facilities for childbirth in the home are woefully inadequate. Preparation consists of collecting old cloths for pads and navel dressings, of getting ready clean sheets and rubber sheeting in some homes, but in others, old, dirty quilts that can be thrown away. A mother's ideas of sanitation were revealed in her telling of a dream she had had the night before. In the dream she suddenly realized that her sister was about to give birth to a baby on the new $12.75 mattress which is the pride of her life—she has never even let the baby wet it.

She loves her sister, but she could not see her mattress ruined. She ran quickly and found some old, torn quilts she was saving for rags, put them on a cot and made her sister get on it. "You can have your baby here," she told her sister, "but not on my fine mattress and clean sheets!" When instrumental deliveries have to be made, the kitchen table is called into service. Hot water is usually available and one or two mothers said they had Lysol, but any other antiseptics or germicides have to be brought by the doctor. Kidney and blood poison, convulsions, milk leg, and other serious conditions were reported as having developed and having been treated at home. . . .

Every one of the mothers with babies of two or under, either explicitly or by inference, expressed the attitude, "I hope this is the last one." . . . In most cases the effecting of the wish was limited to "hoping." . . . Of the sixty-nine mothers questioned as to the use of contraceptives, only eight replied in the affirmative. Three use condoms, two douches, one diaphragm and jelly, and two practice withdrawal. . . . An illustration of the euphemistic phraseology employed occurred when one mother tried to explain that this [withdrawal] was the method she and her husband used. Her answer was metaphorical: "Well, I always say that when you chew tobacco, it don't make so much mess if you spit it out the window." Another described the same method in the words of advice which had been given her by an older woman, "If you don't want butter, pull the dasher out in time!"

Leo Tolstoy: "It Seemed Something Superfluous, Something Overflowing"

There have been few marriages more tumultuous and strife-torn than that of Leo Tolstoy and his wife Sonya. The best approximation we have of the early period—of their courtship and marriage, Sonya's first pregnancy, and the birth of their son Sergei— is the same interval with Levin and Kitty in *Anna Karenina*. But Levin is a Tolstoy without warts, and that singularly appealing story, although accurate in much of its homey detail, plays down the passions and jealousies that were a constant feature of life at Yasnaya Polyana. Sonya's pregnancy was beleaguered by her husband's mercurial temperament, his conflicting enjoyment and rejection of her sensuality, her feelings of neglect, and her jealousy of the servant woman who had once been his mistress. She and Tolstoy were increasingly ill at ease with each other, and Sonya found herself resenting the child within her that seemed to separate them from each other. At other times he relaxed, and one

day, momentarily entranced with approaching fatherhood, he
burst into the room with obstetrical book in hand and the jubilant announcement—"He already has toenails!"

In *Anna Karenina* Kitty's confinement takes place in town
rather than the country; otherwise, as both Sonya's diary and her
sister Tanya's recollections confirm, the following scene is an almost moment-for-moment account of what actually took place at
Yasnaya Polyana on June 28, 1863.

At five in the morning the creak of an opening door awoke him. He
jumped up and looked round. Kitty was not in the bed beside him,
but on the other side of the partition a light was moving, and he
heard her step.

"What is it? What is it? . . ." he muttered, not yet quite awake.
"Kitty, what is it?"

"Nothing," said she, coming candle in hand from beyond the partition. "I only felt a little unwell," she added with a peculiarly sweet
and significant smile.

"What? Has it begun? Has it?" he asked in a frightened voice. "We
must send . . ." And he began to dress hurriedly.

"No, no," she said smiling, holding him back with her hand. "I'm
sure it's nothing. I only felt slightly unwell; but it is over now."

She came back to her bed, put out the candle, lay down, and remained quiet. Though that quietness, as if she were holding her
breath, and especially the peculiar tenderness and animation with
which, returning from the other side of the partition, she had said:
"It's nothing!" seemed to him suspicious, yet he was so sleepy that he
fell asleep at once. Only afterwards he remembered that bated breath,
and realized all that had passed in her dear sweet soul while she lay
motionless by his side, awaiting the greatest event of a woman's life.

At seven o'clock he was awakened by her touch on his shoulder
and a soft whisper. She seemed to hesitate between regret at waking
him and a desire to speak to him.

"Kostya, don't be frightened. It's nothing, but I think . . . We must
send for Mary Vlasevna."

The candle was burning again. She was sitting on the bed holding
in her hands some knitting she had lately been doing.

"Please don't be frightened! It's nothing. I'm not a bit afraid," she
said on seeing his alarmed face, and she pressed his hand to her breast
and then to her lips.

He jumped up hastily, hardly aware of himself and without taking

his eyes off her, put on his dressing-gown and stood still, gazing at her.
It was necessary for him to go, but he could not tear himself away
from the sight of her. He had loved that face and known all its expressions and looks, but he had never seen her as she was now. How vile
and despicable he appeared to himself before her as she now was,
when he recollected the grief he had caused her yesterday! Her flushed
face surrounded with soft hair that had escaped from beneath her
nightcap shone with joy and resolution.

Little as there was of affectation and conventionality in Kitty's general character, yet Levin was astonished at what was revealed to him
now that every veil had fallen and the very kernel of her soul shone
through her eyes. And in this simplicity, this nakedness of soul, she
whom he loved was more apparent than ever. She looked at him smil-
ingly, but suddenly her eyebrows twitched, she raised her head, and
coming quickly to him she took hold of his hand and clinging close
she enveloped him in her hot breath. She was suffering, and seemed to
be complaining to him of her pain. And for a moment from force of
habit he felt as if he were in fault. But her look expressed a tenderness
which told him that she not only did not blame him, but loved him
because of those sufferings. "If I am not to blame for it, who is?" he
thought, involuntarily seeking a culprit to punish for these sufferings;
but there was no culprit. She suffered, complained, triumphed in her
sufferings, rejoiced in them and loved them. He saw that something
beautiful was taking place in her soul, but what it was he could not
understand. It was above his comprehension.

"I have sent for Mama. And you, go quickly, and fetch Mary
Vlasevna. . . . Kostya! . . . No, it's nothing. It's past."

She moved away from him and rang.

"Well, go now. Pasha is coming. I am all right."

And Levin saw with amazement that she again took up the knitting
which she had fetched in the night, and recommenced work.

As Levin went out at one door he heard the maid enter at the other.
He stopped at the door and heard Kitty give detailed instructions to
the maid, and with her help herself move the bed.

He dressed, and while the horse was being harnessed—for it was
early, and no *izvoshchiks* were about yet—he ran back to the bedroom
on tiptoe but, as it seemed to him, on wings. Two maids were busy
moving something in the bedroom. Kitty was walking up and down
and knitting, rapidly throwing the thread over the needle and giving
orders.

"I am going straight to the doctor's. They have already gone for Mary Vlasevna, but I will call there too. Is anything else wanted? Oh yes, to Dolly!"

She looked at him, evidently not listening to what he was saying.

"Yes, yes! Go," she said rapidly, frowning and motioning him away with her hand.

He was already on his way through the drawing-room when suddenly a piteous moan, that lasted only a moment, reached him from the bedroom. He stopped and for a moment could not understand it.

"Yes, it was she," he said and, clasping his head with his hands, he ran downstairs.

"Lord have mercy! Pardon and help us!" he repeated the words that suddenly and unexpectedly sprang to his lips. And he, an unbeliever, repeated those words not with his lips only. At that instant he knew that neither his doubts nor the impossibility of believing with his reason—of which he was conscious—at all prevented his appealing to God. It all flew off like dust. To whom should he appeal, if not to Him in whose hands he felt himself, his soul, and his love, to be?

The horse was not yet ready, but feeling particularly energetic, physically strong and alert to meet what lay before him, so as not to lose a moment he did not wait for it but started off on foot, telling Kuzma to catch him up.

At the corner he encountered a night izvoshchik hurrying along. In the little sledge sat Mary Vlasevna in a velvet cloak with a shawl over her head. "Thank God!" he muttered, recognizing with delight her little blonde face, which now wore a particularly serious and even severe expression. Without stopping the izvoshchik he ran back beside her.

"So it began about two hours ago, not more?" she asked. "You will find the doctor, but don't hurry him. And get some opium at the chemist's."

"So you think it may go all right? God have mercy and help us!" said Levin as he saw his horse coming out of the gateway. Jumping into the sledge beside Kuzma, he ordered him to drive to the doctor's.

The doctor was not yet up, and his footman said he had gone to bed late and given orders that he was not to be called, but the footman added that he would be up soon. The man was cleaning lampglasses and seemed quite absorbed in his task. This attention to his glasses and indifference to what was taking place at the Levins' astonished Levin at first, but he immediately recollected himself and realized that no one knew or was bound to know his feelings, and that it was therefore all the more necessary to act calmly, deliberately, and firmly in order to break through this wall of indifference and to attain his aim. "Do not hurry and do not omit anything," he said to himself, conscious of an increasing uplift of his physical powers and of his attention to all that lay before him.

Having learnt that the doctor was not up yet, Levin, out of the many plans that occurred to him, decided on the following: Kuzma should go with a note to another doctor, while he himself would go to the chemist for the opium; and if the doctor was not up when he returned he would bribe the footman—or if that was impossible, he would enter by force and wake the doctor at all costs.

At the chemist's a skinny dispenser, with the same indifference with which the footman had cleaned his lamp-glasses, closed with a wafer a packet of powders for which a coachman was waiting, and refused to let Levin have any opium. Trying not to hurry and not to get excited, Levin gave the names of the doctor and of the midwife, explained why the opium was wanted, and tried to persuade the dispenser to let him have it. The dispenser asked in German whether he might sell it; and receiving permission from some one behind a screen, took out a bottle and a funnel, slowly poured it from a large bottle into a small one, stuck on a label, and, in spite of Levin's request that he should not do so, sealed up the bottle, and was about to wrap it up. This was more than Levin could stand; he resolutely snatched the bottle out of the man's hands and rushed out at the big glass door. The doctor was not up yet, and the footman, now busy putting down a carpet, refused to wake him. Levin deliberately took out a ten-rouble note, and speaking slowly but without losing time, handed him the note and explained that Dr Peter Dmitrich (how great and important this Peter Dmitrich, formerly so insignificant, now appeared to Levin!) had promised to come at any time, and that he would certainly not be angry and must therefore be called at once.

The footman consented and went upstairs, asking Levin to step into the waiting-room.

Levin could hear the doctor at the other side of the door coughing, walking about, washing, and speaking. Some three minutes elapsed; to Levin they seemed more than an hour. He could not wait any longer.

"Peter Dmitrich! Peter Dmitrich!" he called out in a tone of entreaty through the open door. "For heaven's sake forgive me! . . . Receive me as you are! It's over two hours. . . ."

"Immediately! Immediately!" answered a voice, and Levin was as-tounded to detect that the doctor was smiling as he said it.

"Just for one moment!"

"Immediately!"

Two minutes more passed while the doctor put on his boots and two more while he put on his clothes and brushed his hair.

"Peter Dmitrich!" Levin again began in a piteous voice, but at that instant the doctor came out, dressed and with his hair brushed. "These people have no conscience," thought Levin. "Brushing their hair while we are perishing!"

"Good morning!" said the doctor, holding out his hand and, as it seemed to Levin, teasing him by his calm manner. "Don't hurry! Well?"

Trying to be as exact as possible, Levin began recounting every un-necessary detail of his wife's position, continually interrupting himself to beg the doctor to accompany him at once.

"Don't be in such a hurry. You see you are inexperienced, I am sure I shall not be needed, but I promised, and if you like I will come. But there is no hurry. Please sit down. Won't you have a cup of coffee?"

Levin gave the doctor a look which asked whether he was not laugh-ing at him. But the doctor had no idea of laughing.

"I know, I know," he said with a smile. "I am a family man myself. We husbands are the most miserable of creatures at those times. I have a patient whose husband always runs away into the stable on such occasions!"

"But what is your opinion, Peter Dmitrich? Do you think it may go all right?"

"All the symptoms are favourable."

"Then you will come at once?" said Levin, looking angrily at the servant who brought in the coffee.

"In an hour's time."

"No, for heaven's sake . . . !"

"Well, only let me finish my coffee."

The doctor began on his coffee. Both kept silence.

"Well, the Turks are being seriously beaten! Did you read yester-day's telegram?" asked the doctor, chewing a piece of roll.

"No, I can't stand it!" said Levin, jumping up. "So you will come in a quarter of an hour?"

"In half an hour."

"On your honour?"

Levin got home just as the Princess arrived, and they met at the bedroom door. There were tears in the Princess's eyes and her hands shook. When she saw Levin she embraced him and began to cry.

"Well, Mary Vlasevna, darling?" she asked, seizing the hand of the midwife who came toward them with a beaming but preoccupied expression.

"It's going all right," she said. "Persuade her to lie down; it will be easier for her."

From the moment when he woke up and understood what was the matter Levin had braced himself to endure what might await him, without reasoning and without anticipating anything—firmly suppressing all his thoughts and feelings, determined not to upset his wife but on the contrary to calm and support her. Not allowing himself even to think of what was about to happen and how it would end, judging by inquiries he had made as to the time such affairs usually lasted, Levin mentally prepared himself to endure and to keep his heart under restraint for something like five hours, which seemed to him within his power. But when he returned from the doctor's and again saw her sufferings, he began repeating more and more often: "God, pardon and help us!" sighing and lifting his head, afraid lest he should not be able to bear the strain and should either burst into tears or run away, so tormenting was it for him. And only one hour had passed!

But after that hour another passed, a second, a third, and all the five hours that he had set himself as the longest term of possible endurance, and still the situation was unchanged; and he went on enduring, for there was nothing else to do but to endure—thinking every moment that he had reached the utmost limit of endurance and that in a moment his heart would burst with pity.

But the minutes went by, and the hours, and other hours, and his suffering and terror and strain grew tenser.

The ordinary conditions of life, without which nothing can be imagined, no longer existed for Levin. He lost the sense of time. Sometimes minutes—those minutes when she called him to her and he held her moist hand, now pressing his with extraordinary strength and now pushing him away—seemed to him like hours; and then again hours seemed but minutes. He was surprised when Mary Vlasevna asked him to light a candle behind the partition, and he learnt that it was already five o'clock in the evening. Had he been told it was ten in the morning he would not have been more astonished. He had just as little idea of where he was at that time as he had of when it all took place. He saw her burning face, now bewildered and full of suffering, and now smiling and soothing him. He saw the Princess red, overwrought, her grey hair out of curl, and with tears which she energetically swallowed, biting her lips. He saw Dolly, he saw the doctor smoking thick cigarettes, and Mary Vlasevna with a firm, resolute, and tranquilizing look on her face, and the old Prince pacing up and down the ballroom and frowning. But he did not know how they came and went, nor where they were. The Princess was one moment in the bedroom with the doctor, and the next in the study, where a table laid for a meal had made its appearance; and next it was not the Princess, but Dolly. Afterwards Levin remembered being sent somewhere. Once he was told to fetch a table and a sofa. He did it with zeal, believing that it was necessary for her sake, and only later discovered that he had been preparing a sleeping-place for himself. Then he was sent to the study to ask the doctor about something. The doctor answered him, and then began talking about the scenes in the city Duma. Then he was sent to fetch an icon with silver-gilt mounts from the Princess's bedroom, and he and the Princess's old lady's maid climbed on a cupboard to get down the icon, and he broke the little lamp that burned before it, and the old servant tried to comfort him about his wife and about the lamp. He brought the icon back with him, and put it at the head of Kitty's bed, carefully pushing it in behind the pillows. But where, when, and why all this was done he did not know. Nor did he understand why the Princess took his hand, and looking pitifully at him, entreated him to be calm; nor why Dolly tried to persuade him to eat something and led him out of the room; nor why even the doctor looked seriously and sympathizingly at him, offering him some drops.

He only knew and felt that what was happening was similar to what had happened the year before in the hotel of the provincial town on the deathbed of his brother Nicholas. Only that was sorrow and this was joy. But that sorrow and this joy were equally beyond the usual conditions of life: they were like openings in that usual life through which something higher became visible. And, as in that case, what was now being accomplished came harshly, painfully, incomprehensibly; and while watching it, the soul soared, as then, to heights it had never known before, at which reason could not keep up with it.

"Lord, pardon and help us!" he kept repeating incessantly to himself, appealing to God, in spite of a long period of apparently complete estrangement, just as trustingly and simply as in the days of childhood and early youth.

During the whole of that time he was alternatively in two different moods. One mood when not in her presence: when with the doctor, who smoked one thick cigarette after another and extinguished them against the rim of the overflowing ashpan; when with Dolly and the Prince, where they talked about dinner, politics, or Mary Petrovna's illness, and when Levin suddenly quite forgot for an instant what was happening and felt just as if he was waking up; and the other was in her presence, by her pillow, where his heart was ready to burst with pity and yet did not burst, and there he prayed unceasingly to God. And every time when the screams that came from the bedroom roused him from momentary forgetfulness he succumbed to the same strange error that had possessed him in the first moments: every time, on hearing the scream, he jumped up and ran to justify himself, but recollected on the way that he was not to blame and that he longed to protect and help her. But when, looking at her, he again saw that to help was impossible, he was seized with horror and said, "Lord, pardon and help us!" And the longer it lasted the stronger grew both his moods: out of her presence he became calmer, quite forgetting her, and at the same time both her sufferings and his feeling of the impossibility of helping her became more and more poignant. He would jump up, wishing to run away somewhere, but ran to her instead.

Sometimes when she had called him again and again, he was half-inclined to blame her. But seeing her meek smiling face and hearing her say, "I have worn you out," he blamed God; but the thought of God made him at once pray for forgiveness and mercy.

He did not know whether it was late or early. The candles were all burning low. Dolly had just entered the study and suggested that the doctor should lie down. Levin sat listening to the doctor's stories of a quack magnetizer and staring at the ash of the doctor's cigarette. It was an interval of rest and oblivion. He had quite forgotten what was going on. He listened to the doctor's tale and understood it. Suddenly there was a scream unlike anything he had ever heard. The scream was so terrible that Levin did not even jump up, but looked breathlessly with a frightened and inquiring glance at the doctor, who bent his head on one side to listen and smiled approvingly. Everything was so out of the ordinary that nothing any longer surprised Levin. "Probably it had to be so," thought he and remained sitting still. "But who was it screaming?" He jumped up and rushed into the bedroom on tiptoe, past Mary Vlasevna and the Princess, and stopped at his place at the head of the bed. The screaming had ceased, but there was a change; what it was he could not make out or understand, nor did he want to understand it; but he read it in Mary Vlasevna's face. She looked pale and stern, and as resolute as before, though her jaw trembled a little and her eyes were fixed intently on Kitty. Kitty's burning face, worn with suffering, with a lock of hair clinging to her clammy forehead, was turned toward him trying to catch his eye. Her raised hands asked for his. Seizing his cold hands in her perspiring ones she pressed them to her face.

"Don't go! Don't go! I am not afraid, I am not afraid!" she said rapidly. "Mama! Take off my earrings, they are in the way! You are not afraid? Soon, Mary Vlasevna, soon . . . !"

She spoke very rapidly and tried to smile, but all at once her face became distorted and she pushed him away.

"No, this is awful! I shall die . . . Go! Go!" she cried, and again he heard that scream unlike any other cry.

Levin clasped his head in his hands and ran out of the room.

"It's all right, it's all right! All goes well!" Dolly called after him.

But say what they might, he knew that now all was lost. Leaning his head against the door-post he stood in the next room, and heard some one shrieking and moaning in a way he had never heard till then, and he knew that these sounds were produced by what once was Kitty. He had long ceased wishing for a child, and now he hated that child. He did not now even wish her to live, but only longed that these terrible sufferings should end.

"Doctor, what is it? What is it? Oh, my God!" he cried, grasping the hand of the doctor who had just entered.

"It's coming to an end," said the doctor, with a face so serious that Levin thought that *end* meant death.

Quite beside himself, he rushed into her room. The first thing he saw was Mary Vlasevna's face. It was still more frowning and stern. Kitty's face did not exist. In its place was something terrible, both because of its strained expression and because of the sounds which proceeded from it. He let his head drop upon the wood of the bedstead, feeling that his heart was breaking. The terrible screaming did not cease, but grew yet more awful until, as if it had reached the utmost limit of horror, it suddenly ceased. Levin could scarcely believe his ears, but there was no room for doubt. The screaming had ceased, and he heard a sound of movement, of rustling, of accelerated breathing, and her voice, faltering, living, tender, and happy, as it said, "It's over."

He raised his head. With her arms helplessly outstretched upon the quilt, unusually beautiful and calm she lay, gazing silently at him, trying unsuccessfully to smile.

And suddenly, out of the mysterious, terrible, and unearthly world in which he had been living for the last twenty-two hours, Levin felt himself instantaneously transported back to the old everyday world, but now radiant with the light of such new joy that it was insupportable. The taut strings snapped, and sobs and tears of joy that he had not in the least anticipated arose within him, with such force that they shook his whole body and long prevented his speaking.

Falling on his knees by her bedside he held his wife's hand to his lips, kissing it, and that hand, by a feeble movement of the fingers, replied to the kisses. And meanwhile at the foot of the bed, like a flame above a lamp, flickered in Mary Vlasevna's skilful hands the life of a human being who had never before existed: a human being who, with the same right and the same importance to himself, would live and would procreate others like himself.

"Alive! Alive! And a boy! Don't be anxious," Levin heard Mary Vlasevna say, as she slapped the baby's back with a shaking hand.

"Mama, is it true?" asked Kitty.

The Princess could only sob in reply.

And amid the silence, as a positive answer to the mother's question, a voice quite unlike all the restrained voices that had been speaking in the room made itself heard. It was a bold, insolent voice that had no consideration for anything, it was the cry of the new human being who had so incomprehensibly appeared from some unknown realm.

Before that, if Levin had been told that Kitty was dead, and that he had died with her, that they had angel children, and that God was there present with them—he would not have been astonished. But now, having returned to the world of actuality, he had to make great efforts to understand that she was alive and well, and that the creature that was yelling so desperately was his son. Kitty was alive, her sufferings were over; and he was full of unspeakable bliss. This he comprehended, and it rendered him entirely happy. But the child? Whence and why had he come? Who was he? . . . He could not at all accustom himself to the idea. It seemed something superfluous, something overflowing, and for a long time he was unable to get used to it.

A Sow-Gelder Performs the First Caesarean

The one thing we know absolutely about the Caesarean section in ancient times is that it was not performed on Aurelia at the birth of her son Julius, later Julius Caesar. He arrived in quite the usual manner. The misunderstanding came about because in seventh century (B.C.) Rome one Numa Pompilius decreed that if a woman died while pregnant, the child was instantly to be cut out of her abdomen. This dictum was part of the *Lex Regia,* and was later incorporated into the *Lex Caesare,* from which the operation acquired the label "Caesarean section."

It was practiced in almost all parts of the ancient world, but always after the mother had already died. Frequently the baby lived; Pliny, in fact, was convinced that such children arrived under favorable auspices, and lists several military heroes as confirmation. The first indication we have that it might have been attempted on a living woman occurs in that part of the Jewish Talmud known as the *Mishna,* and later in the Hindu *Sushruta Samhita,* but as the outcome is left unclear, we must assume that the mother in any case did not survive.

The first record of a successful Caesarean comes much later when in the year 1500 the wife of Jacob Nufer, a Swiss sow-gelder, went into labor and could not seem to deliver. By this time the surgical side of the medical profession had degenerated to the point where most surgeons doubled as barbers or, sometimes, as sow-gelders. In his desperation Jacob Nufer at least knew where to begin. Thirteen midwives (so the story goes) had tried and failed, at which point Jacob collected his tools of the trade and did the obvious. Is it possible he had the intuition to clean them first? To wash his hands? To protect his wife from the barnyard flies? We will simply never know. All that is apparent is that at the operation's close, both mother and child were doing well. In fact, Mom Nufer did very well indeed. In time she gave birth to six more children, including twins, all of whom she delivered normally. She lived to the fine age of seventy-seven.

The Nufer incident was widely broadcast, and during the course of the sixteenth century, the operation was attempted by various others—there is no way to guess how many—but with fourteen more successes recorded. Considering all the possible complications, fourteen is a large number, even for a whole century. Two of the fourteen apparently took place in Toulouse where the Italian physician Scipione Mercurio reports visiting the surviving mothers.

Mercurio became an advocate of the Caesarean section, and included a how-to chapter in his obstetrical best-seller *La Commare o Riccoglitrice,* published at the very end of the sixteenth century. He makes it very clear that in spite of sow-gelder Nufer's success, only a skilled surgeon thoroughly grounded in female anatomy should attempt the operation, and then only on a healthy woman with a strong pulse. Everything is carefully spelled out. The instruments required were two sharp razors, one pointed and one round-edged, a needle and thread (waxed), a soft sponge, and fine pieces of soft linen. Six assistants were the minimum—four to hold the poor unanesthetized patient and two to hand the surgeon his tools—and they must be "strong and courageous" (i.e., not likely to faint). The surgeon was to mark the place of the incision with ink and cut along it "about half a foot long, or a little more." Step by step the instructions continue until the child and placenta have both been extracted, the abdominal wall sewn up, and the wound dressed with the linen cloths saturated with a decoction of various substances including flowers of pomegranate, dried roses, birthwort, bulrushes soaked in sour black wine, and "that water which blacksmiths use to extinguish glowing irons." Assuming she survived, the woman was to stay warm and quiet and not drink wine for a duration of two weeks, after which instruction Mercurio concludes rather abruptly: "This is enough about this new method of aiding difficult deliveries to help miserable patients."

The first Caesarean section in America was performed on a bleak day in the second term of George Washington's presidency by a desperate twenty-five-year-old doctor on his own wife.

Jesse Bennett started practicing medicine in the backwoods of Virginia in 1792 and the next year married young Elisabeth Hog of a prominent local family. Elisabeth became pregnant almost immediately, but when it came time for her to deliver, it was discovered that she had a contracted pelvis and that a normal delivery would be impossible. Labor continued to no effect, and Dr. Alexander Humphreys, the "town doctor" from Staunton, was hurriedly called in. Humphreys agreed with Jesse that Elisabeth could not deliver the baby normally and that either a Caesarean or a craniotomy was called for. It seems doubtful that Jesse could have known much about Caesareans, but Elisabeth, convinced she was going to die in any case, begged her husband to save the baby and attempt it.

There is no record of what surgical experience Jesse had as yet acquired, if any. Mindful of his reputation, Dr. Humphreys declined to do more than assist, so Jesse made the necessary preparations. An operating table was devised from two planks laid across a couple of barrels. Elisabeth was given a large dose of laudanum—the closest the eighteenth century would come to anesthesia—and placed on the boards with a Negro woman on each side to hold her. As witnesses reported later, "Dr. Bennett with one quick stroke of the knife laid open the abdomen and uterus." He enlarged the opening in the uterus with his hands and lifted out the baby girl and the placenta.

Elisabeth's sister, who was present, took the baby, and Jesse, remarking "this shall be the last one," reached in again and removed both ovaries. Then with the same strong linen thread that Elisabeth used to make his shirts, he sewed up the wound.

Elisabeth lived for another quarter of a century and her daughter well into the presidency of Ulysses S. Grant, seventy-seven years later.

Sean O'Casey: It Fell to Him To Make Tea Endlessly

The beautiful actress Eileen Carey was appearing in New York when she happened to pick up a copy of Sean O'Casey's *Juno and the Paycock,* then in its first London season. She was so affected by it that on returning to London she immediately contacted O'Casey. Before long she was appearing in *The Plough and the Stars,* and the next year—although she was twenty-three and he more than twice that—they were married. He called her his "unquiet spirit," and they were seldom apart until his death thirty-seven years later.

In the following excerpt from her memoir *Sean,* Eileen recalls a few episodes from her first pregnancy, and the birth of their son, Breon.

Lady Ottoline Morrell, who maintained her own literary salon, invited us to dine in Bloomsbury one evening with Oliver Gogarty and Dr Julian Huxley and his wife. Oliver visited us whenever he was in London, but the Huxleys I had not met. Far on in pregnancy, I wore a dress of black lace which was pleated from the neck and hung round me; it went with an underslip in heavy silk. When we reached the house the maid showed us into a long drawing-room down which Lady Ottoline advanced to meet us: a tall, striking figure wearing a white satin dress to her feet, with a deep lace fichu. As she swept forward, I realised in horror that I had forgotten my silk slip and that the transparent lace revealed all my underclothes. It must have been ridiculous. Sean burst out laughing; so did I; and Lady Ottoline, joining in, sent the maid for my coat which I wore during the rest of the evening. Luckily, we were the earliest arrivals. The dinner itself was a trifle difficult. Sean, his sight being so poor, did not notice that with the fish he had helped himself to lemon which he loathed; tasting it, he gave a horrified squeak. For some reason, the talk switched to music. Oliver Gogarty hummed a few tunes, all on one note, and we inferred, simultaneously but politely, that he was tone-deaf. Still, singing hardly counted, for he was an irresistible talker; Mrs Huxley was pleasantly animated, and Sean in his liveliest mood. In the end, though I sat fairly silently in my coat, the dinner was a success; everyone relaxed in the drawing-room, and the Huxleys, whom Sean liked greatly, planned to visit us in Woronzow Road. . . .

Because of the baby's size, the birth proved to be more complicated than I had thought. After a visit to Dr Harold Waller one afternoon, he told me that he would come round in the evening with a specialist. No, I said, it was not very convenient. I was going to the theatre. Would another evening do? He was sorry but advised me to cancel the theatre. My mother, who was having tea with me that day, told me in her morbid style that I should prepare myself for the fact that the child might be mentally afflicted: my father had been unbalanced, and the child's father was an eccentric. At this I dissolved in hysteria and practically pushed her down the stairs. Sean tore out from his room. My old dresser, Mrs Earle, who was living with us and who had known my mother a long time, rushed up in astonishment. Sean exclaimed, "What the hell are you up to, woman?" and the gentle Mrs Earle led my mother away, saying soothingly, "Now, now, you mustn't upset your daughter at this time." Mother left the house, repeating that she was simply trying to warn me.

When the specialist came that evening, he said that a little risk would be involved, and that he must ask whether, if there were an emergency, the mother or the child should be saved. Sean unhesitatingly declared for me. The anaesthetist arrived; two doctors delivered Breon; and it was over.

Sean during my last weeks of pregnancy had had an ordeal. I was sleepless at night, and it fell to him to make tea endlessly, or play cards, or sit and talk until perhaps in the early hours of the morning I might doze. On the night of Breon's birth, Dr Waller—who was a leading gynaecologist, among the most advanced of his time—proposed that Sean should stay with a friend; they telephoned him later with the news that I was well and that he had a son. Returning in the morning to Woronzow Road, he saw a pile of letters on the hall table, one of them with a Dublin postmark; it was from the Abbey. After reading it, he went upstairs to my room and embraced me. He was excited about the baby; it was a glorious morning, and round us in St John's Wood the lilac and syringa and acacia trees were in bloom. I was glowingly happy. It was not for a week that Sean told me of the shock he had kept to himself; the letter was from W. B. Yeats, and the Abbey Theatre had rejected *The Silver Tassie*.

The Law of the Bush: She May Never Cry Out

Between 1951 and 1955 Elizabeth Marshall Thomas went on three separate expeditions to the Kalahari Desert to study the African Bushmen, a slightly built, yellow-skinned people who live on the thin edge of survival in a hostile land. They eke out a precarious existence by hunting, and consuming, not only springbok and gemsbok, antelope and wildebeest, but tortoise, lizards, mice, and soldier ants. They also scavenge for the veld food—watery roots, berries, spiny cucumbers, melons, even the occasional truffle. In a bad year, however, many die from thirst or starvation.

If the Bushmen survive at all, it is because they are an unpossessive, sharing people. Their children are their pride, and every birth the subject of quiet rejoicing. In her classic work *The Harmless People,* Elizabeth Thomas describes one such occasion.

We were at her werf at the time, sitting in the shade. That day the young woman had not gone out for veld food, but was lying propped up on her elbow in front of her scherm when suddenly, without telling anyone what was happening, she stood up and walked into the bushes, only to come back some time later with her baby in the fold of her kaross. We might not have known what had happened except that she was smiling a sure, sweet smile because she was pleased with herself. Her belly was flatter, and a tiny foot with a pink sole and curled toes stuck out from her kaross.

Day or night, whether or not the bush is dangerous with lions or with spirits of the dead, Bushman women give birth alone, crouching out in the veld somewhere. A woman will not tell anybody where she is going or ask anybody's help because it is the law of Bushmen never to do so, unless a girl is bearing her first child, in which case her mother may help her, or unless the birth is extremely difficult, in which case a woman may ask the help of her mother or another woman. The young woman was only fifty feet from the werf when she bore her daughter, but no one heard her because it is their law that a woman in labor may clench her teeth, may let her tears come or bite her hands until blood flows, but she may never cry out to show her agony. Bushmen say a woman must never show that she is afraid of pain or childbirth, and that is why a woman goes alone, or why a young girl goes only with her mother, for then if she shows her pain and fear, only her mother will know.

When labor starts, the woman does not say what is happening, but lies down quietly in the werf, her face arranged to show nothing, and waits until the pains are very strong and very close together, though not so strong that she will be unable to walk, and then she goes by herself to the veld, to a place she may have chosen ahead of time and perhaps prepared with a bed of grass. If she has not prepared a place, she gathers what grass she can find and, making a little mound of it, crouches above it so that the baby is born onto something soft. Unless the birth is very arduous and someone else is with the woman, the baby is not helped out or pulled, and when it comes the woman saws its cord off with a stick and wipes it clean with grass. Then the mother collects the stained grass, the placenta, and the bloody sand and covers them all with stones or branches, marking the spot with a tuft of grass stuck up in a bush so that no man will step on or over the place, for the ground where a child has been born is tainted with a power so strong that any man infected with it would lose an aspect of his masculinity, would lose his power to hunt. The woman does not bury the placenta, for if she did she would lose her ability to bear more children.

The moment of birth is a very important one for the child and for the mother; it is at this moment that the child acquires a power, or an essence, over which he has no control, although he can make use of it. It will last him all his life; it is a supernatural essence that forever after connects the person born with certain forces in the world around him: with weather, with childbearing, with the great game antelope, and with death, and this essence is called the *now*.

There are two kinds of *now*, a rainy or cold one and a hot or dry one. If a person has a wet *now* and burns his hair in a fire or urinates in a fire, the person's *now* is said to make the weather turn cold (if it is the dry season) or bring rain (if it is the rainy season). If a person has a dry *now* and burns hair or urinates in a fire, the *now* is said to stop a cold spell or a bad storm. When a person dies, too, the weather changes violently according to the person's *now*. After a death, scorching droughts or devastating storms are sure to follow. . . .

The effect of *now* is simple when a person dies, or when a person burns his hair or urinates to change the weather. With childbearing for women and with killing the great antelope for men (as the great antelope also have *now*, although the small ones do not) the *now* has a larger, more complex effect. In these cases the *now* of the hunter interacts with the *now* of the antelope, the *now* of the woman interacts with the *now* of the child newly born, and when the blood of the antelope falls upon the ground as the antelope is killed, when the fluid of the womb falls upon the ground at the child's birth, the interaction of *nows* takes place, and this brings a change in the weather. In this way a mother may bring rain or drought when she bears a child, a hunter may bring rain or drought when he kills an antelope, no matter what kind of *now* the mother or the hunter may have. The mother or the hunter can only watch the weather to see what has taken place.

Now is intangible, mystic, and diffuse, and Bushmen themselves do not fully understand its workings. They do not know how or why *now* changes weather but only that it does. They watch the changes carefully, though, and by observing have discovered the limits of their own *nows*. When the fluid from a mother's womb falls upon the ground the child's *now* is determined, and it is partly for this reason that birth is such a mighty thing. . . .

When the young woman came back to the werf with her baby she sat down and calmly washed the blood from her legs with water from an ostrich eggshell. Then she lay on her side to rest with her baby beside her, and covered the baby from the sun with a corner of her kaross. She put her nipple in the baby's mouth and let her try to nurse. The young woman still said nothing to anyone, but she did open her kaross to show the baby, and one by one we all came by to look at her, and she was not brown, not gold, but pink as a pink rose, and her head was shaped perfectly. At the bottom of her spine was a Mongolian Spot, dark and triangular, and her hair, which she shed later, was finely curled and soft as eider down.

The father had been away, but he came home a little later and sat stolidly down on the man's side of the fire, his hands on his knees. He pronounced the baby's name softly to himself. Later, when he had no audience, he slipped his finger into the baby's hand. Of course the baby grasped it strongly, and the father smiled.

Sartorial Concerns

A loose dressing-gown is best in the earlier part of the labour. This must be exchanged when the patient lies down for good, for a chemise and bed-gown folded up smoothly to the waist, and a flannel petticoat, without shoulder straps, that it may afterwards be readily removed.

A broad bandage, too, must be passed loosely round the abdomen as the labour advances to its close; and its application must not be left until after the delivery, for it then would be attended with some difficulty and some risk. . . . The breadth will depend upon the indi-

vidual size of the female; but it should be wide enough to extend from
the chest to the lowest part of the stomach. The best thing is a new
and sufficiently large towel. . . .

Some persons suppose that wearing their stays during labour assists
them, affording support, but they are improper, being rather in the
way than useful. . . .

The belt must be worn so long as the abdominal muscles appear to
require support, which in some cases will be a few weeks only; in
others (in very fat and stout persons, for instance) it can never in future be dispensed with.

From Dr. Thomas Bull,
Hints to Mothers, 1841

Anne Moody: "Your Mama Brings Big Babies"

Anne Moody—known then as Essie Mae—was just one of thousands
of black girls who grew up in Centreville, Mississippi, in the
1950s. Her earliest memories were of a "rotten wood two-room
shack" and a steady diet of beans. When she was nine she started
working for white folks; by ten she was earning almost as much as
her mother, enough to keep herself and her brother and sister in
school. Two years later their situation showed some improvement—although her mother, Toosweet, was pregnant again, Raymond, the baby's father, had built them all a house. It had five
rooms, all wallpapered except the kitchen, and new mahogany
furniture, so it really didn't matter that the toilet was still outside
and the bathtub was tin. It was there, as Anne Moody recalls in
her poignant testimony to the black experience in America—
Coming of Age in Mississippi—that she arrived home one day to
find her mother about to give birth to her fifth child.

Just before Christmas, I came home from Mrs. Claiborne's one evening and found Mama's sister Alberta at the house. As I walked in,
she was running around like she was lost. Mama was in bed. I looked
at Mama and she had big drops of sweat dropping off her face. Her
eyes were closed and she was biting her lips as though she was in great
pain. I stood there looking at her for a long time before Alberta saw
me standing there.

"Essie Mae, come here and help me find some clean rags," she said
to me.

"What's wrong with Mama, Alberta?" I asked her.

"She is about to have the baby," she answered, plowing her way
through the clothes in the dresser drawers.

"Look in that big box behind the door in Junior's room," I said. "Mama's got a lot of rags in there."

"I hope Raymond hurry up," she said. "Toosweet is going to have this baby and I don't know what to do," she continued, almost crying.

When she said that, I ran back in the room to look at Mama. Her eyes were still closed and she was lying flat on her back clutching the sides of the bed. I looked at her belly and saw it move. I thought sure the baby was coming. I opened my mouth to call Alberta but the words wouldn't come, I was so scared. "Essie Mae! Come out of there! Go outside and see if that water is getting hot!" Alberta yelled to me. But I couldn't move. "What is she going to do with hot water?" I thought. "Get to the yard and look at that water, Essie Mae!" Alberta pushed me all the way through Junior's room to the kitchen door. I walked outside and found a big fire burning around the washpot. It was now dark and the fire lit up the whole yard. I just stood there staring at the pot full of water and the big blaze leaping up around it. The whole scene was like killing a hog at night.

As I was standing there Raymond drove up, hitting the brakes so hard he sent rocks sailing into the air. He ran around to the side of the car and opened the door to help some old woman get out. She was carrying a ragged-looking black medicine bag, and looked so dried up she could hardly walk. Raymond was leading her to the front porch when he noticed me standing in the yard. "Essie Mae," he called to me, "what are you doing here? Go on over to Pearl's where Adline and Junior is."

I walked out of the yard and headed down the road toward Miss Pearl's, but halfway there I turned around and went back. I stood behind Raymond's car for a long time looking and listening. At first it was real quiet. They had cut out all the lights but the one in Mama's room. I couldn't see anyone moving around inside. A little while later I heard Mama screaming and hollering and carrying on. Raymond came running out in the backyard and got a bucket of hot water from the washpot. All I could hear was Mama hollering from the house. Except for her yells everything else was still.

I stood out there thinking how bad it must hurt to have a baby. I would never have a baby if I had to holler and carry on like Mama, I thought. And that old lady. What did she know about delivering babies? Suppose she did something wrong and Mama died from it? I would kill Raymond if she died. "He should have taken Mama to the hospital," I thought. "Instead he went out in the country and got that old woman to deliver Mama's baby."

When Mama finally stopped yelling, I went over to Miss Pearl's. Well past midnight Raymond came over there and told us we could come home. As soon as he said that, Adline, Junior, and I ran all the way home to see the little baby. For the first time we weren't scared to run down that dark road that late at night.

I was the first one to make it home. When I walked in the door, that old lady was sitting beside the bed with her little black bag at her feet. She looked up and smiled at me when I walked over to see the baby, and something started crawling all over me and I started to shake. "Why is she still here?" I thought. "Something must be wrong with Mama." But then I saw that Mama was asleep.

"Is the baby here?" Adline asked as she came in the door with Junior following her.

"Stop all that noise!" Alberta said from the kitchen. Why was Alberta still here too, I wondered.

Adline, Junior, and I were all standing at the foot of Mama's bed and the old lady just sat there smiling. "Mama *must* be sick," I thought.

"Alberta, is Mama sick?" I asked as she walked into Mama's room.

"Is you crazy? Sho' she's sick after just having a baby."

Then Mama opened her eyes and saw all of us, me, Adline, Junior, and Alberta standing at the foot of her bed. "Show them the baby, Toosweet," Alberta said, "so they can go to bed." There it was lying right next to Mama. She lifted the cover back and Adline, Junior, and I walked to the head of the bed and peeped at it. It was a girl. She didn't look like she was just born like most babies. She looked like she was already four or five months old.

"She is some big!" I said.

"She is big," Mama said. "She weigh ten pounds and three ounces."

"That's as much as I weigh, huh, Mama?" that little stupid Junior asked.

"Your belly weigh that much," Mama said to him.

"You weighed that much, Essie Mae, when you came," the old lady said to me.

I didn't know how she knew I weighed that much. I wanted to ask her but I was scared. Something about her gave me the creeps. "Your mama brings big babies," the old lady said. "Every one of her babies weighed from eight to ten pounds." I looked at her shocked this time and I figured she must have delivered all of us. "No wonder she looks so old," I thought.

"Aunt Caroline, you ready to go?" Raymond asked her as he walked in the door.

"Yes, I guess so, and Toosweet is going to be all right," the old
lady said.

"Y'all go to bed!" Raymond said to us, and he and the old lady left.

I got up early the next morning because I wanted to talk to Mama
and get a good look at the baby before I went to work. Mama was
asleep when I went into her room. Her face looked different, I
thought—so calm and young. She hadn't looked young for a long
time. Maybe it was because she was happy now. She had never been
happy before to have a baby. I remembered how she had cried all the
time after Junior and James were born. I thought she'd gotten to the
point where she hated babies.

For a long time I stood there looking at her. I didn't want to wake
her up. I wanted to enjoy and preserve that calm, peaceful look on
her face, I wanted to think she would always be that happy, so I
would never be unhappy again either. Adline and Junior were too
young to feel the things I felt and know the things I knew about
Mama. They couldn't remember when she and Daddy separated.
They had never heard her cry at night as I had or worked and helped
as I had done when we were starving. No they didn't know the misery
Mama suffered. Not even Raymond knew. Mama loved him too much
to fight with him or have him see her cry. . . .

I got myself all flustered standing there thinking about Mama and
all we had been through. Now I didn't even feel like seeing the baby
or talking with Mama. We were out of school for the Christmas holidays and I was helping Mrs. Claiborne do her Christmas cleaning, so I
just left Mama sleeping and went to work.

Covered Wagon Confinements

Pregnancy and childbirth were events so commonplace in the lives
of nineteenth century American women that when those women
chose, or were persuaded, to leave their safe and predictable lives
in the East or Midwest and cross a continent via horse or wagon,
little accommodation was made for their parturient condition.
Narcissa Whitman and Eliza Spalding, the first two white women
to cross the Rocky Mountains, set the standard. Narcissa, a glamorous blonde not inappropriately named, and the plainer Eliza
shared a missionary zeal strong enough to keep their psyches
going even when their bodies balked. Eliza had suffered a still-
birth shortly before their departure and was still ill when they set
out; she had to choose between jolting wagon and tortuous side
saddle for hours of every day, and for breakfast, lunch, and din-

ner, between buffalo meat fresh or buffalo meat dried. Both made her sick. Narcissa became pregnant during the journey but was fortunate in that a buffalo meat diet agreed with her.

Narcissa and Eliza had at least the advantage of a doctor (Marcus Whitman) at their confinements. Few of the women who followed in the next two decades had that certainty. Mary Walker, who came with the missionary reinforcement immediately after the Whitmans and Spaldings, gave birth to her first son, Cyrus, at the Whitman mission at Waiilatpu, but we do not know whether the good doctor was present. Her own words, taken from her journal, give rather a sense of solitary confrontation: "About nine I became sick enough; began to feel discouraged, felt as if I almost wished I had never been married. But there was no retreating; meet it I must." (Much of the same ambivalence was voiced a decade or so later by Susan Magoffin, a young wife pioneering in Santa Fe, who wrote in her journal: "I do think a pregnant woman has a hard time of it. Some sickness all the time, heartburn, headache, cramp, etc., after all this thing of marrying is not what it is cracked up to be.")

Mary Walker's journal was her alter-ego and was kept more faithfully, and honestly, than most. Cyrus had various little brothers and sisters; sometimes the doctor arrived in time, sometimes he didn't. Mary always seemed to have the situation under control. "Awoke about four a.m. Rose at five, helped about milking, but by the time I had done that, found it necessary to call my husband and soon the Dr. Had scarcely time to dress and comb my hair. Before eight was delivered of a fine daughter." Of a later confinement she reported: "Rose about five. Had early breakfast. Got my house work done about nine. Baked six loaves of bread. Made a kettle of mush and have now a suet pudding and beef boiling. My girl [an Indian helper] has ironed and I have managed to put my clothes away and set my house in order. May the merciful be with me through the unexpected scene. Nine o'clock p.m. was delivered of another son."

After the missionaries had shown that westward emigration was manageable by women, more and more young families began to make the trip. Timing was based on avoiding snow in the Rockies, rather than on a wife's current state of fertility. Births en route were therefore not uncommon. Families traveled in company with other families, and a whole wagon train could seldom afford to stop for more than a few hours. One woman told of a trek to California in 1855 in which a column of wagons, which had been followed by Indians all morning, had to stop mid-afternoon to accommodate a woman in labor. When some braves rode in threateningly close, one of the leaders had the foresight to give the sign

for smallpox, which had the desired effect. The mother was able to
deliver in relative peace, and the next day the caravan moved on.

In the early spring of 1853 Virginia Ivins, her husband William,
and their year-old son Charlie set out from Keokuk, Iowa, for
California with three covered wagons, horses, a drove of cattle
plus five "drovers," and Carl, a young German cook. Virginia was
well along in her second pregnancy. In her *Pen Pictures of Early
Western Days* she later described how after months of plodding
across the plains, climbing the Rockies, and traversing the desert,
they arrived in early September at the foothills of the Sierra Ne-
vada range, where she gave birth, somewhat prematurely, to her
second child.

The ascent of the Sierras began now in earnest. The road was very
rough, in many places covered with round boulders which made it almost impassable. I was obliged to lie down most of the day. In the afternoon, as he usually did, Mr. Ivins went forward to look for a camping
place. We often had to leave the road to find good grass. . . . After he
went away, the road becoming somewhat smoother, I went to sleep,
not waking till quite late. . . .

It was dusk when we drove up to what seemed to be a small lake,
and the order was given to unyoke. The cattle were driven to the lake
to drink but turned away without tasting the water. What was our
consternation to find it to be an alkalie lake, which looked like ashes
and water mixed, not fit to be used at all, and all together the outlook
was most distressing. Carl made the fire and cooked the supper by the
light of a dim lantern, making the coffee out of a little water which
was left over in the cans, keeping about a quart to drink. I fixed my
"house" and Carl brought me my supper but I could not eat and spent
the time in tears. Little Charlie was put to bed and Mr. Ivins retired
also. After all was quiet I lighted my lamp and sat down to sew. I had
been quietly at work making a small wardrobe out of some of the
clothes which were in the broken box, for I realized that I might need
it before we arrived in California, or very soon after. There was only
one more garment to finish and I thought that I had better get it done.
I sewed till about ten o'clock. Outside the poor, thirsty cattle lowed,
the coyotes barked and snarled, the owls hooted and the night hawks
screamed. It seemed as if we were deserted by God and man. I thought
that I would go to bed and sleep if possible, but found that I could not
help myself; that now, indeed, trouble was in store for us. I woke my
husband and told him the situation. He would not believe me at first,
but soon was convinced, and God only knows the fear and agony of

that dreadful night. I tried to be brave for the sake of my husband and child, and at three o'clock there came to us a dear little daughter, with no one near to help, comfort or relieve.

After doing what he could for me, my husband wrapped the little one in a blanket and laid her in my arm. It turned very cold and a dreadful chill came on. My husband put warm covers over me and tried to warm me by holding me in his arms. A bed had been made for Charlie on the spring seat. He was put there and we watched for daylight with aching hearts. At the first faint glimmer of dawn Mr. Ivins dispatched a man on horseback with a can for water to Pea Vine springs. It was five miles and breakfast was late that morning. My husband inquired of the first [wagon] train that came past for some elderly woman to come in and see me and the somewhat unexpected guest. About ten o'clock a good Samaritan came in, looked at the baby, said a few kind words to me, and left me to my fate.

What To Do with the Umbilical Cord

The placenta and umbilical cord—organs that seem to us, once the birth is complete, to have served their function and require no more attention—are of major concern among primitive peoples, and their disposal a matter of utmost importance. They cannot simply be tossed away in the bush, forest, or steppe; they are too intimately connected with the fate of the newborn child for that. The Mundurucu Indians of Brazil dig a hole in the floor of the living area and bury them. The Chukchee Indians of Northeast Siberia place them on the ground in a corner of the tent and construct a miniature tent of three sticks tied together over them. The Balinese are more ceremonial; they will place them in a coconut, wrap it in sugar palm fiber, bury it at the entrance of the sleeping quarters, and erect a bamboo altar over the spot. But the Zulu mother has the most exacting task. She hides the umbilical cord from her husband; on the seventh day after the birth she sneaks off to the river, chooses a spot where the mud is nice and deep, and thrusting in her arm as far as she can, buries the cord. Afterward, she walks away with a great show of unconcern, as if she had not been there for any reason in particular. Her object is to fool the evil spirits that wander about which, if they knew of her real intent, might themselves dig up the cord and through it work evil magic on the baby.

6. Nurturing

Once upon a time a beautiful young lady and a very handsome young man fell in love and got married. They were a wonderful, compatible couple, and God blessed their marriage with a fine baby boy (eight pounds, eight ounces). They loved their little boy very much. They raised him, nurtured him, and spoiled him. They raised him in the palm of the hand and gave him everything they thought he wanted. Finally, when he was about seven or eight, they let his feet touch the ground.

Duke Ellington, from
Music Is My Mistress

Helen Hayes: "A Passing Performance" as Parents

Helen Hayes was already an established actress, and star, when she met and married journalist and playwright Charles MacArthur. She assured her disapproving mother that no, marriage would not ruin her career, and, yes, they did plan to wait to have children. Two years later Mary was born. She was their only natural child, and nineteen years later she would die of polio. In an excerpt from her book *A Gift of Joy* Helen Hayes reflects on the birth of this daughter.

When Charlie first saw our child, our Mary, he said all the proper things for a new father. He looked upon the poor little red thing and blurted, "She's more beautiful than the Brooklyn Bridge." On subsequent viewing when we three were alone, he stared at her long and solemnly and then said an odd thing, "We have given her birth and death and that's about all we can give her, really." I thought it morbid at the time because I was feeling all-powerful, as women do after childbirth. He was right, of course. It was life that would give her everything of consequence, life would shape her, not we. All we were good for was to make the introductions. We could introduce her to sights and sounds and sensations. How these reacted on her we must leave to her own private self. It is hard to accept this background position, and like most parents, we did not do it very well at all times. But we did at least understand our roles, and that is a step toward a passing performance.

A Sixteenth Century Dr. Spock Instructs the Nursemaid

Jacques Guillemeau, a sixteenth century Dr. Spock, instructs the nursemaid, to whom the newly born and swathed baby has been handed over, what to do next.

First of all, let the Nurse consider and view al the parts of the childs body, beginning at the head, observing whether it be well fashioned or no: that if it chance to have any ill forme, or figure: that then it may be mended as well as it may, which shall be done by bringing the said head unto the forme of a boule, a little pressed and made flat on both sides: in such sort that neyther the forepart nor hinderpart of the head stand too farre out, nor yet be too flat: which shall be done with such head-cloths, as they use commonly to weare, stroking it by little and little, without much pressing or crushing it, as some Nurses do: but onely handling it in a milde and gentle fashion.

Upon the Mould of the head you shal lay a peece of kotton or kerfey: some use to lay a peece of scarlet.

The eares must bee cleaned: with little rags made like tents: and the Nurse must looke whether the holes be well made, that there may not remain any filth eyther within, or in the wrinkles and folds behind them. . . .

The eyes must be looked unto and wiped with a fine linnen cloth, especially about both the corners, that if there should chance to be any filth gathered in those places, it may be taken away. Avicen puts there a little virgin oyle, because it mitigateth and taketh away the roughnesse and nitrosity which might remaine about the childs eyes, through his long swimming and lying in his owne sweat and urine, while he was in his mothers wombe. . . .

Now concerning the childs nose, it is fit, that it should be opened, and dilated gently, washing and cleansing it with a little warme water . . . and annointed with a little Virgin Oyle, which must bee done with the top of ones finger, the nayles being pared very neer and even. And if you chaunce to find some little membrane, or skinne, that stops up the holes, and passage thereof, it shall be cut asunder, that there may bee a passage for excrements of the braine. . . .

Besides shee shall looke whether the fundament bee well opened, and whether there bee any filth bred there or no: as also, whether the passage of the yard be free: and if it be a wench, whether there be any membrane, that doth stop up the entrance: Not long since, I made a new passage as it were glued together: and an other boy, which had the string of his yard so short and straight, that it made the head of it bow downward, and seemed as though it had no passage, but as soone as I had cut the string, the yard came to the right fashion. . . .

As for the armes and legges, if they bee either crooked or stand awry, they must bee set straight with little swaths, & fit boulsters, made for

the purpose: as likewise if eyther the back bone, or the belly, do stand
out. . . . Looke to these . . . because the bones (through their softness & tendernes) are more easily made straight and are apter to be
set in their right place & forme, than when they are growne dryer: it
being then very hard to amend such errors.

From *Child-birth or, the Happy
Deliverie of Women*, London, 1612

Baby Care in the Third World

Modern mothers who operate in a world of baby powders, oils, lotions
and shampoos, disposable diapers, and terry jumpsuits—all conve-
niences of this century—may be unaware that much of the world still
cares for its newborns in the time-honored ways of centuries past.
There are still Hopi Indians who rub the baby with ashes (not the
volcanic ash formerly used, but ash secured by burning sage), then
bathe it in warm water and suds of the pounded yucca root, finally rub
it again with ash before wrapping it in cloths and strapping it to the
traditional cradleboard. Except for the brief moments when it is
bathed and changed, the Hopi child will spend its first three months
on the cradleboard—nursing from it, sleeping on it, straightening its
little body after the long months curled up in the womb. The Kafirs,
or Zulus, of Southeast Africa "wash" their newborn babies in medicinal smoke that they believe will facilitate closing the anterior fon-
tanelle, make the skull bones firm and hard, and impart vigor to the
child's mind and body. The most important ingredient in the medicine is ground meteorite; other components include the whiskers of a
leopard, the skin of a salamander, and the claw of a lion. These are
mixed and set smoldering under a blanket with the baby so that it
must inhale the concoction, without which it will grow up soft, flabby,
and helpless. The same reasoning is used among almost all Moslem
peoples when they rub their newborns with salt. The application
varies: the baby may be rolled up in clothes that have been sprinkled
with salt, or plunged in a bath of salt brine, dried, and then powdered
with fine salt, or rubbed with salt and then smeared with oil. The
Bedouins even bathe the baby in camel urine before rubbing it with
salt, although now that camels have essentially been displaced by
trucks, this usage may be less frequent. But everywhere it is a poor
baby who goes unsalted; it is thus deprived of the essential strengthen-
ing powers. Little attention is given to food—babies are fed from the

breast as a matter of course—but much faith is still placed in the life-sustaining properties of fine salt, meteoric ash, yucca suds, and cradle-boards.

Golda Meir: "This Eternal Inner Division"

The modern Israeli kibutz offers community baby and child care as a matter of course, but the question was hotly debated among the young women who went to Palestine in the early decades of the twentieth century. These women wanted to be part of the pioneer restoration of the Jewish homeland; at the same time they wanted to ensure that that homeland would afford them the same rights as their brothers and husbands. Paramount in their thinking was the right to work. From this inner personal need emerged a collective demand for child care provisions and an accompanying collective agonizing over the effects of such on their children. The problem is less current than we think.

In the following excerpts from *The Plough Woman: Memoirs of the Pioneer Women of Palestine,* young mothers who were part of the second and third immigration movements (1904–1924) express their conflicting desires and fears.

From the outside it does look as though the children today belong to the kvutzah. In the actualities of life the thing has not gone so far by any means. The commune does try to see to it that its children shall lack nothing, either materially or spiritually. But what we consider of importance is the inner attitude of the group and of every individual comrade toward the children and the inner feeling of responsibility toward every new-born child. . . .

And how is it with the parents? To us the act looks simple and natural enough; but it is not easy for the mother to relinquish her new-born child to the children's home. . . .

The woman who has lived for some years in the commune, and knows our institutions, certainly believes in this group upbringing as the best. And yet she suffers from a deep inner division. Nearly every woman wants to feed and tend her own little one. She wants to look at it every now and then, watch its daily development—particularly during that wonderful period of the first year. And if our mothers must surrender all this they suffer. . . .

The struggle between intelligence and instinct emerges clearly in another case—when one mother comes to the help of another who can no longer give her baby milk. The possibility of this form of mutual aid is one of the strongest points in favor of our baby-homes. And the practice is a usual and accepted one. But sometimes it occurs that the child of the second mother needs more milk—and then it is very difficult for the first mother to ration her own child.

These are the details which make clear what goes on in the heart and mind of a mother who gives up her child to the group. It is unreasonable always to expect complete self-control; and we do wrong to accuse a mother of all sorts of weaknesses when this struggle is going on within her. This, indeed, is the moment for the most intimate kind of understanding. . . .

Nina Richter—*Beth Alpha*

It was before our marriages that we, the first women comrades in the communes, decided in advance that our children would be brought up in the group; not because we considered it a necessity of our life in the commune, but because we regarded it as a high ideal. Later, having become mothers, we still clung to this view. Those first years exacted heavy sacrifices from us—of all the trials we underwent in the country and in the commune, this was the hardest and the most important. . . .

Deep mother instinct no longer suffices to fill our lives, as it once sufficed for our mothers. I do not know whether it is good that this should be so, but so it is. The child does not, by itself, satisfy our life needs, does not answer all the demands which we make of ourselves.

And I also know that there is no road leading back to the one-time mother and one-time wife. Each of us women must now tread her own path, and even the child cannot hold us back. . . .

The hardest time in the life of the child, the period which calls for the maximum care and worry in the mother, is in the first three years. And when, a few days after the birth, the mother must relinquish her child into other hands, and cannot herself tend to all its needs, her sufferings begin. For all these little cares and attentions are so important. The new-born child changes from day to day—and the progress is observed in all of these trifles, when the child is being bathed, when it wakes from sleep, when it smiles for the first time, and when the first glimmer of consciousness lightens in its eyes—in every movement, in every note of its voice, it reveals itself anew.

And in the baby-home, even when it is developed to the highest point, no one will wait for these little events with the same eagerness and tenderness as a mother does. . . .

Eva Tabenkin—*Ain Charod*

The theory has been advanced that, in order to concentrate the impressions of the child, we must provide the children's home with so many comforts and attractions that the child will never feel the need of the room which is the home of its parents. But . . . if we could turn our children's homes into palaces, I still would not relinquish that quiet, peaceful hour which I spend with my child in my own room, after the day's work, for the noisy public contact in the children's homes, in the presence of dozens of other fathers and mothers.

We have been convinced by observation that the more the child loves the room of its father and mother, the more it is satisfied by the life of the children's home. For after the exciting, strenuous day in the latter, the child finds by the side of its parents a deep tranquility which is almost unknown to those children who grow up in private families.

But this restful evening visit raises another painful question. Is it right, after this hour of peace, to make the child return for the night to the children's home, to say goodnight to it and send it back to sleep among the fifteen or twenty others? This parting from the child before sleep is so unjust! . . . The women on the night watch in the children homes take turn and turn about. And when my turn comes to "go on guard" I feel my heart contract every time a child calls out in the night—sometimes out of its sleep, not knowing what it is calling— "Night-sister! Night-sister!" What is taking place in the soul of the child in that moment, between sleeping and waking? And who knows what is more important for the child, the conscious life of the day or the unconscious life of the night?

A. T.—*Ain Charod*

Taken as a whole, the inner struggles and the despairs of the mother who goes to work are without parallel in human experience. . . . In spite of the place which the children and the family as a whole take up in her life, her nature and being demand something more; she cannot divorce herself from the larger social life. She cannot let her children narrow down her horizon. And for such a woman there is no rest.

Theoretically it looks straightforward enough. The woman who replaces her with the children is devoted, loves the children, is reliable and suited to the work; the children are fully looked after. . . . Everything looks all right. But one look of reproach from the little one when the mother goes away, and leaves it with the stranger, is enough to throw down the whole structure of vindication. That look, that plea to the mother to stay, can be withstood only by an almost superhuman effort of the will.

I am not speaking now of the constant worry that haunts the mother's mind that something may have happened. And I need not bring in the feelings of the mother when her child falls sick—the flood of self-reproach and self-accusation. At the best of times, in the best circumstances, there is the perpetual consciousness at the back of the mind that the child lacks the mother's tenderness, misses during the day the mother's kiss. We believe, above all, in education by example; and therefore we must ask ourselves: Whose is the example which is moulding the child of the working mother? A "borrowed" mother becomes the model. The clever things the child says reach the mother at second hand. Such a child does not know the magic healing bruise. And there are times, after a wearying, care-filled day, when the mother looks at her child almost as if she did not recognize it; a feeling of alienation from her nearest and dearest steals into her heart. . . .

But the mother also suffers in the very work she has taken up. Always she has the feeling that her work is not as productive as that of a man, or even of an unmarried woman. The children, too, always demand her, in health and even more in sickness. And this eternal inner division, this double pull, this alternating feeling of unfulfilled duty—today toward her family, the next day toward her work—this is the burden of the working mother.

G. M. (Golda Meir)—Tel Aviv

An Eskimo Incubator

The Eskimo incubator for the premature baby consists of the skin of a large seabird, taken off whole and turned so that the feathers are inside. The tiny newborn is tied carefully inside and hung over an oil lamp in which a low flame is burning. In this warm and infinitely soft cradle the baby exists for the first weeks of its life, fed with milk drawn from its mother's breast and a little oil, until it is large enough to suckle and survive in the Arctic world.

Mary Martin: "It Was All Role Playing"

Later Mary Martin said of her relationship with Larry Hagman: "My son and I were more like brother and sister, or perhaps very close friends who sometimes got to play together." Given the circumstances, it was not surprising. She was only sixteen when she married his father, Ben Hagman, age twenty-one—as much as anything to escape the finishing school to which she had been sent only two months before. The scene was Texas, 1930, the beginning of the Depression. As Mary Martin comments rather woefully in her otherwise very funny biography *My Heart Belongs:*

We spent our honeymoon at my house, our first "wedding night" in my old bedroom. None of it made any sense. We were too young. I was hardly prepared for the physical aspects of marriage. In those days, one rarely spoke to mothers about sex. I didn't know enough to talk to a doctor, a minister. It's difficult to believe, now, how ignorant we were.

Our marriage was not consummated for a week or so, but almost from the moment it was, I was pregnant. Boom. I had morning sickness the whole time. There I was, right back where I had started, but pregnant, with no little white house with roses. Ben liked to hunt and fish and play cards. I tried to keep up, to be the little Texas housewife. I played bridge in the afternoons, when I wasn't throwing up, and I played poker at night with Ben and his friends. But I never really liked games.

On September 21, 1931, our son was born. We christened him Larry Martin Hagman. He weighed eight and a half pounds and was the image of his father. I weighed ninety pounds and was terrified by the baby. I did all the things I longed to do—breast-feeding him for three months, making formula, learning to give him a bath without drowning him, and singing him to sleep.

It was all role playing. I felt that Larry was my little brother, Ben my big brother. Role playing was something I had known since I was born, but it wasn't a good basis for a marriage.

Theodore Dreiser: "You Must Take Him Out in the Full of the Moon"

Theodore Dreiser treated pregnancy, among other subjects, with a realism new to American fiction in the early part of the century, but he himself was born under more fantastical circumstances. His mother, who could not read or write until in later years Dreiser himself taught her, was an earthy and great-hearted, if essentially pagan, woman, forever at odds with her fanatically religious Roman Catholic husband. In case anyone should think that offering a newborn to the sun or moon is limited to primitive cultures, observe what was going on in Terre Haute, Indiana, in the 1870s, as described by Dreiser in his autobiography *Dawn*.

. . . a deeply-rooted vein of superstition . . . was one of the few traits of temperament my father and mother possessed in common and which was the heritage of most of their children. In connection with my own birth, for example, I have heard both of my parents and my eldest sister tell of having seen, at the time my mother was laboring with the birth of me, three maidens (graces, shall we say?), garbed in brightly-colored costumes, come up the brick walk that led from the street gate to our front door, into the room in which my mother lay, pass about the foot of the bed and finally through a rear door into a small, exit-less back yard, from whence they could have escaped only by vanishing into thin air! According to my sister—who still maintains that she saw them—they gave no sign nor made observation of anything, but entered and left most gaily, dancing and laughing, their arms about each other's waists, flowers in their hair! I would like to believe that Fate intended these beauteous apparitions as an august annunciation of my coming and import to this planet, but all things considered, I lack the vainglory as well as sufficient subsequent substantiation. . . .

I was born on August 27th, 1871, at eight-thirty o'clock in the morning—at which time the three Maytime graces are said to have walked. This house on Ninth Street seems to have been associated in family annals with supernatural occurrences and visitations. There were tales of spirits striding through the rooms, previous to my birth and shortly after moving in, so that my father felt obliged to send for the local priest and have him sprinkle the house with holy water. Although the spirits did not vanish completely, so great was my father's faith that he was less troubled after that. This he personally told me.

Once safely introduced into the world, I proved but a sickly infant. For a time it was thought I could not live. My eldest sister, who was my mother's chief assistant at the time, describes me as puny beyond belief, all ribs and hollow eyes and ailing and whimpering. Perhaps because of this I appear to have seized upon my mother's fancy or affection. But indeed, which of her children did not, poor victim of maternal love that she was! She grieved and grieved over my impending fate, and as she herself later told me, finally resorted to what can only be looked upon as magic or witchcraft.

Opposite us, in an old vine-covered, tree-shaded house falling rapidly into decay, lived an old German woman, a feeble and mysterious recluse who was regarded in the neighborhood as, if not a witch, at least the possessor of minor supernatural and unhallowed powers. She may have practised illegal medicinal arts, for all I know. At any rate, in cases of illness or great misfortune, she was not infrequently consulted by her neighbors. One night, when the family feared that my death was imminent, my mother, weeping, ordered my eldest sister to run across the street and ask this old woman to come over. But, knowing of my father's strict religious views, she refused. She did say, however: "If your mother wants my help, tell her to take a string and measure your brother from head to toe and from finger-tip to finger-tip. If the arms are as long as the body, bring the string to me."

This was done, and the measurements proving satisfactory, the string was taken to her, whereupon she smiled and sent for my mother.

"Your child will not die," she announced. "But for three nights in succession, you must take him out in the full of the moon. Leave his head and face uncovered, and stand so that the light will fall slantwise over his forehead and eyes. Then say three times: '*Wass ich hab, nehm ab; wass ich thu, nehm zu!*' "

As a result of this remarkable therapy, I am reported to have improved. In three months I was well.

I report this naïve and peculiar happening precisely as it was told me by my elders.

Prescription: Bone Soup Bath, Once Daily

Sam and Mary Ann Maverick were among the earliest American settlers of San Antonio, were present at the battle of the Alamo, and played an integral part in the growth of the state of Texas. While Sam was out prospecting and acquiring vast tracts of Texas land, Mary Ann stayed home and bore children, ten in all, five of whom lived to adulthood. Eventually Sam would lend his name to the English language because he carelessly did not bother to brand his calves on the open range, so that local cowboys in their round-ups came to refer to all unbranded yearlings as "mavericks"—not part of the herd. But that was later. At the time Mary Ann recorded the following in her diary, they had been living in Texas for fifteen years and had recently lost their two little girls in a cholera epidemic.

On Tuesday, June 17th, 1851, at eight A.M. was born our third daughter, Mary Brown. How glad and thankful were Mr. Maverick and I to have a daughter. . . .

Soon after Mary's birth I wasted until I fainted twice and grew quite helpless and almost speechless. This was caused by the mid-wife Mrs. D., wilfully giving me lobelia—telling me it was raspberry tea. I felt my hold on life very slight, but in my fainting had felt an indescribable peace. For two weeks I could scarcely move without fainting, but after that I grew strong very fast. My precious baby grew thin the while, and Mrs. Beck, who had a baby born on the same day with mine, nursed Mary twice a day. Mary was sent to her each morning and afternoon for five or six weeks. When Mary was seven weeks old, we had to commence feeding her, and I began drinking ale and porter myself to see whether I could provide the proper nourishment—and I recovered my strength rapidly. Baby however, was thin and fretful. . . .

August 23rd. We call in the service of a goat—feed it well—and milk it four or five times a day for baby, and she improves some.

Bone Soup Bath. August 28th, Mrs. Salsmon, an experienced German nurse, came to see baby, and persuaded me to bathe her daily in bone soup. The bone soup is made by boiling beef bones four hours, and then cooling to a temperature of about one hundred, and the bath is ready. Daily I put her into the bath, and kept her there some time, and then, while wet from the bath, rolled her in a blanket and put her to sleep. And when she awaked, I rubbed her well and dressed her. At first the bath did not seem to do any good. But Mr. Maverick asked me to try it one month, and then we saw she had steadily improved. The treatment was kept up for about six months.

Mr. Maverick bought a horse and buggy and drove us out into the country every evening.

September 28th, baby is rosy and playful and good.

Journey to the Cradle

A baby born in old Persia was welcomed as a dear friend returned from a long journey; for six days it lay cosily next to its mother, and when on the seventh preparations were made for its removal to the cradle a few feet away, a little bread or cake was tied up in a handkerchief and fastened to its wrappings as provisions for the trip. Seven women, of whom the nurse was one, would gather around in a circle and hand the baby from one to the other. "Take it," the first would say. "What is it?" the second would ask, to which the response was, "A child." This little dialogue would be repeated seven times until the baby reached the nurse who would conclude with something on the order of "God watch over thee, my precious one," and place the baby safely in the cradle.

Adopting International Style

Anthea and Richard Lingeman are close friends of mine who tried to have children and couldn't, and then found adopting almost as difficult. Anthea, who is English, is a book designer, and Richard, a writer, was working at the *New York Times Book Review* when the following events, as Anthea tells them, took place.

At first Richard hadn't wanted any children. Later we decided we did want to have a child, but by them I had started growing fibroids in my uterus, and the doctor said it would be increasingly difficult for me to have one. After a few years of trying, with nothing happening, the "increasingly difficult" became "impossible." So that was that.

Then I started thinking about adopting a child. Richard was not keen, and I had some doubts, too. I didn't know how it would be—whether I could be presented with a baby from nowhere and love that baby as if it were my own. I wasn't sure that I would. But I *thought* it would be o.k., so we applied to several private agencies, and to the city, and we filled in all the forms and were visited in the apartment and studied by case workers. After about a year the city sent us a letter inviting us to a meeting. There were quite a few couples there. They explained that ninety percent of the babies who used to be put up for adoption were now kept by their mothers, so that it was practically impossible to adopt a healthy infant. They went through a list of adoptable children. These children all had handicaps of one kind or another, or were much older and had lived in foster homes. It could be very rewarding to go that way, as they explained, but it wasn't for everybody. We felt kind of guilty, but it wasn't what I had pictured, and I didn't think it would work for Richard to bring in an older child.

So then we tried the New York Foundling Hospital, and they did a study on us. An agency in Oregon that arranged adoptions for Korean children used their studies, so we got onto that list, and onto the New York Foundling list. We were also in touch with several adoption lawyers whose names we had been given. One lawyer called us with the proposal that we could go to Greece, hire a lawyer there, spend four weeks, and somehow come back with an infant. But since we didn't speak Greek, the thought of going through the courts there sounded a little dodgy. Another lawyer had a woman in Pittsburgh to whom we could send $2,500 on deposit, and in six weeks several thousand more, and in two months there would be a baby. It really made you throw up to think about it. A real black market—it was dreadful. So we rejected those, needless to say.

Then my uncle in England, who knew our predicament, started looking into the situation over there. We were given the name of an obstetrician who ran a clinic in London. The next time we were in England to visit my mother, we went to see him, had a long interview, and sent him the New York Foundling study after we came back. After that it was just waiting, waiting, waiting. Then suddenly one morning

at work I got a call from my mother, which was an unheard of thing
to happen. She asked if I had heard from the London doctor, because
he had sent us a telegram that apparently we had never received. But
he also had my mother's address, so when he didn't hear from us, he
contacted her. He asked her if she knew if we were still interested, or
if we had moved, or what had happened? She told him please not to
do anything until she phoned us. After she reached me, I immediately
phoned him in London to say yes, we were very interested. He said a
baby girl had been born at the clinic five days before, that her mother
was Italian and her father Indian, that she was a very bright baby,
and that if we were interested we should come over very soon. I left
the next day. I quit my job and went straight out and bought some
little night dresses at Bloomingdale's. I didn't know what I was doing,
really. Richard said he would follow as soon as he could. I bought my
ticket, stuffed some things in a suitcase, and went.

I went straight to London to a friend's house in Notting Hill Gate,
and together we went to the clinic. It was a private clinic; a lot of
people have their babies privately in England even though there's a
National Health system. Occasionally foreign girls would come have
their babies there. In our case, this Italian girl had been teaching in
London, and learning English, and her family did not know about
this baby. We were told she was a beautiful, intelligent girl of twenty-
three. Apparently there was no way she could keep the baby.

So as soon as I could change my clothes, my friend and I went in to
the clinic. And I sort of expected that I would walk out with the baby.
My friend took shawls and such—it was December. Of course, I was
being very naive. We walked in and waited in a waiting room for what
seemed like ages until at last we were taken up to see the baby. I held
her, and she was just so gorgeous! I mean, she was just the sweetest
baby!

Of course, I told the doctor that yes, we did want her. We wanted
her very much. But there were a lot of formalities to go through. Although neither of the natural parents were English, the baby had been
born in England, so she was English. All the English adoption laws
applied, and they were very strict. I had to be resident in England for
six months, and Richard had to spend at least six weeks there, too.
They were even more careful because the baby was not going to stay
in the country. The baby had a guardian appointed—someone to speak
for her. Very English—Lincoln's Inn, all that. At the clinic she was in
a little crib with four other babies in the room. The mothers would
go in and out of the room; we all had to wear white gowns and nose

masks. There was one mother who wasn't interested in her baby at all, even though she had a perfectly good husband, and that just horrified me. My baby's natural mother's name was on her wrist and on the crib, and the people at the clinic told me to answer to that name. They said I could go in every day, twice a day if I wanted to, and of course I wanted to. No question.

About two days later Richard arrived, and I took him to the clinic. That was quite, quite wonderful. He got dressed up in the white gown and nose mask—our baby was only about a week old, and some of the others were younger. We went in, and the nurse picked up our baby and gave her to Richard. He held her, and he looked at her, and her little head just fit into the palm of his hand. For a newborn she was very lively. She was moving her little hands, and she had her eyes wide open. She looked like she was looking right at you, communicating. And I could see that Richard was just bowled over! And he was— just in one blow!

So after that, whatever we had to go through, Richard was all for it, whereas before he had been very ambivalent, really. But after that first moment it was all plus. We named her—Jenifer Kate Lingeman—and we went into the clinic every day until he had to fly back four days later. He came over again in April and July for longer periods.

After the decision to adopt was definite, the procedure started. The baby and I would be spending the six months with my mother in Southampton, so we had to alert social workers there. In the meantime I went into the clinic every day and fed her and bathed her. She was three and a half weeks old when all the forms came through and the day finally came when I was allowed to take her out of the clinic. I remember, I just couldn't believe it! I was walking out with her in my arms!

I had planned to spend the night at my friend's house and to go down to Southampton in the morning. We made up a bed for her in a drawer. We went into such a fuss about that bed! My friend's housekeeper thought it should be one way—with a very soft pillow underneath—and I had very strong feelings that it should be firmer. Then we had terrible trouble with the bottle nipples. They didn't seem to have the right size hole. Poor child—she had kind of a rough night. But I put one of my little Bloomingdale's nightgowns on her, and tucked her in real tight in the drawer.

The next day we went down to Southampton on the train. And my mother had collected everything there that a baby could possibly need. My sisters-in-law, my mother's friends—everybody had contributed.

There was a full-sized Marmet pram, dark blue outside, white inside; a little cot already by my bed for her to sleep in; blankets, sheets, nappies—the English terry cloth kind—so much. My sister-in-law had kept about everything my nephews had ever worn, and I had all that, which was for the wrong sex but it didn't matter. The bathroom was full of baby powder and baby oil—everything I could hope to need. Even gripe water for hiccups. In England if a baby has some slight stomach discomfort, you give it a tiny spoonful of gripe water, and invariably it does the trick. My mother met me at the station, and she was nearly dying with excitement. She was almost as excited as I was.

So for the next six—really eight or nine months, we led a kind of three generation life at my mother's. The health visitor came—they're very experienced, motherly kind of people with helpful suggestions. And the social service visited us, talked to my mother, to me, saw that it was a decent house and that the baby was being well looked after. They had to come three times, but they got behind and didn't complete their three visits in the proper time. Our solicitor didn't get his preparation done on time either. And then Jen had a guardian who should have been doing certain things, and wasn't. So the whole process was lengthened by a couple of months. Eventually everything was ready for the judge, but by then the courts had gone off for the summer holidays, so there was another delay. Richard came over in July, hoping to do all the final things, and he couldn't after all. So he went back. But finally in late August the legal adoption came through. As soon as I got home I phoned Richard in New York, at the *Times*. I heard him say "This is it!" and then I heard a cheer go up from everybody at the *Book Review!* She was the *Book Review* baby!

So she was legally adopted, but now we had to get her out of the country and over here, and that was quite a jarring experience. At the American Embassy they pushed you from crowded room to crowded room, and when you finally got hold of some official, he had never heard of such a case in his life and didn't know how to deal with it. All the forms had to be processed through Frankfurt, Germany, and that was a problem until Richard finally got in touch with our congressman, who happened to be Ed Koch, and with the *New York Times* London office. After that things suddenly happened. We got all the okays, and on October 2 Jen and I flew over.

We came home to our railroad flat on East 89th Street, and Richard had done up the little room for Jenifer. There was a porta-crib with a rag doll in it. He'd even bought a high chair and Pampers and such. He was all prepared. And soon afterward we had to go in to the *Book*

Review, and there was a champagne party in John Leonard's office. Jen sat on the floor and everyone stood around and toasted her with champagne. It was a wonderful homecoming!

Transporting Infants on the Santa Fe Trail

Transporting infants and small children across the western plains was never simple, and was usually left to the management of the mother in question. In California during the 1850s one inventive woman discovered that champagne baskets imported from abroad, of which there seemed to be an abundant supply, made ideal baby carriers. A cavalry officer's wife conveyed her month-old infant from Los Angeles across the desert to Arizona in a champagne basket strapped to a wagon seat. She said the wagon acted as a perpetual lullaby and the baby slept soundly except when progress ceased.

There were times, however, when mothers had to walk over rough stretches of trail carrying their babies in their arms for hours. Other times they rode horseback. Sarah Royce describes riding sidesaddle, her baby in her lap, the infant's necessities suspended from the pommel, canteen and diapers in a saddlebag on one side and a little pail on the other, while she bore the weight of the child on one arm and clung to the pommel of the saddle with the other.

Another method used for slightly older babes was a special pack-saddle constructed with fifteen-inch arms around which rawhide strands were woven to make a sort of basket. "Two children could be placed in one of these pack saddles without any danger of their falling out," said Benjamin F. Bonney of Oregon, who claimed that even a bucking horse would not spill the occupants.

"For Infants Are Tender Twigs"

. . . roul it up with soft cloths and lay it in the cradle: but in the swaddling of it be sure that all parts be bound up in their due place and order gently without any crookedness or rugged foldings; for infants are tender twigs and as you use them, so they will grow straight or crooked . . . lay the arms right down by the sides, that they may grow right. When the Navel-string is cut off, . . . bind a piece of Cotton or Wool over it . . . and if the child be weak after this, anoint the child's body over with oil of acorns, for that will comfort and strengthen it and keep away the cold. . . . Carry it often in the arms, and dance it, to keep it from the rickets and other diseases.

After four months let loose the arms but still roul the breast and belly and feet to keep out cold air for a year, till the child have gained more strength. Shift the child's clouts often, for the Piss and Dung . . .

When the child is seven months old you may (if you please) wash the body of it twice a week with warm water till it be weaned. . . .

From Jane Sharp, *The Midwives' Book
or the Whole Art of Midwifery*, 1671

Vladimir Nabokov: "That Slow-Motion, Silent Explosion of Love"

Vladimir Nabokov was eighteen when the Bolsheviks took over Russia and he and his family fled St. Petersburg. After a brief sojourn in the Crimea, they went via London to Berlin. Nabokov took his degree at Cambridge, followed his family to the German capital, married, and remained in Europe until 1940 when he, his wife Vera, and their son Dmitri emigrated to the United States. His autobiography *Speak, Memory* concerns this first, European, half of his life; in the following excerpt he addresses his wife in his inimitable prose on the memories attached to their child's birth.

We shall go still further back, to a morning in May 1934, and plot with respect to this fixed point the graph of a section of Berlin. There I was walking home, at 5 A.M., from the maternity hospital near Bayerischer Platz, to which I had taken you a couple of hours earlier. Spring flowers adorned the portraits of Hindenburg and Hitler in the window of a shop that sold frames and colored photographs. Leftist groups of sparrows were holding loud morning sessions in lilacs and limes. A limpid dawn had completely unsheathed one side of the empty street. On the other side, the houses still looked blue with cold, and various long shadows were gradually being telescoped, in the matter-of-fact manner young day has when taking over from night in a well-groomed, well-watered city, where the tang of tarred pavements underlies the sappy smells of shade trees; but to me the optical part of the business seemed quite new, like some unusual way of laying the table, because I had never seen that particular street at daybreak before, although, on the other hand, I had often passed there, childless, on sunny evenings.[. . .]

Whenever I start thinking of my love for a person, I am in the habit of immediately drawing radii from my love—from my heart, from the tender nucleus of a personal matter—to monstrously remote points of the universe.[. . .] It cannot be helped; I must know where I stand, where you and my son stand. When that slow-motion, silent explosion of love takes place in me, unfolding its melting fringes and overwhelming me with the sense of something much vaster, much more enduring and powerful than the accumulation of matter or energy in any imaginable cosmos, then my mind cannot but pinch itself to see if it is really awake. I have to make a rapid inventory of the universe, just as a man in a dream tries to condone the absurdity of his position by making sure he is dreaming. I have to have all space and all time participate in my emotion, in my mortal love, so that the edge of its mortality is taken off, thus helping me to fight the utter degradation, ridicule, and horror of having developed an infinity of sensation and thought within a finite existence.

Since, in my metaphysics, I am a confirmed non-unionist and have no use for organized tours through anthropomorphic paradises, I am left to my own, not negligible devices when I think of the best things in life; when, as now, I look back upon my almost couvade-like concern with our baby. You remember the discoveries we made (supposedly made by all parents): the perfect shape of the miniature fingernails of the hand you silently showed me as it lay, stranded starfishwise, on your palm; the epidermic texture of limb and cheek, to which attention was drawn in dimmed, faraway tones, as if the softness of touch could be rendered only by the softness of distance; that swimming, sloping, elusive something about the dark-bluish tint of the iris which seemed still to retain the shadows it had absorbed of ancient, fabulous forests where there were more birds than tigers and more fruit than thorns, and where, in some dappled depth, man's mind had been born; and, above all, an infant's first journey into the next dimension, the newly established nexus between eye and reachable object, which the career boys in biometrics or in the rat-maze racket think they can explain. It occurs to me that the closest reproduction of the mind's birth obtainable is the stab of wonder that accompanies the precise moment when, gazing at a tangle of twigs and leaves, one suddenly realizes that what had seemed a natural component of that tangle is a marvelously disguised insect or bird.[. . .]

Throughout the years of our boy's infancy, in Hitler's Germany and Maginot's France, we were more or less constantly hard up, but wonderful friends saw to his having the best things available. Although powerless to do much about it, you and I jointly kept a jealous eye on any possible rift between his childhood and our own incunabula in the opulent past, and this is where those friendly fates came in, doc-

toring the rift every time it threatened to open. Then, too, the science
of building up babies had made the same kind of phenomenal, stream-
lined progress that flying or tilling had—*I*, when nine months old, did
not get a pound of strained spinach at one feeding or the juice of a
dozen oranges per day; and the pediatric hygiene you adopted was
incomparably more artistic and scrupulous than anything old nurses
could have dreamed up when we were babes.

I think bourgeois fathers—wing-collar workers in pencil-striped
pants, dignified, office-tied fathers, so different from young American
veterans of today or from a happy, jobless Russian-born expatriate of
fifteen years ago—will not understand my attitude toward our child.
Whenever you held him up, replete with his warm formula and grave
as an idol, and waited for the postlactic all-clear signal before making
a horizontal baby of the vertical one, I used to take part both in your
wait and in the tightness of his surfeit, which I exaggerated, therefore
rather resenting your cheerful faith in the speedy dissipation of what
I felt to be a painful oppression; and when, at last, the blunt little
bubble did rise and burst in his solemn mouth, I used to experience a
lovely relief while you, with a congratulatory murmur, bent low to
deposit him in the white-rimmed twilight of his crib.

You know, I still feel in my wrists certain echoes of the pram-
pusher's knack, such as, for example, the glib downward pressure one
applied to the handle in order to have the carriage tip up and climb
the curb. First came an elaborate mouse-gray vehicle of Belgian make,
with fat autoid tires and luxurious springs, so large that it could not
enter our puny elevator. It rolled on sidewalks in slow stately mystery,
with the trapped baby inside lying supine, well covered with down,
silk and fur; only his eyes moved, warily, and sometimes they turned
upward with one swift sweep of their showy lashes to follow the receding of branch-patterned blueness that flowed away from the edge
of the half-cocked hood of the carriage, and presently he would dart a
suspicious glance at my face to see if the teasing trees and sky did not
belong, perhaps, to the same order of things as did rattles and parental
humor. There followed a lighter carriage, and in this, as he spun
along, he would tend to rise, straining at his straps; clutching at the
edges; standing there less like the groggy passenger of a pleasure boat
than like an entranced scientist in a spaceship; surveying the speckled
skeins of a live, warm world; eyeing with philosophic interest the
pillow he had managed to throw overboard; falling out himself when
a strap burst one day. Still later he rode in one of those small contrap-
tions called strollers; from initial springy and secure heights the child

came lower and lower, until, when he was about one and a half, he touched ground in front of the moving stroller by slipping forward out of his seat and beating the sidewalk with his heels in anticipation of being set loose in some public garden. A new wave of evolution started to swell, gradually lifting him again from the ground, when, for his second birthday, he received a four-foot-long, silver-painted Mercedes racing car operated by inside pedals, like an organ, and in this he used to drive with a pumping, clanking noise up and down the sidewalk of the Kurfürstendamm while from open windows came the multiplied roar of a dictator still pounding his chest in the Neander valley we had left far behind.

7. *Attending*

O for a few of yon junipers,
  To cheer my heart again,
And likewise for a gude midwife,
  To ease me of my pain!

> Clementina's lament, from the
> medieval ballad, "Willie and
> Earl Richard's Daughter"

Ye'll gie me a lady at my back,
  And a lady me beforn,
And a midwife at my two sides,
  Till you young son be born.

> Maisie's request, from the
> medieval ballad, "Fair Janet"

Jenny Jerome Settles for the "Little Local Doctor"

When Jennie Jerome became pregnant, her husband, Lord Randolph Churchill, second surviving son of the 7th Duke of Marlborough, made arrangements for a leading London obstetrician, Mr. William Hope, to attend her delivery. The event was to take place in the young couple's new London house at 48 Charles Street, Mayfair, sometime after the new year in 1875. It proved, however, another case of best-laid plans. In late November, while Jennie and Randolph were at Blenheim Palace in Oxfordshire for the shooting, Jennie took a fall, and afterwards, undaunted, went for a rather rough drive in the pony carriage. The result is described by her mother-in-law, Frances Churchill, "Duchess Fanny" as she was known in the family, in a letter to Mrs. Leonard Jerome Jennie's mother, then in Paris. The "Boy" to whom she refers was later christened Winston.

30 November [1874]   Blenheim

My dear Mrs Jerome,

Randolph's Telegram will already have informed you of dear Jennie's safe confinement & of the Birth of her Boy. I am most thankful to confirm the good news & to assure you of her satisfactory Progress. So far indeed she could not be doing better. She was in some degree of Pain Saturday night & all Sunday & towards evg of that day we began to see that all the remedies for warding off the Event were useless. Abt 6 of P.M. the Pains began in earnest.

We failed in getting an *accoucheur* from Oxford so she only had the Woodstock Doctor; we telegraphed to London but of course on Sunday ev there were no trains.

Dr Hope only arrived at 9 of this Morg to find dear Jennie comfortably settled in bed & the baby washed and dressed! She could not have been more skillfully treated though had he been here than she was by our little local doctor. She had a somewhat tedious but perfectly safe & satisfactory Time. She is very thankful to have it over & indeed nothing could be more prosperous.

We had neither cradle nor baby linen nor any thing ready but fortunately *every* thing went well & all difficulties were overcome. Lady Camden, Lady Blandford & I were with her by turns & I really think she could not have had more care. She has had an anxious Time and dear Randolph and I are much thankful it is over. I will be sure to see you receive a Bulletin every day.

We expect today a 1st Rate Nurse. Best love to Clara [Jennie's sister] & Believe me,

Yrs sincerely
F. Marlborough

The Court of Eleventh Century Japan Attends the Birth of the Prince

At the same time that Europe was struggling to emerge from the "Dark Ages" and a Norseman called Leif Ericson was exploring the coast of North America, a young Japanese widow of about twenty-five was setting down in elegant calligraphy a fictional account of life in contemporary civilized Kyoto as she knew it. Murasaki Shikibu was a member of the prominent Fujiwara family; like many Japanese women of her period she was beautiful, educated, and economically independent. When her book reached fifty-four volumes, she drew it to a close; it has come down to us nearly a millenium later as *The Tales of Genji*. It is a remarkable work, at once realistic yet romantic, and it brought the author instant fame. And honor—Murasaki Shikibu was called to the court of Queen Akiko to live.

But the lady of letters could not relinquish her vocation. Shortly before her thirtieth birthday she began a diary that she kept for the next three years—1007–1010 A.D.—and in which she depicts court life in exquisite detail. A translation is included in *Diaries of Court Ladies of Old Japan*. In the following excerpts Murasaki portrays with her characteristic delicacy of observation the birth and consequent celebration of Queen Akiko's long-awaited first child.

Note: It was the custom for those in attendance at a birth in Japan to wear white and for all objects—beds, screens, etc.—to be hung with white. The "substitutes" referred to are ladies-in-waiting who occupied nearby couches and pretended to be in

labor in order to attract evil spirits toward themselves and away
from the Queen.

The evening I went to the Queen's chamber. . . . Her Majesty took
out some of the perfume made the other day and put it into an incense
burner to try it. The garden was admirable—"When the ivy leaves
become red!" they were saying—but our Lady seemed less tranquil
than usual. The priests came for prayers, and I went into the inside
room but was called away and finally went to my own chamber. I
wanted only to rest a few minutes, but fell asleep. By midnight everybody was in great excitement.

Tenth day of the Long-moon month.

When day began to dawn the decorations of the Queen's chamber
were changed and she removed to a white bed. The Prime Minister,
his sons, and other noblemen made haste to change the curtains of the
screens, the bed cover, and other things. All day long she lay ill at ease.
Men cried at the top of their voices to scare away evil spirits. There
assembled not only the priests who had been summoned here for these
months, but also itinerant monks who were brought from every mountain and temple. Their prayers would reach to the Buddhas of the
three worlds. All the soothsayers in the world were summoned. Eight
million gods seemed to be listening with ears erect for their Shinto
prayers. Messengers ran off to order sutra-reciting at various temples;
thus the night was passed. On the east side of the screen there assembled the ladies of the Court. On the west side there were lying the
Queen's substitutes possessed with the evil spirits. Each was lying surrounded by a pair of folding screens. The joints of the screens were
curtained and priests were appointed to cry sutras there. On the south
side there sat in many rows abbots and other dignitaries of the priest-
hood, who prayed and swore till their voices grew hoarse, as if they
were bringing down the living form of Fudo. The space between the
north room and the dais was very narrow, yet when I thought of it
afterwards I counted more than forty persons who were standing there.
They could not move at all, and grew so dizzy that they could remember nothing. The people now coming from home could not enter the
main apartment at all. There was no place for their flowing robes and
long sleeves. Certain older women wept secretly.

Eleventh day. At dawn the north sliding doors were taken away to
throw the two rooms together. The Queen was moved towards the
veranda. As there was no time to hang misu, she was surrounded by

kicho. The Reverend Gyocho and the other priests performed incantations. The Reverend Ingen recited the prayer written by the Lord Prime Minister on the previous day adding some grave vows of his own. His words were infinitely august and hopeful. The Prime Minister joining in the prayer, we felt more assured of a fortunate delivery. Yet there was still lingering anxiety which made us very sad, and many eyes were filled with tears. We said, "Tears are not suitable to this occasion," but we could not help crying. . . . The Prime Minister's son, Lieutenant-General Saisho, Major-General Masamichi of the Fourth Rank, not to speak of Lieutenant-General Tsunefusa, of the Left Bodyguard, and Miya-no-Tayu, who had not known Her Majesty familiarly, all looked over her screen for some time. They showed eyes swollen up with weeping, forgetting the shame of it. On their heads rice was scattered white as snow. Their rumpled clothes must have been unseemly, but we could only think of those things afterward. A part of the Queen's head was shaved. [This was done when a woman was considered close to death, in order that she might be ordained a priestess, which would insure her welcome into the next world.] I was greatly astonished and very sorry to see it, but she was delivered peacefully. The after-birth was delayed, and all priests crowded to the south balcony, under the eaves of the magnificent main building, while those on the bridge recited sutras more passionately, often kneeling. . . . As the afterbirth came, it was fearful to hear the jealously swearing voices of the evil spirits. . . . Chiso Azari . . . was overpowered with the evil spirit, and as he was in a too pitiable state Ninkaku Azari went to help him. It was not because his prayer had little virtue, but the spirit was too strong. . . . At noon we felt that the sun came out at last. The Queen was at ease!

She is now at peace. Incomparable joy! Moreover, it is a prince, so the joy cannot be oblique. The court ladies who had passed the previous day in anxiety, not knowing what to do, as if they were lost in the mist of the early morning, went one by one to rest in their own rooms, so that before the Queen there remained only some elderly persons proper for such occasions. The Lord Prime Minister and his Lady went away to give offerings to the priest who had read sutras and performed religious austerities during the past months, and to those doctors who were recently summoned. The doctors and soothsayers, who had invented special forms of efficacy, were given pensions. Within the house they were perhaps preparing for the ceremony of bathing the child.

Large packages were carried to the apartments of the ladies-in-wait-

ing. Karaginu and embroidered trains were worn. Some wore daz-
zlingly brilliant trains embroidered and ornamented with mother-of-
pearl. Some lamented that the fans which had been ordered had not
come. They all painted and powdered. When I looked from the bridge
I saw Her Majesty's first officials, and the highest officers of His Highness the Crown Prince [the newborn baby] and other court nobles. . . .

All the people seem happy. Even those who have some cause for
melancholy are overtaken by the general joy. The First official of our
Queen has naturally seemed happier than anybody, though he does
not show special smiles of self-satisfaction and pride. . . .

The navel cord was cut by the Prime Minister's Lady. Lady Tachi-
bana of the Third Rank gave the breast for the first time [ceremonial].
For the wet-nurse Daisaemon-no-Omoto was chosen, for she has been
in the Court a long time and is very familiar with it; the daughter of
Munetoki, courtier and Governor of Bitchu, and the nurse of Kurodo-
no-Ben were also chosen as nurses.

The ceremony of bathing was performed at six o'clock in the evening. The bath was lighted [by torches]. The Queen's maid in white
over green prepared the hot water. The stand for the bathtub was
covered with white cloth. . . .

There were two stands for kettles.

Lady Kyoiko and Lady Harima poured the cold water. Two ladies,
Omoku and Uma, selected sixteen jars from among those into which
the hot water was poured. These ladies wore gauze outer garments,
fine silk trains, karaginu, and saishi. Their hair was tied by white
cords which gave the head a very fair look. . . . The Lord Prime Minister took the August Prince in his arms; Lady Koshosho held the
sword, and Lady Miya-no-Naishi held up a tiger's head before the
Prince. . . . Two sons of the Prime Minister and Major-General
Minamoto Masamichi were scattering rice in great excitement. "I will
make the most noise," each shouted to the other. The priest of Henchi
Temple presented himself to protect the August Child. The rice hit
him on his eyes and ears so he held out his fan and the young people
laughed at him. The Doctor of Literature, Kurodo Ben-no-Hironari,
stood at the foot of the high corridor and read the first book of
Sikki. . . .

For seven nights every ceremony was performed cloudlessly. Before
the Queen in white the styles and colours of other people's dresses
appeared in sharp contrast. I felt much dazzled and abashed, and did
not present myself in the daytime, so I passed my days in tranquillity
and watched persons going up from the eastern side building across

the bridge. . . . The younger ladies wore much-embroidered clothes;
even their sleeve openings were embroidered. The pleats of their
trains were ornamented with thick silver thread and they put gold foil
on the brocaded figures of the silk. Their fans were like a snow-cov-
ered mountain in bright moonlight; they sparkled and could not be
looked at steadily. They were like hanging mirrors.

On the third night Her Majesty's major-domo gave an entertain-
ment. He served the Queen himself. The dining-table of aloe wood,
the silver dishes, and other things I saw hurriedly. Minamoto Chuna-
gon and Saisho presented the Queen with some baby clothes and diapers, a stand for a clothes chest, and cloth for wrapping up clothes
and furniture. They were white in colour, and all of the same shape,
yet they were carefully chosen, showing the artist mind. . . .

On the fifth night the Lord Prime Minister celebrated the birth.
The full moon on the fifteenth day was clear and beautiful. Torches
were lighted under the trees and tables were put there with rice-
balls on them. Even the uncouth humble servants who were walking about chattering seemed to enhance the joyful scene. All minor
officials were there burning torches, making it as bright as day. Even
the attendants of the nobles, who gathered behind the rocks and under
the trees, talked of nothing but the new light which had come into the
world, and were smiling and seemed happy as if their own private
wishes had been fulfilled. . . .

On the seventh day His Majesty celebrated the birth. His secretary
and Major-General, Michimasa, came as King's Messenger with a long
list [of the presents] put into a wicker box. A letter was immediately
sent from the Queen to the King. The students from the Kangakuin
came keeping step. The list of visitors' names was presented to Her
Majesty. Some may perhaps receive gifts.

The ceremony of the evening was noisier than ever. I peeped under
the Queen's canopy. She who is esteemed by the people as the mother
of the nation did not seem to be in good spirits. She appeared a little
weary. She had grown thinner, and her appearance in bed was slen-
derer, younger, and gracefuller. A little lantern was hung under the
canopy which chased the darkness away even from the corners. Her
fair complexion was pale and transparently pure. I thought her abundant hair would be better tied up. There is great impropriety in writing about her at all, so I will stop here. . . .

It was after the tenth day of the Gods-absent month, but the Queen
could not leave her bed. So night and day ladies attended her in her
apartment towards the West. The Lord Prime Minister visited her

both during the night and at dawn. He examined the breasts of the wet-nurses. Those nurses who were in a sound sleep were much startled and got up while still asleep; it was quite a pity to see them. He very naturally devoted himself with the utmost care, while there was anxiety about the August Child. Sometimes the Honourable Infant did a very unreasonable thing and wet the Lord Prime Minister's clothes. He, loosening his sash, dried his dress behind the screen. He said: "Ah! it is a very happy thing to be wet by the Prince. When I am drying my clothes is my most comfortable moment!" . . .

The day of the King's visit was approaching, and the Lord's mansion was improved and adorned. Beautiful chrysanthemums were sought for everywhere, to plant in the garden. Some were already fading, others in yellow were especially lovely. When they were planted and I saw them through the shifting morning mists, they seemed indeed to drive away old age. . . .

The visit of His Majesty was to be made at eight or nine o'clock in the morning. From early dawn ladies adorned themselves with great care. As the seats of the courtiers were placed in the west side building the Queen's apartment was not so much disturbed. I have heard that the ladies serving at the Imperial shrine dressed very elaborately in the rooms of the first maid-of-honour. . . .

The Royal dais was prepared at the west side of the Queen's. His honourable chair was placed in the eastern part of the south veranda. A little apart from it on the east side were hung misu, and two of the court ladies in attendance on the King came out from behind that misu. The beautiful shape of their hair, tied with bands, was like that of the beauties in Chinese pictures. . . .

The Lord Prime Minister, taking the August young Prince in his arms went before the King. His Majesty took the child himself. The Honourable Infant cried a little in a very young voice. Lady Ben-no-Saisho stood holding the Prince's sword. The Prince was taken to the Lord Prime Minister's wife, who sat on the west side of the inner door. After His Majesty had gone, Ben-no-Saisho came out and said to me: "I was exposed to brightness. I felt discomposed." Her blushing face was beautiful in every feature, and set off her dress delightfully.

When night came we had beautiful dances. The court nobles presented themselves before the King. The names of the dances performed were:

The Pleasures of Ten Thousand Ages.
The Pleasures of a Peaceful Reign.
The Happy Palace.

When they danced the "Long-Pleasing Son," the closing one, they
went out singing and danced along the road beyond the garden hills.
As they went farther away the sound of flute and drum mingled with
the sound of wind in the pine-wood towards which they were going. . . . His Majesty went in beside the Queen, but as the night was
far advanced it was not long before the Prime Minister called the
Royal carriage and the King returned to his own palace.

"I Never Heard of Women Havin' Babies in a Hospital"

In 1968, the year of Martin Luther King's assassination, Josephine
Carson toured the American South interviewing black women in
all walks of life. Billie Dee is a young nurse who works in a Negro hospital where, she says, despite poor and inadequate facilities, the care is far superior to what a black woman will get in a
white hospital. In the following excerpt from *Silent Voices: The
Southern Negro Woman Today* she describes what a pregnant
black woman in the South might encounter.

Thing you gotta understand about this race discrimination and Negro
people living in this South is: a colored got to be tough! Weak
ones dies early. Negro mothers losin' one in eight of their babies and
gettin' pregnant too fast again, not gettin' the right kind of care before *or* after. Prenatal care—shoot, I never heard of it till I became a
nurse. I never heard of women havin' babies in a hospital. Midwife or
else your own mother come around and help out. I and my sisters and
my four brothers, all us born in the house or born in the field. My
people 'croppers. . . .

I'll never quit nursing, never. I had a lotta inspiration from my
grandmother—my mother's mother. She was a fullblood Indian woman.
Kidnapped off the reservation in Oklahoma by my granddaddy. He
was a colored man. He brought her to Louisiana and they raised a big
family together. She was *somethin'*, that old lady. . . . I never saw a
doctor deliver a baby the way she could. . . .

See, the Negro woman have a choice; she going to stay home and
let the midwife bring her through—birth the baby, see, or she go to
the hospital. Now if she don't have a Negro hospital, then she have to
go into the white. And one way she going to do best in the white is
not make any arrangement ahead, because mostly they won't remember that, unless she have a very good doctor there expecting her. But

if she don't have a doctor to get her in the hospital, then what's she going to do? She going to get out on the street and fall down and commence to holler she's 'bout to give out that baby, or get her a taxi and tell him to get her to the hospital emergency cause she's 'bout to deliver, see. That way, she goes in as emergency in some cases. Some cases it don't do any good to do anything at all. Maybe they take you if you unconscious. But don't wake up, Honey! Ooo, no!

But once she get inside that white hospital, her trouble just beginning. My mother's best girl friend livin' in the city and she went for her first baby 'bout twelve years ago in the city hospital. She had a very bad labor and she done an awful lot of yellin'. After she yell for fifteen hours or something, a white doctor come in there and say, "Listen, Nigger, you yell one more time and I chuck you out the window." And then he hit her in the stomach to shut her up! That's the God truth! He hit that pregnant woman in the stomach. And that baby born dead in a few more hours. I *know* that case. See, when you helpless like a pregnant woman, and you got that kinda race-minded mess on your hands, you better off home in the bed with your mother bringing your baby for you.

My *God!* A woman havin' a baby—if you don't respect that, then you not human, that's all.

So, see, that's one problem. Then she got the rest of the problems, like she didn't have no prenatal care. That's one. Twice as many Negro women as white losin' their babies today because of that. Then, she goes home, maybe she's poor, she don't eat right and she don't feed the baby right. She can't keep it clean maybe if she got to haul water from around the cornah or somethin'. Shit! They don't know nothin' 'bout what these mothers trying to do. Welfare goin' to give her some extra money for that baby but it don't get there right away. They got to come over and make sure that's a *real* baby and make sure it not borrowed offa somebody else. . . .

Shoot! It's a mess. But the point is, Honey, you start your life out *crazy* if you a colored around here.

The Ancient Profession of Midwifery

There were two ancient professions for women: prostitution and midwifery.

The names of the great courtesans thread through history; of midwives we know considerably less. Aspasia is remembered as the mistress of Pericles when Athens was in its prime, the woman whose ill advice to her lover triggered the Peloponnesian War. Largely forgotten is her vaguely feminist tract deploring the state of womanhood in her time and instructing her sisters in the finer arts, including midwifery. A contemporary of hers, the "brave and burly midwife named Phaenareta," is mentioned by Plato not because of any special skill in her profession, but because in Athens no woman could qualify as a midwife until she had herself given birth, and the child by which Phaenareta fulfilled her qualification had been named Socrates. The most celebrated physician of antiquity, Hippocrates, may or may not have delivered a child, but he had plenty of sound advice to offer in the fields of obstetrics and gynecology. When his teachings were transported to Alexandria, a highly male chauvinist city, a certain Agnodice (on whom historical evidence is unclear) had to dress up as a man so that she could attend the lectures in order to improve her own midwifery skills.

Greek midwives performed other functions besides the obvious. They were called in to treat various gynecological disorders, and from the inside information thus obtained took it upon themselves to advise eligible bachelors as to which young women were most likely to conceive and to produce the best offspring.

Roman midwives continued the tradition of marriage-brokerage on the side, and were also called upon to verify virginity or confirm consummation. Roman midwifery was really just Greek midwifery imported. Then in the second century A.D. Soranus of Ephesus, who had studied in Alexandria, arrived in Rome and became the first specialist in gynecology and obstetrics. Soranus was a true cosmopolitan; he had seen enough of the world to differentiate between unbiased scientific observation and parochial gobbledygook. He encouraged the clearly beneficial practices of his forerunners, but divested them of their supernatural associations. He could see that washing one's hands before aiding in a delivery and laying a warm hand on the belly of a woman in labor were appropriate and welcome actions in themselves, having nothing to do with magic. He spent two chapters of his celebrated *De Morbis Mulierum* on what was and what was not desirable in a midwife, and another on trying to acquaint that midwife with the anatomy of a woman, a subject of which she, like everyone else in the ancient world, knew next to nothing. He disposed of the belief that the uterus and the vagina were one and the same, as well as the idea that within the uterus there were nipple-like growths on which the embryo practiced sucking. He was the first to describe podalic version—the attempt to turn the child within the womb. He also set down step by step the course of a normal labor, encouraged the use of the birth stool, and warned midwives to pare their nails, take their time, and above all not to ascribe difficulties to supernatural causes. If only little parchment pamphlets of his directives could have been distributed among midwives in the centuries following, but unfortunately most of his writings disappeared and were not unearthed until the nineteenth century.

Through the long twilight time that followed, the midwife was left much to her own devices. On occasion scholars compiled volumes from the obstetrical writings that had gone before, adding theories of their own, as with Paulus of Aegina who in the seventh century attributed inflammation of the breast in the nursing mother to her milk having been converted into cheese. But nothing very new occurred until the eleventh century when a series of works known as the *Trotula* came out of the medical school at Salerno, an ancient city and health resort southeast of Naples. The true author—and whether man or woman—of the *Trotula* has never been determined. Arguments in favor of the latter derive from the fact that both cosmetics and feminine hygiene are discussed exhaustively, and are clearly more original than the sections on pregnancy, birth, and the care of the newborn, which are nearly all taken from earlier sources. One of the few underivative discussions involves the repair of a torn perineum by primary suture: wash the parts with butter and wine, press them back into place, stitch together with silk, and for seven days keep the patient away from draughts or any food or drink that might make her cough. Valuable advice, but for its time probably of less general interest than the hygiene section that describes how lice are to be found not only on the head, but in the pubic hairs, armpits, and even the eyebrows.

In the fourteenth century the *Trotula* was translated into English and its generally useful directives became available to the rare midwife who could read. But on the whole medieval midwifery hung more on songs, incantations, and feminine instinct than on any specialized skills of obstetrics.

Laboring on a Banana Leaf

There is a double advantage to the old tribal custom still widely practiced in Nigeria, West Africa, in which the young woman returns to her family home to give birth. Nothing is quite so pleasant as a mother's care, and then, too, there are no in-laws present to exploit the young wife's vulnerability in labor by accusing her of all manner of crimes and insisting that the baby will not be born until she confesses.

Not that all mothers-in-law are quite so unfeeling. Many will see to it that their sons' wives have all the comforts of home and give birth just as they themselves did—on a banana leaf in the backyard accompanied by the ceremonial chanting of friends and neighbors. Iris Andreski in her book *Old Wives' Tales: Life-Stories from Ibibioland* reports the following story told her by a young Nigerian trained nurse who happened to return to her native village for a visit just as the wife of a relative was about to have a baby.

The news went round that I was in town and in thirty minutes of our arrival men and women of my compound and distant relatives were gathering to see me. They were coming with gifts of all kinds, i.e. pots of palm wine from the men folks, basins of coco yam, coconuts and what have you from the women. Amongst these people, I noticed that the wife of a relative of whom I was very fond was missing from the crowd. After several enquiries it was revealed that she could not be there because she had been under labour for the past couple of days.

On receiving this information I could no longer contain myself and as soon as the crowd dispersed I made straight for the compound where she lived wondering within myself what could be the reason for such delayed labour for a multiparous woman.

On arriving to the scene I made for the back of the house where I was told I would find her. There I saw a group of women chanting songs which they explained would hasten the delivering and at the same time giving her bowls of concocted medicine all to hasten delivery. All by my observation made her look the more weak and her tummy was greatly distended. She indeed looked terribly worn out.

After further enquiries I discovered that she had been out in that open place and on the bare ground with a plantain leaf as her bed for the last two days and juice squeezed out of local herbs as her only food, for according to custom she is not supposed to go into the house nor have any food to eat until the baby is born. The story almost paralysed me and in great anger I dispersed all the women and the native midwife who was supposed to be conducting the delivery and who by my observation had given up hope of anything good coming out of Israel.

This poor lady as I said was very tired and could hardly move her limbs. She could not refuse me. I felt her pulse and glad that it was fairly satisfactory only showing sign of shock. With the help of her husband we moved her into her apartment. I gave her a quick wash down for she was practically covered with dust and sweat and covered her up for warmth. I managed to do a quick abdominal palpation and found the head of the foetus was still high for a multipare labour. This finding further proved that she had been whipped off to the back of the house with a false labour and made to push until she became quite exhausted.

Before long, I noticed that she was fast asleep, so I left her alone to rest as I felt that was what she needed most, in any case it is unlikely that she will deliver for another six to eight hours. With this opportunity I got ready everything I needed for her delivery. Some of these I had with me and some I borrowed from the nearby dispensary. When I came back after a couple of hours or so she was still sleeping, but she woke up in about an hour after my arrival and asked for a hot drink and we offered a small plate of pepper soup made with few pieces of yam and this she ate up as fast as it came. Not quite an hour after she asked for more and this time I gave her a small bowl of pap with plenty of milk and sugar. It was after this that I will say she recognized me and sat up to talk with me and with her husband who was then my only assistant in the business. The next thing that this lady asked for was to go to the toilet and I must say that I was very happy about this and quickly offered her an old bucket that I reserved for my dirty water during delivery. At first she refused to use it and insisted on going to the pit latrine. After much persuasion she consented to use the bucket. Everything was quiet from then on and it was 9 P.M. when I settled her down again and made myself comfortable on the next wooden bed and asked the husband to go off to his apartment, for there was no need for anxiety. In the next few minutes we were both off to sleep.

When she called me again, it was 2:30 A.M. by my watch. This time she said that she felt like going to the toilet again and also complained of pain. I knew that this time, she was truly in labour so I rushed out for the old bucket and by the time I came back she was pushing. I got things ready as quickly as I possibly could, tidied her bed and then encouraged her to push having cleaned her up. Soon the head of the foetus was seen and in less than another ten minutes the baby was born. It was a girl. The cry of the baby was so strong that I suppose it woke her husband who came flying into the apartment where we were. Soon he was dancing and shouting for joy and both his shouts and the cry of the baby brought the nearest neighbors in. Every place was full of joy.

With-Women

The word "midwife" comes from the Anglo-Saxon "mid-wif," meaning literally, "with-woman."

The first mention of "mid-wife" in English history is found in Henry of Huntington's twelfth century chronicle *Historia Anglorum*. As Henry describes it, the ancient Briton woman placed girdles believed to be possessed of supernatural powers about a woman whose labor proved difficult. Noble families possessed more elaborate girdles embossed with mystical figures; these were draped around the waists of ladies of the castle at the onset of labor to ensure the birth of heroes. Henry described the ceremony as a holdover from Druid times.

By the fourteenth century the Church had ousted all remnants of a pagan past. Magic girdles had been replaced by bits and pieces of lace or cloth sold to pregnant women by avaricious friars who assured them their purchase was a true piece of the Virgin Mary's own cloak and would lighten the pains of childbirth. Midwives, on the other hand, were expressly forbidden from using charms or any other sort of "sorcerie, invocations, or praiers, other than suche as be allowable and may stand with the lawes and ordinances of the Catholike Churche" (injunction of the Bishop Bonner, 1554). The friars did not like competition.

In sparsely settled medieval England the midwife might live some distance away from her patient, and no doubt often arrived after the fact. An entry in the account book of the Shuttleworth family steward in Lancashire notes that "Will'm Woode and Cooke" spent four shillings "when they wente for the midwiffe of Wigan, being a day and a night away," and that she received twelve pence remuneration.

Priests being sometimes as scarcely placed, a midwife was frequently required to baptize the baby, just in case, and local curates were advised by the Archbishop of York to "teach and instruct the mydwiefes of the very words and form of baptisme." In the oath taken by one Eleanor Pead in 1567, she promised to serve rich and poor women equally, not to use sorcery or incantations, not to destroy or in any way harm the child, and to baptize it when necessary "in the name of the Father, the Son, and the Holy Ghost."

Almost no record remains of the early midwives beyond what they

swore they would or would not do. We know the name of Margaret
Cobbe because she attended Edward IV's queen, Elizabeth Woodville,
in the dark sanctuary of Westminster where on November 1, 1470, her
son the future Edward V was born. We are told that a midwife by the
name of Alice Massy served Elizabeth of York, queen of Henry VII.
We hear of Elizabeth Gaynsforde because she baptized the child of one
Thomas Everey before the baby was completely delivered. As she testi-
fied later before the bishop, "she saw nothing of the childe but the
hedde, and for perell the childe was in, and in that time of nede, she
christened as is aforesaid, and caste water with her hand on the childe's
hede, after which the childe was born." And we have records of Johane
Hammulden, who practiced during the reign of Henry VIII, because
she was a gossip and indiscreetly passed along a defamatory remark
made to her by a woman in labor. The woman, known only as "Burgyn's
wyff," in praising Johane's skill as a midwife, said that for "her
connyng that she hadd, she might be mydwyff unto the Quene of In-
gland yf hitt were Quene Kateryn; and yff hitt wer Quene Anne she
was too goode to be her mydwyff, for she was a hoore and a herlott."
Johane unwisely repeated the remark before a third party, and was
hauled before the constable, along with Burgyn's wyff, who denied her
part in the conversation. A deposition was sent up to Thomas Cromwell, Henry's hatchet man. There the matter hangs in history: we shall
never know whether the good wyff and mydwyff were pardoned or
whether they met the same fate as Quene Anne the hoore and herlott
(and, for that matter, the fate of Thomas Cromwell himself).

Louise Bourgeois, Midwife, Delivers the Dauphin

In 1599 Henri IV of France dissolved his marriage of twenty-seven
years to Marguerite de Valois whose licentiousness he might have
forgiven (being so inclined himself) but whose childlessness he
could not. The following year he married Marie de' Medici who
had had no lack of lovers but was at least fertile. Six children followed in close succession before Henri's murder in 1610.

In attendance at each of these royal births was a stout Parisian
midwife known alternatively as Madame Boursier or by her maiden
name of Louise Bourgeois. Under the latter she wrote a book on
midwifery (much of it borrowed almost verbatim from the great
French surgeon Ambrose Paré with whom her husband had worked
as assistant for twenty years). In her *Compleat Midwife's Practice
Enlarged* (English translation 1659) she also describes "The Lyings-In of the Queen and the Births and Baptisms of the Children

of France." The most important of these was, of course, that of
the Dauphin, which took place on September 27, 1601, at Fountainebleau:

When I entered the royal chamber, the King exclaimed, "Come to my
wife, who is ailing, and see whether she be in travail." She had great
pains, and I assured him that it was even so. "Dear heart," said the
King, "I have often told thee that the Princes of the Blood have need
be present at thy travail, owing to thy rank and to that of the child,
and I beg thee to submit to it." The Queen replied that she had resolved to do whatsoever pleased him. "I know, sweetheart, that thou
hast resolved to do whatsoever I wish," said the King, "but I'm sure
that unless thou dost summon up all thy courage, the sight of them
will hinder thy travail. I therefore beg thee not to be overcome, for
this is the usage observed at the first labor of a queen."

The pains quickened, and with each one the King supported the
Queen. He kept asking me whether the time had come to summon the
princes, and saying that I must not fail to let him know, for it was
very needful that they should be present. I replied that I should not
fail to give him ample time. Towards one hour after midnight, the
King growing impatient at the sufferings of the Queen, and fearing
she would be delivered before the princes could arrive, sent for the
Princes of Conty, De Soissons, and Montpensier. . . . They came at
about two of the clock, and were in the chamber for nigh half an hour.
The King, then, learning from me that the end was not very near, dismissed them, with the request to hold themselves in readiness for immediate summons. . . .

The Queen was now conducted from her private bedroom to the
grand lying-in chamber. At one end of it under a rich pavilion stood
the grand state-bed draped in crimson velvet fringed with gold. Nearby,
and under a smaller pavilion, were the chair of travail and the bed of
travail, also covered with crimson velvet. On the latter the Queen was
laid, while around her sat on stools and golden chairs the King, Madame his royal sister, and the Duchess de Nemours. . . .

The Queen's travail lasted two and twenty hours and a quarter. . . .
During this long time the King never left her side but for his meals,
and then kept sending messages to learn how she was. Madame his
sister did likewise. . . .

The Queen had often expressed her fears lest little M. de Vendosme
[the natural son of the King by his mistress Gabrielle D'Estrées] come
into the room during her travail, and sure enough he did so, but she
was suffering too much to note him. He stood by my side and kept

asking me if the Queen would soon be well, and whether it would be
a boy or a girl. To quiet him I said . . . "Whichever sex it doth
please me." "What," said he, "is it not already made up?" I replied,
"Yes, it is indeed already a child, but it doth depend on my pleasure
whether it shall be a boy or a girl."

The travail went on apace, and I took note that the Queen repressed her cries. I begged her not to do so, lest her throat should
swell. The King also said, "Sweetheart, do what the midwife doth tell
thee, and cry out lest thy throat should swell." She now wished to be
placed in the delivery chair directly opposite which the Princes stood.
I sat on a low stool in front of her, and when she was eased of her
burthen, placed Master Dauphin in a napkin on my knees and took
good care to wrap him up so well that no one but myself knew his sex.

The King came near me, but I looked earnestly at the child which
was very feeble from what it had gone through. I called for some wine.
Monsieur Lozeray, one of the chief valets-de-chambre, brought me a
bottle. I asked for a spoon, while the King took and held the bottle. I
said to him: "Sire! Were this any other body's child, I should spurt the
wine from my mouth over its body, for fear lest its weakness should
last too long." The King put the bottle to my lips, and said, "Do to it
as thou wouldst to any other child." I filled my mouth, and spurted
the wine over the child, which at once revived and tasted a few drops
that I gave it. The King withdrew from me, sad and downcast, because
he had seen only the face of the child, and knew not its sex. He walked
up to the pavilion-door near to the fireplace and ordered the ladies of
the chamber to get the bed and linen ready. . . .

Then the King . . . strode to my side quite near to the Queen.
Putting his mouth to my ear, he whispered, "Midwife! Is it a boy?" I
answered, "Yes." "I beg thee not to mock me for that would be the
death of me." I so unwrapped Master Dauphin that the King alone
saw that it was a boy. With uplifted eyes and with clasped hands he
returned thanks to God, while tears as big as peas rolled down his
cheeks. He then asked me if I had told the Queen, and whether there
would be any harm in his telling her. I said there would not; but
begged His Majesty to do so with as little emotion as possible. He
thereupon did kiss the Queen, and said to her, "Sweetheart! Thy
travail hath been sore, but God hath greatly blessed us by giving us
what we most wanted; a lusty boy." The Queen at once clasped her
hands, lifted them as well as her eyes toward heaven, shed big tears,
and fell into a swoon. . . .

The King approached the Princes, embraced them, and, not per-

ceiving the weakness of the Queen, threw the door of the chamber
wide open, and called in everybody who was in the ante-chamber and
the great cabinet. It is my firm belief that not less than two hundred
persons came in. They so crowded the room that the attendants could
not carry the Queen to her bed.

I was greatly vexed at this, and made bold to say that there was no
excuse for the admission of such a throng, inasmuch as the Queen had
not yet been put to bed. The King overheard me, and clapping me
on the shoulder, said: "Hold thy tongue, hold thy tongue, midwife!
and fret not, for this child belongeth to the whole world and everyone
must needs rejoice." This happened at ten-and-a-half of the clock on
the evening of Thursday, September 27, 1601, the day of St. Cosme
and St. Damian, nine months and fourteen days after the marriage of
the Queen.

The royal valets-de-chambre were now called in, who carried the
chair to the side of the state-bed, into which she was laid. I rendered
her every needful service, then took Master Dauphin from the arms of
his governess, Madame Montglas, and carried him to M. Eduoard. He
made me wash the babe in wine-and-water, and looked it over from
head to foot before I swaddled it. The King brought the Princes and
many of the nobility to see it. He further bade everyone attached to
the royal household to come in, and then dismissed them to make
room for others. Everyone was beside onself with joy and hugged
one's neighbor without regard to rank. I'm told that even some noble
ladies were so overcome with joy as to hug their attendants without
knowing what they did.

Having dressed my said lord, I handed him back to Madame Montglas who bore him to the Queen. Her Majesty looked at him tenderly,
and then bade my said lady to carry him into her private chamber.
M. Edouard and all the female attendants were there; what with
them and what with the throngs of persons that the King kept bringing in, the room was always crowded. I'm told that in the city the
whole night was spent in one uproar of fire-arms, trumpets, and drums.
Hogsheads of wine were broached to the health of the King, the
Queen, and the Dauphin, and couriers sped with the good news to
all the provinces and the loyal cities of France.

Ambroise Paré and the Hôtel Dieu

From the sixteenth century it was the French who set the style in
childbirth and (witness Lamaze and Lebouyer) still do. Surgeons—

usually barber-surgeons—were everywhere called in when all else failed, when in spite of all the midwife's efforts the baby refused to be born; the surgeon would then proceed with the most primitive of instruments to extract the child. The baby was, of course, always lost, and usually only the most skillful surgeon could save the mother. But in France the surgeon had an advantage that existed nowhere else; he had access to the Hôtel Dieu of Paris, that great municipal hospital founded about the time of Charlemagne, where the poor could go for treatment. In the sixteenth century there were 1200 beds in the Hôtel Dieu: 486 for single patients—obviously those who could pay—and the rest king-size, about five feet wide and meant to hold as many as six patients at a time with various afflictions and in varying stages of decline. But if she could stand the vermin and the smell, and if she could survive being juxtaposed between cases of typhoid and tuberculosis, the indigent parturient woman was assured that her delivery would be attended.

The young Ambroise Paré, later surgeon-in-chief to the royal household, did three years self-appointed internship at the Hôtel Dieu. There he observed a great variety of cases, both surgical and obstetrical. Later he joined the King's army as military surgeon. With his rare empathy for suffering, he constantly sought more humane treatment for the common soldier: he discovered, for example, that amputations did not necessarily fester, and could as effectively be treated with mild salves as with boiling oil. He also demonstrated that hemorrhaging could be controlled by the use of the ligature to tie bleeding vessels. Paré saved so many lives and was so popular that he was the only Protestant spared in the general massacre of St. Bartholomew's Eve in 1572 ("It was not reasonable that he should be massacred," said the King).

His escape was fortunate for the women of France, for his compassion extended to them and their labors in childbirth. In one of his works on obstetrics he described, in his clear, colloquial French, the operation of podalic version. He did not pretend to have invented it; although he apparently did not know Soranus had written of it fifteen centuries before, Paré did mention having seen it practiced by two "master barbers and surgeons in this town of Paris," no doubt at the Hôtel Dieu. This maneuver, used of course only in cases where the child did not deliver normally, allowed it to be turned inside the uterus into such a position that the surgeon could effect the delivery. This was, of course, before the invention of the forceps, and at a time when resort to the Caesarean section was still nearly always fatal to the mother. Paré undertook podalic version with his patient draped head to foot with linen cloths "that the work may be don with more decencie," and he reminded the surgeon to take off his rings, see that his fingernails are well pared, and rub his hands with oil. Then

. . . supposing that the child presents naturally having the head towards the outlet, to duly deliver it by art you must gently push it back in the contrary direction and seek the feet and draw them down. By doing this you will easily turn the child. And when you have drawn the feet into the outlet you must draw one foot outside and tie it above the heel in the manner of a running noose with a moderately long fillet, like that with which women bind their hair. Then you will replace the said foot into the said womb and having found the other foot you will draw it outside and then pull on the fillet. And when you have thus both feet outside the womb you will draw on both equally on one side as on the other, little by little and without violence.

After which, to assist the completion of the delivery, the midwives present were to press the patient's abdomen, and the patient herself was to hold her breath and push, and before long the head would emerge.

It may sound brutal, but podalic version saved thousands of lives—both mother's and child's. Paré's favorite apprentice, Jacques Guillemeau, translated his work into Latin, so it would be more widely available outside France, and later, along with observations of his own, into English under the sanguine title, *Childbirth: or, The Happy Deliverie of Women*. Surely the happiest of Guillemeau's own deliveries was the one he performed on Paré's own daughter Anne whose child he delivered by podalic version just as Paré had taught him some twenty years before.

"I Been a Midwife Ever Since I Was Seventeen"

Izzelly Haines was one of the "Conchs" (the name comes from the shellfish on which they mostly subsisted) who left the Bahamas in the early twentieth century and migrated to Florida. They were of mixed English and Bahamian Negro descent and spoke their own dialect, which could best be described as an amalgam of Cockney and native Bahamian. In 1939 Izzelly Haines, a midwife, was interviewed as part of the Federal Writers' Project—one of many interviews that lay neglected for nearly four decades until Ann Banks collected them into *First-Person America*.

I was born in the Bahamas and I'm still belonging to that country. . . . When I was little I live most of my life with me aunt. She was sure a smart woman, and a real English lady. She worked as a midwife mostly and she ad books that told er ow to tend sick folks. That's ow come me to know what little I do about this work.

I been a midwife ever since I was seventeen. I uster tend all the women around where I lived in the Bahamas. I've tended me own girls as well as meself. I still go when I'm called ere in Riviera, but if it gits beyond me I always calls a doctor. Most of what I know I owe to me aunt, for it was er what ad the books although she kept them under lock and key, cause she didn't want us childrens to read them. I uster steal the key and then open the case what she kept the books in, and sneak them out and ide until I could read them. As I growed up, I got more and more interested, so after reading them books I decided I'd be a midwife too, and sure enough that's what I did.

I was seventeen when I took my first case. This case was sure pitiful, that's ow come me to take it. If I adn't the little mother woulda died. In them days folks was ignorant about sech things, and in the Bahamas there warn't no doctors at all. There ain't many now, and midwife does most everything, but it's better than it was in them days. All I knowed about this work was what I read in them books and what I'd already seen.

This woman ad given birth at about six o'clock in the morning and by four o'clock that afternoon the afterbirth adn't come and she was dying from the poison that sets in. There warn't a soul around that could do nothing about it, so remembering what I could, I took two pounds of onions and pulverized them; then soaked it in a pint of gin. Then I took it all and put it in two cloth bags. One bag I put to the lower part of the woman's stomach and the other to er back. Inside of a alf our it ad come and she was gitting along fine.

I learned a lot of things down there in the Bahamas and I tended a lot of cases. One ome remedy what can be used for the same case I jest mentioned is to boil muddauber nests that still have the worms in them and give the woman the tea. It always works. Another remedy is tea made from the wild peanut; it grows to ome in the Bahamas, and it will start labor pains again if they have stopped and shouldn't. I never practiced under no doctor's orders, and I don't yet unless the situation gets beyond me.

As for pay, I takes whatever they give me. I can't expect much for folks ere is most as poor as they was in the Bahamas, so I'm willing to tend the women for whatever they can afford and as glad to do it. What little I does git out of it elps though, cause there hain't much in fishing now days. Prices hain't so good, but they never is, so that hain't nothing neither. That's another reason how come I'm always glad to make whatever money I can as a midwife. . . .

"I Just Sat There and Caught the Baby"

My friend Richard Serbagi later became a concert cellist, but in 1953 he was a twenty-one year old doing his military service and assigned—when the following event occurred—to a small station hospital on Burtenwood Air Force Base near Manchester, England.

I was a sergeant in the Air Force, and I had been trained to be a surgical technician. When I went to England, I had never been much of anywhere except Brookline, Mass., where I grew up, and then Texas. I was pretty much of a greenhorn. My training had been a lot of general surgery and emergency procedures—mostly on-the-job training.

I remember one night, after I had been at Burtenwood about six months, the ambulance station got a call. I was the surgical technician on duty. There were no nurses to take ambulance runs along with the driver—the surgical technician was it.

We were called to go into Warrington to pick up a woman who was in labor and bring her back to the hospital. Her husband was an American serviceman on duty, and she called the hospital herself. In those days we traveled in very low, slow Cadillac ambulances, American-made, with very low roofs.

We went out about 3 a.m. and picked up this young woman about my own age who was in labor. We went into the house and put her on a stretcher and put her in the ambulance. I was trained enough to recognize, when I examined her, that she was quite dilated, and I realized that she was going to have this baby very soon. I said to the ambulance driver, "C'mon, Harold, let's go!" We had about twenty, twenty-five miles to go to the hospital.

The woman was pretty wild. It was her first baby. She should have called sooner, but she didn't. She had had to be in labor for quite some time by the looks of it. I was trained to take her blood pressure and make sure it was reasonably normal. In order to slow down the whole procedure, I had her cross her legs tight and pant rapidly to see if she could keep from pushing, since obviously if she pushed, she was likely to have the baby in the ambulance. I certainly wasn't prepared for her to do that. Since all O-Bs took place in surgery—we didn't have an obstetrics department—I had been in on both normal births and Caesarean sections. I was well acquainted with the procedure in surgery, but I certainly wasn't acquainted with the procedure out of surgery.

Also, I had never myself been the person responsible.

Along about five or six miles, her blood pressure started showing a little low, and I started getting a little worried. I said, "Harold, I've got to give her something to boost her blood volume, because her blood pressure is going down. I decided to give her some dextrose in water, which I had in the ambulance. I told him to stop the ambulance, because I wanted to put this needle into her arm and get it going fast. So he did, and I got it into her arm, and it started to drip, and everything was going along all right, and we set off again along this dark highway. It was late fall. I had her covered with blankets, and I had the cuff on her arm, and I had the I-V going. I kept watching her blood pressure. We had no intercom with the hospital, so there was no way to get in touch with the doctors there.

Then the I-V stopped running, and I couldn't get it going again. I told Harold to stop the ambulance again. I was afraid that the I-V had infiltrated—that the needle was out of the vein and the fluid was going into the tissues instead of the circulatory system. There she was coming closer and closer to birth, and I had a blood pressure that was dropping and an I-V that was possibly out of the vein. I didn't know what to do. You know, I was a frightened kid. I said, "Harold, stop the ambulance. You've got to come around, and we've got to take the stretcher out on the road. I've got to check the I-V. I think it's still in the vein, but this damn roof is so low that I can't get the bottle up high enough. I've got to get her out on the road so I can get the I V bottle higher." He said, "You've got to be out of your mind," but he stopped the car, and we took the stretcher out and put it on the road, and I said, "Harold, back up and turn around and shine your headlights here so I can see what's going on with this needle." I didn't have a flashlight and I couldn't find a flashlight in the ambulance, so I had him back up and turn the ambulance around and shine the headlights on the woman so I could see if the needle was all right. I got the bottle up as high as I could, and it started to run—I got it going again. When I saw that the needle was still in the vein, we brought her back into the ambulance and had her keep her legs tight and keep panting. She was nearly hysterical. I was doing everything I could to keep her calm and in control, because I thought if she once lost control, she would have the baby there in the ambulance.

Well, we didn't make it to the hospital. The blood pressure now was stable, but she couldn't help the contractions. About six or seven miles from the hospital she said to me, "It's coming! It's coming!" I said, "Harold, I'm sorry, you've got to stop the car again because this lady's having her baby." He said, "That's impossible! We're not prepared to have a baby in this ambulance." But he stopped.

The only thing I had were some towels and a set of basins and some sterile gloves, which I put on, and a little surgical kit. *She* delivered the baby. I mean, I just sat there and caught it. Of course, at that point I knew exactly what to do because I had been through that procedure many times. I took a couple of clamps and clamped it in two places about an inch apart and about a foot from the baby. I knew that was further than it should have been, but I had never done it myself before, and I was afraid of not doing it right. I figured if I left some extra cord, they could do it again properly at the hospital. So I put on the clamps and cut in between. I didn't tie it, because I was afraid of that, too—afraid of tying it too tight or not tight enough.

I had the baby in a towel, and I had a little surgical kit with a bulb syringe and some silver nitrate, and I aspirated the baby and put silver nitrate in its eyes. I didn't have to tip the baby upside down or any of that stuff—the baby was screaming its head off already. The mother was still half-hysterical, too. In fact, Harold was, too. He kept saying, "Holy shit, Richard! Holy shit!"

I had some sterilized water, and I poured it into one of the basins and took some sterile gauze and sponged the baby off. Then I wrapped it in a blanket and gave it to the mother. Sometime in there the placenta came—just came out. I sort of half caught it in the basin. Then I sponged off the mother and covered her with a sheet and we set off again.

We drove up to the hospital, finally. I carried the baby in, and we got some orderlies to come out and carry in the mother on the stretcher. And that's the story. In retrospect, I don't know whether the fact that she was about to give birth was the reason the blood pressure went way down or not—I had no way to judge that. I just did what I thought should be done.

Back at the hospital there was a lot of back-slapping—you know, "you did a great job!"—all the usual thing. But really, I hadn't done much. I just sat there frightened. She did all the work. I don't know if anything I did really made any difference.

I remember that when I went to clean up, I was amazed. I was just full of blood. What with the placenta, and all that stuff, I was just covered up to my elbows. And it was an incredible mess in the ambulance.

But it worked. And the baby was a boy.

"I'm So Proud of Mother"

A friend, Debbie Dickinson, showed me the following passages from her diary written when she was thirteen, as she sat on the stairs of a Midwest farmhouse outside her mother's bedroom.

Nov. 29, 1952

Dear Diary,

It is 11:15 A.M. & my little baby sister or brother is just about to be born. Oh Im so excited.

They have got Mom all proped up on the bed. By the way this is home delivery. I want it to be a girl & name is Lodoska Elizabeth. I hope she will be physically mature.

It was supposed to be here on Dec. 15 but this morning about 3:50 the water broke. Mother didn't wake Daddy till 5.

Dr. Davies has a mask on her face & was just in the bathroom sterilyzing her hands.

I could not stand to be proped up the way she is & she isn't even under either.

Dr. Putnam just said "Now is the time when you push."

Oh I'm so excited. I'm going to listen real

"Relax till another pain & then push."

I wonder if she has any either [ether]?

It's coming out they can see its hair Mom—"Oh that's wonderful. Is it a boy or a girl?"

It's crying. It is a girl. Oh you little punkin

Mother did not have any either.

I'm so proud of Mother. She is so brave.

Men Scale the Barricades

About the turn of the seventeenth century, men began to make a more concerted attempt to get in on the midwife act. Traditionally, they had been unwelcome, if not entirely banished, from the scene of childbirth. Husbands were no doubt occasionally recruited in emergency situations, but only by default. Childbirth was woman's business.

In some countries, in fact, man's presence in a lying-in chamber was strictly forbidden. In 1522 one Herr Wertt, a German physician, put on women's clothes and sneaked in, hoping to observe an ordinary delivery, but he was found out and sentenced by the authorities to be burned to death. An early American colonist, Francis Rayus, tried a similar feat in 1646 and was also discovered and arrested (although the more lenient colonial government only fined Rayus fifty shillings). Percivall Willughby, an English physician whose daughter was a midwife, was more successful at avoiding detection and recorded the following event:

In Middlesex, anno 1658, my daughter, with my assistance, delivered Sir Tennebs Evank's lady of a living daughter. All the morning my daughter was much troubled, and told me that shee feared that ye birth would come by ye buttocks. About seven o'clock that night labour approached. At my daughter's request, unknown to the lady, I crept into the chamber upon my hands and knees, and returned, and it was not perceived by ye lady. My daughter followed mee, and I being deceived through hast to go away, said that it was ye head, but shee affirmed the contrary. . . . I crept privately again the second time into ye chamber, and then I found her words true. I willed her to bring down a foot, the which shee soon did, but being much disquieted with fear of ensuing danger, shee prayed mee to carry on the rest of the work.

The open participation of men in the childbirth process came about as a result of the remarkable invention of an unusual family. Early in the reign of Queen Elizabeth I a Huguenot named William Chamberlen fled from Paris to escape that same St. Bartholomew massacre from which Ambroise Paré had been spared, and arrived in Southampton with his wife, two sons, and a daughter. The sons, for reasons obscured by time, were both named Peter, and were known as Peter the Elder and Peter the Younger. To obfuscate things still further, Peter the Younger died before Peter the Elder, but not before he himself had a son whom he, too, named Peter.

The extraordinary thing about the Chamberlens was not, however, their lack of imagination in regard to nomenclature, but their possession of a major medical secret that they jealously guarded for more than a century. All the Chamberlen men were physicians. William's sons became members of the Barber Surgeons' Company and practiced general surgery in London, which meant that they were from time to time called in when a midwife recognized she had a case she could not handle. One of them, probably Peter the Elder, unhappy at the seemingly inevitable sacrifice of the child and pondering how it might be avoided, hit upon the concept of the forceps. His early invention resembled two large spoons that were inserted separately into the birth canal after which, with the bowls of the spoons cupped around the baby's head, the short straight handles were joined and locked together. The surgeon, gripping the handles and exerting considerable force, could thus pull the baby along.

The instrument was crude, but it worked. Now the surgeon summoned to the lying-in room was not forced to choose between the life of the mother and that of the child. With greater and greater frequency the Doctors Chamberlen were able to save both. Word, of course, got around. The brothers were much in demand, and their fees rose proportionately. Young Peter, recognizing a good thing when he saw it, also took up the calling.

As the Chamberlens began to be enlisted not just by despairing midwives, but increasingly by fearful women or anxious husbands when trouble was merely suspected, they began to deal more and more exclusively in obstetrics and could truly be called the first of the man-midwives or accoucheurs. They were intelligent—perhaps brilliant—men, and no doubt compassionate, but their compassion and their pecuniary interests collided. The clue to a lucrative practice and social advancement lay in keeping the invention within the family circle, so the Chamberlens, in what we would see today as total disregard of the welfare of women in general, did just that. They allowed no one else into the room when they operated or, if that could not be avoided, kept the room in darkness and covered both themselves and the patient with a large sheet under which they performed their miracles. The rumor that their family possessed extraordinary powers was discreetly encouraged.

Young Peter was even more of a charlatan. He attempted to use his reputation to organize midwives into a guild with himself at the head, empowered to examine the midwife applicants and award licenses as he saw fit. Since the transparency of his purpose was obvious to authorities and midwives alike, his petitions were regularly denied, which never seemed to deter him more than temporarily. He subsequently applied for an ordinance that would grant him a monopoly to furnish London with baths and bath-stoves, but once again he was turned down with the reminder that private baths already existed with or without him, and that public baths would be apt to promote the kind of morals associated with ancient Greece and Rome. From baths his schemes proliferated into plans for propelling carriages by wind and for writing phonetically; patents were granted to him for these last.

Peter the Charlatan had three sons—Hugh, Paul, and John—and Hugh had a son, Hugh, Jr., all of whom also practiced midwifery and continued to guard the family secret. But in 1699 Hugh Sr., deeply in debt and fearing imprisonment, fled to Holland where he sold the design to a leading Dutch obstetrician, Hendrik Van Roonhuyze. Van Roonhuyze apparently did not possess the proper dynastic instincts; in any case, the secret soon leaked out. In 1726 William Giffard used the forceps openly in London. Two years later Hugh, Jr., the last of the male Chamberlens, died.

In 1813, during the restoration of Woodham, Peter Chamberlen's former country estate in Essex, the actual Chamberlen forceps and other instruments were accidentally found in a secret place under the floorboards of a closet.

Birth on Easter Island Is Everybody's Business

The population of Easter Island is under a thousand. Everybody knows everybody else; everybody knows all there is to know about everybody else; and when there is a birth on the island, it's everybody's business.

Let a pregnant woman indicate that she believes labor has begun and a whole succession of events is set in motion. First, the husband, if he is elsewhere, is notified. A fire is built, and a black stone heated in it. When the stone is very hot, it is removed, wrapped in bulrushes, and placed under the woman to stimulate her contractions. Meanwhile, from all directions, relatives and friends can be seen crossing the grassy, windswept island in the direction of her house, and as many as can crowd inside to encourage and comfort her. There she is, squatting, kneeling, leaning back against her husband who has grasped her under the armpits and is supporting her while at the same time massaging her stomach with both hands.

When the delivery appears imminent, someone makes sure that the *tangata hahau pito*, the man who will tie the navel cord, has been summoned. This is a sacred ritual, the exact details of which are known to only a few persons on the island. Once the baby has arrived, attention focuses on the *tangata hahau pito* and his string. Three transverse turns around to the right and tie, three more to the left and tie again. Such knots will keep the baby's strength in its body. But to cut the umbilical cord, a young boy or girl is called forward. What, the young person is asked, has he (she) dreamed the night before? If he is so unlucky as to have slept soundly and not dreamed, or if he cannot remember his dream, the honor moves to someone else. Dreams featuring cows or stars are considered favorable for the new child; a falling star—in fact, anything falling—is a bad omen.

Finally, the baby will be turned over to its parents who will accept congratulations all round. Now the event will probably end there. Time was when the paternal grandmother had the concluding role. It was her job to put the placenta and umbilical cord into a calabash and carry them down to the shore (never, on Easter Island, very far away). There she threw them into the sea while intoning the charm— "*Ka oho, kangaro ki hiva!*" "May it be lost in a foreign country!"

Leave the Birth Process to Nature

Women themselves were always the victims of poor midwifery, and those who had any influence begged the English physician to try to help. William Harvey was one who answered the call. When he was not needed to minister to Kings James and Charles I, and when not occupied with his discovery of the circulation of the blood, Harvey found time to write extensively on childbirth. His aim was to provide sound, scientifically based directives for the average ignorant English midwife, a goal that was somewhat thwarted by the general inability of the seventeenth century midwife to read. To put matters in perspective, it should be noted that Harvey did not have all the answers either; conception remained as much a mystery to him as to other scientists of his day, and he believed, like many before him, that the fetus itself possessed the power to induce labor contractions. But he was the first to set down a careful record of that fetus at all stages of its intrauterine life, and the chapter on labor in his famous work *De Generatione Animalium* set new standards for English midwifery. He understood the dangers of interference in natural cause and effect, and he implored midwives to leave the birth process to nature no matter how long it took. He rebuked "the younger, more giddy, and officious midwives, who mightily bestirre themselves and provoke the expulsive faculty, and who, persuading poor women to their three-legged stool before the time, do weary them out and bring them in danger of their lives."

Harvey's friend and colleague, Percivall Willughby—he who crept into the birth room on his hands and knees to aid his daughter in a difficult delivery—also took up the cause. He added to the midwife manuals with his *Country Midwife's Opusculum* in which he condemned "high and lofty, conceited midwives" who employed everything including "pothooks, pack-needles, silver spoons, thatcher's hooks, and knives" to hurry the birth along. He described one poor woman whose first experience with a midwife was so devastating that she refused ever to employ one again. Instead,

. . . so soon as she perceiveth her labour approaching, shee causeth a fire to be made in her chamber, and her husband bringeth her into the chamber, and after the taking of their leaves one of ye other, hee, with her desire and consent, locketh her in the roome, and cometh no more unto her until she knocketh, which is the signe of her delivery to him.

Finally, Hugh Chamberlen translated Francois Mauriceau's *The Diseases of Women with Child, and in Childbed,* and Dr. William Sermon contributed *Ladies Companion, or, The English Midwife.* But all the former were men, and author, Mrs. Jane Sharp—herself a midwife—resented that fact. Although she published her *Midwives Book* with the stated purpose of "directing childbearing women how to behave themselves," her real aim was to put down the notion that "men-midwives" (she is credited with inventing the term) were of any real use in the childbirth process.

A French Midwife Embarks for the New World

Although the typical early colonial midwife was English, one who was not was Marie Grisot, a Frenchwoman of unknown age but determined character who emigrated from France to Louisiana on the royal payroll. In 1704 Louis XIV sent twenty-three young women across the Atlantic as prospective wives for some of the soldiers and settlers who had gone out previously. Marie embarked soon thereafter for obvious reasons. Besides the performance of her duties, Marie conducted a running controversy with Governor Bienville as to whether or not nursing the sick in general was part of her job. Bienville insisted that it was, but Marie refused on the grounds that "the majority of the soldiers were subject to scurvy and that having thus cared for the scurvy patients she could not at all touch the women in childbed or even the children at birth without running the risk of communicating this disease to them." The belief that scurvy was contagious was widely held at the time; what is more interesting is that Marie apparently grasped some idea of carrying infection through touching, and that such infection would be dangerous to both mother and baby. It would be another 150 years before such personages as Oliver Wendell Holmes and Ignaz Philipp Semmelweiss would convince the world at large of the infectious nature of puerperal or childbirth fever.

Instructing Midwives, Male and Female

By the eighteenth century English midwives were having to face the fact that men had entered their sacred field of endeavor, and apparently were there to stay. A few still tried to arrest the trend. Mrs. Sarah Stone, who had learned midwifery from her mother and taught it in turn to her daughter, deplored the ignorance of the average country midwife that brought the whole profession into bad repute. As she described in her *Complete Practice of Midwifery:*

I was sent for to Curry Mallet, to a tanner's wife, about eleven o'clock at night. . . . It being very bad weather, and bad roads as ever were rode, so that before I got there the child was born. I did not go up-stairs directly to see the mother and child. The woman saying all was well, I thought proper to dry my cloaths, being very wet and tired (for 'twas eight long miles). When I had dry'd and recovere'd myself I went up stairs, and to my great surprize saw the child with one eye out, and the whole face much injured, having no skin left on it, and the upper lip tore quite hollow from the jawbone, was extremely swell'd, so that the child could make no use of it. I put some warm water and sugar in the child's mouth, with a small spoon, and resting it upon the tongue the poor infant sucked it down. I asked the mid-wife, how the child's face came to be so miserably hurt? She told me the mother fell down two days before she was in travail, and, as she thought, hurt the child, for she was sure she was born right. I told her I was sensible the child came head foremost, but the face presented to the birth; and the damage the child received was from her fingers. She could not make any defence for herself. I found her extremely igno-rant.

Despairing that the English midwife would ever receive proper instruction, Mrs. Stone published her book for her "sister profes-sors in the art," begging them to study anatomy and observe dis-sections so that they would be more knowledgeable and would not be obliged to call in a man for "every little seeming difficulty."

Not everyone, however, felt that studying anatomy and observ-ing dissections were proper occupations for women, even midwives. Although he admitted his book, *Treatise on the Improvement of Midwifery*, was intended for "experienced attendants," Edmund Chapman refused to include in it either a description of, or plates on, the female reproductive system, which would, he said, only "serve to raise and encourage impure Thoughts in the Reader's Mind." Or perhaps it was the "man-midwife" to whom Chapman was referring. Nicholas Culpeper, author of *Directory for Midwives,* disapproved of man-midwives in general, believing them lazy men among whom "Covetousness outweighs their Wits." The rules in his book were, as he put it, "very plain and easy enough; neither are they so many that they will burden your Brain."

Less chauvinistic was the eminent surgeon John Douglas who, in his *Short Account of the State of Midwifery in London, Westminster, &c.,* pointed out that it was ridiculous for male practitioners to insist they be called in for "every trifling little difficulty." First of all, they were not always available, even in London, certainly not in the countryside. Second, they often charged more than a workingman could pay, and third, many husbands would not allow them to attend their wives anyway. Women, said Douglas, were perfectly capable of dealing with difficult cases in other countries and ages in which they had been properly instructed, and could be in England now if given the chance. Instead of forever blaming them for what they did wrong, one should teach them how to do it right.

Three men, to their infinite credit, tried. Sir Richard Manningham, a leading London man-midwife, set up a "Charitable Infirmary" to serve poor married women during their confinement and at the same time provide instruction opportunities for his students, both men and women. The cost for women was ten guineas, only half what it was for men, although both sexes had access to the "Great Machine"—Manningham's mannequin of a woman about to give brith. But only men were taught use of the forceps.

The giant among midwifery teachers was William Smellie, a Scotsman removed to London, who taught both men and women at his house in Pall Mall. Smellie also had mannequins equipped with uteruses of leather able to contract at will and expel their liquid contents (usually beer). The fetuses were made of wood with movable joints. Even the placenta was represented. By observing the "lady" giving birth, the students were expected to become sufficiently familiar with the process to conduct a birth themselves. But again, only men were taught how to use the forceps.

Smellie also supplied his students with clinical training. Since he had no infirmary at his disposal, he advertised that he would deliver poor women free in their own homes in return for his students being allowed to examine them and assist at the deliveries. He had, apparently, no lack of candidates; one of his students wrote in his journal that in a single afternoon he (the student) had examined twenty-one pregnant women. Smellie almost started a riot one night when, being called to the East End of London to aid in a difficult birth, he was accompanied by some twenty young men all tramping along in his wake.

Smellie was the kind of rough-hewn man to whom it seemed not to occur that twenty strange men crowding around a poor, distraught women in hard labor in the tiny room of a London tenement was at least eighteen too many. "But my students must *learn*," he would say with his soft burr. He had a warm, direct bedside manner, his "improved" forceps were the most efficient of his time, and he was obsessed with imparting knowledge. His goal was the safer delivery of women, and for him almost any means justified that end.

Finally there was Smellie's pupil, William Hunter, who built up a fashionable practice, including the Queen, but still found time for teaching midwifery and for his anatomical studies of the gravid uterus. In the preceding centuries, because the church did not sanction dissection of pregnant women, most knowledge of the human uterus was assumed from dissections of lower animals. But with the dwindling of clerical powers, Hunter was able to obtain the bodies of women in various stages of pregnancy. Twenty years and uncounted bodies later he published his *Anatomy of the Gravid Uterus,* with the major discovery that the internal membrane of the uterus forms the exterior part of the afterbirth and separates from the rest of the uterus every time a woman bears a child or has a miscarriage.

Together Hunter's and Smellie's works transformed the practice of midwifery into the science of obstetrics. Inadvertently, they also widened the breach between the traditional midwife and the new man-midwife or accoucheur. Although they trained women to be more competent than they had been, they trained men to be more competent than women—or at least competent in more situations. Neither of them wished to eliminate good midwives from the scene, but once the focus had turned to men—once all the interesting cases began to go to men—the profession lost its appeal to intelligent women, and the result was the same.

"You Will Preside at the Accouchement"

Madame du Hausset was for many years lady-in-waiting and confidante of Madame de Pompadour, the favorite of Louis XV. Her mistress placed such confidence in her that she allowed Madame du Hausset to spend much of her time in a private nook adjoining her own chamber where she could overhear everything said in the room. Afterwards, Madame de Pompadour would frequently ask for her opinions and discuss matters with her. "The King and I look upon you as a cat, or a dog, and go on talking as if you were not there," she once told her.

Undoubtedly, Madame de Pompadour did not know that her "cat" was, during those years, keeping a journal in which she meticulously recorded all she saw and heard. The Journal was not published until well after the deaths of those persons principally concerned. In 1827 it appeared, anonymously translated into English, from which the following selection has been taken.

Madame callled me one day into her closet, where the King was walking up and down in a very serious mood. "You must," said she, "pass some days in a house in the avenue of Saint Cloud, whither I shall send you. You will find there a young lady about to lie in." The King said nothing, and I was mute from astonishment.

"You will be mistress of the house, and preside, like one of the fabulous goddesses, at the *accouchement*. Your presence is necessary, in order that everything may pass secretly, and according to the King's wish. You will be present at the baptism, and name the father and mother."

The King began to laugh and said, "The father is a very honest man." Madame added, "Beloved by everyone, and adored by those who know him." . . .

The King said, "Guimard will call upon you every day to assist you with his advice, and at the critical moment you will send for him. You will say that you expect the sponsors, and a moment after you will pretend to have received a letter stating that they cannot come. You will, of course, affect to be very much embarrassed; and Guimard will then say that there is nothing for it but to take the first comers. You will then appoint a godfather and godmother—some beggar or some chairman [i.e., litter-carrier] and the servant girl of the house—and to whom you will give but 12 francs, in order not to attract attention." . . .

"Guimard," continued the King, "will tell you the names of the father and mother; he will be present at the ceremony and make the usual presents. It is but fair that you also should receive yours." And as he said this, he gave me 50 louis, with that gracious air that he could so well assume upon certain occasions, and which no person in the kingdom had but himself. I kissed his hand, and wept. "You will take care of the accouchée, will you not? She is a good creature, who has not invented gunpowder, and I confide her entirely to your direction. My chancellor will tell you the rest," he said, turning to Madame, and then quitted the room.

"Well, what think you of the part I am playing?" asked Madame.

"It is that of a superior woman, and an excellent friend," I replied.

"It is his heart that I wish to secure," said she, "and all those young girls who have no education will not run away with it from me. I should not be equally confident were I to see some fine women belonging to the court or the city attempt his conquest."

I asked Madame if the young lady knew that the King was the father of her child.

"I do not think she does now," replied she, "but as he appears fond of her, there is some reason to fear that those about her, who might suspect the truth, will tell her so," said she, shrugging her shoulders. "She and all the other sultanas are told that he is a Polish nobleman, a relation of the Queen, who has apartments in the castle."

This story was contrived on account of the *cordon bleu*, which the King has not always time to lay aside—because to do that he must change his coat—and also in order to account for his having a lodging in the castle so near the King. There were two little rooms by the side of the chapel, whither the King retired from his apartment without being seen by anybody but a sentinel, who had his orders, and who did not know who passed through those rooms. The King sometimes went to the Parc aux Cerfs or received those young ladies in the apartments I have mentioned.

Madame de Pompadour said to me, "Be constantly with the accouchée to prevent any stranger, or even the people of the house, from speaking to her. You will always say that he is a very rich Polish nobleman, who is obliged to conceal himself on account of his relationship to the Queen, who is very devout. You will find a wet nurse in the house, to whom you will deliver the child. Guimard will manage all the rest. You will go to church as a witness; everything must be conducted as if for a substantial citizen. The young lady expects to lie in in five or six days; you will dine with her, and will not leave her till she is in a state of health to return to the Parc aux Cerfs, which she may do in a fortnight, as I imagine, without running any risk."

I went that same evening to the Avenue de Saint Cloud, where I found the Abbess and Guimard, an attendant belonging to the castle, but without his blue coat. There were, besides, a nurse, a wet nurse, two old menservants, and a girl, who was something between a servant and a waiting woman. The young lady was extremely pretty, and dressed very elegantly, though not too remarkably. I supped with her and the mother abbess. . . . The young lady chatted with us after supper; she appeared to me very naive.

The next day, I talked to her in private. She said to me, "How is the Count?" (It was the King whom she called by this title.) "He will be very sorry not to be with me now, but he was obliged to set off on a long journey." I assented to what she said. "He is very handsome," said she, "and loves me with all his heart. He promised me an allowance, but I love him disinterestedly. And if he would let me, I would follow him to Poland."

She afterward talked to me about her parents. . . . "My mother," said she, "kept a large grocer's shop, and my father was a man of some consequence; he belonged to the Six Corps, and that, as everybody knows, is an excellent thing. He was twice very near being head bailiff." Her mother had become bankrupt at her father's death, but the "Count" had come to her assistance and settled upon her 60 pounds a year, besides giving her 240 pounds down.

On the sixth day she was brought to bed, and according to my instructions, she was told the child was a girl, though in reality it was a boy; she was soon to be told that it was dead, in order that no trace of its existence might remain for a certain time. It was eventually to be restored to its mother. The King gave each of his children 4 or 500 pounds a year. They inherited after each other as they died off, and seven or eight were already dead.

I returned to Madame de Pompadour, to whom I had written every day. The next day the King sent for me into the room; he did not say a word as to the business I had been employed upon; but he gave me a large gold snuff-box containing two rouleaux of 25 louis each. I curtsied to him, and retired.

Madame asked me a great many questions of the young lady, and laughed heartily at her simplicity, and at all she had said about the Polish nobleman. "He is disgusted with the Princess," she said, "and, I think, will return to Poland forever in two months."

"And the young lady?" said I.

"She will be married in the country," said she, "with a portion of 40,000 crowns at the most, and a few diamonds."

Men-midwifery and the Morals of Wives

Although man-midwifery might well in the eighteenth century have been considered the trend of the future, husbands were definitely of two minds about it. Journalists of the day, who recognized a good story when they saw one, played on the age-old male fear that wifely fidelity would collapse at the first relaxation of the barriers of propriety. In both France and England, titillating stories of what really went on during visits of the male-midwife to his patient fanned the insecurities of countless husbands. "Virginity is a moral quality, a virtue which cannot exist but with purity of heart," wrote the celebrated French naturalist Count Buffon. "In the submission of women to the unnecessary examinations of physicians, exposing the secrets of nature, it is forgotten that every indecency of this kind is a violent attack against chastity; that every situation which causes an internal blush is a real prostitution." Buffon's friend Voltaire was more concise. A husband who employed a man-midwife for his wife's confinement was, in his opinion, "traveling the road to cuckoldom." The morals of France being what they were in Voltaire's day, one would think it would hardly have been noticed.

Conjugal indignation was not helped by the publication in England of such books as Philip Thicknesse's *Man-Midwifery Analysed* and Francis Foster's *Thoughts for the Times but Chiefly on the Profligacy of Our Women*. According to both men, wives were by nature weak and inconstant and, already corrupted by French novels and dances, would never be able to resist the temptations created by this latest French fashion, the *accoucheur*. Or if somehow one did manage to withstand the advances of the accoucheur himself (who was, of course, occasionally elderly and otherwise less than romantic), it would be only to fall prey to the first seducer who came along and requested similar familiarities. The very citadel of English marriage was threatened, said Thicknesse, and all because of a "slavish desire" on the part of a few aristocratic ladies whose husbands didn't much care one way or the other anyway, and who would be copied in this as in everything else, particularly everything undesirable, by the "middling classes."

So the more conservative men joined forces with the more radical of the women midwives. Mrs. Elizabeth Nihell, the Betty Friedan of the midwife cause, was afraid that the doomsday was at hand when male-midwives would take over entirely, and she rode boldly to the defense of her sex and her profession. In her *Treatise on the Art of Midwifery*, she expressed her "insuppressible indignation at the errors and pernicious innovations . . . every day gaining ground under the protection of Fashion, sillily fostering a preference of men to women in the practice of midwifery." Her first target was the "multitude of

disciples of Dr. Smellie, trained up at the feet of his artificial doll,"
and her second, "those instruments, those weapons of death!" meaning, of course, the forceps. Since it was the male-midwife's almost exclusive right to the forceps that most conspicuously divided him from
his female counterpart in the public mind, it was there that she concentrated much of her attack.

Mrs. Nihell was right, of course, that the forceps in the hands of a
still inexperienced accoucheur was a dangerous instrument. ("Only
ten in a thousand labors require instrumental delivery," was Smellie's
rule.) She was right to protest as she did when men-midwives received
more pay for the same normal delivery than did women. She was right
that the new man-midwives unfairly belittled the female intellect and
stirred up prejudice in the public imagination. And she was right that
midwives of both sexes should have to pass rigorous examinations
before they could practice. But she was a general who failed to inspire
her army—or maybe it was only that her army was dwindling to insig-
nificance as each succeeding year produced a new band of accoucheurs
to tip the scales of power and influence further in their direction.

By the end of the century, however, passions had cooled. Man-
midwives had not displaced women entirely after all; perhaps they
had never really tried. A few die-hards like Margaret Stephen, bless
her, still maintained that a good female midwife was preferable to a
man any day, and Queen Charlotte, who engaged her for her own confinements, apparently agreed. Mrs. Stephen persisted in trying to raise
the standards and competency of her own sex. She set up a training
establishment in London complete with anatomical studies and mannequin, and actually taught women how to use the forceps and other
instruments. But she was nevertheless a realist. Although her students
should know *how* to use the forceps, she did not advise that they actually *do* so. A male-midwife, she said, might get away with employing
instruments and the baby dying anyway; for a woman it would mean
ruin, imprisonment, perhaps hanging. But she insisted that women
were innately as well qualified as men to practice all phases of midwifery, and never ceased to campaign in their behalf.

Colonial Childbirth, the Best Gossip Time

Midwives were highly valued in colonial America right up to the latter
half of the eighteenth century. More than one New England town,
anxious to have one handy, provided a house or lot rent-free. In New
Amsterdam, where they were known "Zieckentroosters" or "comforters

of the sick," they were salaried by the colonial government. They were required to be licensed, and after the early wave of emigrant midwives from Europe had passed along their expertise to apprentices, local systems to license native-born midwives had to be established. The colonial midwife was a busy woman. Death notices in papers of the time credit them with having delivered thousands of infants, and when one considers the time and energy spent in travel by horse or wagon, their dedication becomes clear.

But the midwife was seldom the only attendant on the parturient woman. Childbearing was a community event for women in seventeenth and eighteenth century America, and other mamas collected at the first rumor of a labor beginning. The early stage resembled a party with a table laid with refreshment and the "hostess" doing her best to walk about as the manuals of the day suggested. She, too, might partake of a little broth, or munch on toast dipped in wine. When her pains grew too heavy, she would retire to bed, while her neighbors clustered round. Day or night mattered little; someone else had been assigned the essential tasks at home, and babies still at the breast would have been brought along and put to sleep in a corner somewhere. This was the best gossip time. Although the tenor of the event would depend to some extent on the course of the labor and who was present, some jollity could usually be counted on, and always comfort and support for the young—or not so young—mother.

The colonial papa was almost never present at a birth except in remote areas when labor came fast and no one else was available. But he had his role. It was his job to provide meat, and perhaps ale, for refreshment; he might already have gathered the necessary medicinal herbs from the forest, and if it were winter, it was up to him to keep plenty of firewood on hand. And it was usually papa who afterwards recorded the course of the "travail" and the particulars of the birth in the family Bible.

Medicinal supplies tended to be familiar: herbs for a variety of purposes, fresh butter or hog's fat to lubricate the perineum, a plaster of partially cooked new-laid eggs to be applied to the vaginal area after the birth. If the labor was long, there was supposedly nothing like a draught of another mother's milk to help things along. It was inconceivable that there would not be at least one lactating woman present, and after the birth it would often be she who would first put the newborn to the breast.

For the actual birth the new mama might lie propped up against pillows, but she was more likely to be in the lap of a patient friend or supported by neighbors while squatting on the midwife's stool. The midwife herself, or an older woman if no midwife were present, would receive the child; if the latter, there would be cries of warning concerning the umbilical cord, which must not touch the floor or be cut too short or too long, in fulfillment of this or that superstition. After which, all appearing well, the women would perhaps have a last cup of tea together, and leaving one of their number in charge, would scatter, tired but emotionally replenished, to their separate homes.

"It Wasn't No More Than Three Dollars To Catch a Baby"

Annie Mae Hunt is a large Black woman with white hair, a warm, resonant voice, nine children, and a gift for telling a tale. Her tale is about her family—five generations of it, in Texas—and she told it over some months time to Ruthe Winegarten who put it together into the book, *I Am Annie Mae* (1983). In the following excerpt she speaks of her grandmother, who was born in South Carolina during slavery, came to Texas after the Civil War, lived with her husband on a farm in Washington county, and bore sixteen children, which would seem to have provided ample experience for her own profession.

My grandmother was a midwife. Every white man or black man born in that country that's my age, my grandma *caught him*. They called it *catch em*. Yes, a many a one down there right today.

Grandma would go and stay three and four weeks with a family, according to how rich they was. The Hodes, the Yahnishes, the Wobblers, they all were rich people, Bohemian, German, Polish people. Yeah, that's what that country's made out of.

She was woke up many a night, and stayed right there with that woman until she got up. There wasn't nothing they could do for pain. Grandma kept quinine. Now they had a doctor in there, was a doctor named Kanale, and one that name Wooskie. They'd give them quinine. They knew just how much to give them. Now what that quinine was for, I don't know.

And Grandma had another little medicine in a bottle, real dark red. I don't know what it was. Grandma kept also a black bag, just like a doctor did, she kept it. And we wasn't allowed to touch it. We couldn't even look at it too hard, cause everything she needed was there. She had her scissors and her thread that she cut the baby's cord, and she had it right there. Where the doctors tie the baby's cord now with certain plastic and catguts and stuff, Grandma had big number eight white spools of thread, and she kept it in this bag.

Everybody paid her—except sometimes the colored people didn't. It wasn't no more than three dollars to *catch* a baby. She stayed with the rich white people, doing their washing and ironing, and taking care of the woman's baby and her chores. Those Polish and German people had a hell of a chore. Those women worked like dogs. They'd do anything a man would do, go out and plow. Now the rich women didn't do this, but the rich white woman's daughter got out and plowed like her brother did. And when the mamas didn't have no small babies, they worked in the fields too. Grandma didn't do that; she'd wash and iron.

And when Grandma came home, they would give her 25, 30 dollars, and that was a whole lot of money. She'd have everything she needed, all kinds of clothes and meat, and she'd bring light bread home, and we was there to gobble it up cause we loved it.

She *caught* everybody in that country, white or black. You better know she did. She had a name for herself. She was good and she was recognized.

Victorian Ladies in the Family Way

As in much of Victorian life, there was a curious paradox in the almost universal switch of the middle and upper classes from midwives to doctors (virtually all of whom were male) during the nineteenth century. That time when most emphasis was placed on the delicacy of ladies' temperaments, that period during which the word "leg" could not be mentioned in mixed company and the word "pregnant" not pronounced at all, that was the very time at which these same ladies were expected to submit as a matter of course to being examined and delivered by gentlemen. True, everything was done by "touch." Both examination and delivery were performed under the sheets, sight unseen, and with a careful avoidance of eye contact. But the experience, especially for a primapara, could be distressing. Not all could manage it. A certain Dr. Dewees of Philadelphia told of arriving to attend a lady in labor only to have her pains cease abruptly the moment he entered the room, not to resume for another two weeks. One Samuel Gregory, A.M., published in 1850 a *Letter to Ladies in Favor of Female Physicians* in which he describes a doctor in Woburn who had been engaged to deliver a particular young woman but who discovered that his presence at her bedside had a retarding effect on the progress of her labor and that the only practical solution was to leave. Unfortunately, not all doctors were so sensible. Another, waiting at the bedside of a prospective mother for what seemed to him an inordinate amount of time, decided that a normal birth was impossible and set off to get his forceps, only to find on his return that the young woman had delivered quite handily in his absence.

Sensitive young women were not the only ones unhappy with the replacement of midwives by their male counterparts. Many couples thought midwives not only more sympathetic, but safer, which in the early part of the century, before doctors realized the importance of washing their hands and changing their clothes before going from a sickbed or an autopsy to attend childbirth, was undoubtedly true. Physicians were also accused, often justifiably, of using instruments unnecessarily to hurry along a case because of their own impatience, or of using instruments to increase their personal sense of importance.

"Meddlesome midwife" was the accusation. With obstetrics as with other matters, what was in one week was out the next. Poor Princess Charlotte, in 1817, hit the wrong swing of the pendulum. Charlotte was the only child of the Prince of Wales, soon to become George IV, so when shortly after her marriage to Prince Leopold of Saxe-Coburg she became pregnant, there was national rejoicing. Her mother had always been attended by Midwife Stephen, but Charlotte engaged a physician. That was expected in 1817. Sir Richard Croft was his name—tall, lean, decidedly middle-aged. His colleague, Dr. Matthew Baillie, would assist.

The princess was young, charming, and much beloved, and her pregnancy and its outcome were considered of great importance. All the rules then in fashion were observed: Charlotte was strictly dieted and frequently bled and purged. About seven o'clock on Monday evening (November 3) her waters broke and she went into labor, but the pains, although sharp, were ineffectual. By Tuesday evening Sir Richard was beginning to get nervous, and sent for a colleague, Dr. John Sims, who arrived about two A.M. Wednesday. The progress continued slow. Use of forceps was discussed, but rejected. About six that evening a green discharge appeared, and about nine the princess delivered a stillborn son who could not, despite attempts, be revived. She had been in labor fifty-two hours. She was utterly exhausted, and by morning she, too, was dead.

The country was stunned, horrified. It was hard to blame Croft and his colleagues for letting nature take its course; if they had interfered and used instruments and the princess had died, the outcry would have been overwhelming. Croft, of course, had been aware of that. He had not dared when perhaps he should have. The poor princess, weakened to a practically febrile state by low diet and regular bleeding, had then been allowed to remain in labor for more than three days running. But the team of Croft, Baillie, and Sims was afraid to risk its reputation. The use of forceps was not "in" that year.

Poor Princess Charlotte—but poor Sir Richard, too. "My mind is in a pitiable state," he wrote to a friend the day after the death. "God grant that neither yourself nor anyone that is dear to you should ever have to suffer what I experienced at this moment." He tried to keep up with his work, but three months later, while visiting a patient, he blew his brains out.

For a while the succession was uncertain, until the next year an infant princess was born to Edward, younger brother of George IV, and named Victoria.

The Cows Mooed and the Horses Neighed

My friend Annie Farrell currently assists a midwife in a rural area of upstate New York, which she describes as "a beautiful place of white houses and red barns and black and white cows." In fact, the land, the animals, and the people there would seem to live in a special harmony, as evidenced by the following account.

I believe in the right time and the right place for everything. I've been in births where the mother really had to work, where it was not easy. One mother whose birth I was assisting in really had to work hard to get that baby out. Her first baby had been born by Caesarean section. She had attempted a home birth, but the midwife who worked with her that time was a passive midwife, someone who didn't get involved. A "hands-off" midwife, where you just let the lady do her thing, and whatever happens, happens. You don't really work with her. Whereas the midwife I work with is a "hands-on" midwife; she gets in there and works right with you, and it's just as if she were having the baby. She has pre-natals, and is equipped with fetal monitors and oxygen. If you're going to have a home birth, you should be prepared. And I think it's good to have someone there who knows even more than you do, to tell you if they think there's a good reason that you should transport to the hospital.

This lady, the first time—the time she'd had the Caesarean—she'd worked and worked, and pushed and pushed, and couldn't get anywhere. Couldn't get that baby down. The midwife who was with her thought they ought to go to the hospital, and they did. And they did a Caesarean on her right away. But this time she'd made up her mind that she was going to try again.

This woman was a very strong lady. She was in her late twenties, her husband a little older, and she happens to be a very religious person. She has a lot of faith—a very serious girl. She's not someone who would do anything lightly. So I trusted her judgment. And she is also very strong physically. She has a lot of animals, does her own butchering—very strong. Anyway, she was in labor for two and a half days, but not to the point where she couldn't work or walk around. She worked, she milked her goats, she did everything she normally does up until the last twenty-four hours. In fact they went to the movies Saturday night to try to get things relaxed.

By Sunday afternoon, however, things were pretty radical. She was having contractions very fast. She wasn't milking the goats any more. And she pushed and she squatted and she made loud noises until about ten o'clock Sunday night when she just felt like she could not do it any more. She just wanted to quit. And I thought that if she wanted to quit, she should. That she should feel she had that option. That she shouldn't feel obliged to stick with it if she didn't want to—that she could go any way she wanted. But the midwife was a little more aggressive. "C'mon, stick with it, you can do it!" Whereas my job—you know, "If you want to go to the hospital, you are welcome. Just say the word."

She decided to go. I got the car ready; everything was prepared for her to leave. We went outside with the bags and all, and it was a beautiful starlit summer night. Out she came into the yard, and suddenly all her animals—she has guinea hens, peacocks, goats, horses, chickens, turkeys, pigs, cows—all of them began to carry on. They just made every noise—it was like Noah's Ark, with all the honking and neighing and mooing. And she went to the fence and held on—it wasn't a conscious thing—and got her energy back. All the animals got so excited—maybe they thought they were going to get fed, I don't know. But it was as if they infused their energy into her. And she said, "Maybe I'll try a little longer."

So we went back inside, and she ended up down on the floor on a blanket in her living room. What finally happened was that her waters broke and showed some meconium stain, which means that the baby has pooped inside the womb. Then if the baby starts to come out, any kind of oxygen hitting the baby could make it take a breath;

and if it began to breathe and breathed in some meconium, that could cause viral pneumonia which can be fatal in newborns. It was essential that that baby get out fast. At that point it was really too late to transport. There was no choice but to do it. I get tingles thinking about it, it was so heavy. I was not responsible, but I was there, and I was involved. In the end I actually pushed the baby out with my hands. I was braced with my feet against the wall, pushing. It took all my strength and it sounds brutal, but really you're just pushing the baby's fanny. There must have been a lot of praying going on, because her head came out finally, and once her head was out we were able to suction her, and then the rest of her came. We put her right up on her mother's belly and covered her up and rubbed her, and her mother rubbed her, and finally she began to turn pink. She opened her eyes and looked at everybody, and she was fine. Nine pounds.

Sometimes very curious things happen at a birth. At one I attended the baby was born in what is called a "frontal presentation," which means that the baby's face is born first. It happens about five percent of the time. Her lips came out—we could see something there, but we didn't quite know what it was. The midwife reached in to feel the baby's head, and the baby began to suck on her finger!

An Obstetrician Speaks Out

A friend who practices in a medium-sized hospital in Kansas City, Missouri—surely the heartland of America—shared his views on contemporary birthing.

I'm in private practice in O.B.-gynecology with two other doctors. I'm fifty-three. My associates are fifty-nine and thirty-eight respectively. My younger associate has ideas a little different from myself and my older associate, to some degree. Quite a degree on some.

I would say that the biggest change in obstetrics in the last generation is the involvement, both of the woman and her husband. And, I suppose, the technologic thing. There's so much more technology than there was twenty years ago. There are more tests you can run to prove this or that, and fetal monitoring, that sort of thing. We do fetal monitoring as a matter of course; it gives you a little added advantage. I've reached the stage where I feel uncomfortable if I don't do it.

I would say about eighty percent of our obstetrical patients try natural childbirth. When they tell me that's how they want to do it, I say, "That's fine with me. I'll do anything you want to." And I do.

I'd just as soon not give them a lot of medicine. We use very minimal medicine. When they deliver, we use a little local for stitches. To me, I think that it takes some of the weight off the doctor. Let's say you haven't given them much and the baby doesn't breathe well—they can't say, "The baby isn't breathing right because you gave me a shot." So I kind of like it. And you don't have to pay a lot of attention to them, that's another thing. They're in there with their husband helping them. I didn't expect to like it that well, but it hasn't worked out badly at all—natural childbirth.

There are a lot more doctors than there used to be. One of my partners said, "You can be pretty busy as a doctor unless you are a weirdo, and even some of the weirdos are pretty busy." I'm not sure that's good for medicine, or for the consumer. You turn out a lot of doctors that know how to do things, and man, they'll *look* for things to do, you know. My feeling is that one of the things that used to hold medical costs reasonably in check was that the average doctor in the past didn't have time to do a lot of things. But you turn a lot of doctors loose who know how to do various technical procedures, and they aren't real busy, and they're going to look for those things to do. They know how to do them, and they think they ought to be doing them. There's nothing worse than a doctor who isn't busy.

At this hospital we deliver about 2,400 babies a year, 200 a month. Ours is a nice size obstetrical unit. Our Caesarean section rate is about eighteen percent. It has gone up a lot over the past eight to ten years. I think it's for the good. Golly Moses, we used to let some women labor forever, you know, just forever. They'd try anything not to do a Caesarean section, and that was not in the patient's best interest. The patient got worn out. The doctor got worn out. The baby got worn out. The relatives got worn out. When I was first in residency, I don't think it was unusual to let somebody labor for thirty-six hours. In retrospect, it was terrible. No way would I ever do that now.

We don't have very many unmarried mothers here because this is a private practice hospital. Maybe about five percent. Nobody makes much of an issue about it. The girls tend to keep the babies, of course; they very rarely put them up for adoption. Very rarely. And they certainly don't have to stay pregnant if they don't want to, you know, and I'm in favor of that. I think that's the way it should be.

Midwives? There's one at the University of Kansas Medical Center. I think she's the only one in the area. We do have some nurse practitioners—RN's who have had extra training in OB. There are times when patients take to midwives very nicely, I know. I'm not opposed to that. I think there just probably aren't going to be very many. I'm not sure a nurse midwife can practice here under our present laws. I'm not sure what the status of midwives is in the state of Missouri. Missouri isn't exactly a leader. They're a little behind the times in some respects. They couldn't get the Equal Rights Amendment through; there are just too many conservative senators. So they're not likely to lead out in a business like midwives.

I wouldn't consider delivering at home. No way. There are some home deliveries in this area—not many though.

My most interesting delivery? Sometimes the interesting ones don't turn out very well. I'd just as soon not have those interesting ones. I think the case I remember best was a patient who had triplets. We didn't pick it up until about six months. I knew something was going on. The triplets were big, but she did well and had a normal delivery. They were healthy and have all done well. *That* was exciting.

8. Fathering

It's a girl . . . a little beauty, an angel, and I'm madly in love with her.

Henry Miller, on the birth
of his daughter, Valentine

W. C. Fields: "A Baby Boy, Ain't It Great, Hat?"

W. C. Fields was touring England in the summer of 1904 when he received word of the birth of his first child, William Claude Fields, Jr., and sent his wife Hattie (nicknamed Bricket) this typical response.

Sheffield, 30/7/04

Dear Bricket:

Kitty's cable I recd. yesterday and was speechless for about two hours & then I was speechless as we all had a drink on the head of the kid *a boy too* & last night's show, I was next to the worst thing that ever went on the stage.

It is impossible Hat to tell you how glad I am to know all the worry is over. You are well and we have a little baby boy, aint it great Hat? Bring him over until I kick the stuffing out of him. Have wired all my intimate friends, but have recd. no congratulations, not up to now anyway, but I suppose they will come to & send me some telegrams soon.

You keep well now & get over this O.K. I suppose all the worst is over, don't discharge nurse or Dr. too soon. Keep them until everything is just right. Stay in bed and wrap your Zennie up well. Don't get up too soon. Soon as you are able write me a long letter explaining all. Tell me how it all happened, how you feel, if you are thin or fatter. Tell me *all*.

Am sending fifty for some fine clothes for to bring him over with, will send it next week. . . .

Will close now with lots of love & Kisses & quick recovery to health & strength.

Sod

Piaf: Born on the Sidewalks of Paris

Edith Piaf, the French *chanteuse* who sang her heart out in the
nightclubs of Paris and New York (and later in Carnegie Hall),
learned her trade singing for pennies in the streets, first with her
father, Louis Gassion (sire to nineteen children that he knew of),
and later with her half sister, Simone Berteaut (one of the above).
In her biography *Piaf*, Berteaut describes her sister's birth during
the First World War, as their father had told it to her.

"Edith wasn't born the way everybody else is," my father told me. "It
was right in the middle of the war, after the taxis of the Marne. I was
in the infantry, one of those *poilus* who were supposed to march or
croak—it's always the poor who get the good jobs because there are
so many more of them. Edith's ma, Line Marsa—Anita Maillard was
her real name—was a chanteuse. She was born in a circus, and was a
real sawdust kid. She wrote me, 'I'm going to be having the baby soon;
ask for leave.'

"I was lucky—I got one and made it home.

"See, that business about flowers on our rifles, that had been over
and done with for a year. And that nice, clean, joyous war, nobody
believed in it any more. Berlin was a long way to hoof it. I went
straight to our dump. No coal, black bread full of straw, no coffee,
no wine.

"I found the neighbors' wives yakking around my better half! 'This
rotten war, and her man at the front. . . .'

" 'Beat it, ladies,' I said. 'I'll take care of everything.' It was the
nineteenth of December, 1915."

When Edith told how she was born, she'd add, "Three o'clock on a
December morning's no time to pop out of your mother's belly to see
if it's better outside than in. . . ."

"It happened in a flash," my father went on. "I hardly had time to
say hello, drop my pack, buy a bite to eat and hit the sack, when Line
started to shake me and yell.

" 'Louis, this is it! The pains have started. It hurts like hell! The
kid's coming!'

"Looking so pale, her face all gaunt, it sure was no time to ask her
to marry me.

"Ready for anything, I'd gone to bed in my underpants. So I
jumped into my duds, grabbed Line by the arm, and down we went
into the street. There wasn't a damn cab in sight—they'd either already

gone home or else weren't out yet. It was cold enough to freeze your balls off. We started down the rue de Belleville. Line was nagging and bawling.

" 'Don't let it be a boy—he'd have to go to war!'

"We staggered down the sidewalk like we were loaded. Line was holding her belly with both hands. And right there at the foot of a lamppost, she stopped and flopped down on some steps.

" 'Leave me here and quick get the cops to call an ambulance.'

"The rue Ramponeau police station was a few feet away. I ran into their den yelling, 'My wife's having a baby on the sidewalk!'

" 'Goddamn!' the sergeant said, a guy with a mustache and graying hair. And there were the cops, grabbing their capes off the hooks and rushing to the scene as if they were all licensed midwives.

"My daughter was born on a cop's cape under a lamppost in front of number 72 rue de Belleville."

There was no better way to "arrive" in the world. For putting over realistic songs later in life, Edith was branded the day she was born.

The Cult of the Hero Father

For centuries Western man believed that he was the only progenitor, his wife merely providing the receptacle in which his child spent its pre-birth existence, so it seemed to him mandatory (an appropriately sexist word) to know that it was his child she was carrying. A man perpetuated himself in his children; they were his sole grasp at immortality. Sons were especially important: although a daughter was also entirely of her father's line, she could not carry on that line since the baby she would bear would be exclusively of her husband's making. A daughter was a dead end, genetically. A son, on the other hand, would carry on, through the vessel of his own wife, his, and his father's, and his father's father's, seeds of life.

In most of pre-Christian northern Europe, however, it was commonly believed that women could be, and occasionally were, impregnated by Spirits, and such women were often valued over and above the ordinary wife. Before (and lingering into) the Anglo Saxon period this belief led to the cult of the hero, a noble, semi-divine male figure who would father only superior children, usually male. Ordinary men were not to mind if their wives produced such special offspring while they themselves were detained in far-flung feudal warring. The Frankish king Clothwig set the standard: when making his will, he slighted his own sons and left the major portion of his lands to a child his wife had borne in his absence, reputed to be the son of a hero. The term "bastard" was not at all disparaging. The man we call William the Conqueror called himself William the Bastard; Charlemagne spoke with pride of his like heritage. Roland was a bastard son who went on, in legend, to become a hero, and in legend and no doubt also fact, to sire more bastard sons. Whatever the realities of the sixth century Arthur, the King Arthur of legend was a bastard, as was Gawain, as later was Siegfried.

In the eighth century the Catholic Church set out to counteract this dubious folk glory. The Anglo-Saxon synod of 786 A.D. declared that "the son of a meretricious union shall be debarred from legally inheriting." The Church took the stand that marriage was for life; monogamy was solemn law and not to be devalued by heroic illegitimacy. But it was several centuries before bastardy became a disgrace, before the romantic mystery of not knowing one's father—leaving open the possibility of his having been a hero—wore off.

Nijinsky: "The Supreme Happiness Is To Have a Child"

When Vaslav Nijinsky and the Ballet Russe left on tour for Argentina in the summer of 1913, it was almost the first time impresario Sergei Diaghilev had let his *premier danseur* out of his sight. Nijinsky, only twenty-three, felt like a kid out of school. By the time the ship reached the South American shores he and seventeen-year-old Romola Pulszky, a young woman of the Hungarian aristocracy whose interest in becoming a dancer was, by her own admission, subordinate to her interest in Nijinsky, were engaged. Two weeks later, in spite of a language problem—she spoke Hungarian and French and he Russian—they were married.

For the first weeks of their life together they conversed almost entirely through the translations of Baron Gunsburg, the acting head of the company, and it was he who passed along to Nijinsky his bride's expressed desire that they not have children. He also translated Nijinsky's reply: "For five years we shall live for art and our love, but the supreme happiness and the fulfillment of life and marriage is to have a child, and, after that time, when we will be in our permanent home, we shall have one."

But life is not always so easily arranged. Nijinsky's own mother, also a dancer, had had three children in quick succession after her marriage; one evening she danced through an entire performance and gave birth to him an hour later. So Nijinsky was not at all perturbed—in fact, he was pleased—when Romola, in spite of her resistance, became pregnant almost immediately. He consoled her with the prediction that the baby would be a wonderful dancer. They would call him "Le Petit Negre" in honor of his South American conception.

Back in Europe Nijinsky pretended unconcern when Diaghilev, in retaliation for his rebellion, dismissed him from the Ballet Russe. And when former colleagues who sided with Diaghilev taunted Nijinsky—"This year your creation is a child. . . . The *Spectre de la Rose* chooses the part of a father. . . . How utterly disgusting . . ."—Nijinsky countered: "The entrance of the *Spectre de la Rose's* child will be quite as beautiful as his own entrance, which you always admired."

In *Nijinsky,* her biography of her husband, Romola Nijinsky later touched on the circumstances surrounding that entrance:

Upon Vaslav's return to Vienna, we made all the necessary preparations to receive our baby. We had engaged a suite in the sanatorium, a wet nurse was chosen for the child as well as a nurse for me. The professor awaited our telephone call and we were breaking our heads for a name for *Le Petit Negre*. There was never any doubt that we would have a son. We both intensely wished for it, and it simply could not be otherwise. I wanted to call him Boris or Loris. Vaslav suggested Wladislav, and we decided on this.

The days passed, we visited all the lovely places of the Wiener Wald, but there was no sing of Wladislav. Finally we got tired of waiting. Even my brother-in-law Erik Schmedes, who liked Vaslav immensely, and was with us all the time, declared that this was an unheard-of breach of etiquette! Everybody in Vienna was waiting for the event.

Richard Strauss's new opera *Elektra* was having its premiere at the Opera House, and the intendant of the Hoftheater, Prince Montenuovo, knowing that Vaslav was in the city, sent us an invitation to attend, and had offered us a box, with the remark: "If this modern music won't hasten the baby's arrival, then nothing will!"

The opera was extremely interesting, and Vaslav liked it. Afterwards we dined gaily at the famous Opera Restaurant. Prince Montenuovo's prophetic words proved true. *Elektra* was too much for the baby, and next day, the 19th of June, our child was born.

Kyra Vaslavovna Nijinsky was a girl, and I was very unhappy about it. Vaslav did not show his disappointment. He waited with my sister next door to the operating-room, and, as the nurse announced to him, "It is only a girl, but a nice one," for one second he lost his self-control, and threw his gloves on the floor. But he never said anything about this to me. On the contrary, he tried to console me and praise the loveliness of the baby. Her hair was curled and black, like a *petit negre,* but she had beautiful green eyes, as strangely fascinating, as oblique as Vaslav's very own. At least one of my wishes had been granted. She was extremely muscular and the more she grew the more she resembled Vaslav.

From the very first second the child was shown to Vaslav the adoration which he always had for his daughter began. I think that, after his art, she was the most precious thing to him. . . . He could not admire enough every movement and gesture of the child. She was placed in a lovely white basket which he had near to him in the garden. . . .

James Thurber: He Liked the Idea of It

Not every sensitive man and artist can come to grips with the idea of paternity. One who could not was James Thurber, who, while his wife Althea labored at Doctors Hospital in New York, spent the night on the town with another woman. He did appear the next afternoon, bloody hand bandaged, sober—or anyway, soberer—and apologetic. "He seemed to have other things on his mind, many other things to do," the obstetrician later recalled to Burton Bernstein, Thurber's biographer. "He looked at the child as if she were a puppy." His friend Ted Gardiner, who thought Thurber groped for reasons to excuse his lack of paternal feeling, remembered him screaming at his wife, "The baby's from that chinless wonder you met on the beach!" although clearly the chinless wonder responsible was himself. E. B. White believed him too egotistical to be a proper papa, and Ann Honeycutt, his lady friend of the fateful birth night, said drily, "He didn't behave like a father of a newborn baby. He said that he liked the idea of it, deep down, but then, he was always a good actor."

Once His Wife Is BoofiDo, Goodbye

One of the more extreme examples of fatherly nonparticipation in childbirth is found among the Bororo people, a nomadic tribe of the Niger River area in Africa. Once a wife is unquestionably *boofiDo* (literally, "she who hatches")—that is, about the time she feels the child move within her—she makes preparations to return to her family for a period of two to three years. Her husband provides her with three dresses and a pair of sandals and packs her off. There she re-

mains with her mother and sisters, perhaps one or more of them returned from their husbands for the same reason, through her confinement and delivery and the approximate two years that she will suckle
the child. Although the event is of enormous personal importance to
the young husband—becoming a father is the final step toward man-
hood, after which he sets up his own household and acquires his own
herd of cattle—and although he might actually miss her, visiting her
would not be the thing to do, even after the child has been born. He
makes solicitous enquiries and sends her millet and salt and a handsome gift to her family after the birth, but he must wait out the prescribed time before he can see her again.

When he receives word that the baby has been weaned, the husband
calls into service one of his brothers, supplies him with two new
dresses, and sends him to bring home his wife and child. Their triumphant return marks the completion of the marriage transaction and
the independence of the couple. The women of the husband's camp
have built a little hut for her; the rope for her calf is already attached
at the entrance. The husband waits, and at the appointed time his
wife and brother arrive, complete with her dowry of bed, mats, calabashes, and more dresses. Not to mention the child—whom the father
now meets for the first time.

Napoleon Prepares for the Birth of His Son and Heir

By late summer of 1810 it was clear that Marie Louise, daughter of
Francis, Emperor of Austria, and second wife to Napoleon, Emperor
of France, was pregnant.

Napoleon himself announced the news to all the bishops "with infinite satisfaction" and with orders for "special prayers" for the safe
deliverance of the young Empress. The extent of his "infinite satisfaction" can only be measured against his long-held misapprehension
that he, conqueror of half of Europe, was sterile. Thirteen years of
marriage to Josephine had produced no children. There certainly had
been no lack of trying, and then, too, there were Josephine's two children by her first marriage, Eugene and Hortense, apparent proof of
her fertility. The fault, Napoleon had assumed, must lie with him. It
was not until he began to acquire mistresses, and they in turn began
to bear children—not only children, but *sons*—that the truth occurred
to him. The problem was not his after all. All he needed to produce
an heir—and a successor to the Empire—was a new wife.

Exit Josephine; enter Marie Louise. Plump young Austrian, fairly

exuding fecundity. She was blonde, blue-eyed, almost pretty in a bo-
vine sort of way. But her ancestry was impeccable. Their son, for of
course they would have a son—an heir was what Napoleon required—
would be twice descended from Henri IV, once from Louis XIV, and
would be the great-nephew of that unhappy pair Lous XVI and Marie
Antoinette. That such a heritage might be inappropriate in light of
his past position as First Consul of the Republic did perhaps not occur to Napoleon.

So the bishops were to pray, and if reports came in that their prayers
were not offered with the desired frequency or ardor, they were sharply
reprimanded. Not only Christians, but Jews, too, prayed. The Empire
was all-encompassing.

By October the Comte de Segur, who had been made responsible
for the overall management of the impending event, was deep in his
researches into the details of royal births of the past, such as that of
the Grand Dauphin, Louis XIV's son. Emulation of the past could
only enhance the present in Napoleon's current mood. It had already
been proclaimed (back in February, with the marriage not yet even
consummated) that the first son of the French-Austrian union would
be titled "the King of Rome," in recognition of Napoleon's Italian
campaign. Now it was only necessary to make sure that the new little
monarch would be properly welcomed in all the 132 imperial depart-
ments and various vassal states, with elaborate processions, illuminations, fireworks, artillery salutes, masses, and almsgiving.

Of greatest consequence (considering expectations of the baby's future) was the appointment of a governess. Traditionally, the "Governess of the Children of France" was accountable for considerably
more than the mere book-learning of her charges. In rank she became
second only to the Empress herself, with ultimate responsibility for the
little King of Rome's welfare. Napoleon settled upon Madame de
Montesquiou, a sensible woman of forty-six whose major recommenda-
tion was that she ate no meat. Directly reportable to her would be two
deputy governesses, three children's nurses, three cradle rockers, two
mistresses of the wardrobe, and two maids.

The masculine side of the staff—for as the child would be a boy he
would require male attendants—would consist of a first equerry and
two ordinary equerries, a secretary, a secretary to the governess, two
ushers, two grooms, four valets, a house steward, and a carver. The
aforementioned would be clad in appropriate and colorful uniform.
By Christmas of 1810 all such appointments were complete.

More delicate was the selection of the physician in ordinary and the
surgeon in ordinary, neither of whom, of course, were to be ordinary

in any way. There was much jockeying among the notables in the medical profession for these posts, and for that of physician vaccinator, whose sole duty it would be to inoculate the royal heir against small-pox. But by early March these positions, too, had been filled to the emperor's satisfaction.

Next there was the nursery to be fitted out and the layette to be ordered. Napoleon selected a ground floor apartment with windows looking out on the Carrousel; the interior was rather gloomy and the furniture heavy and elaborate, but then it was considered temporary. A more elaborate establishment, befitting an infant of exalted station, would be built later. The most important item of furniture was the cradle, an ornate gilded affair at the head of which had alighted a winged figure bearing a laurel wreath from which silken curtains hung down, and at the foot of which a rather ominous eaglet perched. The cradle (three rockers would be needed to keep it in motion) cost 158,289 francs. Madame de Montesquiou had also ordered a few simple tables, to be used for changing diapers, etc., and innumerable basins, warming pans, chamberpots, bedside lamps, mugs, and syringes, all of silver-gilt.

By mid-February Napoleon was able to inspect the layette: it consisted of forty-two dozen diapers, twenty dozen vests, twenty-six dozen nightgowns, fifty dozen pilches, twelve dozen fichus and handkerchiefs, and twelve dozen nightcaps, lace-trimmed. Each of these items, diapers included, was marked with the little King of Rome's own emblem, a star, and came from the establishment of one Mlle. Minette, linen draper, of 30 rue de Miromesnil. The same star was also embroidered on the fourteen long dresses of satin, marceline, and percale, also lace-trimmed.

Marie Louise, although only the mother, had not been neglected either. Her confinement trousseau was ready by the designated time, and a special bed for her lying-in had been delivered, entirely covered with Alençon lace, and so elaborate that the poor child (she was not yet twenty) was quite put off and asked if she might not please use her marriage bed instead. So it was there on the 20th of March, 1811, after twenty-six hours of labor and a difficult forceps delivery—with Napoleon pacing about in an adjoining room, the court waiting expectantly, and all Paris listening for the burst of cannon—that the child was born. It was believed at first to be dead, but the First Physician doused it in a basin of warm water, prodded it gently, wrapped it up in hot towels, and dripped brandy into its mouth, after which ministrations it revived. The Empress was allowed to see and even hold it briefly. Then the usual tradition for royal births was carefully ob-

served: the great double doors were thrown open and out in front of
the waiting Court stepped Madame de Montesquiou, baby in arm,
flanked by her deputy governesses and various of her appointed staff.
The usher stepped forward, cleared his throat, and announced—"Napoleon Francis Joseph Charles, the King of Rome!"

Elie Wiesel: "A Name Has Returned"

Elie Wiesel, Rumanian-born chronicler of the Holocaust and its
victims, who remembers a boy stealing a crust of bread from his
father on the train to Auschwitz and who watched his own father
die before he was himself liberated from Buchenwald, admitted
strong reservations (to *New York Times* reporter Samuel G. Freed-
man) about whether fatherhood was an acceptable role in this
world.

My life is a commentary on my books, not the other way around.
When Marion, my wife, told me she was pregnant, my first feeling
was fear. What am I doing? The world is not worthy of children. I
was frantic. But the next wave was joy. Will it be a boy or a girl?
Whose name will it have—my mother's or my father's?

I must confess, I felt something special when I carried him for the
circumcision. The circumcision is a very mystical rite. The rabbi had
a very beautiful way of putting it. He said, "A name has returned."
A name has returned. When I was called to read the Torah by name,
Eliezer ben-Shlomo, now there was Shlomo ben-Eliezer. For weeks and
days and months, I would carry him in my arms. I saw myself when I
was a child. A name has returned. . . .

There was a group in ancient Israel called the Pharisees who decided after the destruction of the Temple not to have children. And
they were over-ruled by the Rabbi Ishmael. He said, "What do you
mean? If you do not have children because the Temple was destroyed,
then you should not drink wine because wine was drunk in the Temple. And you should not eat meat because meat was eaten in the Temple. If you stopped having children, you'd stop life. And you cannot
stop life."

Piute Paternity: He Must Do His Part
in the Care of the Child

At the wedding feast, all the food is prepared in baskets. The young
woman sits by the young man, and hands him the basket of food pre-

pared for him with her own hands. He does not take it with his right hand; but seizes her wrist, and takes it with the left hand. This constitutes the marriage ceremony, and the father pronounces them man and wife. They go to a wigwam of their own, where they live till the first child is born. This event also is celebrated. Both father and mother fast from all flesh, and the father goes through the labor of piling the wood for twenty-five days, and assumes all his wife's household work during that time. If he does not do his part in the care of the child, he is considered an outcast. Every five days his child's basket is changed for a new one, and the five are all carefully put away at the end of the days, the last one containing the navel-string, carefully wrapped up, and all are put up into a tree, and the child put into a new and ornamented basket. All this respect shown to the mother and child makes the parents feel their responsibility, and makes the tie between parents and children very strong. The young mothers often get together and exchange their experiences about the attentions of their husbands; and inquire of each other if the fathers did their duty to their children, and were careful of their wives' health.

Sarah Winnemucca Hopkins,
Life among the Piutes, 1883

Madame du Châtelet est Enceinte
(Voltaire's Mistress Is Forty-three and Pregnant)

It was distinctly embarrassing when at the age of nearly forty-three Madame du Châtelet, wife of twenty-four years to the Marquis du Châtelet and companion of sixteen years to Voltaire, became pregnant, as it was clear to everyone that neither man was responsible.

The Marquis was always at Dijon commanding his regiment. He had done his duty by Emilie and the family line in the early years of their marriage—three children were evidence of that—but his real love was the army. He never quite understood how he had acquired a wife who read Latin, Italian, and English as well as her native French and was admired for her grasp of mathematics. His lineage was faultless and her dowry sizable and the marriage, like all upperclass French marriages of the eighteenth century, was based on just such solid qualities as these. The contract had made no mention of her intellectual gifts, and certainly no mention of love.

So the Marquis had not taken it much amiss when eight years later his wife had announced quite openly that she planned to spend the rest of her life with the much-admired poet-playwright-philosopher who went by the cognomen Voltaire. Such liaisons were acceptable in French society. He did not even complain when they retired to Cirey, has own ancestral home in Champagne to live. Cirey was a bit run-down; it could use some attention. Voltaire could refurbish it from his adequate funds, and they could be philosophers there together, a role to which the Marquis felt inadequate.

Voltaire, for his part, settled contentedly into country life and sel-dom left Emilie except to visit his dear friend, Frederick the Great, who invited only men to the Prussian court. Voltaire wrote his plays, Emilie translated Newton, and the relationship was quite satisfactory except that somewhere along the way Voltaire gave up sex. (There is a difference of critical opinion on this matter: there are those who as-sert that it was not sex, but sex with Emilie that Voltaire renounced.) In any case, it left in Emilie a definite vacuum. Her approach to love may have been metaphysical, but it was nonetheless passionate. She was clearly *malcontent*. None of her friends was, therefore, much sur-prised when during the course of a gay summer at Lunéville with Voltaire, houseguests of King Stanislas of Poland, she should become enamoured of one Saint-Lambert, a man of considerable charm some ten years younger than herself. The attachment was rather one-sided, but Saint-Lambert was too much the gentleman to discourage it overtly, and Voltaire (after the initial recriminations were past) too sensitive to his reputation as a free-thinker to object. Thus it hap-pened that when in late fall the two philosophers returned to Cirey, one of them was unmistakably pregnant.

As soon as she was sure, Emilie confided in Voltaire. He was all sympathy. She was not to worry; such things happened all the time; it would work out. In the meantime they had, perhaps, better send for Saint-Lambert and see what he thought. Saint-Lambert was sum-moned, arrived post-haste, and the three closeted themselves out of hearing of the servants to examine the options.

Actually, in the eighteenth century there were not very many. Abor-tion was available but hazardous to the extreme; Emilie would sim-ply have to go ahead and have the child. She could, perhaps, go into hiding to do it, but retirement was so unlike her that people would suspect the reason, and, besides, it would be so awfully dull. Then too she must name a father for the child, and what name would she give? Voltaire's quip that she simply record the baby as one of the miscel-laneous works of Madame du Châtelet was not appreciated. No, the conspirators finally agreed, the best course would be for her to have the baby openly as simply an untimely addition to the offspring of the Marquis. But how to accomplish that when for seventeen years the couple had lived on amicable but entirely platonic terms?

Clearly it was now time to summon the Marquis. There was no reason to suppose that *he* had renounced sex. He was a hardy old soldier, bless him. A little flattery here, a little flirtation there, and who knew what might ensue? So a letter was sent off at once to Dijon: would not the Marquis join the Marquise at Cirey? The Marquise had been busy collecting the rents and wished to hand them over personally, and besides, she had not seen him in such an awfully long time.

The Marquis came. From our perspective it might seem that the conspirators rather overdid the welcome, but then the Marquis was perhaps a very simple man after all. His reunion with his wife was almost embarrassingly tender. His servants were solicitous, his tenants positively devoted, and all his most affable neighbors were invited to the various planned festivities. Encouraged to ride about his domain in the mornings, he then returned to a good dinner of which his favorite dishes were automatically a part. At supper only the best of wines were served. Madame du Châtelet sat next to him, her low-cut gown showing to best advantage her already expanding bosom (she was otherwise rather flat-chested). After supper the Marquis was pressed to reminisce about his campaigns while Emilie hung adoringly onto every word and Voltaire and Saint-Lambert commented admiringly on the astuteness of his military judgment.

It was all very intoxicating. By the second such evening the Marquis was returning his wife's attentions and, moreover (as the candles burned low and songs alternated with the stories), asking for yet further favors. The Marquise demurred. After so many years? and besides, there were all these guests. Nonsense, said the Marquis, the years were as nothing, and the guests would excuse them. She marshalled forth a few more defenses, he overrode them, and they retired.

This (for the Marquis) charmed existence continued for three weeks. Before he set off again for Dijon, the Marquise informed him, blushing, that she thought perhaps—yes, was really quite certain—that their union was once more to be blessed. The Marquis was overjoyed. His wife was with child! Everyone must know, and soon everyone did, including those who had known for some time. At a final farewell dinner the Marquis and Marquise du Châtelet accepted the warm congratulations of their guests, after which the Marquis returned to Dijon, and Voltaire and Emilie settled down once more to quiet philosophy.

It would be lovely if the story could end right there in this best of all possible worlds, but unfortunately it does not. The two philosophers spent the winter and spring in Paris. Emilie had an uneventful if at times uncomfortable pregnancy, during the course of which she worked doggedly to complete her translation and commentary on Newton. She seldom went out, partly in order to conserve her energies for her work, and partly because she knew that to the world at large a forty-three-year-old woman *enceinte* was laughable. In June they returned to Cirey where they were joined by the Marquis, and in July all three went on to Lunéville. Something in Emilie's mathematically oriented psyche wished to have the event come round full circle, to end where it had all begun. King Stanislas was there, of course, and in due time Saint-Lambert arrived. The house was, in fact, full of guests, but Emilie had been given the old queen's suite, which was more private than most, and which she felt leant an air of respectability to the matter at hand.

During the last month everyone at Lunéville was much concerned about her, because of her age, and because she seemed so exhausted—Voltaire should never have allowed her to work so hard last winter, they said. But when her time came, nothing could have been simpler. She was sitting at her writing table one afternoon when she felt something odd. She called for her maid who, on rushing in, had just time to hold out her apron to receive the baby. It was a girl. Still wrapped in the apron, she was laid on a book while her mother sorted and put away the papers she had been working on. Then, for the sake of appearances, mother and child went to bed and the Marquis du Châtelet was informed that a daughter had been born to him.

For a few days all went well: the other houseguests visited the new mother, praised the child, and congratulated the Marquis. The baby was put out to nurse. Then without warning the action changed from French farce to tragedy. The weather turned hot. Emilie began to run a fever; breathing difficulties set in. Doctors were called. She seemed to improve, and then one evening, as Voltaire and the Marquis supped downstairs and Saint-Lambert, who had been talking with her, left her he thought to sleep, she suddenly hiccupped a few times and died. Her death was as abrupt as the birth had been the week before.

The poor baby also died a few days later, but that fact was hardly noticed in the general mourning over Madame du Châtelet. King Stanislas gave her a state funeral at which all, including Saint-Lambert, cried. The Marquis du Châtelet went about in a daze, and finally returned to Cirey. Voltaire, for his part, plunged into grief. For weeks he did little but write of her to his friends. "It is not a mistress I have lost but half of myself," he wrote, "a soul for which my soul seems to have been made."

At one point in his frustration and despair he turned on poor Saint-Lambert himself. *"Eh! Mon Dieu, Monsieur, de quoi vous avisiez-vous de lui faire un enfant?"* My God, sir, what gave you the idea of getting her with child?

E. M. Forster: "He Is Made Out of Me; I Am His Father"

E. M. Forster had no children himself, but the relationship of father to child recurs with haunting tenderness in his novels. He was twenty-six when he completed *Where Angels Fear to Tread*, not much older than its Italian hero, Gino, of whom he wrote: "He wanted a son. He could talk and think of nothing else. His one desire was to become the father of a man like himself, and it held him with a grip he only partially understood, for it was the first great desire, the first great passion of his life. Falling in love was a mere physical triviality, like warm sun or cool water, beside this divine hope of immortality: 'I continue.' "

When his wife Lilia, who is English and older than he, goes into labor, Gino lies all night on the floor outside the closed door of her room, waiting. The son is born, but Lilia dies. Several months later her brother- and sister-in-law and friend, Miss Abbott, come down from England to try to claim the child. Gino is caring for his son himself, with the occasional help of Perfetta, the maid. He explains to Miss Abbott the difficulties involved in raising a child, but he clearly has no intention of giving him up.

"What is to be done? I cannot afford a nurse, and Perfetta is too rough. When he was ill I dare not let her touch him. When he has to be washed, which happens now and then, who does it? I. I feed him, or settle what he shall have. I sleep with him and comfort him when he is unhappy in the night. No one talks, no one may sing to him but I. Do not be unfair this time; I like to do these things. But nevertheless" (his voice became pathetic) "they take up a great deal of time, and are not all suitable for a young man."

"Not at all suitable," said Miss Abbott, and closed her eyes wearily. . . .

"No, he is troublesome, but I must have him with me. I will not even have my father and mother too. For they would separate us," he added.

"How?"

"They would separate our thoughts."

She was silent. This cruel, vicious fellow knew of strange refinements. The horrible truth, that wicked people are capable of love, stood naked before her, and her moral being was abashed. It was her duty to rescue the baby, to save it from contagion, and she still meant to do her duty. But the comfortable sense of virtue left her. She was in the presence of something greater than right or wrong.

Forgetting that this was an interview, he had strolled back into the room, driven by the instinct she had aroused in him. "Wake up!" he cried to his baby, as if it was some grown-up friend. Then he lifted his foot and trod lightly on its stomach. . . .

The baby gave a piercing yell.

"Oh, do take care!" begged Miss Abbott. "You are squeezing it."

"It is nothing. If he cries silently then you may be frightened. He thinks I am going to wash him, and he is quite right."

"Wash him!" she cried. "You? Here?" The homely piece of news seemed to shatter all her plans. She had spent a long half-hour in elaborate approaches, in high moral attacks; she had neither frightened her enemy nor made him angry, nor interfered with the least detail of his domestic life.

"I had gone to the *farmacia*," he continued, "and was sitting there comfortably, when suddenly I remembered that Perfetta had heated water an hour ago—over there, look, covered with a cushion. I came away at once, for really he must be washed. You must excuse me. I can put it off no longer."

"I have wasted your time," she said feebly.

He walked sternly to the loggia and drew from it a large earthenware bowl. It was dirty inside; he dusted it with a tablecloth. Then he fetched the hot water, which was in a copper pot. He poured it out. He added cold. He felt in his pocket and brought out a piece of soap. Then he took up the baby, and, holding his cigar between his teeth, began to unwrap it. Miss Abbott turned to go. . . .

"Oh, but stop a moment!" he cried. "You have not seen him yet."

"I have seen as much as I want, thank you."

The last wrapping slid off. He held out to her in his two hands a little kicking image of bronze.

"Take him!"

She would not touch the child.

"I must go at once," she cried; for the tears—the wrong tears—were hurrying to her eyes.

"Who would have believed his mother was blonde? For he is brown all over—brown every inch of him. Ah, but how beautiful he is! And he is mine; mine for ever. Even if he hates me he will be mine. He cannot help it; he is made out of me; I am his father."

It was too late to go. She could not tell why, but it was too late.
. . . "May I help you wash him?" she asked humbly.

He gave her his son without speaking, and they knelt side by side,
tucking up their sleeves.

Rousseau, Jefferson, and Marx: Not Acknowledging Paternity

Although fathering an illegitimate child, or children, is seldom other
than a delicate matter, it was especially so for three celebrated cham-
pions of the downtrodden: Jean Jacques Rousseau, Thomas Jefferson,
and Karl Marx. Not one was able to deal with his delinquent fatherhood in a manner that we today would consider adequate, much less
exemplary. All their brilliance and erudition seemed of little help
when challenged by their passions, and their defense of ordinary people did not prevent them from turning to those same ordinary people—in this case serving women, women dependent on them for their
livelihood—for sexual needs they could not, would not, or did not,
satisfy in marriage. When the result was a child, or children, they
avoided acknowledging paternity, and (except for Jefferson) had the
offending babes removed from the scene. It may be unfair to judge
people from one century by the values of another, but all three of
these men were active formulators of those very values they could not
themselves entirely honor.

In the case of Rousseau it is difficult to find a single mitigating factor. At about thirty-five, the French writer-*philosophe* set up housekeeping with a young servant girl, Thérèse le Vasseur, of whom he
had become very fond. She never learned (in spite of his efforts) to
add and subtract, name the months of the year in order, or tell time,
but she was loving and willing and before long pregnant. In his *Confessions* Rousseau reports that he had been quite open with Thérèse
in regard to their liaison—she knew better than ever to expect marriage—but what to do about the potentiality of children had not been
discussed. His quandary—a common one, he discovered—could easily
be solved through the good offices of the Foundling Hospital. "Here
was the expedient for which I was looking," Rousseau wrote in the
Confessions. "I cheerfully resolved to adopt it, without the least scru-
ples on my own part; I only had to overcome those of Thérèse, with
whom I had the greatest trouble in the world to persuade her to adopt
the only means of saving her honor." Poor Thérèse, who would much
have preferred to keep her baby rather than her honor, was forced to

consent to turn the whole matter over to the midwife, one Mlle Gouin
at the Pointe Saint-Eustache. Transporting swaddled newborns to the
Foundling Hospital was matter of course with Mlle Gouin. She did as
much for Rousseau, and repeated the process a year later.

When Thérèse became pregnant for the third time, the philosopher
paused for a moment to reflect on her situation and on what he termed
"the duties of man." "I began to consider the destination of my children and my connection with their mother," the *Confessions* continue.
Then follows a rationalization so self-serving that it reads like a parody
of eighteenth century hypocrisy. "Is it possible," Rousseau asked himself, "that my warm-heartedness, lively sensibility, readiness to form
attachments, the powerful hold which they exercise over me, the cruel
heartbreakings I experience when forced to break them off, my natural
goodwill towards all my fellow-creatures, my ardent love of the great,
the true, the beautiful, and the just; my horror of evil of every kind,
my utter inability to hate or injure, or even to think of it; the sweet
and lively emotion which I feel at the sight of all that is virtuous,
generous, and amiable; is it possible, I ask, that all these can ever
agree in the same heart with the depravity which, without the least
scruple, tramples underfoot the sweetest of obligations? No! I feel and
loudly assert—it is impossible. Never, for a single moment in his life,
could Jean Jacques have been a man without feeling, without compassion, or an unnatural father. . . . My third child was accordingly
taken to the Foundling Hospital, like the other two. The two next
were disposed of in the same manner, for I had five altogether."

The realms of self-delusion are awe-inspiring. And poor Thérèse.
What life must have been like for her during the seven years in which
all this took place can only be imagined. How must she have felt to
read in *Emile,* published soon after this final child-disposal, of Rousseau reproaching mothers for not suckling their children themselves,
for leaving their care to nurses who would simply "hang them on a
hook" when they cried. And to read that no man who did not fulfill
his paternal duties had any right at fatherhood. Of course, Thérèse
probably never read *Emile*. She did not read very well.

Eventually the whole matter became public knowledge and caused
a great scandal. Rousseau's Puritan virtue had appeared so pronounced
(he never lost an opportunity to mention it) that everyone in Geneva,
where by that time he was living, had assumed that Thérèse was nothing more than his housekeeper. Chagrined at being found out, he di-
rected his anger at whomever (he never learned his identity) had
turned him in. He declined to recognize any culpability on his own

part. "My fault is great," he concludes self-righteously, "but it was due to error; I have neglected my duties, but the desire of doing an injury never entered my heart, and the feelings of a father cannot speak very eloquently on behalf of children whom he has never seen. . . ."

Thomas Jefferson was born about the time Rousseau first met Thérèse, and he later based many of his own writings on the French philosopher's theories of man's natural goodness and the desirability of a liberated, humanistic community. But Jefferson was a Southern landholder in a slave society. Theoretically, he was resolved on the emancipation of all slaves, but practically he avoided the issue altogether, not the least when it concerned the woman who bore his child.

Jefferson's private dilemma focused on a mulatto slave his wife Martha had inherited on the death of her father. Sally Hemings was still tiny when she was brought with her mother to Monticello; what set Sally apart from the other 130-plus slaves in the bequest was the fact that she and Martha Jefferson were half-sisters. John Wayles, Martha's father, was also father to Sally—and to five other mulatto children of his slave Betty Hemings, with whom he had formed an easy attachment after the death of his third wife. How their presence at Monticello affected Martha Jefferson's domestic tranquility is not known; they seem, if anything, to have received rather preferential treatment. Situations of the kind were not, of course, uncommon.

Thomas and Martha lived together for ten years in what he later termed "unchequered happiness" until, not long after the birth of their fifth child, Martha died. In her last hours she begged her husband never to marry again, and Jefferson promised he would not. Much grieved, he welcomed the chance to go to France as Minister Plenipotentiary, and took with him his oldest daughter, Patsy, and Sally's brother, James Hemings. Later, when he found that he would be staying in Paris for several years, Jefferson sent for his younger daughter, Polly. A trusted older slave was to accompany Polly across the Atlantic, but she was found to be too close to her confinement, and fourteen-year-old Sally Hemings went as substitute.

Sally was younger than Jefferson's daughter Patsy, but having been less sheltered, she seemed more mature. "Dashing Sally" she was called back at Monticello. She had long black hair, light skin, and Caucasian features, and may even have resembled (since they had the same father) Jefferson's late wife. Beautiful women always brought out the gallant protector in him, but Sally was more than just protected. Before long she was being tutored in French, had clothes made to order by a

Parisian dressmaker, and had been inoculated against smallpox at considerable expense. Because the Jefferson daughters were in a convent school, Sally was often alone; when he had to be absent from the city for some weeks, Jefferson, unwilling to leave her prey to the French servants at the ministry, arranged for her to lodge with a French couple. She was clearly much on his mind. It was also nearly seven years since the death of his wife. When it became time for the Minister Plenipotentiary and his party to return to America, Sally Hemings was pregnant.

At first Sally and her brother James—who had been learning to cook a la Parisiènne—thought they would not go back to Virginia. After all, as long as they stayed in France, they were free. But Jefferson persuaded them otherwise. He promised Sally, among other privileges, that her child—all her children—would be freed at the age of twenty-one, and to James he promised freedom as soon as he had taught another slave at Monticello the French culinary arts. Perhaps Sally did not feel safe remaining in France after Jefferson left; perhaps she was lonely for Monticello, or perhaps she was in love. To have been singled out by the master, whom everyone at Monticello adored, was no small thing, even supposing she knew little of his role in the larger world. What his feelings were for her we do not know. Did he want to take her back because of his characteristic possessiveness, or because of strong personal feeling for her, or was it simply that he did not want her giving birth among curious strangers in gossipy Paris to a very light-skinned and possibly red-headed child? In any case, he persuaded her to return and have her baby in the backwoods of Monticello. Significantly, when Jefferson ordered the passages for the return trip, he misspelled berth, "birth." They arrived home two days before Christmas, 1789, and not long afterward Sally bore a son whom she named "Tom."

After Tom, Sally gave birth to two daughters who died, then to a second son while Jefferson was Vice President, and a daughter and two more sons during the Presidency. Jefferson encouraged his slaves to marry and live in family units, but Sally had no husband. All her children were light-skinned, and their parentage was not discussed. Historian Fawn Brodie, who sees the Sally Hemings situation as the key to Jefferson's lifelong ambivalence on slavery, has documented the fact that Jefferson was at Monticello nine months before the birth of each of Sally's children, whereas certain potential fathers suggested by other historians were not. Paris-conceived Tom, whose resemblance to Jefferson was said to be quite noticeable, was sent off to another family plantation. His name disappears from the *Account Book* the year in which he would have turned twenty-one.

In the second year of Jefferson's presidency, allegations as to immoral goings on at Monticello appeared in the Northern press. Jefferson refused to dignify these stories with any kind of response. Unfortunately, this approach, or non-approach, rather backfired on him; since he refused comment, various Southern papers, hoping to exonerate their man, investigated, and came to the unhappy conclusion that their Northern counterparts were probably right. John Adams up in Quincy, Massachusetts, believed it; he had met Sally during the European sojourn and could testify as to her beauty, and he felt such liaisons "a natural and almost unavoidable consequence" of slavery. His horror at the spread of such stories was such that he sat down almost at once to declare in writing that "my children may be assured that no illegitimate Brother or Sister exists or ever existed."

In 1873, nearly a century after the fateful trip to France, an Ohio newspaper, the *Pike County Republican,* published a "reminiscence" by Madison Hemings, Sally's third son, and another by Israel Jefferson, also an ex-slave from Monticello. Both independently reported Sally's role at Monticello as that of Jefferson's chambermaid and "concubine." After his death Sally had been freed and lived the remaining nine years of her life with her sons Madison and Eston. Apparently believing that after his death it could not matter any more, she affirmed that yes, of course, Jefferson was their father.

In his "reminiscence" Madison Hemings alludes to a double standard in Jefferson's paternal feeling: "He was uniformly kind to all about him. He was not in the habit of showing partiality or fatherly affection to us children. We were the only children of his by a slave woman. He was affectionate toward his white grandchildren, of whom he had fourteen. . . ." Still, the Hemings children were clearly better used than the average slave child. Madison admits that "we were permitted to stay about the 'great house,' and only required to do such light work as going on errands. . . . We were free from the dread of having to be slaves all our lives long."

The biographers who discount the Sally Hemings story do not credit the slave testimony, but have no answer either to the question of how a healthy, vigorous man still in his thirties could go through the rest of his extremely active and creative life without some outlet for his sexual drives. Many of us *prefer* the more human Jefferson that Sally allows us, and feel for the man torn between his ideology and his emotions, who wrote: "The whole commerce between master and slave

is a perpetual exercise of the most boisterous passions, the most unremitting despotism on the one part, and degrading submissions on the
other. . . . The man must be a prodigy who can retain his manners
and morals undepraved by such circumstances."

There can be no historical doubt, however, about the paternity of
the baby that arrived at 23 Dean Street, London, on June 23, 1851.
This in spite of the fact that five weeks later when he was finally registered as Henry Frederick, boy, child of Helena Demuth, the space
for "father" was left blank.

Helena Demuth was a young servant girl who, six years before, had
been sent to Brussels by the Baroness von Westphalen, whom she had
served for ten years, as a "present" to the baroness's only surviving
daughter, Jenny Marx. The wife of Karl Marx was expecting again.
Daily life for the Marxes was in continuous upheaval, and "Lenchen,"
as she was known, was more than welcome. Over the succeeding years
she quite literally held the family together—cooking, baking, brewing,
washing, cleaning, caring for newborns and toddlers, and nursing
Jenny through illnesses and the inevitable lyings-in. It was usually up
to Lenchen, too, to move them all from one cheap lodging house to
another as they were repeatedly evicted or fled. Her only reward (her
wages were seldom if ever paid in those early years) was their complete
acceptance of her as one of them, a valued member of the family,
someone whom they used but also loved.

The event in question took place three years after Marx published,
with Friedrich Engels, the *Communist Manifesto,* which necessitated
flight from the Continent to London. In England Engels provided
much of the family's support. Of their two-room flat in Soho, then a
working-class section of London, a Prussian police spy reported to his
superiors: "two rooms, the one looking out on the street is the living
room and the bedroom is at the back. There is not a single clean or
solid piece of furniture to be seen in the whole place . . . in the centre
of the living room there is a large old-fashioned table covered with oil-
cloth on which lie manuscripts, books and newspapers along with children's toys, bits of his wife's sewing things, a few teacups with chipped
rims, dirty spoons, knives, forks, candlesticks, an ink-pot, tumblers,
clay pipes, tobacco ash. . . . Sitting down is quite a dangerous affair:
here is a chair with but three legs; there another, which by chance is
still intact where the children are playing at being cooks. . . ." Under
such conditions, with Jenny Marx three months into her fourth preg-

nancy and small children always underfoot, the ingenuity required for Marx to have gotten Lenchen pregnant defies imagination. Clearly Lenchen was the hapless victim or she would not have been permitted to stay on. But stay on she did, into what would seem to have been an intolerable situation—wife and ravished servant there together in two rooms, night and day, advancing side by side through the long months to their confinements.

Politically speaking, of course, for the great advocate of the dispossessed to take such blatant advantage of one of those same dispossessed, was a situation that could have discredited Marx and ruined all he was trying to accomplish. This would have been clear not only to Marx, but to Engels and Jenny as well. How else could Engels, who had already done so much for Marx, have been persuaded to accept paternity? How else could Jenny, the beautiful young woman of the nobility who had relinquished position and comforts to marry a revolutionary and live in poverty for his cause, have been persuaded to stay?

There were rumors, but Marx denied them categorically, and the baby, once born, was turned over at once to a foster home. Marx never contributed to its support; at least in this respect he treated all his offspring equally—he couldn't support his legitimate children either. Engels must have taken it as a matter of course to provide for this extra mouth along with the others. Had Engels not set the matter straight on his deathbed, and the Marx daughters, once they knew the truth, not openly acknowledged Frederick as their half-brother, this bit of peripheral history would have remained in obscurity.

Frederick Demuth became himself one of his father's dispossessed, not only economically, but psychically. Although he knew his mother, and thought he knew who his father was, during the formative years of his childhood he lived with neither and was denied any really cherishing affection. In adulthood every work he undertook met with failure, his marriage equally so; he seemed to suffer rejection at all points of his life. In their later years he and Eleanor Marx, Karl and Jenny's youngest child, became very close. Born after the worst times were over, Eleanor received all Lenchen's mothering that should have gone to Frederick. She had adored her father, and for some time would not accept Engels's disclosure of Frederick's true paternity. But disappointed in love herself, she became gradually reconciled to the tricks of fate, and at the end wrote to Frederick as "the only friend with whom I can be quite free. . . ."

What is missing in all three of these stories is, of course, the testimony of the women involved. All of them were attached to exceptional men; each of them must have gained something from that relationship, but surely not enough to make their lives even minimally satisfactory. We are left with Confessions, Declarations, Manifestos—but not a blessed word from the feminine side.

9. Twinning

Maria Whitaker came, all in tears. . . . "Maria, are you crying because all this war talk scares you" said I. "No ma'am."
"What is the matter with you?" "Nothing more than common." "Now listen, let the war end either way and you will
be free. We will have to free you before we get out of this
thing. Won't you be glad?" . . .

"Now Miss Mary, you see me married to Jeems Whitaker
yourself. I was a good and faithful wife to him, and we were
comfortable every way, good house, everything. He had no
cause of complaint. But he has left me." "For Heaven's sake!
Why?" "Because I had twins. He says they are not his, because
nobody named Whitaker ever had twins."

Mary Chesnut, Diary from Dixie

The Universal Dread of Twin Births

Quarreling women of the Niger Delta used to curse each other with a two-finger gesture and the malediction, "May you be the mother of twins!" The threat was not an empty one. The role of "mother of twins" was at best a disgrace, at worst, fatal.

A similar bias could be found in nearly all the rest of Africa, the East Indian archipelago, and Australia; with the greater part of the aboriginal populations of North and South America and northeast Asia; and among the non-Aryan tribes of India and the less sophisticated population of Europe. In other words, there were relatively few parts of the globe where people did not view the birth of twins as a disaster—a crime guaranteed to call down the vengeance of the gods, who could only be appeased by the death of at least one twin, often both, and frequently the offending mother as well.

The dread of twin births was almost universal; the reasoning behind it, however, varied. The Mundurucu of Amazonian Brazil believed the abomination arose from the similarity to the animal world of multiple births. Peoples of Australia, Japan, and India were more apt to view it from the social perspective; in their monogamous societies a twin birth was regarded as proof of infidelity on the part of the wife. As the Tiwi of Australia explained it in their usual meandering poetics: a woman becomes pregnant when a *pitapitui* (unborn person) passes into her body. Since her husband, who "delivers" the *pitapitui*, would never deliver more than one at a time, she could not give birth to twins unless someone else had also delivered a *pitapitui*. She must have "walked in the bush in the dark" (met her lover) and allowed herself to be exposed to the *pitapitui* that flit about there.

The tribes of the Niger Delta area in West Africa carried this same general approach one step further, and a dangerous step at that. It was not a mere lover who was responsible for the other child, they said; it was the evil spirit. One of the twins had been fathered by a tribal approximation of the devil and could not be allowed to live; since it was seldom possible to know which, it was safer to kill both. The Hottentots were one of the few peoples to lay any share of the responsibility on the father; after disposing of the offending mother and twins, they removed one of the father's testicles to prevent a recurrence of the event.

Methods of disposing of twins also varied. Sometimes they just "got lost" somewhere in the bush or out on the frozen steppe. In West Africa they were customarily placed in clay pots and taken to unhallowed parts of the forest to be left to their fate. By the nineteenth century Christian missionaries began to achieve a limited success in reversing African practices, if not opinion. One Mary Slessor, a working-class Scots girl turned Presbyterian missionary, is legendary for stalking the bush, often barefoot, with her faithful retinue, rescuing babies who had been left to die. In her *Travels in West Africa* (1897) Mary Kingsley, niece of novelist Charles Kingsley and a resolute young woman in her own right, describes a visit with the redoubtable Miss Slessor during which she witnessed one such event.

The mother in this case was a slave woman, an Eboe, the most expensive and valuable of slaves. She was the property of a big woman, who had always treated her—as indeed most slaves are treated in Calabar—with great kindness and consideration, but when these two children arrived all was changed immediately. She was subject to torrents of virulent abuse, her things were torn from her, her English china basins, possessions she valued most highly, were smashed, her clothes were torn and she was driven out as an unclean thing. . . .

She was hounded out of the village. The rest of her possessions were jammed into an empty gin-case and cast to her. No one would touch her, as they might not touch to kill. Miss Slessor had heard of the twins' arrival, and had started off, barefooted and bareheaded, at that pace she can go, down a bush path. By the time she had gone four miles she met the procession, the woman coming to her and all the rest of the village yelling and howling behind her. On the top of her head was the gin-case, into which the children had been stuffed, on the top of them the woman's big brass skillet, and on the top of that her two market calabashes. Needless to say, on arriving Miss Slessor took charge of affairs, relieving the unfortunate, weak, staggering woman from her load and carrying it herself, for no one else would touch it, or anything belonging to those awful twin things, and they started back together to Miss Slessor's house in the forest clearing. . . .

A new path had to be cut to save the market road from pollution, but the troop finally arrived and the mother and surviving twin girl (the boy had died of the rough handling) were tenderly cared for. In the ensuing days, however, the natives absolutely refused to take pity on the child.

They would not touch it, and only approached it after some days, and then only when it was held by Miss Slessor and me. If either of us wanted to do or get something, and we handed over the bundle to one of the house children to hold, there was a stampede of men and women off the verandah, out of the yard, and over the fence, if need be, that was exceedingly comic, but most convincing as to the reality of the terror and horror in which they held the thing. Even its own mother could not be trusted with the child; she would have killed it. She never betrayed the slightest desire to have it with her, and after a few days nursing and feeding it she was anxious to go back to her mistress, who, being an enlighened woman, was willing to have her, if she came without the child. . . .

She would sit for hours singing or rather, moaning out a kind of dirge over herself. "Yesterday I was a woman, now I am a horror, a thing all people run from. Yesterday they would talk to me with a sweet mouth, now they greet me with curses and execrations. They have smashed my basins, they have torn my clothes" and so on. There were no complaint against the people for doing these things, only a bitter sense of injury against some superhuman power that had sent his withering curse of twins down on her.

"Madame, Vous Avez Deux Enfants"

My friend Teresa Alfieri-Weinberg told me the following story about the birth of her two beautiful daughters in 1979.

We were living in Verdonnet, a French village where we have an eighteenth century farmhouse and where we moved from New York soon after we were married. Our first child, Nicolai, was born there in the little hospital in Montbard, a nearby village only slightly larger than Verdonnet. The doctor there gave natural childbirth classes, but as I was just learning French, my husband Allan had to come with me every week to translate. The doctor was new—she had only just come to Montbard—and she had the delivery room painted, blue walls, orange ceiling. It was a whole new thing for this ancient French town—natural childbirth classes and painted delivery rooms.

Anyway, Nicolai was born, very beautifully, and a year and a half later I became pregnant again. Seven months into my pregnancy, my doctor wanted me to take a special test because I was carrying so big. She had asked me as far back as the fourth month if I had twins in my family, and I had said, "Oh no, no. Absolutely not." I had to go to another hospital in an even larger village to take the sound wave test. Afterwards, the doctor said to me, "Madame, vous avez deux enfants." And I almost fainted. Allan was in the next room with Nicolai, and when he heard, he almost passed out, too. We drove home trying to figure out how suddenly to get two of everything.

I hadn't suspected it at all, except that with Nicolai I'd had a fabulous pregnancy and felt so good, and this time I didn't. I was so tired, and I kept thinking—well, it's my age. I had Nicky at thirty-three, and I thought—well, I'm getting on. One day I was lying on the couch having a deep nap, and I felt two heartbeats. Two! I thought it was mine and the baby's. That was the only time I ever thought of it.

Another reason the doctor had wanted me to have this test was because I was having contractions by the end of my sixth month, which was very dangerous. She told me that I would have to go to bed. She told me not to get up or walk around or do any exercises. We had to get help. We had a woman come into the house and take care of Nicolai and prepare meals and such. As time went on it got worse, even though I was lying down. I also had medication to take.

Three weeks before the babies were actually born, I went to a special maternity hospital in Dijon. My doctor said that I *could* stay and have the babies in Montbard—she would have been delighted to deliver twins—but I felt, and Allan felt, that I should be in a bigger hospital in case there were any complications. Next door to this special hospital was a hospital for premature babies only—a highly specialized hospital. People come from Paris, from all over to this place.

I went to Dijon by ambulance, because when I rode in a car I would have contractions. I felt terrific when I arrived. I felt secure, and I really wanted to keep these babies. But after three weeks in the hospital, I was anxious to get it over with. The whole place was designed so that you didn't see other mothers in their rooms with their babies, because that was another section of the hospital. But the women who had had Caesareans were on my floor; they were under strict doctor's care and had their babies in their rooms. So you would pass their rooms every once in a while, and your heart would go in your throat. But most of the women on my floor were waiting for their babies, like me. There were anywhere from fifteen to twenty women there at a time. We all had private rooms.

Being an American in France was very special. I was always looked after as a special person, and they would ask me about my country, which I loved to talk about. I had to stay in bed. I was served my food; I had a television set; I read twenty-three books in three weeks. And I studied French—my French improved almost 100 percent. When I went home my friends in the village couldn't believe how fluent I was. Allan would bring Nicolai on the weekends and visit me, but that was hard, because then he would have to leave, and he would cry.

So there I was, wanting to give birth, and the doctors—every time they would come round in the morning, they would say, "Hang on! The longer you stay, the healthier the babies are going to be." There was one young woman doctor who could speak English—not fluently, but she understood better than she spoke. And she would come visit me every once in a while. The doctors were curious about certain birth techniques in America; they would ask me questions in French, and I would answer, which made my visit more interesting. I felt I had a purpose there. Not that I was so knowledgeable, but I knew something of what was going on in American obstetrics. So it was an interesting stay. Difficult, but interesting. But there were many hours when I was lonely for my husband and my child.

It was incredible how big I was, and how uncomfortable. They put me on a salt-free diet. I had lost a lot of weight. I really was not well, which was why I couldn't nurse them after they were born. The French are so into nursing. They told me that if I wanted to nurse, they had special pumps to pump the milk from me, and they would take the milk and put it into bottles to feed the babies. But I didn't really have the strength.

The babies were born on Friday, July 13th. Of course, here in America Friday the thirteenth is a bad luck day. I knew my mother would be worried if she knew. On July 12th, my water broke. They put me on an intravenous, because they were going to try to keep the babies in me even though the water had broken. They really wanted me to go another week. But the next morning I was so exhausted, I said to the doctors that I really couldn't continue. And they agreed. They took off the intravenous, and said we would go on with the birth.

They told me, "If by noon you don't go into labor, we'll induce it." Of course at noon I started my labor. I called Allan, and he came. He said, "I've taken a room, and I'm going to stay with you." Nicolai was taken care of. I said to Allan, "Do you realize today's Friday the thirteenth?" He said, "Yes, but we won't talk about that." Of course, July 15th is Bastille Day, and for nights before there are fireworks and big preparations. And with the French, Friday the thirteenth is a good luck day. Everybody said to me, "How fabulous! Twin births on Friday the thirteenth! How lucky you are!" The French are marvelous that way. They're so pro-babies, so into motherhood. I think if a woman's going to be pregnant, she should be pregnant in France. You feel very fertile.

I went into labor very quickly. They wheeled me down to be X rayed. They weren't sure the position of the babies was correct, and they couldn't hear the heartbeat of the other baby, which frightened me, too. So I was X rayed, which I didn't want to be, and then they wouldn't tell me anything. They just said, "Go ahead; there's no problem." I said, "May I see the X ray?" They said it wasn't necessary. I said to Allan, "Allan, something's wrong!" I was wheeled into the delivery room, Allan at my side with things on his feet and head and a smock—I think it was a soft green. There was a tall, handsome man who was the chief, the director of the hospital. Allan said to another man, "And who are you, Monsieur?" and he said, "I am the surgeon." In French, of course. There was a blood specialist, and another man— there were eight people plus the *sage-femme*, the midwife. She was just watching. And the young woman doctor who could speak some English was there, just to be with me, holding my hand.

I said to Allan, "Something's wrong. Why are all these people here?" I said, "Allan, it's Friday the thirteenth." And he said to them, in French, "My wife is very concerned that you're all here. She's happy to have you here, but she's afraid there's something wrong." And they all laughed, and said, "No-o-o! It's a fête for us. A twin birth is a very exciting thing." The doctor said, "I have asked all my colleagues to come." He invited everyone because that's what they did, that's what they always did. He hoped I wouldn't mind.

I was so tired from having had the intravenous thing during the night, and the anxiety of three weeks waiting for this, and my water breaking and everything, and I said to them, "I'm not sure that I can go through with natural childbirth. I did it with my first child, and it's a wonderful experience, but maybe I'm going to need help." The doctor—the French are so great about this—said, "We'll prepare a needle for you, but the babies are there. One push and your child's

going to be born. For you and for us to experience the two births. . . ."
He went on and on, so I said, "O.K., let's do it." And they all said approvingly, "Good girl."

Then Emily was born. They put her on my stomach, and she was a full grown baby. She was beautiful! They were all applauding in the background; it was just magnificent. You need spirit like that around you. A woman needs that.

Then they said Alexandra was on her way. I just felt like my whole stomach went in. The doctor was poking around very gently, probing my stomach. Emily had been head down, ready to be born, and now Alex—I could feel her turn. I *felt* her turn! The doctor was pushing her over; I could feel him. I said, "Is there a problem? because I felt like my whole stomach had dropped. But he said, "No, it's right there. It's coming out. Now, push!" and I did. And she came right out. I had to work for Emily, but not for Alex. Alex was very small, and they took her away from me right away because she needed oxygen. And they were all crying, "Bravo! bravo!"

They took Allan out and bought him a beer. They brought the babies back to me in a little bed, the two babies together, and they were sucking each other's fingers. It was so sweet. They were wrapped up, and Emily was sucking Alex's index finger, and Alex was sucking Emily's. They left them with me for a while, and then they took them away.

They wheeled me to my own private room, but a different room, because now I had my babies. It was a very comfortable room with a bed like you'd have in your own house—like a hotel. The next morning I was taken to see my children. They were in incubators. Emily had a little infection, because I had had an infection in my uterus. It was nothing serious, but they had to give her an antibiotic. With tiny babies, they put needles in their heads, not in their arms, so there was Emily with needles in her head. I was horrified. She had that for about three days, I guess. But she was fine—they were both fine. They were lovely. They were tiny, like little birds. I photographed them in the incubators.

I stayed there ten days. When I went home, I called every day to find out their weight, because they wouldn't let them leave until they reached a certain weight. After three weeks I brought them home. My mother had come over from America, and she came with us, and we drove home with these two babies. I was still tired, and paper thin, but my head was so happy.

The "Child Blunder" of a Twin Birth

With some primitive peoples it was the incestuous nature of twins of the opposite sex inhabiting the same womb for nine long months that was frightening. Incest was a taboo of the first order. In North American Indian tribes the female member of the duo was killed, usually suffocated; in other areas it was the male. In Bali, where infanticide may also at one time have taken place, the response by this century had been reduced to an elaborate kind of village exorcism. In his book *Island of Bali* the artist Miguel Covarrubias, who lived there for some years, describes the panicked reaction of the Balinese to the "child blunder" of a twin birth.

As soon as the happening is discovered, the alarm drum is sounded to declare the village polluted; the temple doors are closed and hung with forbidding pandanus leaves, and the entire social life of the village is paralyzed until the long crisis that ensues is over. . . .

The guilty parents and the baby twins are rushed to some unholy spot, generally the cemetery or more rarely the crossroads, together with the house in which the twins were born, which is dismantled and hastily rebuilt there. The couple and the twins are condemned to live in exile for forty-two days, guarded by a number of watchmen, who remain with them until the period of banishment is over, when the house is ceremonially burned to the ground before they all return to the village to perform the *metjaru* the great ceremony of purification.

This strange calamity is only for the common people. Among the nobility the birth of such twins is generally a happy omen and people of high caste claim that should the boy and girl twins marry each other, the union would bring prosperity and happiness to the country and they would become rulers. . . . When a couple of [the noble] class has led a model life of faithfulness unto death, they will reincarnate as twins "again married in the mother's womb," returning to their old home.

Two Little Bodies Sewn Up in a Bag

Illicit sex in seventeenth century, predominantly Puritan New England was not at all uncommon. The Word of God may have been in opposition, but the Situation of Man was all in favor. There was little privacy in any but a very few wealthy homes; occasionally heavy curtains might surround the bed of the master and mistress, but even then a child or two might sleep with them, and the other children plus servants of both sexes generally slept well within sight and hearing of each other. Whether this encouraged or deterred sex is probably debatable, but certainly many a young woman went before the courts to sue her master or a fellow servant for support of her bastard child. Although there were punishments meted out for fornication, the same also held true for bearing a child out of wedlock: a five pound fine and ten stripes was an average disciplinary measure. This is not to mention the opprobrium of the community, which was even greater in cases when the young woman was not a servant, but a daughter of the household.

Such was true with Elizabeth Emerson, fifth of the fifteen offspring of Michael and Hannah Emerson. Michael Emerson was a man of some standing in the town of Haverhill, Massachusetts; he was an occasional grand-juryman, and made his living by farming and shoe-making. Of Hannah we know nothing except that she must have been hard-working and over-taxed. Elizabeth was apparently an unruly child; in 1676, when she was eleven, she did something that caused her father to beat her so excessively that he was taken to court and fined for it. Perhaps, as one of the "middle children," she was so desperate for attention that she would do anything, and everything, to get it.

One imagines that Elizabeth's self-image was not very high. In her teens she began to exhibit rather loose behavior, and before long she was pregnant. When she accused one Timothy Swan of being responsible, however, he refused to do anything about it, inferring that paternity might be assigned elsewhere just as easily. In due time Elizabeth gave birth to a daughter.

In the course of the next five years she remained in her parents' house as "Elizabeth Emerson singlewoman." She put on a lot of weight, probably overeating from despondency. Then early in the spring of 1691 it began to look to the neighbors as if Elizabeth was "that way" again. When her mother asked her point blank, she denied it, but some of the townspeople remained unconvinced. Perhaps on Saturday, the ninth of May, someone saw her looking suddenly sleeker; in any case, on Sunday, the tenth, while her parents were at meeting, she was visited by a delegation of both sexes from the town. The women took her aside to "search her condition." The men went to the garden where they were not surprised to find a shallow grave and in it a cloth bag with two little bodies sewn up inside.

The next day, Monday, a town elder came to question her as she lay in the trundle bed at the foot of her parents' larger bed:

Q: What is your Husband's name?
A: I have never an one.
Q: Were you ever married?
A: No: never.
Q: Have you not been a second time Delivered, & had Two Children or Twins this month?
A: Yea, I have.
Q: When were they born?
A: On Thursday night last, before day toward Friday morning. But I am not certain of the time of the night.
Q: Where were they born?
A: On the bed at my Fathers bed foot, where I now am.
Q: Did you call for help in yor travel?
A: No: There was no body to call but my Father & Mother, & I was afraid to call my Mother for fear of killing her.
Q: Did you acquaint you Father or Mother with it afterwards?
A: No, not a Word: I was afraid.

The magistrate found it hard to believe that she had been able to give birth so quietly, not once but twice, and to stifle her own cries so successfully that neither of her own parents, a few feet away, had been aware of what was happening. He also expressed doubts that the babies had not cried, but she insisted they had not.

Q: Did you not do them to death, by violence, sitting down upon them, smothering them, or by any other meanes?
A: No: by no meanes.
Q: Where did you hide them before buried?
A: In the chest there by my bed.
Q: Who helpt you sow them up in the bag they were found in?
A: No body.
Q: When did you sow them up in the cloth they were buried in?
A: On Saturday night last.
Q: Where were your Father & Mother?
A: My Mother was gone to Milking & my Father was abroad.

Then it was the parents' turn, but they too denied any knowledge of the pregnancy, the birth, or its aftermath. In the fall, however, Elizabeth was taken to Boston where she was tried by a jury and

found guilty of murder. "Elizabeth Emerson singlewoman"—she probably never had a chance. On the eighth of June, 1693, she was hanged.

Unusual Fertility Associated with Twins

In some societies twins are believed to bring luck and good fortune to
the tribe. The Mohave Indians believed that twins moved back and
forth from heaven to earth at will, merely "visiting" on earth when
they chose. Newborn twins were loaded with gifts to make them want
to stay there in the tribe. The Yuman Indians of the Colorado River,
where drought was a recurrent problem, treasured twins because they
believed them to possess the ability to make rain. Parents of twins
among the Baganda of Central Africa were esteemed for having produced proof of unusual fertility which it was hoped they would transfer to the land and the plantain trees that provided them with their
staple food. Toward that end a particular little ceremony was conducted as soon after the birth as possible, before the potency of the
reproductive powers should have dissipated. The mother lay down on
her back in the thick grass with a flower from the plantain tree between her legs; the father then approached and knocked the flower
away with his penis. This ritual, the Baganda trusted, could not fail
to transmit increased fertility to their plantain trees.

An Early Woman Doctor Stakes Her Reputation

Helen MacKnight was a young woman of twenty-one when, in
the early 1890s, against unremitting opposition from her fellow
(male) students and professors, she completed her study of medicine in San Francisco. Degree in hand, she returned home to the
Wild Rose Mine on the California-Nevada border. Women doctors were suspect there, too, but at least you had the chance to
prove your skills. That Dr. MacKnight was successful—doubly so—
is clear from the following selection from her autobiography, *A
Child Went Forth*.

There were two physicians in the town. One was an old army doctor,
who refused to consult with me. The other was a man who treated my
degree as a rare joke. He said I might be a good nurse. . . .

I fitted up an office in the front room of the house and put out my
shingle—Helen M. MacKnight, M.D., Physician and Surgeon. . . . I
put in a small stock of drugs (it would be necessary to fill my own prescriptions), bought a medicine case, and started in.

My conveyance was a two-wheeled cart with a jump seat. I harnessed and unharnessed the horse myself. I would stand at the back of
the cart with the reins in my hand, raise the seat, clamber in and
start off. I used to smile sometimes, wondering what those professors
with their carriages and coachmen would think if they could see
me. . . .

Patients came to me, mostly chronic cases at first, who had failed to
get relief elsewhere and were curious to see what the new woman doctor might do for them. Every man, woman, and child in such an isolated place has a personal interest in the health of the community. If
a woman is "expecting," every good wife knows just when, can tell
how long her "morning sickness" lasted, and will venture an opinion
on the sex of the child by the way the mother is "carrying it." When a
woman is known to be in labor a kind of tenseness settles over the
whole community until word is passed about that it is all over. Then
the length of labor, the sex and weight of the child, whether "they"
wanted a boy or a girl, and other important factors connected with the
case are reviewed in detail.

Doctors are supposed to be able to bury their mistakes, but if they
do not wish to have post-mortem discussions of why and how it happened they had best keep to the cities. A young doctor, fresh from
medical college, can pass many embarrassing moments in the presence
of the neighborhood midwife. . . .

My practice flourished. . . . I was engaged to confine a woman
whom the Army doctor had warned not to have any more children, or
she would probably die in the attempt. She had given birth to three
girls and the desire, shared by herself and her husband, for a boy had
inspired her with the courage to defy the ultimatum.

She studied *Tautology,* a book widely read by expectant mothers at
that time, and followed its precepts closely. I have never been sure
how much of the credit for the successful outcome of that case should
be given to *Tautology* and how much to the instruction in prenatal
care that I had received in Toland Hall and the Children's Hospital.
At any rate, Aesculapius could not have sent me a greater boon than
that patient.

I was called. The woman passed through a normal, uneventful
labor, and was delivered of—another girl. I had hoped, as ardently as
the parents, for a boy, and sympathized with their disappointment.
But on examination, I found that the rotundity that disappears so
miraculously when the child is born still persisted. I smiled, remem-

bering the interne who had retired too soon. Without doubt there was another baby, and it might be a boy!

I remember going out to the father, sitting by the kitchen stove, holding his new little girl in his arms. "Don't be too disappointed," I said, "we might have a boy yet!" He looked up at me, entirely puzzled.

"What do you mean?"

"There is another baby, and it might be a boy."

I am sure that the father doubted that I knew what I was talking about. He may have experienced a pang of regret that he had placed his wife in the care of a person with such astonishing lack of the knowledge of the processes of nature. But the twin was born, and it was a boy. I needed no press agents. My patient who had been threatened with such dire misfortune if she ever tried to bring another child into the world had borne twins with no difficulty whatever! Everybody in the valley knew about it.

Where Twin Births Are Perfect Births

It becomes a welcome change then to find any peoples where twins and their mothers are honored, revered, and cherished. Robert Brain found such to be the case among the Bangwa and Dogon tribes of the Cameroon. There twin births are perfect births, the vestige of a primordial world where twins were the rule and single births the exception. In his classic work on the potentialities of human relationship, *Friends and Lovers,* Brain, who spent two years among the Bangwa, describes their approach to twins and twinship.

In Bangwa, a woman who gives birth to twins is fêted by the whole population rather than banished from the village. I have seen elaborate sculptures carved in honor of a mother of twins. Villagers bring her food and ask her blessing. A certain number of days after the birth she and the children are dressed in finery, decked out with beads, and paraded through the market where the people congratulate her on her good fortune and press coins into her hands. More than this, a mother of twins automatically becomes a member of a twin-mothers association and is called in to dance at important ceremonies and funerals. I once saw two hundred of these women dance at a chief's funeral. During fertility rites twin-mothers wearing their special insignia—beads, staffs, leaves—"cool the earth" and offer sacrifices. Twin-mothers are also the most popular diviners and priestesses; having given birth to "little gods" they are themselves in touch with the divine.

More wonderful than the mothers are the children, creatures to be feared as well as admired. They are demanding, selfish, and cantankerous—half human and half spirit. Most twins are thought to despise the world of humans and special rites are performed to accustom them to the rigors and tedium of a mortal life. . . .

Most interestingly, the Bangwa call twins "best friends." Best friends are known as "twins" and elevated to the miraculous status of the products of a dual birth. The Bangwa stress equality in friendship—both in "achieved" friendships (of the heart) and ascribed friendships (of the road)—and the relationship is allowed to cut across differences in rank. If a slave woman has a child at the same moment as the king's favorite wife gives birth, the two children are automatically, inexorably, best friends and twins. Nor is this a formality, since the friendship has its duties and obligations. As among the Kaguru, twins born of one womb are the complete expression of true equality and friends born at the same time approximate this two-in-oneness. Twins in Bangwa are the only persons in a kin group who are allowed to use each other's personal name in conversation and act in a friendly fashion. All other brothers and cousins use the term "elder relative" or "junior relative," since age differentiation is as important as social rank and is given full expression in etiquette.

Twins are best friends, therefore, because they are supremely equal and because they shared the same womb for nine months—or according to Bangwa folklore usually longer since twins are well known for having a much longer pre-natal life than ordinary children, roaming in and out of the womb for an indefinite period before finally consenting to being born. This spirit world of unborn children is described by Bangwa as a vast, black cave, peopled by the spirits of babies which float around in pairs and groups looking for suitable parents. The belief is that the supply of children is replenished by the spirits of dead Bangwa who are reincarnated in their descendants. Spirit children who are great friends and always in pairs are choosy about being born again; life with their friends in the spirit world is comfortable and moreover there is the danger of losing one's twin-friend during the journey, since it is rare for a spirit pair to agree to enter a single womb.

When twins are born a special ritual is immediately performed both to prevent the death of one of the parents or grandparents (thus correcting the imbalance in the spirit world) and to persuade the pair to accept their new life on earth. Even when a single child is born and shows a disinclination to live, he will be called a "twin." Since it is rare for a spirit pair to enter a single womb—tastes differ even in the world of unborn children—twins are often separated at the last minute. Or some may decide to enter a womb, remaining there quite a long time, before one of them is seduced back to the delights of the spirit world. This renegade torments his "friend," lurking in the shadows of the fire burning in the mother's hut, trying to make the child die and go away with him.

I once spent a whole day hearing of one old man's prenatal life. He spent long years traveling in the world of the spirits with his best friend and twin looking around for a luxurious home with agreeable, generous parents. Finally decided, the two entered the belly of a man—this man's father—and from there were eventually transferred in the latter's semen to the womb of his wife. Unfortunately his twin refused to accompany him at the last minute and, furious that he had been deserted, the unconceived child tormented his friend in the womb, bringing considerable strain and pain to the mother who suffered an agonizing pregnancy lasting two years. Toward the end the unconceived twin went so far as to hide in the woman's eyelid where he formed an ugly, swollen sty. Finally he-she left the pregnant woman's eye and entered the womb of a woman in a neighboring village who gave birth to a bouncing baby girl the day after the man whose interminable story I was hearing was born.

The point of this story is to show how . . . children who are born without a twin in Bangwa are considered, in a way, abnormal, at least more abnormal than twins in so far as they are born singly. The pairing of them with a friend of the same age removes any future danger of their being seduced back to the spirit world by a spirit friend or twin.

10. *Resisting*

My mother still thinks I would be happier if I settled down and had a baby.

Billie Jean King

Gloria Swanson: "The Greatest Regret of My Life"

Perhaps more than any other woman, Gloria Swanson personified the original Hollywood. She was part of the Charlie Chaplin-Mary Pickford-Douglas Fairbanks silent screen crowd; her favorite male lead was Rudolph Valentino. It was a time when movie stars were the American royalty and carried that aura with them from Hollywood to New York and across the Atlantic and back in the elegant first class staterooms of ships like the *Homeric* and the *Liberté*. Great crowds met them everywhere; they were pelted with flowers; their most trifling activities were recorded, with scant attention to accuracy, for an insatiable public.

This was Gloria Swanson's scenario in the 1920s and 1930s, and her personal life was nearly as flamboyant as her public one. She had six husbands interspersed with various lovers, most of whom exploited her shamelessly, Joseph P. Kennedy being no exception. One who did not, however, was her third husband, Henri, the Marquis de la Falaise de la Coudraye. This elegant but impoverished French aristocrat served as her translator in Paris during the filming of the otherwise forgettable *Madame Sans-Gêne*. Within weeks they were lovers, then engaged, but inevitably her marriages were held up while her latest divorce became final. In the meantime, she became pregnant.

Beautiful, clever, and entirely professional, Gloria Swanson was not always an appealing figure. One of her lovers referred to her as a "mental vampire," which is as good a characterization as any. Her saving grace was her honesty, her willingness to deal with the ambiguities of life—a trait abundantly apparent in her autobiography *Swanson on Swanson*, published only a few years before her death in 1983. In the following selections Swanson, the woman, already the mother of two, is set in opposition to Swanson, the star, in perhaps the most difficult decision of her life. She is twenty-five; the year, too, is 1925. In another couple of decades, for their own reasons, other movie stars would solve the situation differently. But Gloria's wrestling with her problem will strike a sympathetic note with other, less celebrated, women who also have been faced with the choice between the demands of a promising career and the fact of an unwanted pregnancy.

I spread my contract out before me on the table and turned to the morals clause.

". . . Provided, however, that in the event that at any time in the future . . . First Party shall be charged with adulterous conduct or immoral relations with men other than her husband, and such charges or any of them are published in the public press, the waiver herein contained shall be null and void and of no force and effect. . . ."

Technically, I had already broken the contract, but no one would know that if I married Henri immediately, which I could not do. Before my divorce from Herbert was final, as much as a month could go by. After that, it would be easily provable that I was pregnant when I married Henri, and in the eyes of the press and the public, that would be enough to finish me.

Moreover, if the press didn't destroy my career, Mr. Lasky could. If he didn't, however, he would be able to renegotiate my contract while holding all the trumps in his hand, because I would have broken my contract, with four pictures still to do in 1925. Mr. Lasky could therefore rewrite the contract on his terms, at his price. The awful part was that he could dictate terms to me just exactly at the point when I was at my peak, just exactly when he would otherwise have to accept any terms I chose to name—double my salary at least, plus many dividends.

By having Henri's child under the terms of my present contract, I would forfeit the chance to become one of the highest-paid performers in history. I would also, probably, lose Henri, because we had both gone past the stage where we could be happy in a garret.

By not having the baby, on the other hand, I could begin *The Coast of Folly* on schedule and complete my contract in a year, I could be free to dictate my own terms after that or leave Paramount altogether, and I could provide a rich, happy life for Henri and me.

The contract was a devilish trap. It always had been. But I had helped to build the trap by letting the studio persuade me not to sue Herbert for divorce but to wait until he sued me.

I knew I needed to confide in someone. I couldn't handle this decision alone. The person I trusted most was André Daven. I called him, and when he came to the house late in the afternoon, I showed him my contract and explained the awful dilemma. When I finished, I told him I thought I had to have an abortion.

André said, "You are absolutely right. The situation must be regularized. It is easier perhaps in Paris than in New York or California. You and Henri are both very young. You have all the time in the world to have another child."

The words went through me like an electric shock. . . .

"Have you told Henri?" André asked.

"I've told no one but you, André," I said. "I can't burden Henri with the price of my career. It would change our relationship totally."

"I know."

"But I just had to tell someone, André, that I have such a bad conscience about doing what I'm thinking of doing."

"You mustn't blame yourself," André said. "Leave it to me. I will arrange everything. I promise to get you the very best doctor in France. No one need ever know."

"There's no other way, is there?" I asked.

"Of course not, Gloria," he said.

His voice was reassuring, and I smiled feebly at him in gratitude. Then I heard another voice speaking very clearly. "Don't do this," it said.

The voice, I knew, was inside me. It was the voice of my unborn child. I tried not to listen.

"Your heart is pounding," the voice said. "I know you hear me. Listen to me. I want to live. I am frightened of the sewers."

I shuddered and started to sob convulsively. André came over and held me tightly in his arms. He didn't ask me what was wrong. He thought he knew. But of course he didn't know at all, and I could never tell him what I had just heard.

"I will arrange everything," he repeated. "Do not worry. You are doing the right thing. You are choosing for many people besides yourself."

When he had left, I pulled back the taffeta curtains in my bedroom and stared into the gray, foggy Paris dusk. A face was looking at me from the darkness. It was not a baby's face. I could not have stood that. It was the face of death, beckoning or warning, I couldn't tell which. . . .

By chance, Gloria and Henri are married only the day before the scheduled abortion, of which he knows nothing. She has warned him that she must be out much of the following day.

I wanted to go to sleep in Henri's arms. Instead he dozed off in mine. For me it was the longest, darkest night of the year, and the dawn was gray and bleak too, without a sliver of sunshine. I made a great effort not to waken Henri because I knew I couldn't trust myself to say good-bye. I hurried to put on a dress I had laid out the night before and slip out the door.

André was waiting downstairs. I could tell from the look of him that he hadn't slept either. I followed him to the car, and we drove most of the way to the doctor's without speaking. We took the elevator to the third floor of an elegant apartment building in which the doctor had his offices. In the waiting room, a nurse offered us chairs, and André sat me down and held my hands. He spoke to the nurse in French. She left the room, and when she returned she beckoned for me to follow her. André walked me down the hall to the last door, which the nurse and I entered. Inside the office she helped me off with my clothes and then helped me into a white hospital gown. She had me lie down on a table and she strapped my hands down and put my feet in some sort of stirrups. Then the doctor came in and spoke a few words of heavily accented English in a beautiful voice. He told me to breathe deeply, and as I inhaled the familiar ether, his voice faded to nothingness.

When I came to, André was with me. I could feel my hand in his. My wrists were free. He kissed me on the forehead. I knew from the pain that the awful deed was done. The nurse wanted to give me something for the pain, but I refused. No pill could remove the real pain I felt, of that I was sure.

They helped me to sit up. The nurse slipped on my shoes. I was surprised to find I could walk. The nurse spoke to André and he asked me if I wished to speak to the doctor.

"Oh, no, André," I whispered, "I can't. I don't want to see him."

André assured me he had taken care of everything. He had also telephoned Henri to tell him we would see him at the hotel sometime after lunch. He led me out to the car and took me for a long drive. When I felt recovered, we went back to the hotel.

The room was in chaos, and boxes and baskets of flowers lined the corridors in all directions. Both phones were ringing and cables were piled on the bed. Henri put down one phone long enough to kiss me and ask me if I'd had a good lunch. Jane West was on the other phone. She held her hand over the mouthpiece and said Paramount was furious they hadn't known about the wedding. They wanted to know if we would do it over again so they could film it. My name was on the front page of almost every paper in America.

I asked Henri if he had had lunch. He said no and kissed me again. Then I told André to take him to lunch at the Ritz and I told Jane to have the switchboard turn off the phones and go home. I said I was tired and needed a nap. They argued, but I pushed them out. I said they could all come back in two hours and we would start celebrating again with champagne. But first, I said, I had to have a little sleep. I locked the door after them. . . .

I was crying. There were four or five baskets of flowers in the room, mostly roses, and the sweet smell was almost unbearable, but I was too tired to put them out in the hall with the others. I pulled the shades and turned out the lights. Then I lay down on the bed, rolled over on my stomach, and buried my face in the pillow. . . .

As it turned out, the doctor had bungled the operation. By the next day Gloria was unconscious with fever. She was removed to the hospital where for weeks she lay between life and death. Daily reports of her condition filled the newspapers. At last she recovered, and she and Henri were able to board ship for the United States and the adulation that awaited them there.

Gloria and Henri never did have a child. More than a half century later she wrote at the close of her book:

. . . the greatest regret of my life has always been that I didn't have my baby, Henri's child, in 1925. Nothing in the whole world is worth a baby, I realized as soon as it was too late, and I never stopped blaming myself.

"I Don't Want Anyone To Know I'm in Labor"

Sarah LeVine was in southwestern Kenya from 1974–1976 as part of a field project on parenthood and child development; while there she conducted her own study of rural Gusii women of childbearing age. The following account of the second pregnancy and eventual delivery of Trufena Moraa is taken from her book *Mothers and Wives: Gusii Women of East Africa.*

As is the custom, Trufena lives surrounded by her husband's family and some distance from her own. Ombui is her husband; Francesca, her mother-in-law; Cecilia, Teresa, and Sabera, her sisters-in-law. Johnathan is her son. Mary is the author's assistant and, coincidentally, Trufena's aunt.

Ombui came home unexpectedly for a week's leave and during his stay he told his older brother, Mwamba, that Trufena was pregnant. Mwamba told Mary, who of course told me, a fine example of the indirect way by which news of pregnancy gets about among the Gusii. . . .

When we went to visit Trufena, I asked her laughingly, "When will you give birth?" In fact I had greeted her thus on two previous occasions and she had denied that she was pregnant, just as she did today. . . .

> "But why is your maternity dress hanging on your clothes line?" I ask. Then it becomes obvious that however lighthearted I might feel about the issue, Trufena feels very differently. She is extremely angry and upset. Mary says, "Why couldn't you tell us you were pregnant? When you knew you were pregnant with Johnathan, I was the first person you told." "I don't know if it is so." Trufena refuses to look at either of us. "I had a period last month!" "How could you have?" asks Mary. "You must be four months pregnant at least, or you wouldn't need a maternity dress. . . .

I believe Trufena denied to herself for a very long time that she was pregnant. I do not know whether she conceived without having menstruated after Johnathan's birth or whether she merely "forgot" she had had a period in order to discount the possibility of pregnancy. . . . Her failure to admit her condition to her family, to me, or even to herself must have reflected her ambivalence about her marriage as well as her shame at having two children so close together. . . .

When next I saw Trufena, she was in the fields harvesting finger millet. . . . I asked her whether her mother knew she was going to have another baby.

"Of course not! I haven't seen her since May, and I did not know I was pregnant then. I would not go to my home now. I would be ashamed to appear thus before my parents." . . . Traditionally married Gusii women were expected to experience *chinsoni* (shame) if they should be seen by their fathers or fathers-in-law when they were pregnant, but nowadays young women tended to be less self-conscious. Some reported to me that though they knew they should experience shame; nevertheless, they did not. "My father is used to me. So is my father-in-law." However, Trufena was not so emancipated. She was not prepared to risk being seen even by her mother (who would transmit news of the pregnancy to her father). . . . As far as I know Tru-

fena's mother never did know of this pregnancy until she received
news of the birth. . . .

As the weeks passed and Trufena got heavier and slower, she became moody and depressed. . . . Mary was terrified of the anger un-
derlying Trufena's depression. I had heard much about Trufena's
rudeness, her tantrums, the confrontations into which she forced her
husband's relatives. . . .

At no time did the consequences of her attitude and behavior re-
bound upon her more dramatically than the day on which she gave
birth to her second child. She had convinced me that she would give
birth at the end of November. She was not particularly large, and perhaps she really did not know when she was due. At any rate, in the
first week of October we went to visit her as usual and found her lying
on her bed.

> She gets up and walks into the *eero* [living room] where we are.
> "I was planting beans yesterday, and I'm very tired today. I was
> resting." As she sits she grimaces, and Mary exclaims in astonish-
> ment, "But you are in labor!" Trufena shakes her head. "How can
> I be? I am not due for months." She can barely speak; she is in
> the midst of a contraction.

Trufena, Mary her aunt, of whose jealousy Trufena is so afraid, and
I, the persistent meddling European, were all sitting at the table.
Trufena was in hard labor while denying this fact as vigorously as
she could through teeth clenched in pain. When the contraction
passed, she got to her feet and attempted to fill Johnathan's bottle.
This was the last thing she was able to do and at our urging went back
to bed. Meanwhile nothing was prepared. There was neither water
nor firewood in the house. Mary ran off to the river while I collected
wood from under the eaves and built a fire. Trufena lay mute upon
her bed a few feet away from me when Mary returned from the river.
We heated some water and washed Trufena's back and stomach. It
was a dark, cold afternoon, and we were crowded into a tiny window-
less space. Trufena was completely silent. It was as if there were only
two of us, not three.

> Since I have little experience in the delivery of babies and
> could scarcely be relied on as an assistant, I suggest that Francesca
> be summoned. Whereupon Trufena comes to life and calls out,
> "No, don't tell her! I don't want anyone to know I'm in labor!"

Mary convinces her that we must at least find someone to take care of Johnathan. Trufena eventually agrees that the message should be, "Trufena is sick because she worked too hard yesterday planting beans." Mary goes off to deliver this message, hoping to get Cecilia to come back with her; however, she returns with Teresa, the elder sister. Mary tells us, "Your mother-in-law says she cannot spare Cecilia. *She,* Francesca, is sick also. Mogaka beat her up last week and she is still stiff and sore. She sent Teresa instead." But Teresa, having washed a couple of plates, remarks, "There's nothing wrong with you, Trufena," and leaves summarily.

For a while we are alone again, but then Sabera appears, encumbered by her two small children. By now Trufena has shifted off her bed to a stool. Mary sits behind her on a paraffin tin, and whenever Trufena has a contraction, she reaches backward to grasp Mary round the neck. Mary tells Sabera to hold Trufena's legs apart, and Sabera obeys. However, after one or two contractions, she stands up. "Trufena is afraid." she says, meaning she, Sabera, is not prepared to continue the task, whereupon I am detailed to take her place, and Sabera retires thankfully to the living room on the other side of the matting partition. I hold Trufena's legs apart in case the baby is about to fall out. However, since it is quite dark and Trufena is mute, neither Mary nor I have any idea how imminent the delivery might be.

After what seems like a very long time, Francesca appears, reeking of beer. She brings with her two women who are classificatory mothers-in-law of Trufena. This means that they cannot enter the bedroom of their "son" Ombui, for to do so would be *emoma* [a violation of the laws of *chinsoni,* avoidance]. These two women, therefore, can be of no assistance unless Trufena moves into the living room, a more neutral space, which she shows no sign of being about to do. Francesca, who is also forbidden to enter her son's bedroom, looks around the partition and then retires to discuss noisily with the other women the details of their own multiple deliveries. . . .

Meanwhile I am handed a flashlight by Mary and told to see if the baby is crowning. All I see is the water bag bulging through the vaginal opening. . . . Suddenly Francesca appears in the bedroom, pushes Mary off her paraffin can and sits down in her place. She seizes Trufena, who moans, "Taata, Mama Ominto," that is, "Daddy, Mummy," in fear perhaps as well as pain. It seems obvious that Francesca is the last person Trufena wants helping her at the birth of her child. . . . She scolds Trufena, singing, "You are refusing to deliver, you are afraid! If you can't do your work alone, you must go to the hospital and ask for help." (I.e., what coward runs to the hospital?) . . .

Her [Francesca's] intoxicated state no doubt licenses her to be as hostile as she wishes. She yells repeatedly at Trufena to push, even though my periodic examinations indicate that the time for pushing has not yet come. From my vantage point at one extremity, I do my best to nurture Trufena by talking to her reassuringly, but I doubt if she hears anything I say. Sabera has vanished altogether, but the two older women are still chattering away in the living room and Francesca continues her songs. Trufena groans and writhes with the contractions but never cries out. After an hour or so Francesca announces abruptly that the baby is stuck. Trufena cannot deliver the child without help (i.e., she is a failure) and I should go to find the nurse who works with us on our project.

When we return with the nurse the scene is chaotic. There are many neighbors there. Everyone, regardless of *chinsoni* [shame], is now in the bedroom. They are yelling and beating Trufena, telling her to push. The baby's head is half out while Trufena lies limply in the arms of her mother-in-law. The older women are all arguing and pushing one another, behaving in effect as if none of them has ever been through this ordeal before. Sabera's four-year-old son George is stationed at Trufena's left foot, fascinated by what is going on between his aunt's thighs. No one pays any attention to him. Johnathan, who is being entertained by Cecilia, seems unperturbed by the excitement. Apart from George, no one is within arm's reach of Trufena's vagina. The women are all grouped around her head and shoulders. None shows the least intention of being ready to catch the baby. While I hold the flashlight, the nurse takes out the child and hands it to Mary. Immediately attention is focused entirely upon the child, a son, and Trufena is left in a naked heap by the fire, which has been allowed long ago to go out. Francesca leaps into a wildly erotic dance and appears not to hear when we ask for a razor blade with which to cut the cord. After five minutes a blunt one is brought from a neighbor's house, the cord is sawed through, and the baby is washed by the older women. No one does anything about finding a cloth in which to wrap him, and he lies squalling on Mary's lap. I search about in the boxes under the bed until I find a towel, and the baby is wrapped in that. Meanwhile, Trufena is sitting literally on top of the placenta, vainly trying to wipe her blood-streaked legs with a cloth she pulled out from beneath her mattress.

I left the house forty-five minutes after the baby was born, by which time the matting partition had been jerked down to make a bed for Trufena. She lay on it half covered with a blanket. The placenta was still lying on the hearth, and the fire was still unlit. I had bought some sodas and some tea in the market when I had gone to fetch the nurse. Trufena complained of thirst but was ignored. The other women drank all but one of the sodas, and while I was there no one lit a fire to make tea for Trufena. I urged Francesca to throw the placenta in the latrine, as it is customary to dispose of it there immediately, but we discovered later that it had remained in the house until morning.

I was rather shocked by this experience. For one thing, I had not expected Trufena to give birth so soon. Nor had I expected Francesca and Sabera's hostility toward Trufena to have been so obvious. . . . I wondered how Trufena perceived her experience, but when I later questioned her, she replied nonchalantly, "What else do you expect? Those old mothers always behave in that way."

Casanova as Knight, Seducer, Victim

Almost everything even remotely connected with sex passes at one time or another through the ten volumes of Casanova's *Histoire de ma Vie* (*The Memoirs of Jacques Casanova de Seingalt*), so the story of a beautiful young woman unwillingly pregnant should come as no surprise. The only shock is that the child is not Casanova's. This extraordinary Italian adventurer spent his life traveling about Europe supporting himself variously by writing, fiddling, gambling, spying, and conning those susceptible to his famous charm. He fathered an undetermined number of children and, in at least one case, unwittingly fathered upon her he had fathered. His greatest con was upon his readers who leaf avidly through his pages, consuming the comic, the sentimental, and the erotic alike, caring little where fact ends and fiction begins.

The story of Giustina Wynne, however, whom Casanova disguises here as "Mdlle X—— C—— V——," is known to be true in most of its particulars. She is English—pretty, inviting, and under the watchful eye of a dragon of a mother; Casanova has known them both previously in Venice. Now in Paris, she is about to be forced into marriage with a very rich and prominent old chevalier. What Casanova does not mention, but we know from other sources, is that the suspicious old man, hearing rumors of his fiancée's pregnancy, summons a police officer to come in and place his hand on her belly to determine the truth. Somehow Giustina manages to carry it off—although she is five months pregnant, the verdict is negative.

It is to Casanova, a friend of her lover (although this, too, is not mentioned in Casanova's version), that the poor girl turns for help. He promptly, and predictably, falls in love. For the several months in question he loves her ardently (sustained passion is not his *forte*) and gallantly contrives to rescue her from her situation, while at the same time vying for a share of her attractions. He is at once knight-in-shining armor, seducer, and victim—victim because she whom he loves loves another, and because his own nature allows him really to love only the inaccessible. But his account is, in any case, indicative of the plight of *la jolie demoiselle enceinte* in the beau monde of eighteenth century Paris.

The day after my long conversation with Mdlle. X—— C—— V——, my servant told me that there was a young man waiting who wanted to give me a letter with his own hands. . . . The epistle ran as follows:

"I am writing this at two o'clock in the morning. I am weary and in need of rest, but a burden on my soul deprives me of sleep. The secret I am about to tell you will no longer be so grievous when I have confided in you; I shall feel eased by placing it in your breast. I am with child, and my situation drives me to despair. I was obliged to write to you because I felt I could not say it. Give me a word in reply."

My feelings on reading the above may be guessed. I was petrified with astonishment and could only write, "I will be with you at eleven o'clock." . . .

"Yes," said I to myself, "she can count on me. Her mishap makes her all the dearer to me."

And below this there was another voice, a voice which whispered to me that if I succeeded in saving her my reward was sure. I am well aware that more than one grave moralist will fling stones at me for this avowal, but my answer is that such men cannot be in love as I was.

I was punctual to my appointment. . . . As soon as we were alone she said to me. . . .

"I am four months with child; I can doubt it no longer, and the thought maddens me!"

"Comfort yourself, we will find some way to get over it."

"Yes; I leave all to you. . . . I have not told anybody but you, not even the author of my shame. I tremble when I think what my mother would do and say if she found out my situation. I am afraid she will draw her conclusions from my shape . . . every day increases its size, and for that reason we must be quick in what we do. . . . What I should like you to do would be to take me to a midwife's. We can easily go without attracting any notice at the first ball at the opera."

"Yes, sweetheart, but that step is not necessary, and it might lead to our betrayal."

"No, no, in this great town there are midwives in every quarter, and we should never be known; we might keep our masks on all the time. Do me this kindness. A midwife's opinion is certainly worth having."

I could not refuse her request, but I made her agree to wait till the last ball, as the crowd was always greater, and we had a better chance of going out free from observation. I promised to be there in a black domino with a white mask in the Venetian fashion, and a rose painted beside the left eye. As soon as she saw me go out she was to follow me into a carriage. . . .

On the night of the last ball she recognized me as we had agreed, and followed me out into the coach she saw me enter, and in less than a quarter of an hour we reached the house of shame.

A woman of about fifty received us with great politeness, and asked what she could do.

Mdlle. X—— C—— V—— told her that she believed herself pregnant, and that she desired some means of concealing her misfortune. The wretch answered with a smile that she might as well tell her plainly that it would be easy to procure abortion. "I will do your business," said she, "for fifty louis, half to be paid in advance on account of drugs, and the rest when it's all over. I will trust in your honesty, and you will have to trust in mine. Give me the twenty-five louis down, and come or send tomorrow for the drugs and instructions for using them." . . .

"If madame decides on taking your advice," said I, "I will bring you the money for drugs tomorrow."

I gave her two louis and left. Mdlle. X—— C—— V—— told me that she had no doubt of the infamy of this woman, as she was sure it was impossible to destroy the offspring without the risk of killing the mother also. "My only trust," said she, "is in you." I encouraged her in this idea, dissuading her from any criminal attempts, and assured her over and over again that she should not find her trust in me misplaced. . . .

We separated at the opera, and the vast crowd made me lose sight of her in an instant. Next day she told me that she had danced all night. She possibly hoped to find in that exercise the cure which no medicine seemed likely to give her. . . .

The difficulties I encountered only served to increase my love for my charming Englishwoman. I went to see her every morning, and as my interest in her condition was genuine, she could have no suspicion that I was acting a part, or attribute my care of her to anything but the most delicate feelings. For her part, she . . . was now six months with child, and as her figure grew great so did her despair. She resolved not to leave her bed, and it grieved me to see her thus cast down. . . . She spoke of killing herself in a manner that made me shudder, as I saw that she had reflected on what she was saying. I was in a difficult position when fortune came to my assistance in a strange and amusing manner.

One day, as I was dining with Madame d'Urfé, I asked her if she knew of any way by which a girl, who had allowed her lover to go too far, might be protected from shame. "I know of an infallible method," she replied, "the aroph of Paracelsus to wit, and it is easy of application. Do you wish to know more about it?" she added; and without waiting for me to answer she brought a manuscript, and put it in my hands. This powerful emmenagogue was a kind of unguent composed of several drugs, such as saffron, myrrh, etc., compounded with virgin honey. To obtain the necessary result one had to employ a cylindrical machine covered with extremely soft skin, thick enough to fill the opening of the vagina, and long enough to reach the opening of the reservoir or case containing the foetus. The end of this apparatus was to be well anointed with aroph, and as it only acted at a moment of uterine excitement it was necessary to apply it with the same movement as that of coition. The dose had to be repeated five or six times a day for a whole week. . . .

I resolved to tell her of my discovery, hoping she would need my help in the introduction of the cylinder. I went to see her at ten o'clock, and found her, as usual, in bed; she was weeping because the opiate I gave her did not take effect. I thought the time a good one for introducing the aroph of Paracelsus, which I assured her was an infallible means of attaining the end she desired; but whilst I was singing the praises of this application the idea came into my head to say that, to be absolutely certain, it was necessary for the aroph to be mingled with semen which had not lost its natural heat.

"This mixture," said I, "moistening several times a day the opening of the womb, weakens it to such a degree that the foetus is expelled by its own weight."

To these details I added lengthy arguments to persuade her of the efficacy of this cure, and then, seeing that she was absorbed in thought, I said that as her lover was away she would want a sure friend to live in the same house with her, and give her the dose according to the directions of Paracelsus.

All at once she burst into a peal of laughter, and asked me if I had been jesting all the time. . . .

"If you wish," said I persuasively, "I will give you the manuscript where all that I have said is set down plainly."

I saw that these words convinced her; they had acted on her as if by magic, and I went on while the iron was hot.

"The aroph," said I, "is the most powerful agent for bringing on menstruation." . . .

She was silent for some time, for though she was quick-witted enough, a woman's natural modesty and her own frankness, prevented her from guessing at my artifice. I, too, astonished at my success in making her believe this fable, remained silent.

At last, breaking the silence, she said, sadly,—

"The method seems to me an excellent one, but I do not think I ought to make use of it." . . .

> As time passes, however, and her mother is after her to sign the marriage contract and be measured for her wedding dress, the desperate girl agrees to try the aroph after all, with Casanova's aid. He arranges with her maid for the use of an attic room in her house, and makes his own way there surreptitiously one evening at ten.

I was in a cloak, and carried in my pocket the aroph, flint and steel, and candle. I found a good bed, pillows, and a thick coverlet—a very useful provision, as the nights were cold, and we should require some sleep in the intervals of the operation.

At eleven a slight noise made my heart begin to beat—always a good sign. I went out, and found my mistress by feeling for her, and reassured her by a tender kiss. I brought her in, barricaded the door, and took care to cover up the keyhole to baffle the curious, and, if the worse happened, to avoid a surprise.

On my lighting the candle she seemed uneasy, and said that the light might discover us if anybody came up to the fourth floor.

"That's not likely," I said: "and besides, we can't do without it, for how am I to give you the aroph in the dark?"

"Very good," she replied, "we can put it out afterwards."

Without staying for those preliminary dallyings which are so sweet when one is at ease, we undressed ourselves, and began with all seriousness to play our part, which we did to perfection. We looked—I like a medical student about to perform an operation, and she like a patient, with this difference that it was the patient who arranged the dressing. When she was ready—that is, when she had placed the aroph as neatly as a skull-cap fits a parson—she put herself in the proper position for the preparation to mix with the semen.

The most laughable part of it all was that we were both as serious as two doctors of divinity.

When the introduction of the aroph was perfect the timid lady put out the candle, but a few minutes after it had to be lighted again. I told her politely that I was delighted to begin again, and the voice in which I paid her this compliment made us both burst into laughter. . . .

My situation was a peculiar one, for though I was in love with this charming girl I did not feel in the least ashamed of having deceived her, especially as what I did could have no effect, the place being taken. . . . She often told me during our nocturnal conversations that she was happy and would continue to be so, even though the aroph had no effect. Not that she had ceased to believe in it, for she continued the application of the harmless preparation till our last assaults, in which we wanted in those sweet combats to exhaust all the gifts of pleasure. "Sweetheart," said she, just before we parted finally, "it seems to me that what we have been about is much more likely to create than to destroy, and if the aperture had not been hermetically closed we should doubtless have given the little prisoner a companion."

A doctor of the Sorbonne could not have reasoned better.

Three or four days afterwards I found her thoughtful but quiet. She told me that she had lost all hope of getting rid of her burden before the proper time. All the while, however, her mother persecuted her, and she would have to choose in a few days between making a declaration as to her state and signing the marriage contract. She would accept neither of these alternatives, and had decided on escaping from her home, and asked me to help her in doing so. . . .

Casanova asks advice of a certain Madame du Rumain who some days later informs him of the following:

"After I had pondered over the case of conscience you submitted to me, I went to the convent of C—— where the abbess is a friend of mine, and I entrusted her with the secret, relying on her discretion. We agreed that she should receive the young lady in her convent, and give her a good lay-sister to nurse her through her confinement. Now you will not deny," said she with a smile, "that the cloisters are of some use. Your young friend must go by herself to the convent with a letter for the abbess, which I will give her, and which she must deliver to the porter. She will then be admitted and lodged in a suitable chamber. She will receive no visitors nor any letters that have not passed through my hands. . . . I had to tell the abbess the lady's name, but not yours as she did not require it.

"Tell your young friend all about our plans, and when she is ready come and tell me, and I will give you the letter to the abbess. Tell her to bring nothing but what is strictly necessary, above all no diamonds or trinkets of any value. You may assure her that the abbess will be friendly, will come and see her every now and then, will give her proper books—in a word, that she will be well looked after. Warn her not to confide in the lay sister who will attend on her. I have no doubt she is an excellent woman, but she is a nun, and the secret might leak out. After she is safely delivered, she must go to confession and perform her Easter duties, and the abbess will give her a certificate of good behaviour; and she can then return to her mother, who will be too happy to see her to say anything more about the marriage which, of course, she ought to give as her reason of her leaving home." . . .

After leaving Madame du Rumain I went straight to Mdlle. X—— C—— V—— . . . I gave her all the instructions . . . and we agreed that she should leave the house at eight o'clock with such things as she absolutely required, that she should take a coach to the Place Maubert, then send it away, and take another to the Place Antoine, and again, farther on, a third coach, in which she was to go to the convent named. . . .

"I will set out," said she, "the day after tomorrow at the hour agreed upon." And thereupon . . . we embraced each other tenderly, and I left her. . . .

Three or four days after this date, Madame du Rumain gave me the first letter I received from Mdlle. X—— C—— V——. She spoke in it of the quite life she was leading, and her gratitude to me, praised the abbess and the lay-sister, and gave me the titles of the books they lent her, which she liked reading. . . . I was delighted with her letter, but much more with the abbess's epistle to Madame du Rumain. She was evidently fond of the girl, and could not say too much in her praise, saying how sweet-tempered, clever, and lady-like she was, winding up by assuring her friend that she went to see her every day.

I was charmed to see the pleasure this letter afforded Madame du Rumain—pleasure which was increased by the perusal of the letter I had received. The only persons who were displeased were the poor mother . . . and the old *chevalier,* whose misfortune was talked about in the clubs, the Palais-Royal, and the coffee-houses. Everybody put me down for some share in the business, but I laughed at their gossip.

Emma Goldman: "I Did Not Know How To Help Them"

Emma Goldman was a Russian-born immigrant best remembered for her activities in the anarchist movement prior to World War I and for her deportation back to Russia and subsequent disillusionment with the Bolshevik government. Less well known are her early activities as a midwife among the New York immigrant subculture and her outspoken advocacy of birth control, for which she was imprisoned in 1916. In the following selection from her autobiography *Living My Life,* she describes her first midwifery case and the desperate struggles of the poor against repeated pregnancies.

. . . a violent ring brought me to my feet. It was a call to a confinement case. I took the bag which I had been keeping ready for weeks and walked out with the man who had come for me.

In a two-room flat on Houston Street, on the sixth floor of a tenement-house, I found three children asleep and the woman writhing in labour pains. There was no gas-jet, only a kerosene lamp, over which I had to heat the water. The man looked blank when I asked him for a sheet. It was Friday. His wife had washed Monday, he told me, and all the bed-linen had got dirty since. But I might use the table-cloth; it had been put on that very evening for the Sabbath. "Diapers or anything else ready for the baby?" I asked. The man did not know. The woman pointed to a bundle which consisted of a few torn shirts, a bandage, and some rags. Incredible poverty oozed from every corner.

With the use of the table-cloth and an extra apron I had brought I prepared to receive the expected comer. It was my first private case. . . . Late in the morning I helped to bring the new life into the world. . . .

My profession of midwife was not very lucrative, only the poorest of the foreign element resorting to such services. Those who had risen in the scale of material Americanism lost their native diffidence together with many other original traits. Like the American women they, too, would be confined only by doctors. Midwifery offered a very limited scope; in emergencies one was compelled to call for the aid of a physician. Ten dollars was the highest fee; the majority of the women could not pay even that. But while my work held out no hope of worldly riches, it furnished an excellent field for experience. It put me into intimate contact with the very people my ideal strove to help and emancipate. It brought me face to face with the living conditions of the workers, about which, until then, I had talked and written mostly from theory. Their squalid surroundings, the dull and inert submission to their lot, made me realize the colossal work yet to be done to bring about the change our movement was struggling to achieve.

Still more impressed was I by the fierce, blind struggle of the women of the poor against frequent pregnancies. Most of them lived in continual dread of conception; the great mass of the married women submitted helplessly, and when they found themselves pregnant, their alarm and worry would result in the determination to get rid of their expected offspring. It was incredible what fantastic methods despair could invent: jumping off tables, rolling on the floor, massaging the stomach, drinking nauseating concoctions, and using blunt instruments. These and similar methods were being tried, generally with great injury. It was harrowing, but it was understandable. Having a large brood of children, often many more than the weekly wage of the father could provide for, each additional child was a curse, "a curse of God," as orthodox Jewish women and Irish Catholics repeatedly told me. The men were generally more resigned, but the women cried out against Heaven for inflicting such cruelty upon them. During their labour pains some women would hurl anathema on God and man, especially on their husbands. "Take him away," one of my patients cried, "don't let the brute come near me—I'll kill him!" The tortured creature already had had eight children, four of whom had died in infancy. The remaining were sickly and undernourished, like most of the ill-born, ill-kept, and unwanted children who trailed at my feet when I was helping another poor creature into the world.

After such confinements I would return home sick and distressed, hating the men responsible for the frightful condition of their wives and children, hating myself most of all because I did not know how to help them. I could, of course, induce an abortion. Many women called me for that purpose, even going down on their knees and begging me to help them, "for the sake of the poor little ones already here." They knew that some doctors and midwives did such things, but the price was beyond their means. I was so sympathetic; wouldn't I do something for them? They would pay in weekly installments. I tried to explain to them that it was not monetary considerations that held me back; it was concern for their life and health. I would relate the case of a woman killed by such an operation, and her children left motherless. But they preferred to die, they avowed; the city was then sure to take care of their orphans, and they would be better off.

I could not prevail upon myself to perform the much-coveted operation. I lacked faith in my skill and I remembered my Vienna professor who had often demonstrated to us the terrible results of abortion. He held that even when such practices prove successful, they undermine the health of the patient. I would not undertake the task. It was not any moral consideration for the sanctity of life; a life unwanted and forced into abject poverty did not seem sacred to me. But my interests embraced the entire social problem, not merely a single aspect of it, and I would not jeopardize my freedom for that one part of the human struggle. I refused to perform abortions and I knew no methods to prevent conception.

I spoke to some physicians about the matter. Dr. White, a conservative, said: "The poor have only themselves to blame; they indulge their appetites too much." Dr. Julius Hoffmann thought that children were the only joy the poor had. Dr. Solotaroff held out the hope of great changes in the near future when woman would become more intelligent and independent. "When she uses her brains more," he would tell me, "her procreative organs will function less." It seemed more convincing than the arguments of the other medicos, though no more comforting; nor was it of any practical help. Now that I had learned that women and children carried the heaviest burden of our ruthless economic system, I saw that it was mockery to expect them to wait until the social revolution arrives in order to right injustice. I sought some immediate solution for their purgatory, but I could find nothing of any use.

A Discreet Kind of Anti-Maternity Movement in Seventeenth Century France

They never spoke of being pregnant. Like their Victorian sisters two centuries later, they avoided so explicit a term. The ladies of seventeenth century French society suffered from what they called "the ill effects of lawful love"—and they rebelled. They became fugitives from maternity.

No such notion would have occurred to their grandmothers. During the reign of the bluff, gallant old Henri IV, whose second wife, Marie de'Medici, produced seven children in ten years, and who left behind more bastards than anyone thought politic to record, pregnancy was the accepted state of feminine existence. The only reliable form of birth control was war, which kept the average French nobleman away from home a good part of the year. Besides, childbearing was strongly encouraged. Child mortality was high. In aristocratic circles, where the continuation of the line was the primary if not the only object of marriage, a large family was the best insurance. Children were valued for what they represented. Wives were esteemed as the means to the end.

But after Henri's death in 1610 the tenor of life in the French court changed. Louis XIII was nothing like the virile figure his father had been. On the contrary, he was startlingly unwilling to attend to his obvious dynastic duties. Toward the end of his life he did father two sons, the elder of whom, Louis XIV, inherited the throne at five. A long regency was followed by a groping, tentative rule before the young king finally asserted himself. In 1660 he married, and once again there emerged in France a royal role model as husband and father. But for fifty years that position was vacant.

An early response to the situation came from the Marquise de Rambouillet. Catherine de Vivonne-Savelli had married at the tender age of twelve; at thirty-five she was still beautiful in spite of seven children, which was, she decided, enough. Her social life was what interested her now. All kinds of delightful people frequented her celebrated sky-blue drawing room. The ladies were charming, the men attentive, the conversation elegant, if at times banal. Noblemen learned to discard their rough language with their muddy boots before entering. Poets read their latest verses praising the virtue of the ladies, many of whom had chequered pasts, but all of whom acted with extreme decorum in Madame de Rambouillet's *chambre bleu*.

Understandably, the Marquise was not about to allow yet another pregnancy to interfere with such pleasures. In the next—the eighteenth—century, she and the Marquis would long before have come to an understanding. But the seventeenth was not so cynical. The Marquise needed an excuse, and she settled on the precarious state of her health. It was hard to define exactly what was wrong—an aversion to heat was the most overt symptom—but it was enough for her to take to her bed.

She had it placed in a little alcove off the *chambre bleu,* convenient for intimate visits from those guests otherwise milling about in the main salon. As society came to accept her "illness," her husband (who adored her, in any case) did, too. He attended to her needs and no longer bothered her with his own. The Marquise lived on, presumably in bed, to the ripe age of seventy-seven.

Thus did Madame de Rambouillet simultaneously initiate a discreet kind of anti-maternity movement and a new trend in entertaining. To receive *au lit* became *très chic.* Any lady looks to advantage lying against drapings of satin and brocade. It had not necessarily anything to do with sex: members of the sisterhood were always fully clothed. The point was to transcend rather than invite fleshly passion. A lover lurking in the shadowy corners was always a welcome accessory, but the love engendered was often as not limited to verbal declarations. Conversation, not consummation, was the essential element of life.

As the disciples of the Marquise advanced in the development of their cerebral natures, they enlarged the distance between themselves and their functions as wives and mothers. They could no longer reconcile their poetic sensibilities with, for example, morning sickness. Pregnancy made them captive to their physical state. If in spite of their abhorrence it happened anyway, they made the best of it by welcoming their friends to their bedsides. The clumsiness of their figures was less obvious there, and once the baby was born, they could lie in almost indefinitely. If one were a clever manager, one need hardly miss a single *petite poème* or a *soupçon* of gossip.

We should not malign the ladies unfairly. Their resistance to childbearing was also occasioned by their experience of it, which, in that particularly bloody century, was always distressing and frequently harrowing. But one could not call a halt until that healthy male heir had been provided. Take, for example, Madame de Rambouillet's good friend Charlotte, the Princess de Condé, often considered the most beautiful woman in France. Her husband, first cousin to the king, plotted against his highness, was caught, and landed in Vincennes prison. They had already been married seven years with no issue (because, it was whispered, Condé was a notorious sodomite). Most of her friends considered the turn of events in the princess's favor, but Charlotte thought over the matter, went to the queen-regent, and appealed to be allowed to join her husband in prison to provide for the perpetuation of the Condé line. The queen acquiesced. Since prison life offered fewer diversions, the prince fell into line and in less than three years time Charlotte delivered a premature baby and twins, all three of whom died, produced a daughter who lived, and conceived a son who was born after his father's release. Once free, Condé returned to past habits, but the next generation had been accounted for.

Finally, there is in every group such as the one that gathered regularly in the *chambre bleu* the odd man out. In this case, the odd lady, and very odd she was. The Comtesse de Clermont d'Entragues was not part of the sisterhood of maternity escapees because childbirth presented no trauma for her. Apparently her pregnancy advanced to its final month before she recognized its first symptom. A plain and pious lady, she felt unwell one morning, called for the apothecary, and was amazed when he diagnosed her queasy stomach as labor pains. The midwife barely had time to arrive before the baby was born, strong and healthy. By all accounts of the time, the Count de Clermont d'Entragues was as astonished as his wife, and the blessed event was the subject of comment for at least a week at the *chambre bleu*.

The Ik: Childbearing in a Collapsed Society

With some cultures the old childbirth customs are not merely outmoded, they have become actively contrary to the interest of mother and child. The anthropologist Colin Turnbull found such to be the case with the Ik tribe in mountainous Uganda (bordering Kenya and the Sudan). In his book *The Mountain People* Turnbull describes the change in the Ik people over several generations from a vigorous hunting and gathering tribe of nomads who lived in sympathetic harmony with their surroundings, to a corrupted, victimized, de-humanized race among whom survival of the fittest had become tribal law.

Restricted by modern conservationists to an area much too small to support them, and thereby suffering gradual and inevitable starvation, the Ik have seen their entire family and tribal structure collapse. Turnbull could find left only a few vestiges of normal human caring among husband and wife, brother and sister, even parent and child. He notes the time-honored childbirth taboos—intercourse forbidden during pregnancy, the wife exhorted not to lie on her back or look up at the apex of the roof for fear her child would be born blind, the husband denied entry into the house for a week after the birth. He remarks on the traditional invitation to the paternal grandparents to come see the newborn, the ceremonial quaffing of millet beer at the naming ceremony, the consultation with the priest over which foods should be taboo for the child and which for the mother.

But these were the old ways of a more prosperous, family-oriented time. Now, as Turnbull points out,

. . . not only the recommended actions are fantastic, so are the concepts involved. To suggest to a starving people that they should carefully select their foods, rejecting some and limiting the intake of others, is not likely to make much sense. A mother in labor, racked by the additional pains of hunger, thirst and fever, is not going to listen with much sympathy if you tell her not to lie in the one position in which she can get a moment's respite, least of all if you say the consequence is that a child whom she does not particularly want and is likely to die soon anyway will be born blind. As for calling in a priest or inviting grandparents to stay, with what are such visitors to be fed and compensated, and for doing what?

> But surprisingly, not only were such ritual observances recited many times to Turnbull as being in common usage, he even saw them all, at one time or another, being practiced. No matter how impractical they had become, they retained some measure of validity in the Ik mind. Parental concern may no longer extend much beyond the infant stage—the same child who half a century before had remained within the family circle until puberty, is now put out at the age of three (four at the latest) to fend for itself. Most mothers still make the attempt to succor the baby, but once at large with members of his or her own age group, the Ik child has to grope for new attachments. If a girl, and if she survives to young womanhood, she can count on no more than a repetition of the cycle—intercourse without love, marriage (if at all) without ritual, childbirth with the old fears and dangers intact, but with no family structure within which to rear, nurture, and cherish the child.

Virginia Woolf on Flush: "For a Whole Fortnight He Fell into Deep Melancholy"

Flush: A Biography is Virginia Woolf at her most light-hearted. It is the portrayal of a segment of the life of Elizabeth Barrett, both before and after her marriage to Robert Browning, from the perspective of her little spaniel, Flush. Actually, it is that and more—it is also Flush's story of his own world, from the green fields of the English countryside, to the dim interiors of 50 Wimpole Street, London, and finally to the sun-splashed rooms, streets, and markets of Florence. It was there at the Casa Guidi that Flush was "thrown back on his haunches" by the sense that something momentous was about to occur.

At first it was nothing—a hint merely—only that Mrs. Browning in the spring of 1849 became busy with her needle. And yet there was something in the sight that gave Flush pause. She was not used to sew. He noted that Wilson moved a bed and she opened a drawer to put white clothes inside it. Raising his head from the tiled floor, he looked, he listened attentively. Was something once more about to happen? He looked anxiously for signs of trunks and packing. Was there to be another flight, another escape? But an escape to what, from what? There is nothing to be afraid of here, he assured Mrs. Browning. They need neither of them worry themselves in Florence about Mr. Taylor [an evil man who had abducted Flush in London] and dogs' heads wrapped up in brown paper parcels. Yet he was puzzled. The signs of change, as he read them, did not signify escape. They signified, much more mysteriously, expectance. Something, he felt, as he watched Mrs. Browning so composedly, yet silently and steadfastly, stitching in her low chair, was coming that was inevitable; yet to be dreaded. As the weeks went on, Mrs. Browning scarcely left the house. She seemed, as she sat there, to anticipate some tremendous event. Was she about to encounter somebody, like the ruffian Taylor, and let him rain blows on her alone and unaided? Flush quivered with apprehension at the thought. Certainly she had no intention of running away. No boxes were packed. There was no sign that anybody was about to leave the house—rather there were signs that somebody was coming. In his jealous anxiety Flush scrutinised each new-comer. There were many now— Miss Blagden, Mr. Landor, Hattie Hosmer, Mr. Lytton—ever so many ladies and gentlemen now came to Casa Guidi. Day after day Mrs. Browning sat there in her armchair quietly stitching.

Then one day early in March Mrs. Browning did not appear in the sitting-room at all. Other people came in and out; Mr. Browning and Wilson came in and out; and they came in and out so distractedly that Flush hid himself under the sofa. People were trampling up and down stairs, running and calling in low whispers and muted unfamiliar voices. They were moving upstairs in the bedroom. He crept further and further under the shadow of the sofa. He knew in every fibre of his body that some change was taking place—some awful event was happening. So he had waited, years ago, for the step of the hooded man on the staircase. And at last the door had opened and Miss Barrett had cried "Mr. Browning!" Who was coming now? What hooded man? As the day wore on, he was left completely alone. He lay in the drawing-room without food and drink; a thousand spotted spaniels might have sniffed at the door and he would have shrunk away from them. For as the hours passed he had an overwhelming sense that something was thrusting its way into the house from outside. He peeped out from beneath the flounces. The cupids holding the lights, the ebony chests, the French chairs, all looked thrust asunder; he himself felt as if he were being pushed up against the wall to make room for something that he could not see. Once he saw Mr. Browning, but he was not the same Mr. Browning; once Wilson, but she was changed too—as if they were both seeing the invisible presence that he felt.

At last Wilson, looking very flushed and untidy but triumphant, took him in her arms and carried him upstairs. They entered the bedroom. There was a faint bleating in the shadowed room—something waved on the pillow. It was a live animal. Independently of them all, without the street door being opened, out of herself in the room, alone, Mrs. Browning had become two people. The horrid thing waved and mewed by her side. Torn with rage and jealousy and some deep disgust that he could not hide, Flush struggled himself free and rushed downstairs. Wilson and Mrs. Browning called him back; they tempted him with caresses; they offered him titbits; but it was useless. He cowered away from the disgusting sight, the repulsive presence, wherever there was a shadowy sofa or a dark corner. ". . . for a whole fortnight he fell into deep melancholy and was proof against all attentions lavished on him"—so Mrs. Browning, in the midst of all her other distractions, was forced to notice. And when we take, as we must, human minutes and hours and drop them into a dog's mind and see how the minutes swell into hours and the hours into days, we shall not exaggerate if we conclude that Flush's "deep melancholy" lasted six full months by the human clock. Many men and women have forgotten their hates and their loves in less.

But Flush was no longer the unschooled, untrained dog of Wimpole Street days. He had learnt his lesson. Wilson had struck him. He had been forced to swallow cakes that were stale when he might have eaten them fresh; he had sworn to love and not to bite. All this churned in his mind as he lay under the sofa; and at last he issued out. Again he was rewarded. At first, it must be admitted, the reward was insubstantial if not positively disagreeable. The baby was set on his back and Flush had to trot about with the baby pulling his ears. But he submitted with such grace, only turning round, when his ears were pulled, "to kiss the little bare, dimpled feet," that, before three months had passed, this helpless, weak, puling, muling lump had somehow come to prefer him, "on the whole"—so Mrs. Browning said—to other people. And then, strangely enough, Flush found that he returned the baby's affection. Did they not share something in common—did not the baby somehow resemble Flush in many ways? Did they not hold the

same views, the same tastes? For instance, in the matter of scenery. To
Flush all scenery was insipid. He had never, all these years, learnt to
focus his eyes upon mountains. When they took him to Vallombrosa
all the splendours of its woods had merely bored him. Now again,
when the baby was a few months old, they went on another of those
long expeditions in a travelling carriage. The baby lay on his nurse's
lap; Flush sat on Mrs. Browning's knee. The carriage went on and on
and on, painfully climbing the heights of the Apennines. Mrs. Browning was almost beside herself with delight. She could scarcely tear
herself from the window. She could not find words enough in the
whole of the English language to express what she felt. . . . But the
baby and Flush felt none of this stimulus, none of this inadequacy.
Both were silent. Flush drew "in his head from the window and didn't
consider it worth looking at. . . . He has a supreme contempt for
trees and hills or anything of that kind," Mrs. Browning concluded.
The carriage rumbled on. Flush slept and the baby slept.

11. Feigning / Fantasying

I used to dream of having a child. Dreams are like pictures. I would dream of being on a beach with a little boy beside me. Inside my head I could see it. A picture of me, a man and a child. . . .

Children are very important, but a woman is still a woman, even if she never has children. She's a woman as long as she loves someone. A selfish old woman with an old cat is still a woman and goes on having imaginary children.

Francoise Sagan, *Night Bird*

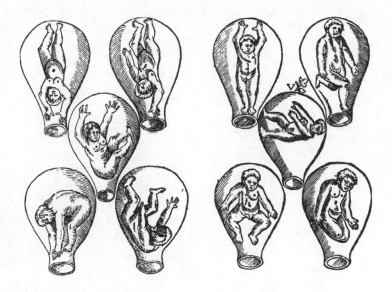

Mary Tudor: The Queen's Belly Expanded
But No Baby Came

"In this kingdom," said Simon Renard, Ambassador to England from the Holy Roman Empire, "the Queen's lying-in is the foundation of everything."

Renard's prediction was by no means an overstatement. He was referring to Mary Tudor, Henry VIII's older daughter, who ruled England for five years after the death of her brother Edward VI in 1553. In 1554 she married Philip II of Spain. Had she, as she so ardently wished, borne a child, and the child been baptized Catholic and lived to rule, England might have completed its return to the Church and continued Catholic to this day. The whole course of European history would, without question, have been greatly altered. But although the Queen's belly expanded and the royal cradle lay ready, no baby came. A phantom pregnancy can produce no more than a phantom child, and only a real child can succeed to the throne.

The marriage of Philip and Mary took place in July; by autumn the Queen was sure she was pregnant. On the 24th of November, the day that marked Cardinal Pole's return from exile and England's return to the Catholic fold, Mary reported feeling the child "quicken and leap in her womb." By her calculations the baby would be due the following April, and it was in that firm belief that she went, at the beginning of that month, to Hampton Court to prepare for her lying-in. All over England the people waited with expectation and concern for the news of the royal birth.

The concern was real despite the fact that the marriage was itself unpopular. Mary had been betrothed to a variety of men—beginning with the little Dauphin of France when she was two and he a babe still in the cradle—and any one of them would have been more popular than Philip. A Spaniard on the English throne was almost unsupportable. But Mary, once the choice was hers—and despite the fact that he was more than ten years her junior—would have no other. Spain had been her beloved mother's country; Spanish, the language she spoke as easily as her own. So the event had taken place, and afterward had come that unexpected dividend; the Queen, at thirty-eight, by contemporary description "not at all beautiful, small, and rather flabby," had fallen passionately in love with her husband.

So to the political and religious considerations for having a child was added a personal one. Mary wanted to give birth not just to a Catholic heir, but to Philip's child. In the furthest recesses of her mind she could remember a time when her father, at about Philip's age, had borne her about in his arms and spoken with tenderness to her mother. That was before Anne Boleyn had come to court. Mary yearned to retrieve something of that familial feeling. She longed to devote herself to this man who returned her passion with a deferential courtesy that she willingly misread as love. She ached to be pregnant, to bear his child (which she imagined blond and blue-eyed like him), and thus to reconcile her people to Philip, to the Spanish marriage, and to a Catholic England.

Hampton Court, where the Queen retired, had been built by Cardinal Wolsey and completed by Henry VIII, and reflected the lack of restraint in both their natures. The palace was a profusion of gilded medallions, terra-cotta escutcheons of arms, and crocketed pinnacles sporting an entire menagerie of beasts in painted wood or stone. The interior was resplendent with its brilliantly painted Great Hall and long windowed gallery with ceiling of burnished gold. There Mary retreated at the beginning of April, and there gathered numerous noble- and gentle-women from all parts of England who either wanted to be present out of love for the Queen, or felt it impolitic to be absent. There, too, waited the doctors and midwives, nurses and cradle-rockers, ready to serve.

These people spoke positively and encouragingly to the Queen as the days passed, but out of hearing some were less optimistic. Mary was now thirty-nine—middle-aged by the standards of the day—and not in good health. There were whispers that it was, after all, "only a tumor, as often happens in women," and someone (who was paid 200 crowns in gold) assured the French ambassador that the Queen's doctor said that on what she ate she could not have kept a bird alive. But Mary heard none of this. When days passed with no indication of oncoming labor, there was always someone handy to comfort and reassure her.

One day a woman of the neighborhood much like Mary in size and age, if not in rank, gave birth to healthy triplets. The babies were brought to the palace for the Queen to see, to give her heart that all things were possible. Then on the last day of April the rumor got out—no one knew how—that the Queen had given birth to a fine son, and in London there was much ringing of bells and drinking of toasts before it could be officially denied. The word even leaped the Channel. In Brussels, too, people celebrated for several days before the refutation arrived.

After the first week in May the Queen, becoming daily more anxious, would hardly leave her chamber. The Venetian ambassador, who on May 15 had written home of the "swelling of the paps and emission of milk," by the 21st was reporting ominously that "Her Majesty's belly" had "greatly declined." Doctors and midwives vied in their calculations and prognostications. Apparently the moon was a governing factor. The Queen could now expect to deliver either at the new moon—May 23—or after the full moon on June 5th. But both dates passed uneventfully.

With June began prayers and processions for the Queen's delivery. But the scuttlebutt was otherwise. Most pernicious was the story that certain persons were scouting for a suitable child to spirit into Hampton Court on a dark night and "have delivered" of the Queen. Years later, after verification was no longer possible, a man named John Foxe declared that on Whitsunday (June 11th that year) Lord North and a friend had asked one Isabel Malt to give over, for goodly recompense, her newly born son Timothy, and to deny ever after that she had borne any such child, but that doting Isabel had not complied. Mary, however, was honesty incarnate; it is unlikely she would have supported such subterfuge had the question been raised with her. And the cradle remained empty.

June advanced to July. The daily walks had ceased now, and Mary no longer moved busily about her rooms, but sat for long hours on a cushion on the floor, knees drawn up to her chin—a position that would have been impossible for a nine-month gravid woman. But even after most of the inhabitants of Hampton Court had begun to believe they were taking part in an elaborate, if unplanned, charade, Mary would not quite relinquish hope. When from Brussels the English ambassador reported rumors that the Queen was not pregnant after all, she had the Council forward an official contradiction, which they did although privately and individually they wrote their true minds— that the poor Queen was greatly deceiving herself.

The tragi-comedy (for it had elements of both) went on through July and into the first week of August. Then without explanation it was announced that the Court was moving to Oatlands. Oatlands was a smallish, unprepossessing house. There would be no accommodation for doctors, midwives, nurses, and cradle-rockers there. It was a way of saying that the Queen was facing reality at last.

Not long afterward Philip left England "for a fortnight"—a month at most. Mary went with him as far as Greenwich, and on the last morning they walked side by side through the chambers and long galleries of the palace there. At the head of the stairs leading to the wharf, as the French ambassador later recorded, the Spaniards who were accompanying him kissed her hand, and Philip kissed each of her ladies in turn. After that he "took his leave of her and went down to the barge." She never saw him again.

The Queen took up her old life again. She read her dispatches, dictated letters, received ambassadors, attended Mass. She kept close beside her—in those three sad years that she had yet to live—a woman of hers, Mistress Frideswide Strelly, the only one of her intimates who had never professed to believe in the pregnancy. "Ah, Strelly, Strelly," she said, "I see they be all flatterers, and none ever true to me but thou."

Mimicking Childbirth

Feigning childbirth has had prescribed ceremonial uses from ancient times. Diodorus Siculus, a contemporary of Julius Caesar and rival historian, tells us that the "barbarians" (meaning practically everyone of his day not Greek or Roman and therefore not civilized) employed it as a way of publicly recognizing adoption, and such usage has continued in various parts of the world down to the twentieth century. In Turkey and Bulgaria when a couple wished to adopt a son, the wife would pull the boy up under her dress, press him to her, and then push him out below. The adopted mother among the Dyaks of Borneo seated herself on a high chair in front of the assembled company while the adopted child crawled backward through her legs. In a similar version practiced by the Berawans of Sarawak (Malaysia), a woman adopting a grown man or woman would prepare a feast for the people of the village and then seat herself on a kind of bench with legs spread so that her adopted son or daughter might crawl through from behind. As soon as he or she appeared on all fours in front of the woman, the adopted person would be tied to the new mother and the two, thus united, would waddle clumsily the length of the room and back again in front of the assembled guests. The new relationship was thus formally recognized.

Similar imitations were performed in ancient Greece and India when a man thought to be dead, and who had been given a proper funeral *in abstentia,* suddenly reappeared alive and well. Symbolically, he had to be reborn. In Greece he was passed ceremoniously across a woman's lap, after which he was washed, wrapped in swaddling bands, and "put out to nurse." In India a tub was filled with a mixture of water and fat, and there he had to spend the first night after his return, doubled up in the position of a child in a womb, not speaking, while the sacraments ordinarily performed over a pregnant woman were performed over him. In the morning he was officially reborn, but in order to return to the state he had been in when he "died," he had to repeat all the ceremonies that he had gone through from boyhood on, including remarrying his old wife (were she still available).

But the most widely practiced ceremony of childbirth was, and still is, the one employed by a woman who has been unable to conceive. There are a number of variations on the basic theme; the one practiced in the Babar Archipelago goes like this: A couple who have tried unsuccessfully to have a child sit together, the woman holding in her arms a red cotton rag doll and pretending to nurse it. A man who is the father of many children has been invited to take part; he prays to Upulero, the spirit of the sun, asking him to grant the woman fertility. Then he takes a chicken, and holding it upside down by its legs close to the woman's head, asks Upulero to make use of the fowl and let a child fall into his hands. After some period of entreaty, he asks the woman if the child has come, and she replies, "Yes, it is already sucking." Then the father-of-many-children moves to the husband, holds the fowl above his head, and intones again to Upulero. Finally, the chicken is killed and laid with some betel on the home altar. The ceremony is thus concluded, and as word circulates that the woman has been confined, her friends in the village gather to congratulate her. The hope is that by mimicking childbirth and offering sacrifice, the symbolic will become reality and the woman will conceive.

The success-failure rate is not known.

The Curious Custom of Couvade

The fantasy of the couvade—that curious practice by which during childbirth the father takes to his bed and affects to be in labor himself—is intriguing for the very universality of the impulse behind it. Herodotus mentioned it among African tribes of his day. Diodorus observed it among the Corsicans in the first century B.C., and his contemporary Strabo saw it practiced among the Celto-Iberians of Spain. (Persons familiar with the Basques of the Pyrenees say it goes on there still.) Marco Polo reported it among the mountain tribes of the Miautse. In fact, couvade either has until recently or still exists in societies, both cultured and uncultured, in Sibera, the Malay Archipelago, Africa, China, India, Europe, and South America.

Although in many primitive cultures the mother will give birth alone, the couvade is never known to be a solitary occupation. At the first sign of labor pains in his wife, the husband will retire to his bed, hammock, mat, or whatever, where he will lie moaning and writhing and carrying on generally, always well within hearing. Usually he will require considerable attention—warm compresses, cool cloths, and the like. After the birth he will take on the same restrictions, dietary and otherwise, assumed by his wife, often considerably more than his wife, and until he has had his ritual bath (perhaps hours, perhaps weeks after the birth), he will consider himself, like her, unclean and unfit to return to normal existence.

To some extent the couvade may be the mere attention-getter it appears, but it exists on deeper levels as well. The father is attempting to establish a fundamental connection with his child. In many cultures he will already have sought this during the long months of gestation. If he is Chinese, for example, he will have avoided any violent movement that might be felt by the embryo in his wife's body. If Jambin, he will forgo fishing, because to stir the sea with the beating of the oars would have a like effect on the fecund waters of the womb. A Philippine father will abstain from sour fruit because it might give his unborn child a stomach ache; a Borneo man will not use a cork for fear of making the child constipated. Men in Malaya will kill no animals nor use a knife or sharp implement for any purpose for fear of injuring their unborn child.

These, of course, are taboos imposed by the culture; more interesting are the involuntary sensations experienced by men in contemporary Western society. It is not at all uncommon for a man to go through a pregnancy with his wife in a quite literal fashion. In analyses of her male patients Karen Horney was surprised to find repeated cases in which intense envy of pregnancy and childbirth was expressed. British psychiatrist W. H. Trethowan found that one man in seven suffers pregnancy symptoms—nausea and vomiting, craving for a particular food, even abdominal swelling and toothache—along with his wife. The acceptance of this phenomena was underscored in an episode of the recent popular television comedy $M*A*S*H$ when surgeon Henry Blake in Korea undergoes various physical symptoms in identification with his pregnant wife back home.

From the ailments of pregnancy to the couvade is a short step, but the couvade is seldom, if ever, involuntary. It is interesting that it occurs almost exclusively in matriarchal societies, almost as if the father were doing everything in his power to establish his own claim to the child which would otherwise be negligible. The Swiss historian J. J. Bachofen, who made extensive studies of the couvade in the nineteenth century, believed it to be essentially a "birth-giving gesture" on the part of the father who found mere procreation emotionally insufficient, and who sought to share the birth experience to bind himself more closely to his child. The anthropologist Malinowski extended that idea one step further to imply a desire for a mystical connection. Austrian sociologist Richard Thurnwald differentiated between the usual couvade and the "real couvade," in which the father was not acting, but actually felt the birth pangs. The Celts in Ireland were known to practice this kind of couvade for centuries. The idea was that all pain would be transferred from the wife to the husband; for it to work the husband had willingly to consent to take on the pain. The eighteenth century Welsh naturalist Thomas Pennant believed that was what he was observing when he reported: "I saw the progeny of such a childbed come into this world gently, without causing his mother the slightest inconvenience, while her poor husband roared with pain in a strange, unnatural anguish."

Two final interpretations of the couvade should not be neglected. One is an outcome of Freudian psychoanalysis; the other, of the feminist movement. In the former theory man, instead of duplicating the actions of the woman in giving birth, is simulating those of the child in being born. Man's real desire, said Freud, is to return to the womb, and his moans and contortions are thus portrayed as his enactment of his own birth relived. This suggestion skirts dangerous areas, since metaphorically it turns the wife into the mother, but in a matriarchal society the lines are fudged in any case.

In the feminist theory, the father practices the couvade out of "womb envy" or "parturition envy." He fantasies the birth process from an overwhelming unconscious wish actually to be able to give birth—to become a mother—to be, in fact, a woman rather than a man.

Joanna Southcott: Delusions of Procreative Grandeur

Joanna Southcott was an ordinary English woman with delusions of procreative grandeur. Born in 1750, she never married but at the age of forty-two announced that it was she who was referred to in the twelfth book of Revelations:

And a great portent appeared in heaven, a woman clothed with the sun, with the moon under her feet, and on her head a crown of twelve stars; she was with child and she cried out in her pangs of birth, in anguish for delivery. . . . She brought forth a male child, one who is to rule all the nations with a rod of iron, but her child was caught up to God and to his throne, and the woman fled into the wilderness, where she has a place prepared by God, in which to be nourished for one thousand two hundred and sixty days. . . .

An apparently charismatic prophetess, Joanna attracted thousands of followers. Quite a cult formed around her. At the age of sixty-four—perhaps surmising that if she were ever to fulfill her prophecy, the time had come—she announced that she was with child and would give birth on October 19, 1814, to a second Prince of Peace. Her belly and breasts enlarged and she felt, she said, movements of the child inside her. Several doctors of repute examined her and confirmed her pregnancy. Her disciples (reports number them over a hundred thousand) awaited the day with reverent awe, but Joanna merely fell into a trance and died two months later. A post-mortem was performed, revealing that she had no tumor of any kind, and was, as she had claimed, a virgin. But faith defies fact. Many of her followers remained true; they were not yet quite extinct at the beginning of the twentieth century.

Rere-ao-toki-poki

The following popular Easter Island story was told to Alfred Metraux as if it had only recently occurred; he included it in his *Ethnology of Easter Island* (1971).

A woman named Rere-ao slept with her husband but saw that she would never have a child. One day she noticed a woman who was pregnant. She pretended to be pregnant too. She also pretended to suffer when the pregnant woman felt the first pains of labor. The other woman gave birth to a child. Rere-ao said to the midwives, "You stay here. I must go out to defecate." She went to the house of the woman to whom the child had been born. She said, "Give me this child. I want to suckle it." The woman passed the child to her and she stole it. She put it in front between her tapa skirt and her waist. Then she returned to her house and said to the women sitting there, "Hurry and take my child." They came to deliver the child and it was born from the front part of her bosom. The real parents looked for their child who had been stolen by Rere-ao. They came to the house of Rere-ao and said, "The child is ours. Why did you steal him?" Then they said to the people, "She only pretended to have a child and for that reason she has taken our child. She is Re-ao, stealer of the child." The parents took their child back, and thereafter the people made fun of Re-ao and called her Rere-ao-toki-poki (Rere-ao-the-stealer-of-the-child).

A Pregnant Princess Must Marry—Soon

Eleanor, youngest daughter of King John, was born in 1215, that same year in which the nobles gathered and forced her father to sign the Magna Carta. At the unripe age of nine she was married off to the Earl of Pembroke (an advanced thirty-two). The marriage was child-less. When the Earl died seven years later, the young widow, deter-mined to forestall another arranged match, took a vow of chastity before the Archbishop of Canterbury and, without formally entering a convent, put on her finger a ring to symbolize her marriage to Christ.

But Eleanor soon found the quiet life not to her taste. She began to visit her older brother's court—Henry III was now king—and at the celebration of his marriage at Canterbury in 1236, she met one Simon de Montfort, a twenty-eight-year-old French baron come to England to press his claim to the earldom of Leicester. Simon had a practiced French charm about him that the rough English barons lacked. He laid seige, and Eleanor capitulated with hardly a struggle. But what to do about—(a) the fact that she was the king's sister while Simon was neither royal nor English, and (b) that troublesome chastity vow?

The lovers conferred and reasoned the obvious: if Eleanor were with child, the world, including the English nobility and clergy, must ac-cept the *fait accompli* of a broken vow and a French father. It would not be necessary to wait until pregnancy were certain. The merest hint that such might be the case with a royal princess would be more than adequate to promote a hasty marriage with the king's blessing.

So Eleanor feigned pregnancy, and during Christmas court at Westminster, she and Simon were secretly married in the king's private chapel. Of course, word leaked out. The local barons, who had thought her off-limits because of her vow, were incensed, and the clergy was outraged. The archbishop took it as a personal affront. To amend matters, Simon, that spring, established his supposedly *très enceinte* wife at Kenilworth Castle and sailed to Rome with a suitable hoard of treasure to beg the pope for a dispensation to Eleanor's vow.

The trip was predictably successful. Less easily explained was the fact that although Simon did not return to England until October, he was in plenty of time to attend the birth of his son in November, a full eleven months after the precipitate wedding at Westminster. Now it was the king's turn to be affronted. But Simon and Eleanor, ever the resourceful pair, named the baby Henry for the king, who eventually not only forgave them but rewarded them with Kenilworth Castle for their own.

Drs. Breuer and Jung: Pregnancy as Wish Fulfillment

In 1882 in Vienna a young patient of Dr. Josef Breuer imagined herself in the throes of childbirth in consequence of her treatment for hysteria. A generation later another young woman in Zurich fantasied herself pregnant with the child of her doctor, C. G. Jung. Both were, by chance, brilliant and in many ways remarkable women whose deepset longings to have a child by the man to whom they had entrusted their very souls augured what would later become a not uncommon dilemma in the psychoanalytic world.

Breuer's patient was Bertha Pappenheim, a member of a wealthy Jewish family of Frankfurt, who later became a noted philanthropist, social reformer, and outspoken denouncer of Naziism. For a long time her identity was guarded; in *Studies in Hysteria,* the first book on psychoanalysis, published jointly by Breuer and Sigmund Freud in 1895, she appears under the pseudonym of Anna O. Anna/Bertha was twenty-one when she first came under Breuer's care. She was suffering from partial paralysis, poor vision, inability to hear or speak, cough, and headaches—typical hysteria symptoms she had acquired during the time she was nursing her terminally ill father. Under hypnosis, she was encouraged to talk about experiences from her past that were connected with her various symptoms, to remember the first time the symptom had appeared and what emotional state had provoked it. In each case, when she awoke, the symptom had vanished.

But the treatment had its own side effects. Over the course of a year and a half Breuer visited his patient almost daily, toward the end, twice a day. Only forty himself, he became very fond of this beautiful young girl who was so intelligent, spoke four languages fluently, and while under hypnosis spun stories of such charm and imagination. He could not help but be aware that her attachment to him, especially after her father's death, was sufficiently intense to give cause for some alarm, but he was also aware that this very attachment was making the cure possible. Where previous doctors had failed, he was succeeding. The "talking cure," as Anna herself named it, was working.

Breuer's wife, however, became jealous of the time he spent at the Pappenheim residence. For her sake he was glad when he could pronounce the patient "cured." One morning she bade him a cheerful—and final—farewell; that evening he was hurriedly summoned again to her bedside. He found her thrashing about in the apparent agonies of childbirth. Through clenched teeth she gasped that the baby was coming—"Dr. Breuer's baby!" Breuer's first reaction was astonishment; his second, panic. Never for a moment had he expected a denouement such as this. Mindful of his wife, his children, his solid reputation as Vienna's leading physician, he controlled his own emotions long enough to hypnotize his patient back into a sleeping state, impressing upon her that when she awoke she would remember it all as an imaginary experience. Then he escaped. They never met again.

Few doctors today would find Bertha Pappenheim's reaction particularly upsetting, or even surprising, but for some time Breuer could not speak of her at all, in spite of the quite amazing cure he had effected. Five months later he mentioned the case to a young colleague, Sigmund Freud. It did not take Freud long to recognize that Breuer had made a revolutionary discovery in the treatment of hysteria. It was Freud who later concluded that "hysterics suffer mainly from reminiscences"—reminiscences that grow out of situations where the person had felt an urgency to act but had repressed the feeling. And although Breuer never wanted to discuss what had happened that last fateful night in his patient's room, Freud gathered enough details from that and subsequent observations of his own to theorize the process of "transference."

During psychoanalysis, Freud said, a patient will "transfer" to the psychoanalyst any number of emotions—love, hate, fear—that originally he felt for his father or mother. Clearly Bertha Pappenheim—Anna O.—had a "repressed attachment" to her father, and the stresses of nursing him as he lay dying left her particularly vulnerable. In her case, said

Freud, "after the work of catharsis had seemed to be completed, the girl had suddenly developed a condition of 'transference love'," which her fancies had then carried to the next logical step of pregnancy and childbirth.

Anna O./Bertha P. spent some time in a sanitarium, but she recovered and returned to Frankfurt to take on a varied career in social philanthropy. Although she worked extensively with orphans, she never married or had children of her own.

Jung's patient had more substantial cause for her fantasies.

The case of Sabina Spielrein, herself a pioneer in psychoanalysis, has come to light only recently with the publication of some of her newly discovered papers by Jungian psychoanalyst Aldo Carotenuto (*A Secret Symmetry*, 1982). The eldest child of a well-to-do Russian Jewish family, Sabina suffered as an adolescent from what was diagnosed as either "a schizophrenic disturbance" or "severe hysteria with schizoid features." Her parents took her to the famous Burghölzli mental hospital in Zurich for treatment, where she became quite possibly the first patient on whom Jung himself tried psychoanalysis. Apparently he had some success, for she had been in Zurich less than a year when she enrolled as a medical student at the university, continuing her treatment with Jung as an outpatient.

She was eighteen or nineteen when the treatment began. Jung was thirty, and married. He was apparently strongly attracted to her from the start; if one can advance anything in Jung's defense, it would be that Sabina Spielrein was a formidable personality to have as a first patient. He may never again in his long career have had another so highly intelligent, intuitive, and articulate. Over the seven approximate years of their relationship, she came to exercise a pivotal influence on his thinking; they also fell in love. Like Breuer before him, Jung did not know what to do with such feelings. He simply capitulated. Somewhere along about the middle of the analysis, they became lovers, and from their letters and the diary that Sabina kept at this time, it is clear that she loved him deeply and passionately. She began to fantasy having a child by him—a gloriously exceptional son whom (she was a devoted Wagnerian) they would call Siegfried.

There are many references to Siegfried in the diary and letters. In the beginning he is their child; later, a paper she has written that she sees as a product of their combined thinking; later yet, as she moved away from Jung and closer to Freud, a new psychoanalytic approach combining Freud's and Jung's theories. In 1912, feeling (with good reason) betrayed by Jung both personally and professionally, she severed their relationship. The following year she married.

Nearly five years passed. Then late in 1917 Sabina resumed a correspondence with her old analyst-lover, whom she now addresses formally as "Dr. Jung" where before he had been "dear one." She writes
primarily of psychoanalytic matters but, perhaps despite herself, the
phantom Siegfried keeps reappearing. In one letter she informs Jung
that Freud, with whom she is also in correspondence, agrees with her
interpretation of Siegfried as "a fulfillment of the wish to create a
great Aryan-Semitic hero"—her fantasy of the child she had wanted to
have with Jung. In another letter she speaks of Freud cautioning her,
"You could have the child, you know, if you wanted it, but what a
waste of your talents." For herself, however, she "came to recognize
that the long-suppressed demands of my nature had a right to exist."

Sabina becomes pregnant, but Siegfried has not yet quite finished
with her. She writes to Jung, referring back first to her early birth
fantasy, then to an intermediate stage during which Siegfried took on
various disguises, and finally to the point at which she began to dream
of the child directly. After she becomes pregnant in all actuality, she
finds that in her mind the real and imagined child are locked in a
bitter struggle, each seeking the promised life.

> My subconscious *thinking* and *feeling* were influenced by you to
> such a degree that I thought to find a solution to the Siegfried
> problem in the form of a real child. The subconscious was not
> taken in by this putative possibility for realization and advised
> me to put up no resistance, since one could only regard this ten-
> dency as a "higher" one. The realization of my dream was blocked
> by the difficulties of everyday life. The "real" Siegfried complex
> therefore had to be drained of its energy and in order to keep this
> energy alive, it had to be channelled into another task, that of the
> "Siegfried" in sublimated form. What this new "Siegfried" is—I
> do not know. Strange to say, I no longer dream of "Siegfried" . . .
> No—that is not quite true! He appeared once more in a dream
> during my pregnancy, when I was in danger of losing my baby.
>   . . . until I had gone through many, many analyses I never
> dreamed of "Siegfried" directly. It was sometimes a candle (light)
> which you gave me, sometimes a book which grew with colossal
> speed, sometimes there were dreams containing elements of Wag-
> ner's *Siegfried,* sometimes music, sometimes prophetic dreams and
> prophecies which only yielded "Siegfried" as a real child upon be-
> ing subjected to analysis. Not until I was in Vienna did I begin to
> dream of the child directly, and even then not quite directly, since
> it was not a child born to us; rather, sometimes I was Siegfried in
> disguise, sometimes it was an Aryan-Semitic minstrel, Aoles; some-
> times a song implied that it was a child born out of wedlock and

deserted by its father, whom it resembled down to the slightest feature. Life arranged things in such a way that Siegfried was lived out in another way. . . .

As you know, I have already written to you that during my pregnancy I almost lost my daughter, simultaneously with or as a result of the appearance of a powerful Siegfried dream. Finally my child proved victorious in reality, and I called her Renate, as another dream instructed me. Siegfried was vanquished. But is he dead?

12. *Politicizing*

It is fraudulent to maintain that through maternity woman becomes concretely man's equal. The psychoanalysts have been at great pains to show that the child provides woman with an equivalent of the penis; but enviable as this manly attribute may be, no one pretends that its mere possession can justify or be the supreme end of existence. There has also been no dearth of talk about the sacred rights of the mother; but it is not as mothers that women have gained the right to vote, and the unwed mother is still in disrepute; it is only in marriage that the mother is glorified—that is, only when she is subordinated to a husband.

Simone de Beauvoir, *The Second Sex*

Children More or Less, Mostly Less

There was a time in the ancient world when everybody was having children, and then there was a time when people wanted to, but seemed not to be able to. They had done their best to keep the population down, but it had gone down too far, and they couldn't bring it back up again. Sparta, Athens, Rome—each in its turn was affected.

The most common and effective form of birth control was the practice of exposing a newborn child on a bleak hillside. In Sparta, after the sixth century B.C., every boy baby was examined at birth by a committee of "elders" who determined whether he was, or was not, likely to grow up into good soldier material. If not, out he went. In Athens and other Greek city states, one son per family was considered preferable to keep the patrimony together, and one daughter, or at most two, all that was necessary to provide company for the house-bound wife. Any child after that was an "extra" and likely to meet the common fate. Similarly, in the Rome of the Republic and early Empire, exposure was the conventional way of dealing with an unwanted child. In Roman society a father chose a wife for his son, but a son could select his own mistress; many young men therefore avoided marriage all together. Because it was a nuisance for one's mistress to have a child, much less keep it, such babies were taken to the hills as a matter of course—as, for that matter, were the children Roman wives routinely bore to their gladiator lovers.

But all this paring down of the population at will had its consequences. By the fourth century B.C., Spartans were becoming concerned about their dwindling numbers. Two centuries later, when all that was left of the battered Greek city states had fallen to Rome, the wealthier Greeks, who had deliberately limited their family size in order to maintain their standard of living, found that disease and war could play havoc with family planning. The upper class, from which came the administrators and officers for the army, was rapidly becoming extinct.

Rome, too, had not become the supreme power of the world without paying for it—more often than not with the lives of prospective fathers. The ruling class came to realize that a concerted effort was needed to arrest the downward trend of the male population. For some time there had been fewer and fewer legitimate Roman children being born. Smaller families were more—civilized. Then, too, many Roman men spent the major part of their wives' childbearing years on military campaign in distant lands. If Rome were to have the manpower to rule the world for generations to come, some changes would have to be made.

A few leaders (and their wives) tried to set an example. In 131 B.C. the censor Q. Metellus Macedonicus adopted a positive course; he strongly urged young men to marry and have children. He and his wife had six. Cornelia, wife of Tiberius Sempronius of the famous Gracchus family, gave birth to twelve, although few survived to adulthood. Marc Antony surpassed himself. He was never very interested in his children, but he was reassured by frequent proof of his virility. He started off with two children by his Roman wife Fulvia. After his long Egyptian campaign he left Cleopatra carrying what would be twins, and returned to Rome where, after Fulvia's death, he married the recently widowed Octavia. Her brother, Octavian, divorced his second wife and married Livia. Both brides were noticeably pregnant with the offspring of their late husbands and had to sit down through much of the ceremony. When Octavia's child was born, a girl, her new father named her Antonia after himself, and when the next year Octavia bore his child, also a daughter, he named her, too, Antonia. After having made Octavia once again pregnant, Antony left for the East. The East, of course, meant Cleopatra. He joined her in Antioch, and, as if Roman and Egyptian matrimony could exist in legal juxtaposition, he married her at once and made her, too, again pregnant. After that he left on campaign. After that, in his view, it was always a woman's matter.

Although few others were quite so flamboyant, later Roman rulers also did their part for the population gap. Germanicus and Agrippina (the elder) had nine children. Faustina (the younger) had at least twelve, most of whom are credited to her husband, Marcus Aurelius, and Vistilia, mother-in-law to Caligula, had children by each of six successive husbands.

But such fecundity was not the norm among the Roman aristocracy.

Much more common were marriages with a single issue, or none at all. Julius Caesar married Cornelia (Cinna's daughter) when he was about eighteen; they had one child—Julia. Although famous for his sexual prowess, Caesar had no children by either his second wife, Pompeia, or his third, Calpurnia, and the child he is reputed to have had by Cleopatra (the unlucky Caesarion) was probably not his. Augustus Caesar (Octavian) followed the same pattern: one daughter by his first wife in his youth, but none by his second or by Livia, his third. Nero had only one child, also a daughter, who died at four months. Trajan had no children. Hadrian had no children. And yet despite the poor example their leaders were setting, the Roman people all through this period were being exhorted to marry and have children for the good of the state.

Whether this dearth of empiric offspring was due to chance or to some as-yet-unascertained cause has never been determined. We know very little of the personal lives—much less the gynecology—of Pompeia or Calpurnia, of Livia, of Poppea or Statilia Messalina (Nero's wives) or Plotina (Trajan's) or Sabina (Hadrian's). We are unaware whether they had stillborn children, or suffered miscarriages, or simply never conceived. We do not know what percentage of the upper classes suffered the same sad childlessness, or to what extent the afflictions sifted downward to the common people. (It would be interesting to speculate whether or not the high preponderance of lead present in the water might have played a factor).

It was Augustus who first made an effort to reverse the trend. Assuming that when family limitation was by choice, it was due to economic reasons, he announced that three children was the minimum size for a proper family, and initiated legislation awarding a children's allowance to poor parents. Subsequent rulers provided similar incentives. A mother, if she was a slave, became free with the birth of her third child; the father, if he was in public life, received an automatic promotion. These were the standards within the city; outside Rome the advantages commenced with four children, and in the provinces with five. It is probably safe to conclude that the legislation was at least somewhat effective—that fertile couples had larger families than they might have otherwise—but the matter nevertheless inspired a certain cynicism. "People marrying and breeding," Plutarch observed wryly, "not in order to produce heirs, but in order to qualify for inheritance."

There were limits, however, to the state's powers of intervention. There always are. Simple human emotions get lost in the retelling, but they do exist. Even when Rome was at its most decadent, parents could be found who kept and cherished all their children, and some husbands and wives remained deeply attached to each other. A certain Roman wife known to history as Turia is an example. While a young woman, engaged, her fiancé away on campaign, her parents were murdered and she had to bring the culprits to justice herself and then to thwart the attempts of others to deprive her of her inheritance. No sooner had her fiancé returned and the marriage taken place than Julius Caesar was assassinated, and her young husband, a Republican, managed to escape death only through her brave endeavors. She shared his exile; later Octavius granted him pardon, but Lepidus refused to honor it until she had degraded herself before him in a most humiliating manner. After this the couple managed to live their private life in comparative peace, but no children came of the marriage. Turia assumed, as did all women of the time, that the fault lay with her. She suggested to her husband that he divorce her and take another, younger, wife who could provide him with heirs. She asked only to be allowed to live nearby and serve as a second mother to his children. His response, preserved in his eulogy to her on her death, reassures us that conjugal love and loyalty were not unknown commodities in Rome. "I must admit," he said, "that at this I exploded; I went out of my mind; I was so horrified by your suggestion, that I could scarcely pull myself together. The very idea of your even imagining the possibility of ceasing to be my wife, when you had once clung so firmly to me when I was an exile, and as good as dead. How could having children matter to that degree?"

"Our Women Fruitful"

"Our Land free, our Men honest, and our Women fruitful," was a popular slogan used to entice emigrants to the New World. Why the colonial female should be any more procreatively inclined than her European counterpart is not entirely clear, but it did appear to be the case. And men approved. That such propaganda should have been thought an inducement to women is more mysterious, since it was an accepted fact that the average man ran through more than one wife in his lifetime. Counterbalancing the effect of such unpleasant demographics, however, was the prospect that when a wife died, that husband needed another—few women in the New World lacked mates.

If the case histories themselves had been more faithfully broadcast, women considering emigration for marital purposes might have thought twice about the matter. For example, in the early days of the Virginia settlement John Thruston, age twenty-three, married Thomasine, a widow and already mother of three. Together they produced sixteen children in as many years. Then Thomasine died, let us not ask of what, and before two months were out, John remarried. Wife Number Two bore John eight more, making, by his own reckoning, "12 sons and 12 daughters." Clearly, if a man had dynastic inclinations, and a woman sacrificial ones, Virginia was the place to go.

Among prominent Virginians of the next (eighteenth) century, William Byrd III and Robert "King" Carter both had five children by their first wives and ten by their second. Warner Washington had sixteen by two wives and Charles Carter, twenty-three. John Page had twelve children by his first wife and eight by his second, while his son Mann, with but one wife, had fifteen. Chief Justice John Marshall was the eldest of fifteen children, and "Parson" Weems (inventor of the George Washington cherry tree story), the youngest of nineteen. Matters in the Carolinas were no different: Anthony Alexander had nine sons and eight daughters living when he made his will, George Moore's offspring numbered twenty-seven, and Thomas Smith fathered an even ten by each of his two wives.

These were not, remember, the poor Irish Catholics of another century to come. These were the ruling families, the aristocrats of the land, mostly Protestant, God-fearing and good-faring men and women whose plantations easily accommodated as many offspring as came along. The women, too, seemed often to feel fecundity desirable. Martha Jefferson Randolph, living mostly at Monticello with her father, was the mother of twelve children, and Martha Laurens Ramsey, wife of Dr. Ramsey, of eleven. "The act of getting them with the sweet Dr must be very delightful," her friend Catherine Vanhorne Read wrote her (Catherine's) sister, although she (Catherine) thought Martha foolish to indulge him to that extent. Mary Heathy of South Carolina reversed the usual trend and married three times herself; her first and second husbands she provided with seven children each, and still had time to bear three to the third.

By southern standards, New Englanders must have appeared strangely inhibited. Northern mothers tended to suckle their own children rather than hand them over to slave wet nurses, thereby increasing the time span between pregnancies. An even dozen was considered sufficient progeny for any man, and women tried to pare down even these modest aspirations. Wives sought out methods to limit their pregnancies, although the popular New England preacher, Cotton

Mather, himself father of ten, cautioned his Puritan flock to rejoice in the birth of each and every child as the generous gift of God.

Napoleon Bonaparte: "I Was Cradled by the Cries of the Dying"

Napoleon is perhaps the only great soldier to have had prenatal experience of battle. In the spring of 1769 French troops were sighted off the Corsican coast. The rebellious islanders found themselves facing three cavalry regiments, forty-five infantry battalions, artillery, and engineers. Equipped with little more than their horses and a few rifles, they fled to the hills, Carlo Buonaparte among them. At his side—because Corsican girls were taught from childhood that their first duty in times of danger was to load their husbands' rifles—rode eighteen-year-old Letizia, six months pregnant with their second child.

The refuge chosen was a network of caves high in the wildest part of the Corsican terrain. To reach it the rebels had to ride up the gorges of Restonico, through a dense pine forest, and finally up the steep slopes of Monte Rotondo. There they hid, with forays down to the scene of action. "To obtain news of the army," Letizia recalled some sixty years later, "I used to leave the steep rocky hideouts assigned to the women and make for the battlefields. Bullets whistled past my ears, but I trusted in the protection of the Virgin Mary, to whom I had consecrated my unborn son." (How Letizia knew the child she carried was a boy she did not say.)

Against such odds, the inevitable rebel defeat was not long in coming. But the outcome was much the same. The French were less interested in punishing the resisters than they were in assimilating them and, since the Corsicans had nobly defended their cause, they could now honorably return home.

By contrast, the summer in the little market town of Ajaccio was dull. Then on August 15 came the Feast of the Assumption, always enthusiastically celebrated in Corsica. Bells pealed from daybreak and the town was festooned with flowers and banners. Letizia, accompanied by her sister-in-law and little brother, walked the brief space from the family home to the cathedral, but as she knelt before the altar, she felt the first pangs of labor. Surprised by their intensity, she decided to return home, and only just made it to the sitting room couch when the baby was born. His small body made his head appear particularly large; his voice, too, seemed of unusual proportions.

When in later years Frenchmen looked back for miraculous signs to augur the birth of their heroic emperor, they seized upon this scene, certainly remarkable for its brevity. Napoleon's admirers—Stendhal among them—tried to amplify the legend by claiming that Letizia had not made it to the couch at all, but that Napoleon had been born on the carpet in the antechamber, directly on top of an embroidered representation of Julius Caesar. Fortunately, Letizia was still around to set history straight. *"Farlo nascere sulla test di Cesare!"* she said scornfully. "Pretending he was born on Caesar's head!" That, she said, was utter nonsense. Besides, Corsican homes did not have carpets even in winter—certainly not in mid-summer.

It is doubtful though that she ever had much effect on her son's penchant for legend over truth. "I was born when my country was perishing," he years later told the commander of yet another band of Corsican resisters. "I was cradled by the cries of the dying, the groans of the oppressed, the tears of despair."

The Rise and Fall of the Birth Rate in the Third Reich

"Can woman conceive of anything more beautiful than to sit with her beloved husband in her cosy home and to listen inwardly to the loom of time weaving the weft and warp of motherhood through centuries and millennia?"

No, not the question of a complacent Penelope celebrating Odysseus's return. The above is a quote from the 1933 edition of *The ABC of National Socialism*—Nazi propaganda at its most poetic. Fifty years ago the *ABC* was being read, mulled over, absorbed by hundreds of thousands of German working women. The aim of such loaded rhetoric was to will the German woman—the German *Aryan* woman, of course—back into the home from where she had so contrarily strayed. Back to producing children.

Changes in feminine *raison d'etre* have their own cyclical patterns, but in 1933 Adolf Hitler said that the very existence of the Teutonic race hung in the balance, and he was in no mood to wait for the turn of the tide. The sixty-year decline in the birth rate had reached alarming proportions. The women of Germany must be persuaded to the cause, infused with the urgency of the situation, seduced from their emancipated, modern lives back to *Kinder, Kirche, Küche*. And Hitler was a master seducer. Also, he understood that after World War I there were three million more women than men in Germany, nearly two million of marriageable age, and that working outside the home was not something most of them had any choice about.

Two of Hitler's particular bogeys were abortion and radical feminism. He hated with a vitriolic passion those women who had dared to demand sexual satisfaction for women as well as men, and who distributed birth control information. Abortion pre-dated feminism, of course, but he held feminists responsible anyway. He was sure it would be legalized if they had their way—was it not they who had promoted the test case in 1927 by which abortion was ruled permissible if the life or health of the mother were endangered?

Otherwise, Hitler was not entirely unsympathetic to women—Aryan women who knew their place, and especially the victims of the lopsided post-World War I demographics. When visited by a delegation of working women who wished to know just how a Nazi victory in the upcoming election might improve their lot, he cavalierly promised that in the Third Reich every woman would have a husband. The delegation did not ask for particulars.

In fact, Hitler had surprising appeal to women, especially the unmarried. They were attracted by his peculiar blend of aggressiveness and monkish asceticism: he did not indulge in cigarettes, liquor, meat, or—at that point in his life—women. He became the repository of a lot of (mostly unconscious) sexual yearning—the knight on the white charger who never dismounted, who never found his Cinderella, so there was always the chance. Women besieged him with letters begging him, among other things, to father their children. In time, hundreds of such requests would arrive every week.

The Führer also appealed to men, especially to the *Lumpenproletariat* opposed to the inroads women had made into the salaried labor force (no one minded a woman working unpaid next to her farmer husband in the field, or beside her baker spouse over the hot oven). Men stomped their approval when Hitler said that woman's place was in the home. And it was no mere campaign promise. When he became Chancellor in 1933, he told Germany's women, in only slightly couched language, to go home and have babies. "It must be considered reprehensible conduct," he had written in *Mein Kampf*, "to refrain from giving healthy children to the nation." The campaign to return the German woman to her proper biological role was inaugurated.

1933. When Hitler assumed power in January, the birth rate had reached the all-time low of 59 per 1,000 women of childbearing age.

Birth control organizations were immediately banned and their centers closed. Stores could sell but not display contraceptives. In May a law was passed sentencing anyone convicted of providing abortion facilities, except under certain medical conditions, to two years imprisonment. That summer women began to be dismissed from the civil service, from the medical and legal professions, even from teaching. The word went out—"A university education will not be useful." Gratification was to be found in the home.

The feminine side of the Hitler Youth movement began to expand its membership at the same time that it narrowed its horizons. The *Jungmaedel*—"Young Maidens" of ten to fourteen—were indoctrinated with the idea of motherhood as the ideal, indeed the only reasonable goal of their lives. Mind-conditioning increased when they graduated to the *Bund deutscher Mädchen* (League of German Maidens), ages fourteen to eighteen.

Two could not live as cheaply as one, so the Marriage Loan scheme was set up. Engaged couples were eligible for a tax-free loan of 1,000 Reichsmarks (payable in vouchers for household goods rather than in cash) to set up a home suitable for bringing up a child. The money for the loans was to be raised by a tax on single persons. With each new blessed event twenty-five percent of the loan was automatically cancelled.

The Marriage Loan was, of course, offered only to healthy Aryan couples. In *Mein Kampf* (free copies, paid for by the municipalities, were given to all newlyweds) Hitler said that it was "infamy" for persons who "are ill or show hereditary defects to bring children into the world." By July the "Law for the Prevention of Hereditarily Diseased Offspring" was passed. It was widely referred to as the "Sterilization Law."

1934.   Hitler's aim was to erase from the collective feminine mind the very notion of abortion as an alternative to an unplanned pregnancy. Abortion was, he said, "an act of sabotage against Germany's racial future"—with a few exceptions, of course. In March, in a test case, the Hereditary Health Court in Hamburg ruled that a pregnancy might lawfully be terminated if it were determined that the "health of the nation" would be affected adversely by the birth of that particular child. Among the hereditary risks listed were mental illness, congenital physical defects, and alcoholism (the children of women alcoholics, it was claimed, were usually handicapped either mentally or physically, or grew up to become delinquents or prostitutes).

With the focus on fecundity at the expense of morality, increasing numbers of young women were prematurely in the family way. Party members could not agree as to policy. Each unmarried mother contributed to a rise in the birth rate; on the other hand, she tended to raise it only by one. It was unusual for her to contribute twice. The November 24 issue of the *Völkischer Beobachter,* the official party newspaper, reported disapprovingly: "Non-marital liaisons are, as a rule, liaisons of frivolity or of the selfish exploitation of one partner by the other. Because of this, the illegitimate child is generally racially below par." Particularly suspect were those women who had several children by several fathers; one could not predict what unfortunate characteristics might later emerge. On the other hand, such children often gave every appearance of being quite acceptable, indeed, racially valuable in every way. The Party would continue to grapple with the problem; in the meantime, they made one concession—they declared the unmarried mother exempt from the single persons tax.

The word *Kindersegen*—"blessed with children"—came into frequent and emotionally charged use. Happy was the couple that was *Kindersegen;* fortunate were the towns with many such couples. In Camburg, near Halle, large families paid only half the normal water rate. In Darmstadt mothers of a brood were issued free theater tickets for certain evenings. Some town staged exhibits of prominent men who had come from large families or had fathered them, J. S. Bach affording a notable example. The *Völkischer Beobachter* announced that it would award Honor Cards to mothers with three or more children under the age of ten; such cards would entitle them to move to the head of the line in shops or government offices. The face of the card displayed a mother, very Aryan in aspect, surrounded by similarly endowed children, with the caption: "The most beautiful name the world over is 'Mother.'" Although the minimum was put at three, the *Völkischer Beobachter* reminded its readers that it took a family of six children to compensate for every childless couple if the declining birth rate were to be reversed. In 1934 there were few families so *Kindersegen* as that, and the problem was not made easier by the Führer's non-example. Where was the role model for the Hitler Youth?

Still, not all women drank in the Party line unresisting. A little book titled *German Women to Adolf Hitler* came out in 1934—one of the last overt expressions of feminine frustration. In its pages women complained that Nazi party activities systematically shuttled men this way and children that, nearly destroying home life. "Married people have less in common now," one woman said. "Women shrink back further and further into the shadow of loneliness." Said another, "We see our daughters growing up in stupid aimlessness, living only in the vague hope of perhaps getting a man and having children. If they do not succeed, their lives will be thwarted." How widely the book was circulated, or what effect it had, is not known. Most women seemed to be joining the *NS Frauenschaft*, the Nazi party women's auxiliary, and reading *Mein Kampf*. In 1934 the birth rate jumped from 59 to 73 live births per 1,000 women of childbearing age.

1935. That year the Nazi government launched an all-out effort to improve maternity and child welfare services. Various existing midwife organizations were nationalized. The Mother and Child Bureau was set up to dispense advice on having, caring for, and affording babies. Temporary homes were provided for unmarried mothers (after it had been determined that the pregnancy would result in a "hereditarily valuable" child).

Meanwhile, the Party announced that marriage in the Third Reich was no private matter. First priority was to prevent marriages between Aryans and non-Aryans, since the procreative assets of a perfectly good Aryan citizen were thereby lost to the state. The Nuremberg Laws of September 15, 1935, forbade (a) marriage between an Aryan and a Jew, (b) sexual intercourse between same, and (c) the employment by Jews of female Aryan servants under 35 years of age. The employment by Aryans of Jewish girls apparently gave no cause for concern.

A whole network of marriage bureaus, listing racially eligible candidates, was set up; those who applied had to pledge themselves to the principle of massive reproduction. In October the Marriage Health Law was passed. No person with an illness, physical or mental, that might be transmitted to either spouse or offspring, could marry. Couples who wanted to marry must not only be examined by a local health officer, but also take genealogical tables of their family's history to an SS doctor for scrutinization. If no hereditary defects were discovered, the couple would be issued a certificate of approval. Marrying without such, or marrying abroad, was punishable by a minimum of three months imprisonment, and the marriage was annulled. In December a county court dissolved a marriage in which the wife refused to have children on the grounds that she was consciously refusing to comply with the national view of marriage.

"Mothering Sunday," previously a minor holiday in May, took on

major significance. "How fine and noble it is to be a mother," said
Minister of the Interior Wilhelm Frick at that year's celebration. Said
Hitler, "The woman, too, has her battlefield."

1936. By this year professional women found themselves almost
completely excluded from public life; they would soon also be dis-
barred from jury duty on the premise (a throwback to Schopenhauer
of a century before) that their reasoning faculties were weak. A few
young women could still enter the universities, but not to train for
university teaching. Not a single university chair was held by a woman
during the Third Reich. In the church the reforms of the Weimar period that had admitted women to certain ecclesiastical functions were
rescinded by the Bishop of Hamburg. The feminine sphere was noticeably shrinking. According to Dr. Josef Goebbels, Minister of Propaganda, "Woman has the task of being beautiful and bringing children into the world, and this is by no means as coarse and old-fashioned
as one might think. The female bird preens herself for her mate and
hatches her eggs for him."

As for who that mate should be, the Racial Policy Office launched a
public relations campaign for its "Ten Commandments for Choosing
a Spouse." "Racially and hereditarily healthy" persons were to avoid
even considering marriage with anyone not "equally valuable." One
should "marry only for love," but one could not be too careful about
whom one loved. Meanwhile, promising results were accruing from
the Marriage Loan Scheme. At a party rally it was announced that
some 620,000 marriages had been assisted and had produced 425,000
children. Not a bad start, Interior Minister Frick said, but by this
time next year each of those 425,000 children should have a brother or
sister.

The *Bund deutscher Mädchen*—the post-puberty section of the girls'
youth movement—began to receive considerable criticism for unmaid-
enly behavior. Parents were increasingly reluctant to have their daughters take part. American historian William Shirer, then a reporter in
Berlin, describes personally witnessing meetings of the B.d.M. in which
women leaders, "invariably of the plainer type," lectured the girls on
their moral and patriotic duty to bear children for the Reich, within
marriage if possible, but if not, then without. Apparently the Party
had abandoned its theory that the illegitimate child was racially below par. In September, 1936, 100,000 members of the Hitler Youth and
B.d.M. attended the annual party rally in Nuremberg. Nine hundred

members of the B.d.M. returned home pregnant. Subsequent efforts by
the authorities to locate the unsuspecting young fathers were successful in less than half the cases, and even where paternity was established, many of the offenders were under age. Hitler had not anticipated the problem of adolescent fatherhood, but not to worry. A
young man's minority status would be overlooked if he signed the following application:

> I ask to be declared of full age. I have been engaged since . . . to . . . ,
> who has borne a child on the . . . , whose father I am. I want to marry
> my bride, who is an orderly, industrious and thrifty girl, as soon as pos-
> sible, so that I can care for her and my child better than I am able to do
> at the moment. My weekly income is . . . , which means that I can take
> care of a family. We have/are going to get a flat. I know what marriage
> means.

Premarital intercourse was fast reaching epidemic proportions (in
Munich it was estimated at 90 percent). The so-called "duty year" provided new stimulus. Young graduates of the B.d.M. were required to
do one year of unpaid farm labor or domestic household service. But
there was more than one way to define "duty," especially since, once
pregnant, they were excused from heavy work. The result was a plethora of "duty babies."

The question of the unmarried mother also recurred in the salaried
labor force. Should she or should she not be eligible for, or continue
to hold, public employment? The Minister of Posts favored severity—
i.e., dismissal. The government should not appear to condone immoral
sexual acts. Heinrich Himmler, head of the SS, and Deputy Fuhrer
Rudolf Hess were more inclined to leniency. "The unmarried mother
is," Himmler said, "during and after her pregnancy, not a married or
an unmarried woman, but a *mother*." He arranged for her to spend
her confinement in the *Lebensborn* (Fount of Life) homes for expectant and nursing mothers that he had established for wives and girl-
friends of his SS men. In his enthusiasm Himmler went one step further: he himself would assume legal guardianship of all illegitimate
children born in the *Lebensborn* homes.

1937.   An undercurrent of feminine revolt was noted in the matter
of conjugal obligations. The domestic charm Hitler had pictured to
lure women back to the proverbial fireside was less attractive when the
husband was constantly absent from that fireside on party business.
But lonely wives received little sympathy. "It is a husband's duty to

participate in National Socialist activities," a Berlin paper editorialized, "and a wife who makes trouble on this score gives grounds for divorce."

Hitler had, in fact, several reassessments to make that year. One was that women employees would, after all, be quite useful in some of the new arms-related industries such as the manufacture of chemical, rubber, and electrical goods; the stipulation that working women would not qualify for marriage loans was therefore dropped. Another unwelcome truth emerged when investigation showed the abortion rate to have declined little, if at all. Clearly many women were not attentive to party policy, although the SS was having trouble identifying them. In yet another encouragement to the unmarried woman to bear her child rather than abort it, an order went out in May that all unmarried mothers were to be addressed as "Frau," rather than "Fräulein"— a substitution the radical feminists had long advocated.

Not only women, but men, too, were admonished for not conforming. *Das Schwarzes Korps,* the house organ of the SS, felt impelled to censure bosses who publicly scolded employees for their childlessness, apparently a common gesture of patriotism. A 1937 Ministry of Interior memorandum advised that unmarried applicants for promotion in the (by then almost entirely male) civil service must set down in writing why they were still unmarried and when they intended to alleviate that situation. Those married but childless had also to supply reasons. The birth rate had been holding steady at 77 live births per 1,000 women of childbearing age for three years. Seventy-seven was insufficient, Hitler said.

1938. The so-called Marriage Law was passed, although all its significant provisions concerned divorce. Partners in mixed (Aryan and non-Aryan) marriages were urged to separate at once. Either husband or wife might sue for divorce if his or her spouse would not cooperate in the begetting of a child, or if, once a child was conceived, either spouse attempted by illegal means to prevent normal birth from occurring. Premature infertility was another ground for divorce, but not if the family already included "hereditarily healthy" children. "Paragraph 55" provided that a couple who had lived apart for at least three years might apply for divorce, it being assumed they were unlikely to produce children at a distance, whereas if they were free to remarry, new offspring might result. Thousands of long-estranged couples immediately took advantage of "Paragraph 55."

New statistics showed the number of premature births and subsequent infant mortality to be on the increase; to amend this situation, the Midwives Law was passed. Not only did every German woman have the right to the assistance of a midwife, but she had the duty to call her in promptly. Doctors were not regularly summoned for child-birth, and anesthetics were seldom used. Mothers of the Third Reich were expected to suffer proudly. It was not uncommon for women in labor to call out the name of the Führer as an analgesic for their pains.

There was progress on the birth rate in 1938. By the end of the year it had risen to 81 per 1,000.

1939.   A decision was finally reached on the unmarried mother and public employment. Early in the year the Minister of Justice an-nounced that the bearing of an illegitimate child was not in itself reason for dismissal, although he might be forced to reconsider if it were learned that the conception of said child had taken place on offi-cial premises. Discretion was expected of all government employees.

The annual Mother's Day celebration (now held on August 12, Hit-ler's mother's birthday) was particularly festive that year. Three mil-lion German mothers were honored with the newly minted "Honor Cross of the German Mother." On the back of the cross were inscribed the words, "The child ennobles the Mother!" Only mothers with at least four children were eligible, and there were three levels of distinc-tion—bronze, silver, and gold—depending on the number of children involved. The order went out that all members of the Hitler Youth were to salute when they met a woman wearing the cross.

In September open war began with the invasion of Poland. The paradox of the German people needing *Lebensraum* at the same time that there were not enough of them adequately to populate the Fa-therland was discussed behind closed doors, if at all. The army went into full gear. Young men not already serving were called up. Provi-sions of the Marriage Health Act (genealogical tables, etc.) were tem-porarily suspended so that nothing would stand in the way of a new recruit marrying his current girlfriend and begetting a child before he left for the front. Only a fraction of the eligible conscripts leapt at the opportunity, but large numbers of couples previously unable to marry because of the restrictions of the Act took advantage of its suspension to regularize their situations.

With men now in combat, Deputy Führer Hess spotted a new prob-lem—the plight of the pregnant fiancée whose intended was killed at the front. In December he forwarded to Frick a copy of a letter he had written to just such a young woman in distress with the request that Frick arrange for some sort of regulation of her legal position. Hess then took it upon himself to announce that the Party would assume guardianship of all children whose fathers had been killed in combat. These innocent children, he said, whose valiant fathers gave their lives before they could return to marry their mothers—of course the Party would cherish and succor them all.

1940. Hitler was pleased. The war was going well, and the birth rate for the preceding year had risen to 85 per 1,000 women of childbearing age. Although it would hold its own for another year—the largesse of all those young men who had done their best for their country the previous fall—the future prospect would not be favorable. War is not conducive to sustained population growth.

In January *Das Schwarzes Korps* printed SS Chief Himmler's notorious procreation order to his troops. How could a soldier in wartime go to the front, knowing he might die, without leaving an heir behind him? For his own personal satisfaction, not to mention his country, he should be sure of that, and "German women and girls of good blood, acting not frivolously but from a profound moral seriousness," should accept that "sublime task." It was a time of national emergency. There were those who served their country by bearing arms and those who served by bearing children. A marriage certificate was not a prerequisite for either of the above. Moreover, girls who refused such patriotic services were in a class with army deserters. Money was not the issue. The state could and would support its children. What was important was an across-the-board commitment to the national survival.

Motherhood was more prestigious than ever. "I have donated a child to the Führer" became the battle cry of pregnant women across the Reich. But reaction began to set in. The Catholic Church, more of a force since the annexation of Catholic Austria, strongly opposed the Sterilization Law and other pronouncements of the Nazi regime, especially those of Herren Himmler and Hess. Cardinal Faulhaber contended that the Church's views on the sanctity of marriage and the sin of unchastity had survived many other wars and would survive this one as well. Himmler's SS agents reported that in some areas the priests were confusing the people by maintaining that the war was not the glorious struggle they had been led to believe, but God's punishment on a country rapidly falling into depravity and moral corruption.

1941. As the war progressed, women began to leave their homes to replace men at such drudgery duties as train conductor, custodian, and air raid warden. Pants were adopted as the appropriate sartorial solution to night hours and awkward physical tasks. Traditionalists in the party voiced objections, but with the courage of her new semi-independence, the German woman wore her pants to work anyway.

The party hierarchy was also unhappy because statistics showed there still to be about 600,000 abortions annually in spite of eight years of pro-natalist conditioning. Apparently many women who might have "donated a child to the Führer" had reconsidered. The party, always seeking anti-abortion incentives, voted to provide cash grants to new mothers when fathers were not on the scene. The government was in turn dismayed at what it saw as the irresponsible attitude of the SS with government funds, which were in short enough supply. It agreed to provide funds to "needy" unmarried mothers on a continuing basis, but sifted carefully through the applications. Relatively few qualified.

Until this year contraceptives had been discouraged but not prohibited, partly because of the assumed usefulness of the condom in protecting against venereal disease. Although such precaution would seem even more necessary in wartime, a Himmler Police Ordinance now unconditionally banned the production and sale of all contraceptives.

1942. By this year—a middle point in the war from the German standpoint—40 percent of the female labor force were those same married women whom Hitler had confined to their homes for the good of the country and was now pulling out again for the same reason. For most there was no longer a man on the other side of the hearth anyway.

In what must have seemed to him the logical extension of Hitler's procreation policy, SS Chief Himmler let it discreetly be known that he could provide "racially pure" men as *Zeugungshelfer* or "conception assistants." Interested women had only to come to one of his *Lebensborn* homes, above which flew the symbolic white flag with the red dot in the center, and about which circulated the most prurient rumors. We are never likely to know the extent of the services offered and how many took advantage of them. One young woman who did accept Himmler's invitation later left the following brief account: "At the Tegernsee hostel I waited until the tenth day after the beginning of my period and was medically examined; then I slept with an

SS man who also had to perform his duty with another girl. After my pregnancy was diagnosed, I could either return home or go straight into a maternity home."

1943. As the war contributed to mental and nervous strain, more and more women took up smoking, in spite of the fact that the party published medical reports linking nicotine with infertility. Women also began to ignore previous party policy favoring the broad-hipped figure, plain dress, and no cosmetics. Booty from France, Belgium, and the Scandinavian countries arrived regularly now in the form of high-style dresses, stockings, perfumes, and furs. Some of these items had hardly been seen in Germany for ten years.

An efficiency gap was threatening to clog the war machine. Albert Speer, now Minister of Armaments, drew Hitler's attention to the fact that the foreign workers Germany hired for war production were insufficiently motivated; patriotic young German women could do the job much better. Five million were out there, he said, waiting to be mobilized. But Hitler hesitated. Fritz Sauckel, Commissioner of Manpower, was opposed—Fraupower was not his idea of how to win the war. He reminded the Führer of the physical and moral harm to which young German women might be subjected in the armaments works. The present may have its drawbacks, he said, but there was the future to be considered, the mother-potential to be kept in mind. Hitler agreed.

1944–45. As the "killed-in-action" numbers accelerated, so did the national fixation over the birth rate. The government voted the death penalty to anyone convicted of performing an abortion—except, of course, on Jews, although that exception was by now almost entirely moot. In what seemed all too *déja vu,* the Ministry of Justice in the summer of 1944 recorded a complaint against B.d.M. leaders for encouraging their young charges to—you guessed it—donate a child to the Führer.

Conventional morality seemed almost entirely to have disappeared. Women consorted more or less openly with prisoners-of-war. *Ménages à trois* were not uncommon. By 1945 23 percent of young Germany had contracted venereal disease, and prostitution was four times its pre-war level. Looking ahead, Himmler and party crony Martin Bormann worked out a post-war social system in which bigamy—or polygamy—would supercede monogamous marriage in order to ensure an expanding population with improved racial characteristics in spite of the imbalance of the sexes.

As the war dragged on, however, other matters took precedence in the national consciousness. Survival, for one. Many women worked a 56-hour-week, and by the war's end, in spite of their mother-potential, three-quarters of the labor force was female. Neither abortion nor contraception diminished appreciably. Most of the women unmarried when Hitler was promising out husbands, remained so. Concern over the birth rate among the party hierarchy, even with the Führer himself, was temporarily shelved. Postponed, as it turned out, permanently.

In the course of the immense failed experiment that was the Third Reich, women were persuaded of their inferiority as reasoning, thinking beings. Domesticity was their terrain; their childbearing years were the crown, the zenith of their lives. Historian Richard Grunberger put it best: "Women basked in Nazi public esteem between marriage and the menopause, after which they imperceptibly declined into a twilight condition of eugenic superfluity."

Some rebelled. A few women joined active resistance forces; many more were part of that element of quiet uncooperatives known as the Inner Emigration. But the great majority capitulated before the hypnotic power of the man who asked them to swap their basic rights for that cosy home and the weft and warp of motherhood. At the time they seemed not to regret the exchange; some did not even notice they had made one.

Childbirth Before and After the Cultural Revolution

In 1962 Swedish novelist and anthropologist Jan Myrdal spent a month living in an ordinary village in northern China—Liu Ling—and interviewing the inhabitants. He spoke to old peasants and young "ganbus," to farmers, schoolteachers, and party officials. In the following excerpts from his *Report from a Chinese Village*, a young woman pioneer describes the new approach to childbirth and birth control, a young housewife tells of women's work, and in a lighter vein another villager makes a comment on the traditional desire for sons. The same themes from a more urban perspective recur a decade later in Bulgarian-born French historian Julia Kristeva's *About Chinese Women*.

Li Kuei-ying, woman pioneer aged 32:
I was head of the women's organization in Liu Ling from 1955 to 1961. It wasn't a real organization. It automatically comprised all the

women in the village. It was one way of activating the women in social work and getting them to develop and accept responsibility. . . .

We have continued our work with hygiene and public health. . . .
We go to see the women who are pregnant and talk with them about
what to do in their pregnancy. We instruct them in the new delivery
art and tell them how to look after their infants. Before, a woman had
to be sitting straight up and down on her kang three days after having
her baby. And you can understand how that must have felt. Now we
say to them: "That is all just stupidity and superstition. Lie down
with the child beside you and rest. You're not to sit up at all." We
tell the women to let themselves be examined regularly and follow the
doctor's advice. We instruct them in birth control and contraceptive
methods. The women follow our advice because they have found that
with the old methods many children died, but with our new scientific
methods both mother and child survive.

Birth control is primarily a matter of propaganda. Firstly, many
say: "We want to have more children"; secondly, after all birth control is voluntary. We have discussed which contraceptives are best. . . .
A lot of women still believe that they can't become with child as long
as they are suckling. And each time, they are as surprised as ever, when
they find they are pregnant again. But we are working to enlighten
them.

In certain families with lots of children, the women would like birth
control, but their husbands won't. In those families the husbands say:
"There's not going to be any family planning here!" Then we women
go to them and try to talk sense into them. We say: "Look how many
children you have. Your wife looks after the household and sees to all
the children and she makes shoes and clothes for both you and the
children, but you don't think of all she has to do or of her health, but
just make her with child again and again. Wait now for three or four
years. Then you can have more if you want." Usually, they will eventually say: "If it isn't going to go on all one's life, then all right. But
if she's going to go on with birth control for ever, then I'm not having
any." In those cases, all goes well and usually they do not decide to
have any more afterwards. But in other cases, the husband just says:
"No." Then we women speak to him about it every day, till he agrees
to birth control. No husband has yet managed to stand out for any
length of time, when we are talking to him. Actually, of course, they
know that we are right. They know, of course, that they are responsible. It's only their pride that stands in the way, and we have to tell
them that such pride is false and not at all right. But there are, too,

families, where both husband and wife are agreed that they want to have children all the time. We can't do anything there. The whole thing's voluntary. The chief thing is to have a healthy family, and that the mother feels all right."

People say of Li Kuei-ying: "She is always clear and sensible. She speaks in a low voice, but she always knows what she wants, and when she says a thing, then it is so. . . . All the women admire her, because she has always decided exactly when she is to have children or not to have children. Chi Mei-ying said: 'I am not like Li Kuei-ying. We too, tried to be clever and plan, but it went wrong and so I had my last child. Not everyone can be as decided as Li Kuei-ying.' "

Li Yang-ching, housewife, aged 29:
I'm from Liu Ling here. I learned how to run a cave from my mother and sister-in-law. . . .

I was married when I was eighteen. I was betrothed when I was thirteen. My husband was then fourteen. It was our parents who decided it, but we were shown to each other and accepted it. I have never thought of anyone else. . . .

Life became more difficult for me when the children started coming. It isn't easy being a woman. My husband brings up four buckets of water a day from the well. I myself go down to the river to wash clothes once or twice a week. We often go down, a lot of us together. We do that when we have our day off. Or we do it during the midday rest, when our husbands are asleep. When we have our rest out in the field, we take out clothes to make or shoes to sew. The men either sleep then or walk about collecting fuel.

Women work much more than men. We have two jobs: we work both in the fields and in our caves. I know my husband helps me, we're a young family, of course, but he isn't as particular about housework as a woman is. Life is a lot of hard work. . . .

People say of Li Yang-ching: "She loves a chat and jokes a lot. She is a gentle, well-brought-up woman and talks lovely Chinese with elegant phrases. . . . Everything in her cave is well looked after, and her children are well brought up and she works hard. She does more than other women. Most other women stop working in the fields when they have their first child, and don't find the day long enough even to look after the children; but she does work in the fields and sees to her home and the children, and has time to chat with her friends and run her home properly.

"Her husband, Liu Chen-yung, is good. Most men here, or at least

half of them, anyway, go straight to the kang and lie down and sleep
when they get home from work; but he helps her and does things in
the home. He is calm, quiet and doesn't speak much. They never quar-
rel; everyone considers them a happy family. He was anxious during
her last pregnancy, in case she wasn't going to give birth to a son. She
had had two girls before, you see. But she just told him not to worry,
because she had decided to have a son. Then, when she did give birth
to a son, all the women in the village were talking about her and en-
vying her for being able to decide about such things herself. But, of
course, she had been just as anxious in case it should be another girl."

   In the early 1970s Julie Kristeva toured China in preparation
for her book *About Chinese Women*. She visited the tractor factory "The East is Red" at Xi'an in northwest China where at that
time 6,700 women were employed. Pregnant women worked from
wheelchairs, and new mothers stopped work for half an hour,
twice a day, to go nurse their infants in one of the twenty rooms
set aside for that purpose. Later she visited the Shanghai Hospital,
from where she reports:

In a three-bed room there are three women who have just given birth:
one saleswoman, one radio factory worker, and one accountant. For
the worker, this is the second child. She says: "This will be the last, so
that I can give them enough time and still devote myself to my work.
Two daughters—their grandparents will certainly want a boy, but we
won't listen to them. The factory paid for me to give birth, but they
distribute birth control pills for free as well." Zhu Chuangeng has already used them, and will be able to use them again. Still tired, but
most radiant of the three, is the awkward Chan Beiyin, the accountant
from the north who has returned to Shanghai with her husband, so
that she could be near her parents when the baby was born. Many
women do the same, sometimes crossing the whole of China; their husbands are also granted paid holidays under such circumstances. It's
now been a week since she had her baby by Caesarian section, anaes-
thetized by acupuncture: "No pain" she laughs. "In two days I'll be
up on my feet."
   The baby, a boy, is obviously the hero of this story. But she affects
a curious detachment when the talk turns to him—modesty or ritual?—
and prefers to speak of her work as an accountant, her study of the
Critique of the Gotha Programme, and of the campaign against Lin
and Kong [Confucius], who was "an eater of women. . . ." The baby
still has no name, and his "christening" is far from the first thing on

his mother's mind. She does have one idea, though: Xiao Di, "Little Arrow." And it's not just any little arrow—it comes straight from a poem by Mao, "Fei Ming Di":

> Vibrant arrows flying
> There has always been so much to do
> Earth and sky in revolution—Time short—
> Ten thousand years too long
> Speed on your way. . . .

Toni Cade: "Chance Fertilization, Chance Support, Chance Tomorrow"

Toni Cade is a New York writer "preoccupied" (her terminology in 1969) with the contemporary Black woman in American society. In the following excerpt from "The Pill: Genocide or Liberation," a 1967 essay that appears in her anthology *The Black Woman* (1970), she explores the reasons for childbirth by choice— when, how, with whom—as the only "righteous" response to the Black woman's predicament.

After a while meetings tend to fade, merge, blur. But one remains distinct, at least pieces do, mainly because of the man-woman pill hassle. . . . We were offered a medley of speakers dipping out of a variety of bags, each advocating his thing as the thing. One woman, the only female speaker out of twelve speakers, six group leaders, two chairmen, and three moderators, spoke very passionately about the education of our children. She was introduced as so-and-so's wife. Others were for blowing up the Empire State, the Statue of Liberty, the Pentagon. A few more immediate-oriented types were for blowing the locks off the schools if the strike ever came to pass. Finally, one tall, lean dude went into deep knee bends as he castigated the Sisters to throw away the pill and hop to the matresses and breed revolutionaries and mess up "the man's" genocidal program. A slightly drunk and very hot lady from the back row kept interrupting with, for the most part, incoherent and undecipherable remarks. But she was encouraged finally to just step into the aisle and speak her speech, which she did, shouting the Brother down in gusts and sweeps of historical, hysterical documentation of mistrust and mess-up, waxing lyric over the hardships, the oatmeal, the food stamps, the diapers, the scuffling, the bloody abortions, the bungled births. She was mad as hell and getting more and more sober. She was righteous and beautiful and accusatory, and when she pointed a stiff finger at the Brother and shouted, "And when's the last time you fed one of them brats you been breeding all over the city, you jive-ass so-and-so?" she tore the place up.

Since then I've been made aware of the national call to the Sisters to abandon birth controls, to not cooperate with an enemy all too determined to solve his problem with the bomb, the gun, the pill; to instruct the welfare mammas to resist the sterilization plan that has become ruthless policy for a great many state agencies; to picket family-planning centers and abortion-referral groups, and to raise revolutionaries. And it seems to me that once again the woman has demonstrated the utmost in patience and reasonableness when she counters, "What plans do you have for the care of me and the child? Am I to persist in the role of Amazon workhorse and house slave? How do we break the cycle of child-abandonment-ADC-child?"

It is a noble thing, the rearing of warriors for the revolution. I can find no fault with the idea. I do, however, find fault with the notion that dumping the pill is the way to do it. You don't prepare yourself for the raising of super-people by making yourself vulnerable—chance fertilization, chance support, chance tomorrow—nor by being celibate until you stumble across the right stock to breed with. You prepare yourself by being healthy and confident, by having options that give you confidence, by getting yourself together, by being together enough to attract a together cat whose notions of fatherhood rise above the Disney caliber of man-in-the-world-and-woman-in-the-home, by being committed to the new consciousness, by being intellectually and spiritually and financially self-sufficient to do the thing right. You prepare yourself by being in control of yourself. The pill gives the woman, as well as the man, some control. Simple as that. . . .

"Raise super-people" should be the message. And that takes some pulling together. The pill is a way for the woman to be in position to be pulled together. . . . Nobody ever told that poor woman across the street or down the block, old and shaggy but going on longsuffering and no time off, trying to stretch that loaf of bread, her kitchen tumbled down with dirty laundry and broken toys, her pride eroded by investigators and intruders from this agency or that, smiling and trying to hold the whole circus together—nobody ever told her she didn't have to have all those kids, didn't have to scuffle all her life growing mean and stupid for being so long on the receiving end and never in position even to make decisions about her belly until finally she's been so messed with from outside and inside ambush and sabotage that all the Brothers' horses couldn't keep her from coming thoroughly undone, this very sorry Sister, this very dead Sister they drop into a hole no bigger, no deeper than would hold a dupe. And what was all that about? Tell her first that she doesn't have to. She has choices. Then, Brother, after you've been supportive and loving and selfless in the liberation of your Sisters from this particular shit—this particular death—then talk about this other kind of genocide and help her prepare herself to loosen the grip on the pill and get a hold of our tomorrow. She'll make the righteous choice.

13. Mourning

There was no medical care to speak of in Vendrell at the time of my mother's marriage. When children were born, a woman who was the wife of the coal dealer acted as midwife. No doubt he was a good man at his trade, but his wife knew little about delivering children. Many infants died from infections and other complications. Seven of my mother's eleven children died at birth. I myself almost did not survive. I was born with the umbilical cord twisted around my neck. My face was black, and I nearly choked to death. Though my mother had a tender heart, she never spoke of her grief at the death of her children.

Pablo Casals, *Joys and Sorrows*

Sophia Loren: "Oh, God, Please Let Me Be Pregnant"

For most of us, film stars are our modern-day royalty, and they accordingly spend most of their lives in the proverbial goldfish bowl. Sophia Loren has been no exception to the rule. When she left her apartment on the eighteenth floor of the Hotel Intercontinental in Geneva, Switzerland, at five A.M. on December 29, 1968, for the hospital, it was via an automobile that had been secretly driven into the hotel ballroom through a rear door. This subterfuge was made necessary by the hundreds of reporters and photographers camped out in the hotel lobby. There are times when deception is necessary.

To make journalistic amends, on the day after the safe delivery of Carlo Ponti, Jr., by Caesarean section, a huge press conference was held in the hospital amphitheater. The attending physicians and Carlo Ponti, Sr., answered a barrage of questions. The actress's bed was wheeled in and for several minutes cameras clicked and flashed so that newspapers all over the world could next day display pictures of the new mother and child.

Much of the fanfare was caused by the fact that Sophia Loren had been trying for years to have a child. To conceive was in itself difficult for her, and to carry the baby to term even more so. Her final success was only made possible by the regular injections of estrogen that she received to correct a hormone imbalance and by her willingness to spend nine months in bed. Her joy and relief at the birth of her son, as she describes it in her autobiographical *Sophia* (written from interviews by A. E. Hotchner), is therefore understandable. More poignant, somehow, is her account of the first of her several miscarriages, which occurred in 1964 during the filming of *Yesterday, Today and Tomorrow* with Marcello Mastroianni.

Yesterday, Today and Tomorrow was composed of three segments, the first of which we shot in Rome, the second in Naples, the third in

Milan. While I was doing the Naples section, I began to feel strange, not at all like myself. After several days of mounting concern, it finally occurred to me that I might be pregnant. I consulted a local doctor, who took tests which he said were negative. But my feeling persisted, so I asked a physician to come down from Rome. He came to my apartment in Naples bearing a frog he had brought with him from Rome. He injected my urine into the frog and we both watched anxiously for the result. If the frog dropped dead, I was pregnant— at least that's what the doctor said—and if the injection didn't faze the frog, then I was not.

After a while, the frog began to act a bit strange. He listed to one side, and then to the other, and he appeared to be in a state of dizziness. When he jumped, he lost his equilibrium. But he did not die. After a few hours of frog observation, with the frog getting no nearer to the grave, the doctor solemnly announced that I might be pregnant—and then again I might not.

I thanked him and bade him good-bye. Afterward I took a walk and released the poor frog into a little pond.

That night I prayed that I was pregnant. Oh, God, please let me be pregnant. Please, God, I really want a baby. I am twenty-nine and it is high time for me to be pregnant.

My prayers were answered. Shortly before our shooting schedule ended in Naples, it was officially confirmed that I was indeed pregnant. It was a moment of great joy for me. The fact that Carlo and I were not married didn't bother me at all. If it worsened our situation, so be it. All that mattered to me was that I had Carlo's child in my belly. For years I had felt a strong, insistent desire within me to have children. When Carlo and I first started our relationship, I would talk to him about having children. I was just starting my career then and he was married, but that made no difference to me. I would have raised a child by myself. Of course, when a woman is sixteen, or even nineteen, she has no understanding of what it means to have a child, no understanding of the responsibility a child brings. When you are young it is easy to conceive a child and give birth to it, but it took Carlo's forceful advice to impress upon me the realities of raising a child. It certainly would have been wrong for us to have a child early in our relationship.

But by the time we went to Hollywood, our relation was better defined, so I was no longer careful about becoming pregnant. But I was making four pictures a year, working hard, so I had little time to brood about the fact that I had not become pregnant.

When we returned to Italy, my urge to be pregnant intensified. The actress part of me was happy and fulfilled, but the other half of me, the Neapolitan, childbearing, Mother Earth half of me, was fiercely unsatisfied. At twenty-nine, I had become obsessive about turning thirty without having produced a child. I think thirty is the big turning point in a woman's life, not forty, as many people think, because by the time a woman is forty she has formulated, more or less, her life plan. But at thirty, you feel suddenly old, although you are not old, and there is upon you a chilling realization that you must then and there begin to fulfill your dreams or else they are likely to remain just that—dreams. Every woman I've known has experienced a certain fear at turning thirty. If she is not married, then on her birthday she is a self-ordained spinster. If she is childless, she fears that she will be forever barren. I had never known a woman who happily greeted her thirtieth year, but it looked as if I was going to be the exception.

But, curiously, even when I was reveling in my pregnancy, I felt something was not quite right. Something about how I felt, a few little physical reactions, worried me. I didn't mention anything to Carlo, who shared my happiness over my pregnancy, but by the time we were finished with the Naples segment, I was deeply concerned over my condition. I knew that it was not normal for a pregnant woman to have the symptoms I was experiencing. So I went to Rome by car and saw my gynecologist. After examining me, he said I should spend two or three days in bed, after which I would be all right and could go to Milan to film the third and last segment of the film. But he cautioned me to be careful, to go to Milan by train so as to avoid the bumpiness of an automobile ride. I did go by train, but the trouble with his advice was that most of the Milan segment was to be shot with Marcello and me inside an automobile that would be mounted on a mechanically powered cradle, which bumps around much more than an automobile on a highway.

But my pregnancy never even got that far; it didn't even survive the start of the filming. The first night in Milan, I experienced great pain. Carlo wanted to keep my pregnancy a secret, because the press would have made so much out of it, so he called a local doctor to our hotel. The doctor gave me an injection, said that everything was going to be all right but that I must stay in bed and not work for the time being. De Sica, who was directing the film, came to see me; we were much too close for me not to tell him the truth. He knew how much I yearned for a baby; my anxiety over the possible loss of my baby upset him very much and brought tears to his eyes.

That night the pain suddenly intensified and I told the nurse, whom Carlo had hired to stay with me, that I had to go to the hospital immediately. She started to call an ambulance; although I could barely stand up, I insisted that we go by car so as not to attract attention. I just barely managed going down in the elevator, and I almost passed out getting into the automobile. At the hospital I was rushed to an emergency room, but I knew that my situation was hopeless, that the baby was gone and there was nothing anyone could do. . . .

The doctor came the following day and performed a curettage, and the day after that I went back to work. Carlo, as shaken and depressed as I was, asked me to keep the whole thing a secret. I felt as if I had been physically beaten. As soon as I came on the set, Mastroianni came up to me and said, "What's with you? You look very strange." I tried to smile, and I gave him a little Neapolitan shrug.

"Now, don't fool around," he said. "Tell me what happened."

There was no way to pretend anything with Marcello. We knew each other much too well for that. So I said, "Well, I had a baby, and I lost it." I felt relieved to be able to tell someone. Marcello didn't say a word. He looked at me and then he turned and walked away. He never again mentioned it.

I worked every day, full days, and we finished the film on schedule. I had constant pain, but my physical pain was nothing compared to the pain in my heart. In all my years, I had never doubted myself. I had faced discouraging obstacles but always with a certain will, a confidence that I could overcome them. But now, facing the fact that for no apparent reason I had lost a baby that was three and a half months old, I felt a twinge of doubt about myself. What if I could not bear a child? What then?

Three Out of Nine Children Lived

Except for the fact that she wrote her autobiography and thus ensured her immortality, Alice Wandesworth Thornton was a pretty average seventeenth century gentlewoman. She was devoutly religious and wrote always in terms of being delivered from this or rewarded with that. She had intended never to marry, having been put off in her girlhood by experiences, all too personal, with the "wicked Irishmen" and "mad Scots" who during that turbulent time in English history occupied northern England, and from whom she was only by divine intervention delivered "from being destroyed and deflowered." At last she was persuaded to accept the proposal of one William Thornton, Esq., a gentleman less well-to-do than various other suitors, but more pious. Alice became pregnant almost immediately, and over the next fifteen years bore nine children, three of whom lived—a typical survival rate for her time. She remembers her pregnancies in terms of fevers, sweatings, nosebleeds, faintings, and agues; her deliveries were inevitably perilous, and her recoveries of many months duration. The babies who lived were subject to diarrhea, convulsions, or being rolled upon by their wetnurses. The following account of the birth, and subsequent death, of her fifth child is a grim example of seventeenth century childbirth.

Upon the Wednesday, the ninth of December, I fell into exceeding sharp travail in great extremity, so that the midwife did believe I should be delivered soon. But lo! it fell out contrary, for the child stayed in the birth, and came cross with his feet first, and in this condition continued till Thursday morning between two and three o'clock, at which time I was upon the rack in bearing my child with such exquisite torment, as if each limb were divided from other, for the space of two hours; when at length, being speechless and breathless, I was, by the infinite providence of God, in great mercy delivered. But I having had such sore travail in danger of my life so long, and the child coming into the world with his feet first, caused the child to be almost strangled in the birth, only living about half an hour, so died before we could get a minister to baptize him, although he was sent for.

I was delivered of my first son and fifth child on the 10th of December, 1657. He was buried in Catericke church the same day . . . this sweet, goodly son. . . .

"They Should Know Who They're Crying For"

Alma McKenzie, the young head nurse in the obstetrical ward of a Kansas City hospital, told me the following story:

I work with a lot of moms who have stillborns. We really try hard to see that they at least get to see their baby. We take pictures of the baby so that if later on they decide they'd like to have one, they can— and a lock of hair, and their footprints. Before, they never wanted you to see a stillborn, but it works out better if you do. When a woman doesn't see her baby, she cries and she doesn't know who she's crying for, and she imagines all sorts of horrible monsters, whereas if she's seen her baby, and held her baby, then she's had a chance to say goodbye.

One of my favorite cases—I had a young woman here, and her baby was a little bit premature. And the baby was born dead. She was kind of an independent little lady. She saw her baby, and held her baby, and then she wanted her son to come back and see it, too. Her son was five. I thought, "Oh, God, I can't do this." The baby was all bruised. I thought, how is a little five-year-old going to handle this? But I went back and talked to her, and I thought, well, it must be important to her.

Anyway, this young woman, after her delivery, went home and drove back with her son that same day. This was so important to her. She wasn't married, and I guess she didn't have anybody to bring her back. I thought, God almighty, you'd think she could have found someone. Anyway, she brought her little boy back, and he was really cute. And I got him in here, and I talked to him before I brought in the baby. I said, "You know, you had a little sister, and we'd like to have you see her. But you know what it feels like when you fall down and hurt yourself? You know how you get bruised?" The baby was black and blue, and her skin was peeling off in places, and it really was an unpleasant sight for an adult, much less a child. But I said, "You know, your little sister was hurt when she was delivered, just like you're sometimes hurt when you fall down, only she was hurt so bad she couldn't live, and she had to go to Heaven." I said, "We want you to see your little sister, to say goodbye to her, all right? And you have to remember that although she's bruised and hurt, she's real pretty."

I had the baby wrapped up in a blanket, and I brought her in holding her in my arms. I thought I'd present the part that was normal first. So I said, softly as if the baby were asleep, "See her little feet? Doesn't she have cute feet? Look at all her toes—aren't they tiny? They're littler than yours, aren't they?" Then I said, "Look at her hands. Can you hold her hand? Her hand seems so small in yours, doesn't it?" And he was really responding positively. He said, "Her hands are so tiny. I wish she could come home with me. I wanted to change her diapers." I said, "Yes, that would have been nice." Then I said, "And here's her face. Isn't she pretty? She's been hurt real bad, and you can tell where she has bruises, but she's still real pretty."

And I think the thing that made it all worth while, was that when he was leaving, he looked at his mom who had been standing there all the time, and he said, "You know, Mom, we really had a pretty sister." He didn't seem to see that she was bruised with her skin peeling off. He said, "We sure had a pretty sister."

So that mom taught me something. I want the moms with stillborns to have the opportunity to hold their baby, so that when they go home, and they cry, they know who they're crying for. I think sometimes in our society we think there's something abnormal in wanting to hold a dead person, but after all, you've carried that baby as part of you for nine months. Wouldn't you wonder what it looked like? Wouldn't you want to know? At first, it's such a shock that you think, God, I can't look, I can't see. But later on, if you haven't seen, then you wish you had. Talk to anyone who's lost a baby—that's the one baby they've never forgotten.

Have a Shallow Grave Ready

Birth is usually joyous. Bushmen of all ages adore their children and grandchildren, placing a child's health and wishes uppermost in their minds. Orphans are eagerly adopted by their aunts or grandparents, and a newborn baby is welcomed as though it were the first baby the werf had ever seen. Sometimes, though, a baby is born that cannot be supported, and if this happens the baby is destroyed. If a woman bears a child that is crippled or badly deformed, she is expected to destroy it, and if the season is very hard and she already has a baby under a year old depending on her milk, she is forced to kill her newborn child. Bushman women can hardly bear this, but they do.

If a woman knows that she must kill her baby, she braces herself for this as best she can, and when the time comes to do it she must act immediately, must take advantage of the moment after birth before the infant has "come to life," that moment between the time the baby is born and the time her love for the baby wells up in her so that the act would be impossible forever after. She must think of the child she has already and act quickly, before she hears her infant's voice, before the baby moves or waves its feet; she must not look at it for long or hold it, but must have a shallow grave ready for it and must put it in at once and cover it and never think of it again. In times of extreme deprivation she can do this, or she can wait to watch both her children die. All this is very hard, and Bushmen, who have no mechanical form of contraception and know no way to cause miscarriage or abortion, prefer to abstain from intercourse for long periods rather than to suffer such pain.

We knew one woman who had been forced to destroy a baby to save an older child, and we knew one woman who had borne a crippled child and had been persuaded to destroy it by her mother, who had been present at the birth. Such things are very rare, though, and this is fortunate.

From Elizabeth Marshall Thomas,
The Harmless People, 1958

14. *Reconsidering*

If one but realized it, with the onset of the first pangs of birth pains, one begins to say farewell to one's baby. For no sooner has it entered the world, when others begin to demand their share. With the child at one's breast, one keeps the warmth of possession a little longer.

Princess Grace of Monaco

I had eight birds hatcht in one nest,
Four Cocks there were, and Hens the rest,
I nurst them up with pain and care,
Nor cost, nor labour did I spare,
Till at the last they felt their wing.
Mounted the Trees, and learn'd to sing.

Anne Bradstreet, c. 1656

Peter Ustinov: "I Believed the Embryo To Be a Very Small Woman Indeed"

Most of us could answer the question "Where do babies come from?" at a reasonably middle point of our childhood. Playwright-actor-director Peter Ustinov would have us believe he was completely uninformed until—well, almost until he was drafted into the British army in 1942. In any case, it makes a good story—one of many in his charming autobiography *Dear Me*.

There is in existence a photograph of me at the age of one year holding a Russian toy comprising ten wooden women, one within the other, from a great bulbous earth mother to a woman the size of a pea. I am brandishing two halves of this educational toy with evident pleasure. It apparently occurred to me at an early age that a pregnant woman had another pregnant woman inside her, and then another one right down to the smallest. I don't think I ever really suspected that this smallest might be a baby. I like to believe I did, simply because I like to believe I was what the Americans so depressingly call "bright," but in my heart I consider it more likely that I believed the embryo to be a very small woman indeed—dressed, of course, in peasant costume.

The truth of this probability is given further credence by the fact that when my mother informed me of the facts of life at an embarrassingly late stage of my youth (my father being too shy to talk about men, although more than willing to banter about women), I underwent a long moment of utter incredulity. My first reaction was one of horrified claustrophobia. I didn't understand how I had survived nine months of incarceration in a belly, without a breath of fresh air. Then I got used to the idea and quickly accepted such a process as being distinctly odd, but no odder than some of the other phenomena which had been brought to my attention.

It seems to me that I was always half a step behind the others, having no brothers or sisters and being brought up in an atmosphere of rare sophistication without any of the basic hurdles so essential to mental and physical balance. It was as though my cerebral diet were composed entirely of delicatessen and vintage formula.

I was, if anything, overprepared for a life of inconsequential refinement within extremely narrow horizons and . . . it was only when I had children of my own to appreciate and to study that I finally realized the full extent of the distance I had traveled.

"Nothing's Private Here, Not Birth, Not Death, Not Anything"

Ann Cornelisen is an American who spent ten years in the mountainous villages of Lucania in southern Italy with the Save the Children Fund. Her job was to set up nurseries for the children of impoverished families; in carrying out her work, she achieved a rapport with the cautious, brooding women that few outsiders realize. In the following excerpt from her book *Women of the Shadows* an older woman looks back to her childbearing days, and the author follows with her comment on the "improved" conditions of the present.

"Nothing's private in a one-room house. The street's your second room, so the neighbors know when the sheets need mending again and how ragged your underwear is and when you fight with your husband and—like today—when you 'pare' your feet. No way to do it inside where nobody'd see you. It's too dark. Nothing's private, but that doesn't mean you get used to it. You don't!

"I had nine children in that room, back there, and I suppose I'll die there the same way—with all the men in the family sitting around the fire, muttering, 'Why doesn't she hurry up about it.' When my time came and the pains started, I'd send my husband to call my mother—after she died, he called my sister—whichever it was would tell the midwife, and they'd come and stand by the bed and wait to see how far apart the pains were. I'd hear the shuffling in the room and know the men were arriving, one by one. My father, my brothers, my husband's brothers, they all sat there by the fire and drank wine and waited. If you make a sound, if a pain catches you by surprise, or the baby won't come out and you can't stand it and you moan, you've disgraced yourself. You keep a towel shoved in your mouth, and everytime it hurts so bad, you bite down on it and pray to God no noise comes out. I always tied a knot in one end so I could bite real hard, and my sister had a way of crooning and stroking me that made it better.

"I suppose I'll die the same way. The men used to say, 'She's a brave one, she is.' But I'll never forget the pain. I remember all nine times, just how they felt—and every one is different, I can tell you— and you just lay there and bite the towel and never let out a sound. Not once. So many times it was all for nothing too. Six of mine died. I could have wailed then—that's all right—but there are some hurts that stay inside. Every time one of my babies was about to be born I'd think to myself, You're going to die! This time, you're going to die! Then it'd come out. Somehow—I don't know how to explain it—but somehow it was like I had been born again. Maybe that's what gives a woman strength when she finds out she's pregnant. At least some part of her will go on. I tried to think of that when I wanted to scream. Nothing's private here, not birth, not death, not anything. No matter what anyone says though, you never get used to it."

Postscript: Now many peasant women have their babies at the hospital, or at least they have *one* there. Often they refuse to go back a second time. The young midwife assigned to the hospital, who has time for only a small outside practice, told me once that peasant women feel less pain and suffer less from what they do feel than "other women"—a nice bit of medical snobbery which assumes that either peasant sensitivity is blunted by work, or there is some mystical ratio between nerve ends and socioeconomic class heretofore unrecognized. I have always wondered if she understood anything of the peasant woman's strict code of behavior or of the shame she brings on herself if she flails about in pain. To her the shame is a brand as conspicuous, as permanent, as a strawberry birthmark or a scarlet letter. She feels and remembers every cramp, every searing barb that has plucked at her spinal column and made her writhe, those same cramps and barbs that "other women," more pampered and more complaining, have mercifully forgotten. And too the young midwife probably never thought of the delivery "thrones," facing each other in one communal delivery room, as the final indignity a modern world could force upon innately modest women. So the stolid peasant woman half lies, half sits, her knees held high and splayed out by leather slings in the most humiliating position medicine has yet invented. She is fortunate if she is alone. Usually at least one other "throne" is taken, often all three. There, in silence, they wait, trussed up like prisoners in a medieval torture chamber, their teeth clamped firmly on those clean white towels they brought from home and their heads turned aside that they may neither see nor be seen. Down the way in separate cubicles their more sensitive sisters groan and cry out for painkillers.

I was in that communal delivery room only once, at the insistence of the midwife.

"You know all of them. They'd love a visit. It will help them pass the time," she had said. It seemed improbable, but I went with her.

As we opened the door two of the women hid their faces with their arms, the third pulled the towel over hers and I fled, remembering what the older woman "paring" her feet has said to me: "Nothing's private here, not birth, not death, not anything. No matter what anyone says though, you never get used to it."

"But Where Would My Children Be Now?"

Maria and Will are typical of the thousands of American couples who postpone having children only to find that the choice was not theirs after all. Today they know the joys as well as travails of parenthood, Maria's day now taken up with school plays, baseball practice, ballet lessons. But in this short piece Maria recalls how eight years ago the struggle to become a mother took her on a roller-coaster ride of emotion, and finally to a small hospital in Latin America.

When did I first know that I wouldn't be conceiving? There wasn't any one particular moment. We both had our careers, there was no rush about starting a family, and at first we were careful. And then we started to talk about the day we'd have kids, and in the back of our minds we must have started to think that it might be time because there were occasions when we'd be careless. But we were always "lucky." And then we were really careless, and that frightened us because we knew that nobody could be that lucky that often. And gradually the sense grew that something was wrong.

I'd rather not go through the details of all the tests I underwent. From our family doctor to the great fertility centers of New York City I carried my body for poking, prodding, examination. Everyone knew some doctor, some center that was doing new work, and I chased after every lead. I was overweight, and one doctor said, "Lose the weight, you'll conceive." I lost the weight and I didn't conceive. "It's too soon," he said. "Wait a bit and hold your weight. You'll conceive." I waited and didn't conceive. I waited half the day to see one specialist who had had an article published in a prestigious medical journal, and when I came face to face with him, I poured my heart out. He was kind; he listened to me, and conducted more tests, and I knew he knew his business when he never once gave me a word of encouragement.

We started to think of adopting. We tried agencies, lawyers, doctors. The lawyers wanted $25,000 and no guarantees. We called the county agencies every Monday morning for two years, as we had been told to do, and nothing came of that either. My family is of Italian background, and someone encouraged us to believe that there were Italian children for adoption. We wrote, called long distance, made plane reservations. A distant relative, we were told, knew a judge in Italy and we were going to get a child. Then we were told the law had changed. Six children a year could be placed outside the country and our name was at the end of a long list of people who knew Italian judges.

That was when we decided: no more. For us—four years and five countries after we had started—it was over. We were going to put a business together, travel, enjoy the best of life without the cares of child rearing. But we reckoned without my mother. My mother never gave up.

No matter how far-fetched the possibility, she pursued it—relatives, neighbors, friends of friends. Each time she saw us she told us not to give up hope. Then one day she called and told me that she had made an appointment for me to see someone who knew someone who had actually adopted two children from a South American country. I said no, but my mother said she had made the appointment and I had to go. I won't mention the name of the country, because it is a sensitive issue with many people there—some see it as giving the country's children away to rich Americans—and I wouldn't want the door to close in some other couple's face.

I met the people and three months later, on September 18, 1974, I sent off the application. But to tell the truth I did not hold my breath. There had been too many disappointments and I didn't want to set myself up for yet another.

On May 1, at 9 A.M. our time, I received an overseas call collect. The caller said, "We have a four-year-old boy. But you must come right now." I called my husband at work and we cried together on the phone, warning each other not to get our hopes up too high. Could it be that I was going to get on a plane and when I came home I was going to be holding our boy? Just as other mothers go to the hospital and come back with a child? The miracle of parenthood, jet-age style.

Once at the hospital in South America I was put into an empty room and left to wait. My heart raced but not the clock. It ticked away its minutes as if they were months. Then the door opened and a skinny little boy ran across the room and literally jumped onto my lap. I didn't know Spanish. In an Italian called up from memories of long-ago conversations with grandparents I could hardly remember, I said to him, *"Io sono tu Mama."* I showed him a photo of my husband and said, *"Papá. Tu Papá."*

From that moment he was ours. I wasn't allowed to take him home until all the paperwork was done. Paperwork, paperwork, paperwork. It made the Motor Vehicle Bureau seem efficient. But we were together. Between appointments I bought him clothes. Even had I wanted to, I could not wait for that until we got back to New York; the clothes he was wearing had to be left for the next child. His haircut could have waited, but it didn't. On our errands we talked, he in Spanish, I in a mixture roughly 60–30–10 English, Italian, and newly acquired Spanish. I hugged him and when I cried he thought I was disappointed and might turn him back. I held back my tears.

One night, after I had put my boy to bed, and before going back to my hotel, there was a knock on the door. "We have a little girl too," the nun told me. "Do you want her?" I didn't even call my husband. The next day I was back in the room sitting on a chair, again waiting for the door to open. When it did, the smallest, roundest little two year old somersaulted toward me saying, "Yes, yes." I learned later it was her only word of English.

I disembarked at Kennedy on June 18, 1975. There was my husband, the typical expectant father shifting weight foot to foot, tears in his eyes. Behind him was a multitude I can only describe as my Italian family. Mothers, fathers, brothers, cousins. It wasn't till the next day that we were home alone, just the four of us. Nine months to the day after I had sent off the application, I was home with my children, and we were a family.

There are tactless people and once I was asked, "But don't you miss not seeing the traits of your husband, yourself, your family come out in the children?" I don't recall what I said to that person, but I did think about it and look for it. And there it was all around me. My son pouting when he hasn't had his way, just as my husband occasionally does, pushing the peas to the side of his dish, just as my husband does. And my daughter and I trading jokes, her love of fun the match

of mine, the faces she makes at my corny mommy jokes the same face
I made at my own mother's corny mommy jokes.

Do I regret that I never had the pleasure of giving birth? Of course,
at times I do. But I also know that if I had, I would not have gone to
South America, and where would my children be now? Would they
be warm, would they have nourishing food to eat? Would they be
cared for? Would they be loved?

Mormon Childbearing

Mary Ann Hafen was a devout young Mormon girl who migrated
to Utah with her family in 1860, and who at the age of nineteen
became the second wife of John Hafen. The first wife, Susette,
objected, but John Hafen followed the Word, set Mary Ann up in
a two-room adobe house, and spent one night with her, the next
with Susette. Later on two more wives were added to make the
full complement of four. In *Recollections of a Handcart Pioneer
of 1860* (so-called because the Mormon converts had literally
pushed and pulled their belongings across Iowa, Nebraska, Colorado, and Utah in handcarts), Mary Ann looks back on her life,
in particular on the births of her children. Although she was os-
tensibly a good Mormon, uncomplaining, never outwardly re-
gretting her shared existence, it was clearly the human element—
her children—rather than the divine that gave her life its richness
and meaning.

At the time that my first baby, Albert, was born—September 4, 1874—
I nearly lost my life with a hemorrhage. Sister Listen attended me. But
I got out of bed on the tenth day, for that was the prescribed time
when a woman should resume her household duties after childbirth.
For three months the baby cried with colic. Often I rocked his cradle
with my foot while I did my washing, sewing, and cooking. One night
he cried so much that my husband took him away and gave him a
whiskey sling. He slept soundly the rest of the night. . . .

We moved into a little one-room, sod-roofed house below town . . .
just before Mary, my second child, was born. . . . Sister Frehner attended me. As usual I got up on the tenth day. I suppose I caught cold
from the draughts that came up through the loose boards in the floor.
At any rate I had to go back to bed for three weeks and came very
close to dying. My sister Rosie brought her young baby with her and
did up my work each day. I drank barley gruel morning, noon and
night, and it helped me. . . .

At the birth of my third child, Bertha, November 24, 1881, I was troubled with sinking spells, nearly suffocating at times. Sister Frehner attended me again. My sister Rosie came and did up my work each day, and my husband took care of me at night. About six months after this John moved me into a better house. . . . In 1884 he married a young emigrant girl whom he had known while on his mission to Switzerland—Anna Huber. He sent her to live with me. Here she stayed for two years. In February, 1885, he married my sister Rosie, who was then a widow with two children. . . .

On the twelfth of March, 1885, Selena was born. Sister Keller, a neighbor who lived across the street, attended me and came each day to wash the baby, and Anna looked after the housework. . . .

A child was born to Anna in August, so they called him August. He was a fine, husky boy. One morning when he was eight months old we awoke to find the little fellow was dead. He must have smothered in the bed clothes. It was an awful blow to the young mother, but I comforted her the best I could. The next year Anna was given a house to herself.

In 1887 my son Wilfred was born—August 12. When he was about two months old I dreamed that I went to a big celebration at the public square in Santa Clara. Some women were preparing a picnic under the trees. I looked up and saw a large beautiful bird flying around. All at once it came down to where I stood with my baby in my arms. Then it seemed to be a young woman dressed in white. She reached out her arms for my baby, but I said I could not let it go. Then she snatched it from me and flew away. I had no power to hold it. When I awoke I feared I would not have him long, and I prayed the Lord to lengthen out his stay with us. And He did. [Wilfred, however, later died in a measles epidemic.]

. . . On July 14, 1890, Lovena, my sixth child, was born. . . . My last child was born December 8, 1893. He was a fine husky boy, weighing 12½ pounds. Aunt Mary Bunker, wife of the Bishop, was the acting midwife of the town. She came the customary ten days to bathe the baby while I was in bed. We called him Reuben LeRoy. As soon as his father learned of the birth, he came down to Bunkerville [John Hafen was now Bishop of Santa Clara]. I have never had a doctor at the birth of any of my children, nor at any other time for that matter, and I have never paid more than five dollars for the services of a midwife. . . .

I did not want to be a burden on my husband, but tried with my family to be self-supporting. I picked cotton on shares to add to our income; would take my baby to the fields while the other children were at school, for I never took the children out of school if it could possibly be avoided. That cotton picking was very tiresome, back-breaking work but it helped to clothe my children.

I always kept a garden. . . . With a couple of pigs, a cow, and some chickens, we got along pretty well.

[The years passed, Mary Ann's children married and set up their own (monogamous) households] and I was left alone. In the quiet evenings I used to sit and think of the times when my children were all at home and everything was so lively. . . .

My husband, who was still living in Santa Clara, died on May 4, 1928, in his ninetieth year. . . . He was a good man, reared fine children, and did the best he could by us all—27 children, 131 grandchildren, and 53 great-grandchildren.

How Oscar Wilde Got the Name "Oscar"

In *Son of Oscar Wilde* Vyvyan Holland describes how his father acquired the name "Oscar."

It has been said that my father was named after a son of Ossian, the third-century heroic poet of the Gael. That earlier Oscar was killed in single combat with King Cairbre at the battle of Gabhra. This is a fine romantic attribution, but it does not tally with the story told by my family, which is as follows:

In the year 1854 my grandfather read in a medical journal that King Oscar I of Sweden had been blind for some years. His symptoms were described; although he could not distinguish any forms, he could not only tell the difference between light and dark, but could also distinguish certain colors. This, then, was no disease of the optic nerve and, acting upon impulse, Dr. Wilde, as he then was, wrote to the king and suggested that he might be able to do something for him. The King of Sweden, desperate about his blindness, was naturally interested in anything that held out a hope of recovery. So my grandfather traveled to Stockholm, where he immediately diagnosed cataract and performed his operation.

When the bandages were removed and the king found that he had recovered his sight, he was naturally immensely grateful. Then came the question of what fee should be charged. My grandfather, no doubt reluctantly, refused to take any, on the ground that the whole expedition had been undertaken at his own suggestion. The king was at a loss how to show his gratitude in a practical way, and asked the doctor if there was anything he could do for him; to which my grandfather replied: "I have just learned that my wife has given birth to a son, and I would feel highly honored if your Majesty would consent to be his godfather." So Dr. Wilde returned to Ireland no richer than by a name to give his son.

"My Babies Came to Me in Troublous Times"

Pregnancy and poverty are never good combinations; they certainly were not so in England in the nineteenth and early twentieth centuries. Just before the outbreak of World War I, the Women's Co-operative Guild sought to aid working class women by lobbying for the inclusion of a maternity benefit clause in the Insurance Bill soon to go before the House of Commons. To obtain evidential material for their use, the Guild solicited information from 600 of their nearly 30,000 members. These were women who picked up work when, where, and however they could to supplement their husbands' meager incomes, which averaged less than a pound a week. They were asked to comment in general on their pregnancies and how they had affected, and been affected by, the economics of their lives. The three letters that follow were among many published in 1915 in a little book called *Maternity: Letters from Working Women* (Margaret Llewelyn Davies, editor).

I have not had children as fast as some, for which I am thankful, not because I do not love them, but because if I had more I do not think I could have done my duty to them under the circumstances. I may say I have had a very good partner in life, and that has made it better for me. But seeing my husband is only a weaver, I have not had a lot of money to go on with. I have been compelled to go out to work. I have worked when I have been pregnant, but I have always given up when I have been about six months, and then I have done all my own work up to the very last, and I can tell you it has been very hard work. Then when it has been over I have had to begin to do my housework at the fortnight end, and I think that is too soon, but what can women do when they have not the means to do it with? Of course, I am not half so bad as some. I have never carried a baby out to nurse. I have always managed to stop at home one year and get them walking. But I think if we as women had our right, we should not have to work at all during pregnancy, because I think that both the mother and baby would be better. I never knew so many bottle-fed babies as there is now. Nearly all the young married women cannot give breast. How is it? Now, I think because they work so hard before, do not get enough rest, therefore have no milk. And then, some will not begin with their own milk, because they know they have to go out to work. Hence the baby has to suffer. Mother's milk is the best food for baby. I heard a young mother with her first baby say the other day her husband's mother had told her not to bother with her breasts, it made a young woman look old giving her baby breast. What a mother! I think it is one of the grandest sights to see. So you see we have a lot of educating to do yet when we hear such things as these.

My first girl was born before I attained my twentieth year, and I had a stepmother who had had no children of her own, so I was not able to get any knowledge from her; and even if she had known anything I don't suppose she would have dreamt of telling me about these things which were supposed to exist, but must not be talked about. About a month before the baby was born I remember asking my aunt where the baby would come from. She was astounded, and did not make me much wiser. I don't know whether my ignorance had anything to do with the struggle I had to bring the baby into the world, but the doctor said that my youth had, for I was not properly developed. Instruments had to be used, and I heard the doctor say he could not tell whether my life could be saved or not, for he said there is not room here for a bird to pass. All the time I thought that this was the way all babies were born.

At the commencement of all my pregnancies I suffered terribly from toothache, and for this reason I think all married child-bearing women should have their teeth attended to, for days and nights of suffering of this kind must have a bad effect on both the mother and child. I also at times suffered torments from cramp in the legs and vomiting, particularly during the first three months. I hardly think the cramp can be avoided, but if prospective mothers would consult their doctors about the inability to retain food, I fancy that might be remedied. At the commencement of my second pregnancy I was very ill indeed. I could retain no food, not even water, and I was constipated for thirteen days, and I suffered from jaundice. This had its effect on the baby, for he was quite yellow at birth, and the midwife having lodgers to attend to, left him unwashed for an hour after birth. She never troubled to get his lungs inflated, and he was two days without crying. I had no doctor. I was awfully poor, so that I had to wash the baby's clothes in my bedroom at the fortnight's end; but had I had any knowledge like I possess now, I should have insisted at the very least on the woman seeing my child's lungs were properly filled. When we are poor, though, we cannot say what *must* be done; we have to suffer and keep quiet. The boy was always weakly, and could not walk when my third baby was born. He had fits from twelve to fourteen, but except for a rather "loose" frame, seems otherwise quite healthy now.

My third child, a girl, was born in a two-roomed "nearly underground" dwelling. We had two beds in the living-room, and the little scullery was very damp. Had it not been for my neighbours, I should have had no attendance after the confinement, and no fire often, for it was during one of the coal strikes. My fourth child, a boy, was born under better housing conditions, but not much better as regards money; and during the carrying of all my chlidren, except the first, I have had insufficient food and too much work. This is just an outline. Did I give it all, it would fill a book, as the saying goes.

In spite of all, I don't really believe that the children (with the exception of the oldest boy) have suffered much, only they might have been so much stronger, bigger, and better if I had been able to have better food and more rest.

Cleanliness has made rapid strides since my confinements; for never once can I remember having anything but face, neck, and hands washed until I could do things myself, and it was thought certain death to change the underclothes under a week.

For a whole week we were obliged to lie on clothes stiff and stained, and the stench under the clothes was abominable, and added to this we were commanded to keep the babies under the clothes.

I often wonder how the poor little mites managed to live, and perhaps they never would have done but for our adoration, because this constant admiration of our treasures did give them whiffs of fresh air very often.

My husband's lowest wage was 10s., the highest about £1 only, which was reached by overtime. His mother and my own parents generally provided me with clothing, most of which was cast-offs.

Although I have had eight children and one miscarriage, I am afraid my experiences would not help you in the least, as I am supposed to be one of those women who can stand anything. During my pregnancy I have always been able to do my own work.

With the boys labour has only lasted twenty minutes, girls a little longer. I have never needed a doctor's help, and it has always been over before he came. I have never had an after-pain in my life, so the doctors don't know what I am made of. I always had to get up and do my own work at three weeks' end. I work all day long at housework until six or seven, and I then take up all voluntary work I can for the sake of the Labour Cause. I am sorry and yet glad that my lot has not been so bad as others. My idea is that everything depends on how a woman lives, and how healthy she was born. No corsets and plenty of fruit, also a boy's healthy sports when she is young. I had the advantage of never having to work before I was married, and never have wanted for money, so when the struggle came I had a strong constitution to battle with it all.

My two last babies came to me in troublous times, the boy, four years since, when my husband (through being too prosperous and false friends) gave way to drink, although he never tried to strike me, or any of the outward cruelty that I know many wives have to contend with; but it was so different to what I had been used to, and three months before the baby came, I was practically an invalid. Up till dinner I could manage to get about, but after dinner I had to lie or sit as best I could. I could not get on nine in men's shoes, my feet swelled up so, and every night my hands were in agonies; the only relief I got was when I used to hammer them on the wall, to try and take the awful dumb pain out of them. Then when I started in labour, I was in it from eleven o'clock on the night of Thursday, the 17th of February till Saturday, the 19th, at 10 A.M. The waters broke at eleven o'clock on Thursday night, and baby came at ten o'clock on Saturday. The doctor had to put it back, as it was not coming naturally. Of course, I had chloroform; indeed, I had it with all my seven children, except two, as I have always such long and terrible labours, although I am a big woman—5 feet 8 inches, and I weigh over 13½ stone. I flooded with two. By the way, I am never able to get up under three weeks after confinement, as I always start to flood directly I make any movement, and I have to keep my nurse from five to seven weeks after. I always have terribly sore breasts, although the doctor treats them three months beforehand, but it makes no difference. My last confinement was the worst, as I found, five months before baby was born, that my husband was having an immoral going-on. The shock was so great, I could not speak when first I heard it. A cold shiver went over me, and my body seemed to go together in a hard lump. I was never right after, till she came. Indeed, I was never right till my operation last October. I always had a weary bearing-down pain in my body all the time I was carrying babies, and suffer a great deal in my back. . . . And yet I know many women who can go right up to a few hours before, and then tell me they think nothing about it, while to me it is like a time of horror from beginning to end. I suppose we are differently made, somehow.

My husband earned 6d. an hour . . . but we never went into debt.

What we could not pay for we did without, and I can assure you I have told my husband many times that I had had my dinner before he came in, so as there should be plenty to go round for the children and himself, but he found me out somehow, and so that was stopped, although I had been many times only half filled, and I am glad to say during the worst of the pinch time I was not pregnant.

Margaret Mead: When an Anthropologist Gives Birth

Margaret Mead was married to her third husband and had had numerous miscarriages in various parts of the South Pacific when on return to New York in 1939 she discovered she was once again pregnant. She was an old hand at birth, and made careful preparations, as she details in *Blackberry Winter: My Earlier Years*.

From the moment it was certain that I was pregnant, I took extreme precautions. I took a leave of absence from the Museum and gave up riding on streetcars, trains, and buses. I was given vitamin E as an aid to nidification, and I kept the baby. . . .

I looked for a pediatrician first, and talked with Ben Spock, a young pediatrician who had been psychoanalyzed and who was recommended to me by my child development friends. I explained to Ben that I wanted him to be present at the birth, so that he could take over the baby's care immediately, that I wanted to have a film made of the baby's birth, so that afterward it could be referred to with some degree of accuracy; that I wanted a wet nurse if my milk was slow in coming in, and that I wanted permission to adjust the feeding schedule to the baby instead of the clock.

Ben replied genially—for after all he was dealing with someone more or less of his own age with a reputation in his field—that he would come to the delivery and that I could feed the baby as often as I pleased. He also knew of a good obstetrician, Claude Heaton, who had some odd ideas and might be willing to listen to me. . . .

And so it came about that at thirty-eight, after many years of experience as a student of child development and of childbirth in remote villages—watching children born on a steep wet hillside, in the "evil place" reserved for pigs and defecation, or while old women threw stones at the inquisitive children who came to stare at the parturient woman—I was to share in the wartime experience of young wives all around the world. My husband had gone away to take his wartime place, and there was no way of knowing whether I would

ever see him again. We had a little money, a recent bequest from
Gregory's aunt Margaret, so I would not have to work until after the
baby was born. But that was all. Initially, we had thought that I might
join Gregory in England, but my mother-in-law wrote that they were
sending away busloads of pregnant women. Obviously it was better to
stay in America than to become a burden in Britain as the country
girded itself for war. . . .

The day before the baby was born . . . a cable came from Gregory
telling me that he had applied for a permit to come to America. . . .
The following night my father came over from Philadelphia and took
me out to dinner. Soon after he brought me home, the water broke. It
is astonishing how seldom things of this kind, which are apparently
innerly determined, happen in the wrong place and at the wrong
time. Six weeks earlier, I had spoken at Barnard's seventy-fifth anni-
versary celebration. When my former professor, Miss Howard, telephoned to ask whether I would do this, I had said, "But I'm expecting
a baby at about that time." Her response came crisply, "Well, you
won't have it at the dinner, will you?" And as I was getting ready to
go to the hospital, Dr. Beatrice Hinkle telephoned to ask me about
acepting an award and did not see any reason why the imminent birth
of the baby should interfere with my speaking to her.

At the hospital I was made to time my own pains with an ordinary
watch, and I remember my annoyance at not having a stopwatch. They
were convinced that as a primipara I could not be so ready for birth
and I was given medication to slow things down. In the end the baby's
birth had to be slowed down for another ten minutes while Myrtle
McGraw, who was making the film of the birth, sent for a flashbulb
that had been left in her car. . . . And I was fascinated to discover
that far from being "ten times worse than the worst pain you have ever
had" (as our childless woman doctor had told us in college) or "worse
than the worst cramps you ever had, but at least you get something
out of it" (as my mother had said), the pains of childbirth were altogether different from the enveloping effects of other kinds of pain.
These were pains one could follow with one's mind; they were like a
fine electric needle outlining one's pelvis.

Today, preparation for natural childbirth gives women a chance to
learn and to think about the task of labor, instead of simply fearing
how they will endure the pains. In fact, the male invention of natural
childbirth has had a magnificent emancipating effect on women, who
for generations had been muffled in male myths instead of learning
about a carefully observed actuality. I have never heard primitive

women describe the pains of childbirth. But in societies in which men were forbidden to see birth, I have seen men writhing on the floor, acting out their conception of what birth pangs were like. In one such society, the wife herself had squatted quietly on a steep hillside in the dark and had cut the cord herself, following the instructions not of a trained midwife but of the woman who had most recently borne a child.

Mary Catherine Bateson was born on December 8, 1939, and looked very much herself.

A Pioneer Child Remembers

I was born in Florence, Arizona Territory, on December 15, 1878. My birth was really an experience for my father since I came while he was scouring the town looking for the only doctor, whom he found later drunk and playing cards in the back room of a saloon. The small house in which I was born had dirt walls, a dirt floor, and a dirt roof. There was only one board floor in the village, and that was in the most prosperous saloon. Once in a while the townspeople would clear out the bar and hold their dances in this saloon. All the mothers brought their babies and put them to bed on a long bench. Mother was a New Englander, but she did go to these dances until some man sat on me. After that, she refused to go any more.

Edith Stratton Kitt, *Pioneering in Arizona: the*
Reminiscences of Emerson Oliver Stratton
and Edith Stratton Kitt

Birthing in the African Bush and on the Scottish Isles

Faith Aitken, a Scottish friend who chose particularly remote parts of the world for her children's births, sent me the following report:

Our first two children were born at Hilltop, a colonial period wooden bungalow in Calabar, Nigeria, built on stilts and with wide overhanging eaves and verandahs on every side to withstand the tropical heat and rains. The old bungalow was then used as a nursing home attached to the government hospital. On neither occasion was the African doctor present at the actual birth. When Jean-Marion, our eldest, arrived, the doctor was away up country serving as a witness in a ritual murder case. Instead the birth was supervised by the immensely experienced Miss Iso, the midwife. "It will be all right, it will be all right," she would say over and over again as she wiped away the sweat.

Both were hot season babies. You might say my sense of planning was not all that it might have been.

This was particularly true of Sally, the youngest, who was born in Scotland while we were on leave from Nigeria. During that summer we were staying with my parents on the tiny island of Iona in the Inner Hebrides. Iona is where St. Columba landed in 563 A.D., bringing Christianity to Scotland from Ireland. Only three miles long and half as wide, it is separated from Mull, its neighboring and much larger island, by a mile of often very rough water. It takes at least four hours to reach the mainland, whether you go by sea or across Mull. Iona has a year-round population of less than a hundred, greatly inflated in the summer months when the Iona Community, who were restoring the ruined buildings of the Abbey, were there. There is a resident Church of Scotland minister, and someone to mind the post office and the shop, but policeman, doctor, and district nurse visited only when required from Mull.

That summer my parents, a friend with two small daughters, and our family of four were all crowded into a small cottage in the village. By August I was, according to my calculations, in my eighth month of pregnancy, and we planned to return to Glasgow (where the baby clothes and nappies were) well in time for the birth a month later. One morning I felt some indigestion and backache which, as the morning wore on, I began to realize was perhaps not indigestion and backache. The district nurse on Mull was contacted by phone. I was moved into the front room. Bill, my husband, took three-year-old Jean-Marion and nineteen-month-old Robin to a friend's for lunch. My father produced stacks of newspaper and kept checking on the hot water. The district nurse arrived just in time to deliver the baby, Sally, who when weighed on one of those meathook type scales, was a hefty eight pounds, ten ounces. Hardly premature. She was washed, put into borrowed nightgown and nappies, and spent her first night in traditional fashion wrapped in a blanket in the bottom drawer. The nurse was triumphant. She hadn't had a baby to look after in years, and she came over on the ferry every day for the next ten days to bath her. When neighbors asked Jean-Marion if her baby sister would be called Iona, as several other little girls not even born there had been named, she replied indignantly, "She's a girl, not an island."

Postscript: Faith's sister-in-law, Carol Morton, when asked about births on the neighboring island of Eigg, wrote: "All births now take place in Glasgow—or are meant to. Apparently last summer a well-built sixteen-year-old felt a bit sick to her stomach after pony trekking. You've guessed it, the baby arrived, very "natu-rally" according to the doctor, with new Granny rather gaping, not having even suspected her daughter was pregnant."

"My Grandmother Taught Me All These Things"

Delfina Cuero is an elderly member of the Diegueño Indian tribe of California, a woman whose life spanned the primitive and "modern" in Indian life. In the following selection from her auto-biography she looks back over her childbearing days. She deplores the fact that having missed an initiation ceremony, she did not know what to do to save her first child (born when she was barely thirteen herself), and she regrets the decline of other old customs by which births were celebrated in the Diegueño tribe.

. . . I was told by my grandmother . . . when a lady is pregnant, she must not look at anything that is bad, or even see a fox or a snake. You must not look at anything like that or it will mark the baby. You try not to see anything when you are pregnant. The oldtimers would not let a pregnant woman or a menstruating woman go into a garden. She had to stay by herself and not bother anything. She could not gather wild greens, or wash and do things like that. She could not go near sick persons or garden plants without hurting them.

Grandmothers taught the girls that when they were pregnant they must not eat too much or the baby will be born big or have some kind of trouble. They can eat anything they want unless it makes them sick, except they must stay away from salt. Women are weak nowadays. Long time ago, they just kept on doing regular work, they went out and gathered food and whatever was needed, even heavy things, and it didn't hurt them. They just had to be careful not to see bad things.

In the real old days, grandmothers taught these things about life at the time of a girl's initiation ceremony, when she was about to be-come a woman. Nobody just talked about these things ever. It was all in the songs and myths that belonged to the ceremony. All that a girl needed to know to be a good wife, and how to have babies and to take care of them was learned at the ceremony, at the time when a girl be-came a woman. We were taught about food and herbs and how to make things by our mothers and grandmothers all the time. But only at the ceremony for girls was the proper time to teach the special things women had to know. Nobody just talked about those things, it was all in the songs.

But I'm not that old, they had already stopped having the cere-monies before I became a woman, so I didn't know these things until later. Some of the other girls had the same trouble I did after I was married. No one told me anything. I knew something was wrong with me but I didn't know what. Food was becoming hard to find then and we had to go a long way to find enough greens. My husband was away hunting meat. Sometimes the men were gone for several days before they found anything. One day I was a long way from Ha-a looking for greens. I had a terrible pain. I started walking back home but I had to stop and rest when the pain was too much. Then the baby came, I couldn't walk any more, and I didn't know what to do. Finally an uncle came out looking for me when I didn't return. My grandmother had not realized my time was so close or she would not have let me go so far alone. They carried me back but I lost the baby. My grandmother took care of me so I recovered. Then she taught me all these things about what to do and how to take care of babies.

After that, I had my babies by myself. I didn't have any help from anybody. My grandmother lived near us but she knew that now I knew what to do, so she never helped me. I did what I had been taught. . . . I dug a little place and built a hot fire and got hot ashes. I put something, bark or cloth, over the ashes and put the baby in it to keep the baby warm.

So that the navel will heal quickly and come off in three days, I took two rounds of cord and tied it, and then put a clean rag on it. I burned a hot fire outside our hut to get hot dirt to wrap in a cloth. I put this on the navel and changed it all night and day to keep it warm till the navel healed. To keep the navel from getting infected, I burned cow hide, or any kind of skin, till crisp, then ground it. I put this powder on the navel. I did this and no infection started in my babies. Some women didn't know this and if infection started, I would help them to stop it this way.

When each baby was new born, I bathed it in elderberry blossom or willow bark tea. Then after I had washed the baby's face with elderberry blossom tea, I burned some honey real brown, then put water with it and cleaned the baby's face all over. This takes any stuff off the baby's face. The afterbirth is buried in the floor of the house.

Some people are not careful and they eat right away and then the mother nurses the baby and it gets infected. The mother must wait a while to eat, then first eat atole. Next, the mother eats lots of vegetables and drinks lots of herb or mint teas. Never drink water! Never eat beans when nursing a baby, it will ruin the baby.

I did all this myself. When my children were older, if they got sick, I used herbs. That is all I used and my children got well again. There are herbs for stomach pains, colds, tooth aches, and everything that the Indians knew. There is a real good one to stop bleeding right away from a bad cut. There is another good one for bad burns and to stop infection. If a woman drinks lots and lots of xa'a'nayul she can keep from having babies, but there is another herb, even better, that the Indians used to use to keep from having babies every year. They are hard to find now because we can't go everywhere to look for them any more.

I named all of my children myself. I didn't know anything about baptizing them then; I just went ahead like the Indians did and gave them names. When my oldest child was a year or two old, they had a party to welcome him to the group. Everybody got together and they built a big ramada for me and they brought their food together. We had a big fire. . . . They circled around the fire hand in hand and following each other, and jumping with both feet and singing. They were glad because they would have more Indians, another baby added to the group. All the people brought presents for the baby—baskets, ollas, food, mud dolls, or bow and arrows and different things, whatever was right to start the child. Sometimes they also brought tiny things like the real ones, tiny ollas and baskets and bow and arrows. The child was given its name at the party.

By the time my second child who lived was old enough, we didn't have parties for the new children any more. I don't know why, maybe it was too hard to get enough to eat. I'm just telling what happened to me, what I know.

My grandmother told me that a long time ago it was different. The people used to be stronger, she said. They did not have to use hardly anything to eat when they had those dances. They made a juice from the willow, like Kool-aid, not fermented. They would drink that and dance for days, she told me. They were naked too, a long time ago, things were so bad and they had so little.

The fire dance was religious; they danced all night, till the sun came up. The songs that go with it have to be sung in the right order, from early evening until dawn. There is a song for each time of the night and as the sun is rising. It was danced at the death of a person and also to welcome a new child. My grandfather said they used to have dances for going hunting, to bring blessings on the hunt; but I never saw one. The dance for a child brings good luck and blessing to the child and to all the people who dance. That is what they did for me and my first child to live. They might have done more before, but they don't even do this now.

15. Fictionalizing

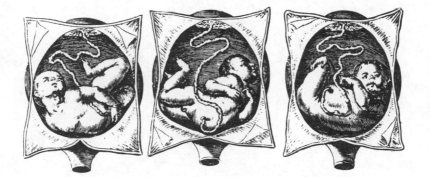

The reticence that once cloaked the physical and psychological aspects of childbirth in fiction began to dissipate in the 1930s with women writers like Anaïs Nin, crumbled further in the 1950s and 1960s with Mary McCarthy and Doris Lessing, among others, and dissolved completely in recent years with a host of excellent writers who spoke out of a new awareness of childbirth as a peculiarly feminine experience. In the following excerpts a few contemporary women deal with the maternal urge in modern society.

Anne Tyler: Celestial Navigation

Motherhood is what I was made for, and pregnancy is my natural state. I believe that. All the time I was carrying Darcy I was happier than I had ever been before, and I felt better. And looked better. At least, to myself I did. I don't think Guy agreed. He was funny about things like that. He didn't want to feel the baby kick, wouldn't even touch me the last few months, acted surprised whenever I wanted to go out shopping or to a movie. "Won't it bother you, people staring?" he asked. "Why would it bother me?" I said. "Why would they stare?" *He* was the one that was bothered. He didn't even want to come with me to the labor room the night she was born; my mother had to do it. She had thawed out some since I got pregnant. She stayed with me all through the pains, talking and keeping my spirits up, but most of my mind was on Guy. I thought, Wouldn't you think he could go through this with me? He'll worry more, surely, out there in the waiting room not knowing. The doctor had been upset about my age. He had told Guy I was still growing, much too young to have a baby of my own. What if I died? Shouldn't Guy be there holding my hand? But no— "I'm scared I might pass out or something," he said, and laughed, with his face sharp and white. Then he whispered, "I'm scared the pain will make you angry for what I done to you." "Oh, but *Guy—*" I said. Then my mother said, "Never mind, honey, Mama's here." She sat by my bed and rubbed my back, and sponged my forehead, and read aloud from yesterday's newspaper—any old thing she came across, it didn't matter, none of it made sense to me anyway. When it came time to wheel me into the delivery room she said, "I'll be right here praying, honey, everything's going to be fine," but I saw that she was worried. I suppose she had taken to heart what the doctor said. Well, doctors don't know everything they claim to. Having that baby was the easiest thing I ever did. I was *meant* to have babies. Age has nothing to do with it.

Anne Roiphe: Torch Song

The next day was a Sunday. Jim slept most of the day, but in the early evening, as he often did, he became frightened and anxious. "What if nobody thinks the new book is any good?" he said. "Marjorie, you're the one who thinks I have genius. Maybe it's stupidity that keeps this illusion alive in your decaying brain. Why do you have to be such an angel? You're driving me crazy with your martyrdom. You make me feel guilty all the time. It's your fault I need to drink. I'm not as good as you think I am." "Yes, you are," I said, as I had said a thousand times before. It was hardly the moment to tell him I wanted a baby. But suddenly, perversely, I told him just that.

"A baby?" he said incredulously. "A child? You must be out of your mind. Why would I want that? Who with any intelligence wants this globe to keep spinning?" He thought I was teasing. Then he realized I was serious. "For Christ's sake," he said, "isn't it enough for you just to take care of me? It was enough for my mother, enough for my grandmother. What's the matter with you? Anyway, you certainly shouldn't have a child. You never wanted to be an ordinary Scarsdale woman. You want to be a part of a larger, more glamorous world." "But I want a baby," I said softly. I was risking his disapproval, his withdrawal, losing him. But I did hold some good cards in this game, his various needs for me and my services. It wasn't just that he owed it to me. I knew he, like a deaf man listening to music, wanted to love me, make me happy too. I made his breakfast and dinner, listened as he read me his work in progress and discussed it with him, sat at the edge of the bathtub and absorbed his rages at other writers. He liked the apartment he and my mother's decorator had designed. He was by now totally attached to the idea of my presence in his life. He couldn't,

I hoped, say no to me when at last I chose to demand something for myself. "Are you serious, Marjorie?" he asked.

"I must have a baby. You owe me that." "Why? What for?" He went in the bathroom and closed the door, giving me time to prepare my answer. But I didn't have an answer he would be able to understand. I didn't think I had an irresistible maternal instinct, or that I would achieve immortality through genetic extension. I had no religious conviction of any sort. When he emerged from the bathroom I said only, "Trust me. It's the right thing to do." He looked at me with the expression of a chicken eyeing a hawk. "I'm not sure I can do it," he said mildly. "Of course you can," I said. "All right," he said resignedly, "we'll try." . . .

I was lucky. It took only that night and one other. I started to throw up on my way to work. Jim got some money from the paperback sale of his book, and from articles. I quit my job, ignoring his increasing fears that success would desert him. . . .

The baby grew inside me, and I spent more and more of my newfound freedom fighting the nausea that signaled hormonal happenings. Could I be allergic to the new being, its fingerless hands clenched over unseeing eyes? Sometimes I lay on my bed while Jim was sleeping into the late morning and I cupped my hands over my round belly and tried to imagine what I couldn't see. I had bought every book on the subject I could find, and week by week looked at pictures of fetuses the age of mine. I was an encyclopedia of information on normal gynecology, and yet sometimes I felt cold terror. I imagined horrors: the baby would grow enormous and its head would push into my lungs and stop my breathing. All the blood in my body would be sucked into the dormant infant and I would, like an exposed Egyptian mummy, crumble into dust. The baby would die within me and the release mechanisms fail, and the baby's body would decompose and putrefaction would spread through my blood and I would, like a gangrene victim, grow stiff, foam at the mouth, choke for breath, and die.

At other times I thought of how I would hold the baby, the new soft skin against my breast. My nipples would be the center of the baby's life, and my arms folding around the infant would fold around myself, holding the two of us together. Never would I allow a Gretchen to touch my child. Never would other hands wash or clean or cut the fingernails of my child. Never would I allow my baby to cry out in the middle of the night and see a stranger appear at the bedside. Never would I, like my mother, go to parties or shopping, never would I leave the child to reach out its arms for the reassuring touch that had disappeared. Never would my child wait outside my door for me to finish a nap, a phone conversation, a card game. I would undo, I would redo my childhood. I would do for my child what had never been done for me. It seemed so simple a way to achieve purification, to make one's way steadily over the debris of the past. I was for the most part confident of the future. These first kicks seemed timid, so light I wasn't certain expectation had not created them, but then, as the weeks passed and they grew stronger, even visible as the mounting flesh of the stomach shook and shifted from the movements within, I grew more confident. As the baby kicked I welcomed this tremor that told me it wasn't a false pregnancy. It was not an illusion. The baby was still only a collection of raw tissue, little knees pulled up, helpless to stop the forces that were causing it to grow, propelling it and the bloody tissue it survived on into the world. I and I alone would, with the power of a feeling so great I sometimes felt crushed and exhausted by it—this love I was readying would make a universe.

Tillie Olsen: "I Stand Here Ironing"

She was a beautiful baby. The first and only one of our five that was beautiful at birth. You do not guess how new and uneasy her tenancy in her now-loveliness. You did not know her all those years she was thought homely, or see her poring over her baby pictures, making me tell her over and over how beautiful she had been—and would be, I would tell her—and was now, to the seeing eye. But the seeing eyes were few or non-existent. Including mine.

I nursed her. They feel that's important nowadays. I nursed all the children, but with her, with all the fierce rigidity of first motherhood, I did like the books then said. Though her cries battered me to trembling and my breasts ached with swollenness, I waited till the clock decreed.

Why do I put that first? I do not even know if it matters, or if it explains anything.

She was a beautiful baby. She blew shining bubbles of sound. She loved motion, loved light, loved color and music and textures. She would lie on the floor in her blue overalls patting the surface so hard in ecstasy her hands and feet would blur. She was a miracle to me, but when she was eight months old I had to leave her daytimes with the woman downstairs to whom she was no miracle at all, for I worked or looked for work and for Emily's father, who "could no longer endure" (he wrote in his good-bye note) "sharing want with us."

I was nineteen.

Marge Piercy: Small Changes

Neil was trying to explain the Lamaze method and how he would be helping Miriam through her labor. Emily was so shocked at the idea of him being present throughout in the labor room—it was as if he had said that he used the women's lavatory in a theater—that she expressed herself loudly. That did it. Miriam could sit back and watch.

All of that Saturday the argument continued. Neil was determined to extract from his mother an acknowledgment that their way of birth was superior. He was after his initial desultory agreement committed to it. He identified with the Lamaze method more heavily than she did. She remained a little skeptical, saying to herself, Well, if it gets really bad, I can always ask for something. But Neil cared. The ideology appealed to him: birth could be beautiful and natural if only you wanted it to be and mastered the proper techniques. They would give birth according to the rules and together. It was almost scientific. It gave him a role and a purpose. . . .

The labor went on and on. Sometimes she felt exhausted and just wished the whole damn thing would end and forget the idiot panting and counting and carrying on. Contractions, my ass. It was pain and big pain and it hurt like hell. However, she continued. Partly she was ashamed to act as if she couldn't handle it, having gone this far. And she wanted to be awake, she wanted that desperately. What was the use in giving birth if she let them deprive her of experiencing it?

"But, Neil . . . it does hurt. It hurts. I'm telling you."

"You're fighting me. Go with the contractions. Don't panic now, Miriam. We're so close."

"I'm not panicking! I'm just telling the truth, damn it. Neil, it hurts."

"Contractions aren't pain. Don't forget now, don't tighten up and hurt yourself. Let me help you."

It was rhetoric. Pain was pain and calling it contractions didn't make it hurt any less. Wave upon wave upon wave. She panted and did her relaxations and did what she had been taught and she was angry. She did not scream, she did not cry out, she did not do any of the things she had been taught were shameful and ignorant. She panted instead of screaming. She counted instead of crying. She bit her lips and bit her cheeks and did what she had been taught and went on. On, in the ridiculous little hospital gown designed to rob her of all dignity. On, among the nurses and residents and doctors doing their business and processing her with as little nuisance to them as possible. On between the blank anonymous walls. She remembered Sally's birth. Perhaps she was not as scared as some of the women around her because at least she had seen birth herself, taken part in the birth of Fern in a roomful of women, singing and rubbing Sally's belly and kissing her and talking softly. Neil was with her, she held his hand, she held tight to him, but she could feel always his fear that she would not be good enough, that she would not be committed enough, that she would back down from the way they had chosen.

It went on and it went on and it went on. She still wanted to stay conscious though often, sinking in the pain she sought to go with, she could not remember why. Could remember nothing. Had no notion who or why she was. She felt herself weakening. Her body was big and strong but it was weakening. Yet she went on. To give up, to go under, would be to lose all the advantage of her hours of suffering, ten hours, twelve hours, thirteen hours, fourteen hours, fifteen hours since she had come into the hospital. Her stubbornness was a rock. She sucked the rock in her mouth along with a sponge. She felt she would die rather than let them knock her out. She had her rag of life gripped in her teeth. She wanted to stay in the light. She would not let go.

It went on and it went on and it went on. Finally, seventeen hours from the time she had checked in, she was taken into the delivery room. . . . She experienced a strong urge to sit up, to get off the table and down on the floor. To squat. But they were strapping her down. That felt all wrong. She felt a strong compulsion to get off her back, to squat, but could not. She bore down where she was, although the urge to raise her whole body forward seemed almost as strong as the urge to push, to thrust. It was moving very fast now, it was plummeting heavy as a truck downhill: huge and heavy and out of control. It carried her, no longer worried, no longer afraid, no longer weak. Now, finally, she pushed. She watched in the mirror overhead except when he was cutting her with the scissors. Then she looked away because it was terrible to see her tender genital flesh sliced through.

When she looked back, she stared and cried out because the head, the head was blooming there. Huge coming through her. Ridiculous. A dark wet head emerging from the nest of towels and large sheet that swathed her blood-dabbled, strained and still swollen thighs. In the mirror a pile of laundry was giving birth. A person was emerging. Then she was laughing, because it looked ridiculous in the mirror. Oh! For real, at last. The child! "I did it!" she cried out and Dr. Foreman said, "Of course you did." Foreman was reaching up, pulling, and the shoulder was out. The baby turned its head. She could not tell yet whether Ariane or Jeffrey was coming from her to the light. Red shoulder, slippery, glossy, moving, alive. The baby turned its head toward its shoulder, it was for real, alive, she saw it move! The other shoulder. Gradually, gradually, the baby slipped out of her, oh beautiful creature thrust into the world glowing and bright.

Upside down he held her baby, using a rubber tube in its mouth and nose, and already—they had not even struck the baby if they really did that—her baby was crying.

"You have a girl, Mrs. Stone."

"Ariane!" She was flooded with joy. Her own, her child, her darling, her flesh and blood. "Give her to me." My daughter. . . .

She was weary and spent. She had expected to feel good afterward. She had expected to be rewarded for doing the birth the right way. The baby out, her body back, joy to the world. But she felt like something a truck had run over. Her breasts hurt, huge and swollen and sore and hot to the touch. She had not expected it all to feel so messy. She could not quite rise to the moment but felt as if she were hanging in dim tepid water not quite able to break through the surface to fresh air. . . .

She was glad to get out of the hospital, but she felt numbed still. Felt alienated from herself, her body, Neil, even Ariane. Least perhaps from Ariane. They were connected through her breasts. Every few hours Ariane cried for her, every few hours her breasts ached to be suckled. They were bound in animal linkage and that bond was the most real thing she could still feel. But she was frightened. She did not feel that she loved her baby. This strange animal in her lap with its smells and its loud cries, the fierce desires that shook it, she was not quite sure what she was doing with it. They belonged to each other through an animal bond but she felt so little else, she was terrified.

When she looked sideways at Neil, she felt distant and alien from him too. He was not bound to the baby by the chain of feedings and hours, yet she could feel love loosed in him toward Ariane. He hovered over her, crooning and gazing, and very gently with the tips of his fingers caressed her nose, her ears, her fingers. He babbled over her, he loudly rejoiced, he truly found her outrageously beautiful. He demanded of everyone within range that they admire her. But soon he

left Miriam in the house that felt too big around her and went to the
office where she had used to go. She thought of her old desk. She sat
and wept for her baby, for herself, because she was a bad mother. She
did not love Ariane, she did not love Neil, and she could not stand
herself. She was empty and harried and oozing and spent. Poor
Ariane! Poor Miriam! They had all gone off and left her and what
was she to do? All but this creature grasping her breast for food.
Feeling like the youngest sister punished by the wicked witch in a
fairy tale, the youngest sister turned suddenly into a crone for punishment, she clutched her baby and wept in the bedroom chair.

Alice Walker: Meridian

She might not have given him away to the people who wanted him.
She might have murdered him instead. Then killed herself. They
would all have understood this in time. She might have done it except
for one thing: One day she really looked at her child and loved him
with as much love as she loved the moon or a tree, which was a considerable amount of impersonal love. She wanted to know more about
his perfect, if unplanned-for existence.

"Who are you?" she asked him.

"Where were you when I was twelve?"

"Who *are* you?" she persisted, studying his face for signs of fire,
watermarks, some scar that would intimate a previous life.

"Were there other people where you were? Did you come from a
planet of babies?" She thought she could just imagine him there, on
such a planet, pulling the blue grass up by the handfuls.

Now that she looked at him, the child was beautiful. She had
thought him ugly, like a hump she must carry on her back.

"You will no longer be called Eddie Jr." she said. "I'll ask them to
call you Rundi, after no person, I hope, who has ever lived."

When she gave him away she did so with a light heart. She did not
look back, believing she had saved a small person's life.

But she had not anticipated the nightmares that began to trouble
her sleep. Nightmares of the child, Rundi, calling to her, crying, suffering unbearable deprivations because she was not there, yet she knew
it was just the opposite: Because she was not there he needn't worry,
ever, about being deprived. Of his life, for instance. She felt deeply
that what she'd done was the only thing, and was right, but that did
not seem to matter. On some deeper level than she had anticipated or
had even been aware of, she felt condemned, consigned to penitence,

for life. The past pulled the present out of shape as she realized that what Delores Jones had said was *not*, in fact, true. If her mother had had children in slavery she would not, automatically, have been allowed to keep them, because they would not have belonged to her but to the white person who "owned" them all. Meridian knew that enslaved women had been made miserable by the sale of their children, that they had laid down their lives, gladly, for their children, that the daughters of these enslaved women had thought their greatest blessing from "Freedom" was that it meant they could keep their own children. And what had Meridian Hill done with *her* precious child? She had given him away. She thought of her mother as being worthy of this maternal history, and of herself as belonging to an unworthy minority, for which there was no precedent and of which she was, as far as she knew, the only member.

Rosellen Brown: "Mustard Seed"

The baby is in her carriage for the first time. Under her fist-tight head is a fancy pillow-slip, lace all around, with a satin stripe like Miss America's, announcing her name before anyone asks. It is not Molly Dugan's style, rather a gift of her mother, whose way of making the best of things tends toward the grandiose in exact proportion to her misery.

Molly looks at her baby and thinks again, Yes, a child can come as though by parcel post. A knock at the door, she's yours, given like a gift. Fairy tales are full of that, children delivered from hand to hand, prizes, forfeits, always someone's to give. . . . She has signed a paper that says I am sane. *Promises* I am sane (which in the first place is not sane). Says I will apportion my moneys into two piles, a small one for myself, a tall one for this child's shoes and cereal. It's a contract, she thinks, stamped, sealed and filed somewhere, and I have married a daughter. . . .

Molly is pushing the carriage through the front door. She gets the front wheels down the doorstep onto the welcome mat and stops. Good God, how do you get a carriage down the steps with a baby in it? She had arranged Carie Lyn so carefully, as though for an ocean voyage. She looks around, flushing, to see if anyone has been watching. All the women on this block who were born to this.

Molly has fair skin, freckled like a lawn full of clover. It prickles now, carbonated. She is about to think the worst thought she knows, it gathers in her exactly as her migraines do, a twitch of imminence be-

fore she even knows it's there. She is pushing it away almost with her
hands, her breath held, averting her eyes from herself as the quick
dumb tears press forward. Who says, who says, any other mother would
know better? How would she know, any other, any real, how will I do
this, this is not my baby who ended in a bottle, what difference does it
make whose baby, she walked out holding him (the ones who don't
make it, the nurse said, are more often hims) stiffly away from her
white cotton cleanness like something unclean, unnatural as the pain,
in a labeled jar my bulbous clot of a child, unchild, the best in me
purple, blue, brown, red, like something that exploded. Where do
they bury the little yolks that are not even corpses, do they burn them
back to ash-flecks the size of sperm and egg, or flush them down, or
chop them up in a bowl? She asked and the nurse, making out the
death certificate in her name, patted her arm as though she were
insane.

She turns her close-cropped head against the door frame but does
not remove her hand from the cool carriage handle. Her tears seem to
make their way like an underground spring up through inches of
dirt, the rigid silence she has enforced on herself since Verne made her
weep that one last time, turning his purie-marble eyes on her. "No we
will not, no, what the stinking world does not need is a child who
smells like we do. You and me, separately and together." Did he celebrate the death, the non-life of that one, then? Did he wish it? *Did he
cause it?* Were all the children of his stone body stone? Or was she, old
flesh, just past its prime, so rotten inside she could not warm anything
growing there but her own death?

Molly jerks the carriage up the doorstep again, brakes it, very carefully lifts the baby out, Carie Lyn Dugan swathed in the softest pink
and white blankets, and—suddenly casual—rests the bundle on the hall
floor, sleeping face up, and rackets the carriage down the cement steps,
one-two-three. She marches back, picks up the baby, who stirs with a
comfortable moan, and before she has blinked her eyes open, has her
deep under the carriage hood again, the CARIE LYN pillow ("Really
dear," her mother had said, seizing on a focus for her disapproval,
"they had to special-order this! Couldn't you have picked a more
everyday name?" Always different, Molly, is what she was thinking, of
course; always up your own tree, alone) pressed to the back, all sweet
sixteen ruffles flapping down George Street. Sometimes these days,
mood alternating with mood, she frightens herself a little. It is like
living with a stranger. . . .

An absurdity. Molly Fry Dugan, B.A., M.A., French with honors, divorcee, WASP, dreamer of adolescent dreams, keeper of her own body, gratefully knowing it is in better hands now than it has ever been before, her canvas shoes on large feet, her long legs attached to a pale and hollow trunk that no one seems much inclined to want to come near or look at in light or darkness (Verne having said that her small wan nipples were like owls' eyes, sad and round and too lonely to be helped)—that Molly Dugan is wheeling, jerkily, a borrowed carriage with (it is becoming apparent) an incipient squeak; the carriage containing the delicious curled body, all new cells, some never sloughed yet! of the baby she found by irrevocable legal means in a basket one day at her body's closed gates. An absurdity.

She is walking in a fog of humiliation, bumping into the dangling carriage basket every few steps, she is so out of phase with her own stride. This is not the way things were supposed to be! It is all falling apart, falling down, ashes, ashes, can she keep the baby alive a day? It awes her that people, teen-agers even, who can't pass her French exams, seem to manage to keep such tender bones attached. Can you be mortified before yourself? Yes, she sees it, if you spend enough time alone, you make a good enough audience and judge. She wants to go and cry behind a tree, like a kid who has to pee.

No trail blazer, ladies and gentlemen, no historic landmark case, whose name was not in the evening edition, hardly the first single woman in the state of New York to be allowed to adopt a baby alone, still she is standing on Atlantic Avenue, corner Fowler Street, covering her prickling eyes with her hands, having forgotten how to set one foot before the other. She is flushed, sweat pokes down between her unuseful breasts. At a standstill, swaying, her face is in her hands. . . .

Carie is stirring, protesting because the carriage has stopped. She is thrusting her head from side to side like a turtle. She has, or will have, the head of a little blackberry. Though the hair is still thin there are very tight shiny curls laid one above the other, blue-black, purple-black. Her skin, a light pinky-brown when she was born, is darkening now day by day; at the folds of her elbows, behind her knees, the places her mother drips the tickly water from her cloth, for fun, she is very dark, graying toward black, just as you might expect in shadowy places. Molly is not dismayed at how much browner she is turning, but she feels guilt in exchange for her curiosity: Who is this stranger? (Hey lady, she is your daughter. We hereby give her to you because she is—even to you who intend to love her—strange, if not ugly. To the state she is worthless, less even. A burden. Therefore she is yours for the asking. If you can give her some worth, fine though not so much it

will ever come home to the state to roost. And keep the little bastard
off the welfare rolls, will you?)

So Molly begins to move again. Fowler has narrowed by now, near
the Projects, and gotten a bit patchy, and the carriage rides the waves
of broken sidewalk like a small ship. Every now and then she rams the
front wheels against a protruding square and it nearly bounces out of
her hands. It's a bad time of day to be walking here—school must just
be over and the sidewalk is awash with teen-agers. This end of the
street the stores are random and grubby, many of indeterminate nature, every face is black, and the children are exuberantly at home.
Girls go past her in clots calling out to their friends walking across
the street. Most of them are clutching their notebooks to their chests
in that crook-armed protective hug no boy has ever needed. . . .

Carie Lyn blinks, her eyes open. They are still looking inward.
Gross shadows draw them but not Molly's smile, yet, not the tumult
of her people, anyone's people, on Fowler Street. The mother who
bore her—her other mother? her real? her unreal?—was a few, but not
so many, years older than these high school girls. Her father might
have been anyone, no record will ever bear his name: he was a magic
wand indifferent (presumably) to its power. Would they be angry if
they knew their daughter was going to grow up in a white lady French
teacher's duplex, with soulless food and pottery on the shelves, Mozart
on the phonograph? Their daughter? But there is no such person,
there *is* no "they." Her skin is a question of physical substance, pig-
ment, her culture a matter of chance. A baby this new lies in the light
of her beholder's eye. . . .

She is back on George Street. . . . Carefully she brakes the carriage
and peeks inside at Carie, who is looking up lazily, back at the edge of
sleep. Someone's long lashes she'll have; they are curled so tight they
look mascaraed. Molly smiles—because one does? Because babies drink
in smiles with their milk and grow on them? Because the smile just
comes, she sees the soft curve of chin, the eyelash shadow on her
cheeks, and wants to smile?

Nora Ephron: Heartburn

I could feel the diamond ring . . . pressing against my breast. Mark
had given me the ring when Sam was born. We had gotten to the hospital when the contractions were coming only five minutes apart, and
Mark sat in the labor room, next to me, holding my arm, whispering,
singing, making little jokes, doing everything right. I'd been abso-

lutely positive that he wouldn't—that he'd turn into the kind of hope-less father who goes through the whole business under the delusion that it's as much his experience as it is yours. All this starts in Lamaze classes, where your husband ends up thinking he's pregnant, and let me tell you he's not. It's not his body, it's not his labor, it's not his pain—it's yours, and does any man give you credit or respect for it? No. They're too busy getting in on the act, holding their stopwatches and telling you when to breathe and when to push and taking pictures of the kid coming out all covered with goo and showing them to your friends at dinner parties and saying what a beautiful and moving ex-perience it was. Not Mark. He just sat there helping me to get through, and he stayed completely calm when the doctor said there was something wrong, perhaps the umbilical cord was around the baby's neck; and he looked so impassive when he glanced over at the fetal monitor and saw that the baby had stopped breathing that I didn't even realize how serious the situation was; he just kept on whis-pering and singing and making little jokes as they rushed me into the operating room and knocked me out for the emergency Caesarean.

When I came to, he was standing next to me. He was wearing a green surgical smock and a mask, and he was crying and laughing, and in his arms was Sam, our beautiful Sam, our sunray, pink and gold and cooing like a tiny dove. Mark laid him on me, and then he lay down next to me on the narrow slab, and held us both until I fell asleep again.

Two hours later, when I woke up, he gave me the ring. He'd just gone out and bought it. The diamond was in an antique setting sur-rounded by tiny little diamonds; it looked like a delicate ice flower. The next day Mark took it back to the jeweler and had it engraved: "Rachel and Mark and Sam."

16. Birthing in the 1980s, with Reference to Times Past

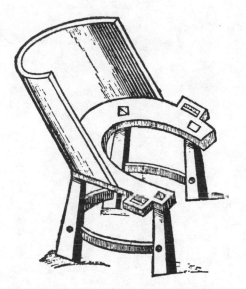

Joan, Annie, Teri, and Liseli have in common that they have each had a baby in this decade and have, with the aid of their husbands, participated with some pain but great pleasure in the birth process. Joan, at thirty, gave birth in a hospital with an obstetrician attending; Annie, at twenty-nine, chose to deliver at home with a general practitioner; Teri, thirty-four, delivered in a hospital with a team of certified midwives; and Liseli and her husband Michael, both twenty-six, opted for a home birth with a lay midwife—although, as they explain below, the midwife never quite made it. Their stories are happy ones; they seemed, in their talks with me, to have given much to the experience and to have received much in return.

Joan:
At the time that John was conceived, I had had a lot of dreams about wanting to have a baby. There was some very, very strong undercurrent going there.

I am an only child. I'm an only grandchild on one side of my family, so it was an excitement for my grandfather in his nineties and my parents who were turning seventy. He was a very welcome child. I gave birth to John in the same hospital where I was born nearly thirty years before.

Jim and I attended natural childbirth classes, and I read a lot. Strangely, the book that left the greatest impression on me is one I had bought for fifty cents at a book sale five or six years before—a midwifery book published by the Edinburgh Birthing Pavilion. It had all the gruesome pictures of polyps and warts and a prolapsed uterus and fetal messes—all the horrible stuff that you know can happen. But it also included suggestions for what to do in an emergency, which was very comforting. And pictures of all these stout-hearted, competent Scottish nurses saying firmly, "If a mother is handled well, she will not have post partum depression." So I had that tucked away in my mind.

I also had my mother's anecdotes about childbirth, both first-hand and ones she had accumulated from her mother and her aunts and grandmother, all about birthing. When she had me, she had the standard 1950 spinal delivery where she could see everything and feel nothing from the waist down. She was a thirty-eight-year-old mother who had had several miscarriages and was determined this pregnancy was going to be successful. She had lost one child at seven months—a breech birth where the legs were hanging out and kicking and they took their time about getting the baby out. Now we know that a seven-month breech delivery would be a healthy delivery. We have the equipment for it. But at that time she had the feeling that the doctors were just letting the baby die because they couldn't handle it, and she was very angry about that. So she had gone into the hospital for me very early. She was very assertive with doctors, which in the fifties was not very common. She told off the residents when they came in *en masse* and wanted to examine her. She said, "I want to know who you are, and in any case I'm not going to give you permission to examine me." It's persons like her that paved the way for me so that I got a lot more TLC and personal respect. She remembers it sort of like a warrior remembering a battle.

I wanted to be a part of the birth. I wanted to know what was happening. I assumed that a little bit of pain was natural. And I very much didn't want somebody interfering, coming in between me and my husband and my baby at that time.

My G.P. held on to me until the seventh month of pregnancy because she herself was a grand multiparous mother who had gone back to work five times after having children and she didn't want to let go of me, but she lived too far out of town. She very reluctantly handed me over to an obstetrician.

I didn't consider having the baby at home. I thought, a first birth, you don't know what complications might develop. Maybe on a second or third birth, with someone who's very experienced and comfortable with doing it, but for my first birth, I thought, there are medical unknowns about me that I don't want to explore at home. So what we found was a birthing room plus short-term stay—twenty-four hours in and out if both pediatrician and obstetrician concur that the baby and mother are both ready to go home.

The obstetrician who actually delivered John was just filling in and was a very quiet, non-verbal type person, but I felt he really cared, so I felt I could trust him in situations. We did have a nurse during delivery who seemed to be emotionally not with it. She was sort of like "Go, go, go! Slam, slam, slam!" I was angry at her cheerleading me. But other than that, the hospital experience was pretty good. There was a time when a resident came in and offered medication. I was having a lot of spikey contractions and it was really tempting. Jim was there and he had been doing back pressure, so that he was able to relieve a lot of the pressure. I think that if I had been alone, I would have said yes at that point because it's a lonely experience unless you have some other voice, another body, even something beautiful to look at outside yourself.

One of the mechanical things I enjoyed a lot was the fetal monitor. The baby's heartbeat was very close-rhythmed to my breathing. I thought, "Isn't that great. Here we are sort of singing along together, his heartbeat and my breathing." It gave me something to work with during contractions. There were certain signs I knew to watch for. If his heartbeat didn't pick up after my contraction or didn't remain steady, then we should alert a nurse right away, but his heartbeat was steady as a clock and that was really good for me. The fetal monitor gave him a voice. You know, it was encouraging to hear from the third party involved.

They had to puncture the membrane. My waters were not going. And when they did, it was a little green with meconium and that worried them, so they really pushed me in the final stages. They wanted to get him out real fast and aspirate him. So they moved me from the birthing room into a regular delivery room so they had enough space for a full pediatric staff. And then when he came out and they were aspirating him, he yelled bloody murder and peed all over the pediatricians, and we were cheering, "Hey, right on, kid!"

I was glad it was a boy, because I had been an only daughter, and I thought it would be good for me to have a child not totally in my own tradition. And I thought at thirty, this might be the only child I have. It would be good to have somebody whom I am going to have to recognize as different so I won't be pushing off onto the child too many of my own attributes.

I think there's a natural anesthesia that occurs during birth—it's really amazing. I think it's given me a special confidence in my own life, a confidence that peace and comfort are given to us in those times when we need it. This also affects my feelings about death. What I understand about death is that the person who is experiencing it has this feeling of comfort and floating out of the body and of seeing the situation in a clear, crystal, tranquil way. And of rushing through a tunnel, and of light, and of being enveloped and making a choice at that time whether to come back into life as we know it or to go on. And it sounded so much like my own feelings of giving birth. Of being there and yet of being a little bit out of my own body. Of being able to talk in a normal voice even while these tremendous contractions were happening, and of being able to laugh and enjoy what was going on. I think it was a sign to me that I shouldn't fear life. I think as a teenager I was often afraid that processes were too big for me. But having had a child, I realize that they're not too big for us. That we always have enough to get through.

Annie:

I ended up having babies at home because my husband Jerry's first child had been born at home twelve years before. I had a very nice doctor, a general practitioner, who had never done home births but had ten children himself and was really wonderful. He finally agreed that if I insisted he would come out and help me have the baby at home. But when the time came, I called his house and his wife told me he was at the hospital with an emergency—a patient was dying and he couldn't leave—and could we go there? So we did; we got there at one in the morning, and Carver was born at 1:10.

Then four years later when Heather was coming—the only one I actually planned—my doctor agreed again to do it at home. He'd delivered a thousand babies and never one at home, but he said, "Oh, I still make house calls. Why don't you tell me how to get to your house, and I'll come out."

When the time came, it was a January night, very frigid and icy, and he's an older man. But we have a neighbor who's a dairy farmer and gets up at four in the morning, so we called him at 4:30. He was up, and he went and got the doctor, brought him to our house. He got there about five-thirty, Heather was born at six, and another neighbor dropped him back at his office by seven. It went very well. Just the doctor and Jerry and our son Carver were there. Carver was just four at the time, but a very mature four. He helped hand the surgical gloves and things, and when the baby was coming out, I remember he said, "Wow, Mom, it looks just like a planet!" To this day he'll deny having said that, but he was just so enthralled. We had told him what birth was about; it wasn't as if he was uninformed. He was really excited, and he got to hold her right away. He's very protective of her now, I think because of that.

My grandmother always knew when I was having a baby. She'd had her babies at home, in New York; she was a very metropolitan lady, very sophisticated, but she didn't like hospitals. She always insisted on having them at home. My grandfather was Chief Inspector of the New York Police Department. And my grandmother's grandmother had been a midwife herself in New York—free, for poor women. My mother wasn't so adventuresome; she had me at New York Lying-In. But my grandmother was very pleased when Heather was born at home. She always tuned in to what was going on.

Anyway, on that morning of Heather's birth, she came out bright rose! The aura was all over the room. The whole room actually turned pink. It was about 6:30 in the morning—January 3, the dead of winter—and it was still pitch dark out, so it wasn't the sunrise. The doctor noticed it, too, and he's as straight as an arrow, just a regular old G.P. He said, "What's happened? Did you turn on a different light in here?" He didn't understand it either—this rose-colored light absolutely filling the room. It went away, faded away, pretty soon afterward. People have told me that's an artistic aura. Heather is already very artistic; she's a lot like her dad.

Anyway, the doctor left, and when I brought the baby in to the office the next morning, he said that that had been the best birth he'd ever been at. He was convinced there was something really magical about it. But I think there's something really magical about every birth.

Teri:

I'm a video producer and editor. I expect to go back to it, but I don't have it planned right now when I'll go back. Since having my first child, I have found that being a mother has really influenced the development of my career. It's such a great investment of time and energy, that it just by its very nature has diluted my interest and involvement in work. I did get a job as an editor at ABC. I didn't tell them at the interview that I had a child. They give the message that you have to give a thousand percent commitment, especially in the communications world. You've got to be accessible. You've got to be willing to work overtime. I felt if they knew I was a mother, that might have kept them from hiring me. I was on the job for a while before I started telling people the "dark secret." I ended up leaving there and trying to do free lance work, and passed up an opportunity to return there because I don't want to work fifty hours a week.

So motherhood is affecting my work. I've gone through a period of disappointment, but I think I've become more realistic. I find I can't do everything fully. It's still important to me to have a work identity whether I'm actively out doing it or not. I feel it's a thing I'll go back to. But I'll go back to it in a modified way—more modified than I would if I didn't have children. I have a lot of women friends who have made the choice to hire full time caretakers for their children and continue with their careers. It's a very, very personal choice. I think however women want to combine children and work, or children without work, or work without children, they should have the support for that.

When you have your first child, you're not prepared for so many things. I both wanted to work right away and didn't want to work right away. A lot of ambivalence enters in. Your identity's really changing.

My first birth was with an obstetrician, and I had some unexpected complications. I had toxemia during labor. I had drugs to deal with the toxemia, but I was still awake and aware and able to push the baby out myself. But I was left with the feeling that the obstetrician was not as tuned in and sensitive as I would have liked him to be. There happened to be a midwife on duty during labor, and she was the key person that both my husband and I related to. Not only her emotional support, but her specific advice on pushing and such—she was the most valuable person there. I'd heard a lot of very good things about this midwifery program at Roosevelt Hospital. They have a team of five certified midwives; they may even be a model group within the country. The program was well established four-and-a-half years ago when my older daughter Kendra was born, but I was just a little bit conservative. I thought, well, my first child, and I'd been trying to get pregnant for a long time—I'd play it safe. But I felt after coming through that experience that having an obstetrician doesn't necessarily guarantee playing it safe. So both my husband and I were determined this time to go with midwives.

Throughout the pre-natal care, I found them so highly informed and accessible. I could ask them questions very easily. Some gynecologists—men, and women too—you'd ask a question, and to them it would imply either a criticism or an unnecessary anxiety. Mostly you just wanted to know as much as you could about the situation. With the midwives it was easy to thoroughly discuss anything on my mind.

So I went through my whole pregnancy feeling very confident. In this neighborhood—the upper West Side of New York—there's a sort of baby boom among thirty-year-old-and-up professionals. I was constantly running into people who had given birth at Roosevelt; it's become very well known. What I liked about it was the back-up of the hospital. Since in my first labor I had unexpected emergency complications, I knew that was possible. I knew that if everything went well, I would be with a midwife in the birthing room, but if there were any complications, I was right next door to a regular delivery room, obstetricians on call, within a hospital setting, and wouldn't have to be moved by ambulance. To us that just seemed the best of both worlds. People would ask, "Are you going to have natural childbirth?" and I would say, "I'm going to have *prepared* childbirth. You don't know what's going to happen, and you hope you'll be awake and aware and it'll be wonderful, but anything can happen."

My parents would question, "Are they trained? Are they certified?" I have a brother who's a radiologist, nothing to do with obstetrics, and they'd say, "Well, what does Jim think about it?" But it never occurred to me to question their skill. I felt that they really gave it enough attention to understand all the subtleties that are just not textbook knowledge. The kind of sensitivity you'd bring to the whole human experience of birth.

Roosevelt Hospital has a very standard hospital obstetrics floor except for the birthing room, which looks like a typical room in a Holiday Inn. It's not what you'd choose in terms of decor, but it has a bed with a bedspread, and drapes, and plants. It's like a little stage. But it's how they use the room that really makes the difference. When I came in, in labor, I was taken right into the birthing room and told, "This is where you'll be. Take your things off, sit down and relax, walk around, have some juice." There was a midwife there when I went in, about 4:30 A.M. A midwife was either with us or accessible to us at all times.

Periodically, the midwife would check me out, giving me choices of things that could be done, to speed up labor or to continue at the pace I was on. Dan and I always felt we were in control. We could walk around, joke around with another couple that was there. That was very nice—a feeling of comraderie.

About nine o'clock when the midwife checked me, I was dilated to five-and-a-half, maybe six centimeters. Jean, the midwife, said, "Well, you're progressing, but if I broke the membrane now, it would really speed up. It would get very intense, but move much faster." The contractions had been getting harder, but I was still coping pretty well. So I said, "Oh, what the hell. Let's do it. Let's go for it." So she broke the membranes, and everything came gushing out. I said, "Ugh! I really feel disgusting! I would love to take a shower." And she said,

"Well, why don't you take one?" I said, "What? Do you mean I can?" and she said, "Sure. There's a shower right across from the birthing room, and there are some towels, and Dan can go in there with you." There was a little ante-room with a bench.

So I went into the shower, and it felt so great. The contractions really picked up: I'd get one, and I'd hang onto Dan and we'd breathe through it, and then when it stopped I would just stand there letting the warm water run down my back. It felt so great; it really took my mind off of the intensity. Then I'd get another one, and I'd hang onto Dan—I think we were in there for half an hour. Jean, the midwife, came to the door and looked at me as if to say, "I'd better get her out of the shower. It could happen right here." They got me out and put warm towels around me and got me to the bed.

After that it was hard and heavy. Jessica was born about 10:30, and that last hour was a really rough stretch. Dan was right in front of me, and the midwife was in back of me. She was a voice, giving me directions. And I was hanging on to Dan—I bit him, I scratched him, I pinched him, I pulled his hair. The midwife could tell when I was losing control, and she would say, "It's almost over. It's almost over. Relax. Just keep breathing. You're doing great." Just a continuous stream of support. Which you need; otherwise, it seems like one long stream of pain. She helped me relax and then go with it again. And Dan came out of it bruised and battered, but he felt so involved. With the first child, all the details of "being a coach" seemed to interfere with what's necessary, which is just being there as a supportive, loving person.

Then I started feeling the urge to push. In the natural childbirth class, they say, "Then you'll feel the urge to push," and you think about it so much in terms of the mind. You think, "At some point I'll feel like pushing." But with me it was just, "Oooohhh!" It was so primal. I was lying on my side. Jessica was nine pounds, six ounces, so it wasn't such a breeze pushing her out. I think it took about fifteen minutes. In class they say, "Don't push through your rectum; push through your vagina," but that's a very subtle distinction when you only do it once or twice in your life. I said, "Oh, I've forgotten how to push," and she said, "Don't worry about it. Just push!" Dan was right there, and it was such a different feeling from when I was draped on the delivery table. I just willed myself to do whatever Jean said was necessary—breathe, or push, or pant through it until she got the baby's head out, and then the shoulder. She was half out, and already she was crying. Jean eased the shoulders out, and then she said, "Reach down! Here's your baby!" And, oh gosh! I reached down and pulled her onto my chest. It was wonderful.

Dan cut the cord, and we had a lovely time alone with her for about an hour. My parents had sneaked into the hospital, and they happened to bump into one of the midwives who said, "Don't say anything, just follow me." And she brought them right to the birthing room. They got to see Jessica before she was an hour old. We drank champagne, and then the next day we took her home.

My mother had questioned the training of the midwives at the beginning, but she was very supportive of the whole thing. She had six children herself, and I think she had the whole range of childbirth experiences, including one caesarean. She would have loved to be there, too. She's very sensitive to considerations like rooming-in, and bonding, and nursing, and she's very loving with a newborn. She says the more you love them, the more you hold them, the better.

Liseli:

When we first started thinking about having children, we were rather appalled by the cost. I'm an R.N. and Michael's a biology teacher, and we don't make a lot of money. I think this is what started us thinking about home births. We knew a midwife in the area—a lay midwife, a registered nurse but not a certified midwife—who works basically underground. We talked to her, and she was relatively non-commital, saying, "The decision is really up to you." But she said she couldn't deliver us at home unless everything was right, and she urged us to have prenatal care with a doctor, which we did. He was a very comfortable person. When we told him we wanted a home birth, he didn't really say one way or the other how he felt. They never do. But I saw him regularly, and then at my last visit right out of the blue he said, "Why don't you draw me a map to your house. And I'll give you my home phone number. If anything comes up, just give me a call." It doesn't sound like a whole lot, except that it was coming from a doctor.

Michael:

We had gone to the natural childbirth classes that the doctor organized. We thought that if everything continued to go right, and the pre-natal care showed there to be no problems, we would deliver with the midwife. She had several attendants, and we chose two we felt comfortable with.

In the classes that the doctor offered, the first thing they said was that ninety-five percent of all births are normal. Then they spent about ninety-five percent of the classtime on the five percent of things that could go wrong. After those classes we both felt that maybe we'd better not do this thing at home after all, that maybe the hospital would be better. There were a lot of unknowns and fears that people were voicing. It wasn't until we went to the home birth classes that the midwife gave that we really made up our minds that that was the way we wanted to go. There was such a difference in the attitude. The home birth classes were so positive and so full of good feeling. Everyone in that class became close to the others, which never happened in the doctor's classes. Out of ten couples though, only three actually delivered at home. The others went to the hospital, but they were all long labors or had other complications.

Liseli:
Both sets of our parents knew we were planning to have the baby at home, and none of them ever said too much about it. I think my mother felt relatively good about it. I think she's interested in that kind of thing, and doesn't trust hospitals too much. We didn't get any negative response from our parents really, even from Michael's parents, and I expected a lot more from them.

Michael:
We live in an old farmhouse which we're rebuilding. We have wood heat, with no oil or gas back-up, and no plumbing in the house. We were working on that, but there wasn't any there yet. We just had a handwell out in the front yard. I think my parents had adjusted to the way we live and thought a home birth would be typical, considering our life style.

Liseli:
I think it does need careful screening in terms of any physical problems that the mother has or that the fetus seems to have. There are also psychological reasons why a woman should not have her baby at home. She has to be comfortable at home.

Michael:
I think if the woman gets a lot of negative feelings from her own mother, that can be a factor. Some mothers are really strongly opposed and keep telling their daughter, "You should go to the hospital."

Liseli:
Or sometimes the husband does that.

Michael:
Both people have to feel comfortable with it. In the beginning I felt much more strongly about having the baby at home than Liseli did.

Then I realized that I couldn't push her into it, that really she had to make the decision. Which she finally did, and became enthusiastic about it.

We made all the preparations. We had a list of things that the midwife wanted us to have. We sterilized towels and sheets, so I played the traditional role of boiling the water. As soon as Liseli said she thought she was in labor, I put a bucket of water on the stove and started heating it. It was April, and I fired up the wood stove, because we didn't know whether it might not get really cold that night. We had a bulb syringe for suctioning—the midwife also had a syringe, but she suggested we have one on hand, too. She had most of the instruments. But we did have oxygen, a small tank of oxygen.

Liseli:

We had sterilized receiving blankets, a shower curtain to put under the bedsheets, and little things for comfort. The midwife had come over earlier and looked around and made suggestions. For instance, she said the birth really should be on the first floor—just in case there's a problem, and it's hard to carry a woman in labor down the stairs.

Michael:

The doctor knew we were going to call the midwife, that the hospital was purely a back-up situation. We were trying to be very up-front with him, because if he saw the slightest thing wrong, we wanted him to say, "Look, I really don't think you should do this." He never really gave any approval or disapproval. Whenever we mentioned having the baby at home, he would just listen, without saying anything.

Liseli:

Whenever we went in, the doctor would feel the position of the baby, and we'd say, "Head still down?" And he'd say, "Ye-a-u-p!" And I'd say, "Everything going O.K.?" And he'd say, "Ye-a-u-p!" He didn't talk much.

After the birth I wrote out a whole long thing about it, because I wanted to remember how I felt at the time. When I thought afterwards about where my labor began, I thought way back to when the uterus first began to prepare itself, which was really the third month, when I felt a kind of contraction almost like cramps. And I would think, "This uterus is working awfully hard already." And I would think, "How long is this labor going to take? Is it going to go awfully fast? Am I just going to drop this baby?" Then, I think it was two weeks before the baby was due, the doctor did an internal exam to be positive the baby's head was down, and at that point he said I was dilated to about fifty percent of fist. And that was encouraging. I hadn't expected it to be anything like that. I had thought, "Well, I'll start dilating when I start going into labor." I felt that my uterus really must have been working as hard as I had felt it was. I told the midwife that I sort of felt it might be a short labor, and she said, "Yeah, well, everyone fantasizes about that." On the other hand, I was also telling myself, "Well, it'll be a twenty-four-hour labor, and you can just go with it. It'll start slow and build up, and you'll be in for a nice long time of it." So that I wouldn't be too depressed.

The day that she was due—April 27th—I made sure that I went out and did a couple of things, went to the lumber yard. And the next day, the day after it was due, I wasn't feeling at all as if anything was going to happen. The midwife was due to go to work at three o'clock in the afternoon—she worked the three-to-eleven shift at a hospital about fifteen miles from our house—and I called her at two and said, "I'm not going to have the baby this evening. You don't have to worry about it. You can go to work." If I had been in labor at that point, she would have called a substitute. So she went to work.

Then about five-thirty I stood up on a chair to get something off a shelf, and I felt this cramp. And I thought, "Oh!" It felt stronger than the old kind, but I thought well, maybe I just have to go to the bathroom. So I went out to the outhouse. I came back, and within ten minutes I had another one. At that point I said to Michael, "If this isn't it, I don't know what it is." So we started making preparations right away, started a fire going to get the house warmer, got some water going on the stove. My second contraction was ten minutes after the first, the third was eight minutes after the second, and pretty soon they were four minutes apart.

Michael:

I called the hospital, but the midwife was at supper. I called the first attendant, but she wasn't home. I called the second attendant, and she was babysitting for the midwife's kids along with her own, and said she would have to find someone to take over, and then she would be along. Liseli was roaming around, and every time a contraction hit, she'd kneel down on a chair and go through the contraction and say, "This is terrible!"

Liseli:

I was thinking, if this is going to go on for ten hours, and get worse, I'm going to be in a bad way.

Michael:

I was thinking the same thing. We didn't verbalize this to each other, but Liseli has a very high tolerance for pain, and I could tell that the contractions were hurting her. I was thinking, if this is going to go on all night, forget it.

Liseli:

I didn't want to get into bed, because I figured if I'm walking around it's going to go faster. So I was afraid to get into bed.

Michael:

At about quarter to seven the contractions were two minutes apart, lasting for at least a minute. I called the attendant again, and she said, "Hang in there," she was getting things arranged and would be right over. She called the hospital and reached the midwife and told her Liseli was in labor, but not to worry, she was heading over. When the attendant came in, Liseli was kneeling on the living room floor with her head in the pillows. The attendant was really organized and that helped, because Liseli was panicking, afraid we'd have to do the baby by ourselves.

Liseli:

By the time the attendant got there, I'd had an urge to push, and I knew that that shouldn't come until I was almost completely dilated, and I couldn't tell.

Michael:

And I had no idea.

Liseli:

I thought it was going too fast. I knew that when it went too fast it could be dangerous for the mother and the baby, and the baby could could come out all bruised. This was only an hour and a half after my labor had started, and already I was going to push, or wanted to—was trying hard not to. And I was kind of scared.

Michael:

The attendant came in then and took Liseli's blood pressure, and listened for fetal heart count, and was breathing with her through the contractions, which was great, because Liseli just focused on her and breathed with her through each contraction, which helped a lot.

Liseli:

And when she checked, I was almost completely dilated, except for a small lip of the cervix.

Michael:

At about quarter after seven the midwife called from the hospital and wanted to know how things were going. The attendant told me to tell her that Liseli was feeling the urge to push, that the contractions were two minutes apart, very strong, and to get there as quickly as possible. And the midwife was saying over the phone, "Oh, my God! Oh, my God!" We hung up, and then she realized that she'd been dropped off at work and didn't have a car. I realized it, too. I called the other attendant, who was home by then, and asked her to go to the hospital and pick up the midwife. By that time it was about seven-thirty. The attendant suggested that we get Liseli into bed.

Liseli:

My waters broke while I was still roaming around the living room.

Michael:

So we got her up into bed and things started progressing rather quickly. The contractions seemed easier after the water broke. There was a lot less pressure. Within about fifteen minutes after we got her into bed, we could see the head crown. Five minutes after that there were a few wisps of hair off the top of her head coming out, just standing straight up. And then at 7:55 Jessie was born.

Liseli:

The entire time I was trying not to push. I never once pushed. I was almost in agony trying not to. I was still afraid it was going too fast. I thought the baby was going to fly right out the window if I pushed. The head came out in one contraction, and the attendant got the syringe—our syringe, the one the midwife had advised us to have just in case—and was going to suction out the mouth. Before she could do that though, I had the next contraction and the body came out, and she started crying. She finally got suctioned a little later sometime.

Michael:

I remember that you didn't push, and the attendant kept blowing with you so that you wouldn't, and I got so confused that I kept saying, "Push!" I had planned on delivering her myself, but things moved too quickly for that. I had gone to a class given by the midwife for the husbands, so I was prepared to do that, but Liseli wanted me up by her head with her. She was holding on to me. And then when Jessie was born, we laid her down on Liseli's stomach for a little while. I told her it was a girl, and she kept asking me if I was sure. I think it was about at that point that the midwife pulled up. I heard her come in the door, and I went running into the kitchen yelling, "It's a girl! It's a girl!" She was thrilled—really happy. She came in and checked everything—the muscle reflexes, and all. And the baby cried—even gave us a couple of tears!

In retrospect, I think knowledge is important. Liseli being an R.N. and having an interest in maternity, and my being a biologist, helped. We were able to understand from what we already knew what was happening. I think we might have recognized if something wasn't going right.

As for whether we'd do it again, we can't imagine doing it any other way. Still, neither of us is fanatical about it; if there was the slightest problem, we'd pack right up and go to the hospital.

Liseli:

It's hard at the time, but it doesn't matter after it's over. You come out with such a nice result!

Selected Bibliography

Abbe, Kathryn McLaughlin, & Frances McLaughlin Gill. *Twins on Twins.* New York: Clarkson N. Potter, Inc., 1980.

Andreski, Iris. *Old Wives' Tales: Life-Stories from Ibibioland.* New York: Schocken Books, 1970.

Angelou, Maya. *I Know Why the Caged Bird Sings.* New York: Random House, 1969.

Arms, Suzanne. *Immaculate Deception: A New Look at Women and Childbirth in America.* Boston: Houghton Mifflin, 1975.

Arnaz, Desi. *A Book.* New York: William Morrow & Co., 1976.

Aveling, J. H. *English Midwives: Their History and Prospects.* London: J. & A. Churchill, 1872.

Ayscough, Florence. *Chinese Women Yesterday & Today.* New York: Da Capo Press, 1975.

Bacall, Lauren. *By Myself.* New York: Alfred A. Knopf, 1976.

Backer, Dorothy Anne Liot. *Precious Women.* New York: Basic Books, Inc., 1974.

Balsdon, J. P. V. D. *Roman Women: Their History and Habits.* New York: John Day Co., 1962.

Banks, Ann. *First-Person America.* New York: Alfred A. Knopf, 1980.

Bartlett, Richard A. *The New Country: A Social History of the American Frontier 1776–1890.* New York: Oxford University Press, 1974.

Beard, Mary R. *The Force of Women in Japanese History.* Washington, D.C.: Public Affairs Press, 1953.

Beauvoir, Simone de. *The Second Sex.* New York: Alfred A. Knopf, 1952.

Beck, Lois, & Nikki Keddie. *Women in the Muslim World.* Cambridge, Mass.: Harvard University Press, 1978.

Belloc, Hilaire. *Louis XIV.* New York: Harper & Row, 1938.

Berg, Barbara J. *Nothing to Cry About.* New York: Seaview Books, 1981.

Bergman, Ingrid and Alan Burgess. *Ingrid Bergman: My Story.* New York: Delacorte Press, 1980.

Bernstein, Burton. *Thurber.* New York: Dodd Mead, 1975.

Bertaut, Simone. *Piaf.* New York: Harper & Row, 1972.

Berton, Pierre. *The Dionne Years: A Thirties Melodrama.* New York: W. W. Norton & Co., 1977.

Bradford, William. *Of Plymouth Plantation,* Samuel Eliot Morison, Ed. New York: Random House, 1967.

Bradstreet, Anne. *The Works of Anne Bradstreet,* John Howard Ellis, ed. Gloucester, Mass.: Peter Smith, 1962.

Brain, Robert. *Friends and Lovers.* New York: Basic Books, 1976.

Brandes, Georg. *Voltaire,* Vol. 2. New York: F. Ungar, 1930; 1964.

Brasch, R. *How Did Sex Begin?* New York: David McKay Co., 1973.

Briffault, Robert. *The Mothers.* London: George Allen & Unwin, Ltd., abridged 1959.

Brodie, Fawn M. *Thomas Jefferson: An Intimate History.* New York: W. W. Norton & Co., 1974.

Brown, Dee. *The Gentle Tamers.* Lincoln: University of Nebraska Press, 1958; 1968.

Brown, Rosellen. *Street Games.* New York: Random House, 1972.

Bruce, Marie Louise. *Anne Boleyn.* New York: Coward McCann & Geohegan, 1972.

Cade, Toni. *The Black Woman.* New York: New American Library, Inc., 1970.

Caffrey, Kate. *The Mayflower.* New York: Stein & Day, 1974.

Carotenuto, Aldo. *A Secret Symmetry: Sabina Spielrein Between Jung and Freud.* New York: Pantheon Books, 1982.

Carson Josephine. *Silent Voices: The Southern Negro Woman Today.* New York: Delacorte Press 1969.

Casals, Pablo. *Joys and Sorrows: Reflections by Pablo Casals,* as told to Albert E. Kahn. New York: Simon & Schuster, 1970.

Casanova de Seingalt, Jacques. *The Memoirs of Jacques Casanova de Seingalt.* Vol. 3, Arthur Machen, tr. New York: G. P. Putnam's Sons, Inc.

Castelot, Andre. *King of Rome.* New York: Harper & Bros., 1960.

Castelot, Andre. *Napoleon.* New York: Harper & Row, 1971.

Chesnut, Mary Boykin. *A Diary from Dixie,* Ben Ames Williams, Jr., ed. Boston: Houghton Mifflin Co., 1949.

Churchill, Randolph S. *Winston S. Churchill: Vol. I: Youth 1874–1900.* Boston: Houghton Mifflin Co., 1966.

Coles, Robert. *Children of Crisis: A Study of Courage and Fear.* Boston: Little, Brown & Co., 1964.

Colette. *Earthly Paradise: An Autobiography,* Robert Phelps, ed.; Herma Briffault, tr. New York: Farrar, Straus & Giroux, 1966.

Cormack, Margaret. *The Hindu Woman.* Westport, Conn.: Greenwood Press, 1953.

Cornelisen, Ann. *Women of the Shadows.* Boston: Little, Brown & Co., 1976.

Covarrubias, Miguel. *Island of Bali.* New York: Alfred A. Knopf, 1938.

Craig, Gordon A. *The Germans.* New York: G. P. Putnam's Sons, 1982.

Cuero, Delfina. *The Autobiography of Delfina Cuero,* as told to Florence C. Shipek. Los Angeles: Dawson's Book Shop, 1968.

Cullingworth, Charles. *Charles White, FRS.* London: H. J. Glaisher, 1904.

Cunnington, Phillis, & Catherine Lucas. *Costume for Births, Marriages & Deaths.* London: Adam & Charles Black, 1972.

Cutter, Irving S., & Henry R. Viets. *A Short History of Midwifery.* London: W. B. Saunders Co., 1964.

Czaplicka, M. A. *Aboriginal Siberia.* London, Oxford University Press, 1969.

Davies, Margaret Llewelyn, ed. *Maternity: Letters from Working Women.* London: G. Bell & Sons, Ltd., 1915.

Demos, John. *A Little Commonwealth: Family Life in Plymouth Colony.* New York: Oxford University Press, 1970.

Diner, Helen. *Mothers and Amazons,* John Philip Lundin, tr. New York: The Julian Press, Inc., 1965.

Donegan, Jane B. *Women and Men Midwives: Medicine, Morality and Misogyny in Early America.* Westport, Conn.: Greenwood Press, 1978.

Donnison, Jean. *Midwives and Medical Men.* New York: Schocken Books, 1977.

Doyle, Helen. *A Child Went Forth: The Autobiography of Dr. Helen MacKnight.* New York: Gotham House, 1934.

Dreiser, Theodore. *Dawn.* New York: Horace Liveright, 1931.

Duffy, John, ed., *The Rudolph Matos History of Medicine in Louisiana.* Louisiana State University Press, 1958.

Duncan, Isadora. *My Life.* New York: Horace Liveright, 1927.

Edwards, Anne. *Sonya: The Life of Countess Tolstoy.* New York: Simon & Schuster, 1981.

Ellington, Edward Kennedy. *Music Is My Mistress.* Garden City, N.Y.: Doubleday & Co., 1973.

Ephron, Nora. *Heartburn.* New York: Alfred A. Knopf, 1983.

Erickson, Carolly. *Bloody Mary.* Garden City, N.Y.: Doubleday & Co., 1978.

Ewell, Thomas. *Letters to Ladies.* Philadelphia, W. Brown, 1917.

Faragher, John M. *Women and Men on the Overland Trail.* New Haven: Yale University Press, 1979.

Fields, W. C. *By Himself.* Englewood Cliffs, N.J.: Prentice-Hall, 1973.

Fischer, Christiane, ed. *Let Them Speak for Themselves: Women in the American West, 1849–1900.* Hamden, Conn.: Archon Books, 1977.

Forbes, Thomas R. *The Midwife and the Witch.* New Haven: Yale University Press, 1966.

Forster, E. M. *Where Angels Fear To Tread.* London: Edward Arnold, Ltd., 1905.

Frazer, Sir James G. *The Golden Bough.* New York: Macmillan, Co., 1951.

Freeman, Lucy. *The Story of Anna O.* New York: Walker & Co., 1972.

Freuchen, Peter. *Peter Freuchen's Book of the Eskimos,* Dagmar Freuchen, ed. Cleveland: World Publishing Co., 1961.

Freud, Sigmund. *A General Introduction to Psychoanalysis*. Joan Riviere, tr. New York: Horace Liveright, 1963.

Fulford, Roger, ed. *Dearest Child: Letters Between Queen Victoria and the Princess Royal 1858–1861*. New York: Holt, Rinehart & Winston, 1964.

Gies, Frances, and Joseph Gies. *Women in the Middle Ages*. New York: Thomas Y. Crowell, 1978.

Gill, Brendan. *Here at The New Yorker*. New York: Random House, 1975.

Gilot, Francoise, and Carlton Lake. *Life with Picasso*. New York: McGraw-Hill & Co., 1964.

Goldman, Emma. *Living My Life*. New York: Alfred A. Knopf, 1931.

Goodale, Jane. *Tiwi Wives*. Seattle: University of Washington Press, 1971.

Goodell, William. *A Sketch of the Life and Writings of Louyse Bourgeois*. Philadelphia, 1876.

Goulianos, Joan, ed. *By a Woman Writt*. Indianapolis: Bobbs Merrill Co., 1973.

Graham, Harvey. *Eternal Eve: The History of Gynaecology and Obstetrics*. Garden City, N.Y.: Doubleday & Co., 1951.

Gregory, Samuel. *Letter to Ladies in Favor of Female Physicians*. New York: Fowler & Wells, 1850.

Gregory, Samuel. *Man Midwifery Exposed and Corrected*. New York: Fowler & Wells, 1848.

Guillemeau, Jacques. *Child-birth or, The Happy Deliverie of Women*. London: A. Hatfield, 1612 (facsimile ed., W. J. Johnson, 1972).

Haggard, Howard W. *Devils, Drugs and Doctors*. New York: Harper & Row, 1929.

Hagood, Margaret Jarman. *Mothers of the South*. New York: W. W. Norton & Co., 1977.

Hartland, E. Sidney. "Twins." *Encyclopedia of Religion and Ethics*, Vol. 12. New York: Charles Scribner's Sons, 1922.

Hayes, Helen. *A Gift of Joy*. New York: M. Evans & Co., 1965.

Hemingway, Ernest. *A Farewell to Arms*. New York: Charles Scribner's Sons, 1929.

Heuer, Berys. *Maori Women*. London: A. H. & A. W. Reed, Ltd., 1972.

Holland, Vyvyan. *Son of Oscar Wilde*. New York: E. P. Dutton & Co., 1954.

Hopkins, Sarah Winnemucca. *Life Among the Piutes; Their Wrongs and Claims*. Boston: 1883.

Horney, Karen. *Feminine Psychology*. New York: W. W. Norton & Co., 1967.

Hotchner, A. E. *Sophia*. New York: William Morrow & Co., 1979.

Hunt, Annie Mae. *I Am Annie Mae*, Ruthe Winegarten, ed. Austin: Rosegarden Press, 1983.

Hunt, Irma. *Dearest Madame: The Presidents' Mistresses*. New York: McGraw-Hill & Co., 1978.

Hutheesing, Krisha Nehru. *Nehru's Letters to His Sister*. London: Faber & Faber, 1963.

Ivins, Virginia. *Pen Pictures of Early Western Days*. 1905.

Jameson, Edwin M. *Clio Medica: Gynecology and Obstetrics*. New York: Hafner Publishing Co., 1962.

Jeffrey, Julie Roy. *Frontier Women: The Trans-Mississippi West 1840–1880*. New York: Hill & Wang, 1979.

Jones, Rex L., & Shirley Kurz Jones. *The Himalayan Woman*. Palo Alto: Mayfield Publishing Co., 1976.

Kapp, Yvonne. *Eleanor Marx*. New York: International Publishers, 1977.

Katznelson-Shazar, Rachel, ed. *The Plough Woman: Memoirs of the Pioneer Women of Palestine*, Maurice Samuel, tr. New York: Herzl Press, 1975.

Kessler, Evelyn S. *Women: An Anthropological View*. New York: Holt, Rinehart and Winston, 1976.

Kidd, Dudley. *Savage Childhood: A Study of Kafir Children*. London: Adam & Charles Black, 1906.

Kingsley, Mary H. *Travels in West Africa*. London: Macmillan & Co., 1897.

Kitt, Edith Stratton. *Pioneering in Arizona: The Reminiscences of Emerson Oliver Stratton and Edith Stratton Kitt*, John C. Alexander, ed. Tucson: Arizona Pioneers' Historical Society, 1964.

Kitzinger, Sheila. *Women As Mothers*. New York: Random House, 1978.

Klonsky, Milton. *The Fabulous Ego*. New York: The New York Times Book Co., 1974.

Kristeva, Julia. *About Chinese Women*, Anita Barrows, tr. New York: Urizen Books, 1974.

Kulsum Naneh. *Customs and Manners of the Women of Persia and Their Domestic Superstitions*, James Atkinson, tr. New York: Burt Franklin, 1832, 1971.

Landes, Ruth. *The Ojibwa Woman*. New York: W. W. Norton & Co., 1971.

LeVine, Sarah. *Mothers and Wives: Gusii Women of East Africa*. Chicago: University of Chicago Press, 1979.

Litoff, Judy Barrett. *American Midwives 1860 to the Present*. Westport, Conn.: Greenwood Press, 1978.

Ludwig, Emil. *Cleopatra*. New York: Viking Press, 1937.

McLellan, David. *Karl Marx: His Life and Thought*. New York: Harper & Row, 1973.

Magoffin, Susan S. *Down the Santa Fe Trail and into Mexico: The Diary of Susan Shelby Magoffin 1846–1847*. New Haven: Yale University Press, 1926, 1962.

Makarova, Natalia. *A Dance Autobiography*. New York: Alfred A. Knopf, 1979.

Malcolm X. *The Autobiography of Malcolm X*, assisted by Alex Haley. New York: Random House, 1964.

Malinowski, B. *The Family Among the Australian Aborigines*. New York: Schocken Books, 1963.

Martin, Mary. *My Heart Belongs*. New York: William Morrow & Co., 1976.

Martineau, Gilbert. *Madame Mére*. London: John Murray, 1978.

Masters, John. *Casanova*. New York: Bernard Geis, 1969.

Maverick, Mary A., & George Madison Maverick. *Memoirs of Mary A. Maverick*. San Antonio: Alamo Printing Co., 1921.

Mead, Margaret. *Blackberry Winter*. New York: William Morrow & Co., 1972.

Mead, Margaret. *Male and Female*. New York: William Morrow & Co., 1949, 1967.

Meltzer, David. *Birth: An Anthology of Ancient Texts, Songs, Prayers and Stories*. San Francisco: North Point Press, 1981.

Metraux, Alfred. *Ethnology of Easter Island*. Honolulu: Bishop Museum Press, 1940, 1971.

Mitford, Nancy. *Voltaire in Love*. New York: Harper & Bros., 1957.

Mittler, Peter. *The Study of Twins*. Harmondsworth: Penguin Books, Inc., 1971.

Moody, Anne. *Coming of Age in Mississippi*. New York: The Dial Press, Inc., 1968.

Morgenstern, Julian. *Rites of Birth, Marriage, Death, and Kindred Occasions Among the Semites*. Cincinnati: Hebrew Union College Press, 1966.

Murasaki Shikibu. Diary, in *Diaries of Court Ladies of Old Japan*, Annie Shepley Omori and Kochi Doi, trs. New York: AMS Press, 1970.

Murphy, Yolanda and Robert F. Murphy. *Women of the Forest*. New York: Columbia University Press, 1974.

Myrdal, Jan. *Report from a Chinese Village*. New York: Pantheon, 1965.

Nabokov, Vladimir. *Speak, Memory*. New York: G. P. Putnam's Sons, 1966.

Nijinsky, Romola. *Nijinsky*. New York: Simon & Schuster, 1934.

Norton, Mary Beth. *Liberty's Daughters*. Boston: Little, Brown & Co., 1980.

O'Casey, Eileen. *Sean*. New York: Coward, McCann & Geoghegan, 1971.

O'Faolain, Julia, and Lauro Martines, eds. *Not in God's Image*. London: Maurice Temple Smith, Ltd., 1973.

Olsen, Tillie. *Tell Me a Riddle*. New York: Dell Publishing Co., 1956.

Packard, Francis R. *History of Medicine in the United States*. New York: 1931.

Packard, Francis R. *Life and Times of Ambroise Paré*. New York: Paul B. Hoeber, 1921.

Papyrus Ebers, The. Cyril P. Bryan, tr. New York: Appleton & Co., 1931.

Paulme, Denise, ed. *Women of Tropical Africa*. Berkeley: University of California Press, 1960.

Payne, Robert. *Marx*. New York: Simon & Schuster, 1968.

Piercy, Marge. *Small Changes*. Garden City: Doubleday & Co., 1973.

Plath, Sylvia. *The Journals of Sylvia Plath*. New York: Dial Publishing Co., 1982.

Pomeroy, Sarah B. *Goddesses, Whores, Wives and Slaves: Women in Classical Antiquity*. New York: Schocken Books, 1975.

Prescott, Hilda Frances Margaret. *Mary Tudor*. New York: The Macmillan Co., 1953.

Roiphe, Anne. *Torch Song*. New York: Farrar, Straus & Giroux, 1976.

Ross, Nancy Wilson. *Westward the Women*. New York: Random House, 1944, 1970.

Rousseau, Jean Jacques. *The Confessions of Jean Jacques Rousseau*. New York: Random House.

Rush, Benjamin. *The Selected Writings of Benjamin Rush*, Dagobert D. Runes, ed. New York: Philosophical Library, 1947.

Ryan, Mary P. *Womanhood in America: From Colonial Times to the Present*. New York: New Viewpoints, 1975.

Sagan, Francoise. *Night Bird: Conversations with Francoise Sagan*. New York: Clarkson N. Potter, 1980.

Sheean, Vincent. *Dorothy and Red*. New York, Houghton Mifflin Co., 1963.

Shirer, William. *Berlin Diary*. New York: Alfred A. Knopf, 1941.

Shirer, William. *The Rise and Fall of the Third Reich*. New York: Simon & Schuster, 1960.

Sills, Beverly. *Bubbles*. New York: Bobbs Merrill Co., 1976.

Smith, Page. *Daughters of the Promised Land*. Boston: Little, Brown & Co., 1970.

Spencer, Herbert R. *The History of British Midwifery from 1650 to 1800*. London: John Bale, Sons, 1927.

Spruill, Julia Cherry. *Women's Life and Work in the Southern Colonies*. Chapel Hill: University of North Carolina Press, 1938.

Stannard, Una. *Mrs. Man*. San Francisco: Germainbooks, 1977.

Stephenson, Jill. *Women in Nazi Society*. New York: Harper & Row, 1975.

Stirling, Monica. *A Pride of Lions*. London: Collins, 1961.

Swanson, Gloria. *Swanson on Swanson*. New York: Random House, 1980.

Teague, Michael. *Mrs. L: Conversations with Alice Roosevelt Longworth*. Garden City, N.Y.: Doubleday & Co., 1981.

Thomas, Elizabeth Marshall. *The Harmless People*. New York: Alfred A. Knopf, 1958.

Tolstoy, Leo. *Anna Karenina*, Louise and Aylmer Maude, trs. Oxford: Oxford University Press, 1980.

Turnbull, Colin M. *The Human Cycle*. New York: Simon & Schuster, 1983.

Turnbull, Colin M. *The Mountain People*. New York: Simon & Schuster, 1972.

Tyler, Anne. *Celestial Navigation*. New York: Alfred A. Knopf, 1974.

Ulrich, Laurel Thatcher. *Good Wives*. New York: Alfred A. Knopf, 1982.

Ustinov, Peter. *Dear Me*. Boston: Little, Brown & Co., 1977.

Walker, Alice. *Meridian*. New York: Harcourt Brace Jovanovich, 1976.

Wertz, Richard W., and Dorothy C. Wertz. *Lying-In: A History of Childbirth in America*. New York: The Free Press, 1977.

Williams, Selma R. *Demeter's Daughters: The Women Who Founded America 1587–1787*. New York: Atheneum, 1976.

Woodham-Smith, Cecil. *Queen Victoria*. New York: Alfred A. Knopf, 1972.

Woolf, Virginia. *Flush: A Biography*. New York: Harcourt Brace Jovanovich, 1933.